TOP
BIRDING
SPOTS

IN BRITAIN & IRELAND

WRITTEN AND PHOTOGRAPHED BY

DAVID TIPLING

HarperCollins*Publishers*

AUTHOR'S ACKNOWLEDGEMENTS

HarperCollins*Publishers*
London · Glasgow · New York
Sydney · Auckland · Toronto
Johannesburg

First published 1996

ISBN 0 00 220035 X

Photograph previous page:
Displaying male Capercaillie in the
Abernethey Forest, Scotland.

All photographs supplied by
Windrush Photos.
Photographs © David Tipling
except for the following: page 32
(Richard Brooks); page 38 upper
(Brenda Holcombe); page 100
(Howard Nicholls).

Edited and designed by
D & N Publishing,
Ramsbury, Wiltshire

Cartography by Carte Blanche,
Basingstoke, Hampshire

Colour reproduction by
Colourscan, Singapore

Printed and bound by
Rotolito Lombarda SpA, Milan, Italy

During my travels and research help has come from many individuals and organisations. I am grateful to the following for arranging photographic opportunities that would have been impossible otherwise. Stuart Potter introduced me to a Capercaillie lek, an unforgettable experience. The Orkney Flying Club gave me a migrant's eye view of North Ronaldsay. Donald Wilkie, skipper of the *Annag*, took me to St Kilda, sailing under the archipelago's majestic sea stacks. Roy Coles has allowed me unique opportunities to erect hides at my local reservoir where he is warden; many of the waders pictured throughout the book are the result of his help.

The staff at RSPB headquarters and at regional offices have been invaluable. Numerous RSPB reserve managers, too many to mention, have assisted with access and information. The following individuals and organisations have helped in various ways, from the supply of information to commenting on drafts of the text and maps: Hugh Harrop, Malcolm Ogilvie, John North, Tracey Barlow, Jo Williams, Jo Thomas, Eddie Franklin, Liam McFaul, Tony Walker, Norman Russell, Robin Tipling, Richard Rutter, Michael Betts, English Heritage, Scottish Natural Heritage, Trinity House, Lough Neagh Discovery Centre, Suffolk Wildlife Trust, Landmark Trust, Wildfowl and Wetlands Trust, The National Trust, The Scottish National Trust, Bardsey Island Trust, Irish, Northern Ireland and English Tourist Boards, Irish Ferries and P&O Ferries.

Special mention must be made of the following: Myles Archibald of HarperCollins Publishers, greeted my idea for this book with enthusiasm, and I thank him for the opportunity to write it. Tom Ennis escorted me around both Northern Ireland and the Republic passing on his wealth of knowledge on Irish birds and sites. Tom also commented on drafts of the Irish section and has been invaluable in making this chapter as complete as possible. Great encouragement and assistance has come from David Tomlinson over the past few years as my photography has developed. I also thank David for the loan of numerous reference books, and his advice and comments to early drafts of the text. Roz Gordon adorns the cover of this book, and shared many trips to sites around the country. Roz also commented on drafts and created maps. Perhaps her greatest contribution was the encouragement she gave me to get it finished.

And finally I dedicate this book to my parents, for their support and encouragement over the years.

P R E F A C E

In compiling this book I have visited more than 150 sites throughout Britain and Ireland. Before embarking on my travels, the idea of travelling to so many sites seemed daunting. As a photographer, the vagaries of our weather was a big worry. Would I reach Shetland to be greeted by rain for two weeks, or never reach St Kilda due to the moods of the Atlantic? My worries were unfounded, as although some trips did not always go to plan, I fortunately picked a year that was one of the warmest and sunniest on record.

I first envisaged picking just 50 of the best places to visit. This proved impossible and even trying to choose 100 sites was unsatisfactory. As a result I went through over 500 sites, picking out the cream. The selection that follows is my own personal choice. No doubt some readers may question why some sites are either omitted or treated as additional sites in preference to others. However, a book like this could run to several volumes and so space dictates the treatment that has been given to each site. The additional sites listed are not necessarily inferior to those dealt with in greater detail. They have been down-graded for a variety of reasons, some due to ease of access, others due to their restrictive interest for just part of the year. But all are top sites in their own right.

The growth in bird-watching over the past 10 years has been dramatic. At certain times, some reserves even suffer from traffic jams on their feeder roads. Magazines and books cover every conceivable subject, and there are a number of 'where to watch' books. Up until now though, no such book has covered, in one volume, both Britain and Ireland in such detail. I have attempted not only to highlight the very best places to visit, but to convey the beauty of many of our wild places and the birds that inhabit them through photographs. My hope is that this book will appeal to both expert and novice alike, and will inspire those with a limited interest to discover the pleasures of watching birds.

Skokholm Island, off the Pembrokeshire coast in Wales.

C O N T E N T S

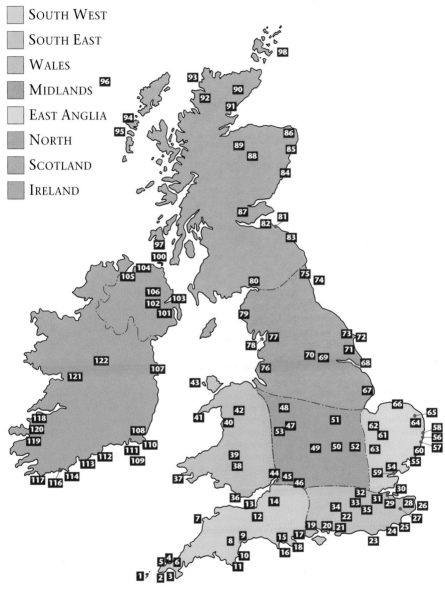

HOW TO USE THIS BOOK

The book is separated into geographical regions, with a general introduction and map to each one. Each site account starts with a general description of the habitat, and what is of particular interest to bird-watchers. Further information is given on the typical birds of the area, accompanied by a brief summary of the highlights that may be enjoyed during the course of a year.

OTHER WILDLIFE & FLORA
These sections are included when I have felt there are species of special interest which are likely to be encountered, or where there is a uniqueness to the site that adds greatly to its wildlife value. For some sites this information has been omitted either because there is little of interest other than the birds or more commonly because such information has not been readily available.

BIRDS THROUGH THE SEASONS
This is a summary of the more interesting species that occur. It is not an exhaustive list of species likely to be seen, but in many cases is highly selective. Furthermore, it is most unlikely you will see all the species listed for a season during one visit. With regard to my selections, I have been conservative in listing rarities.

The seasons are split into four: *Spring* covers the period from mid-March through to mid-May; *Summer* from mid-May to mid-July; *Autumn* from mid-July to the beginning of November; and

Winter from November to mid-March. There are occasional exceptions to this within the text. Birds do not keep to strict timetables, and at many sites wintering species may be present well into the spring period. Conversely, returning winter visitors can start to arrive during early autumn, so these listings should be used with the likelihood of overlap. There is an additional section for birds that are resident *all year*, and usually breed on the site.

ACCESS
Sections on access include detailed directions which can be used in conjunction with the maps. Also included are opening times to reserves and visitor centres. Most of the popular RSPB reserves and all Wildfowl and Wetlands Trust centres have toilets.

Most reserves have information at their entrance on walks and facilities, and many have leaflets providing detailed information. Some reserves charge an entrance fee. Non-members are charged to enter most RSPB reserves and all Wildfowl and Wetlands Trust centres.

When visiting reserves, under no circumstances should designated paths be left. Most sites are sensitive areas susceptible to disturbance. A well-used line, but one worth repeating, is: 'take nothing but photographs and leave only footprints'. When bird-watching from hides, ensure noise levels are kept to a minimum. Talking loudly, banging doors and sticking

hands out of viewing slots to point at something are all to be discouraged as birds will react either by keeping their distance or flying away.

DISABLED ACCESS
This section is mainly directed towards those people confined to a wheelchair. Disabled facilities are constantly being upgraded and introduced on many reserves. On some sites no facilities are listed, but this may of course change and it is worth contacting the controlling body of a specific reserve to check on any developments.

OTHER ATTRACTIONS
Space does not permit anything more than a very brief description or suggestions. This is meant to be of help, especially for the family, where perhaps not everyone wants to go bird-watching.

Key to Maps

—	Road	🅿	Car Park
—	Railway	✈	Airport
⋯	Footpath	♨	Marsh
—	Reserve Boundary	⛴	Ferry
🛖	Hide	☀	Viewpoint
𝒊	Information Centre		
⛳	Golf Course	🌲	Coniferous Forest
🦌	National Nature Reserve	🌳	Deciduous Forest

S O U T H - W E S T E N G L A N D

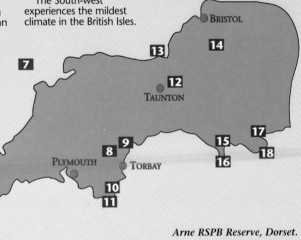

I T IS easy to see why the South-west is Britain's most popular holiday region. Fishing villages nestled in picturesque coves, rugged cliff scenery and long, golden, sandy beaches are just a few of the attractions.

Venture west from Land's End and you arrive in the beautiful Isles of Scilly. For the rarity hunter, Scilly is a mecca. American, European and Asian vagrants show up annually in October, in turn attracting hundreds and sometimes thousands of 'twitchers' (rare-bird enthusiasts).

Back on the mainland, the Cornish headlands at Land's End and St Ives allow the very best sea-watching in Britain.

On autumn days when the weather is right, thousands of seabirds can be pushed close inshore. On the edge of Dartmoor in neighbouring Devon, tranquil oak woodlands attract the western specialities of Wood Warbler, Redstart and Pied Flycatcher.

The South-west experiences the mildest climate in the British Isles.

This helps to attract a multitude of wildfowl and waders to the numerous estuaries along the south coast. Such a climate assists the Dartford Warbler and the Cirl Bunting, the latter now restricted almost exclusively to south Devon.

Arne RSPB Reserve, Dorset.

THE ISLES of Scilly lie 28 miles off Land's End. There are around 150 islands, with approximately 40 that have plants growing on them. Only five of the islands are inhabited. These five are characterised by sand dunes, long sandy beaches, low cliffs, heather moorland, small hedged fields and pockets of woodland.

There are few places more tranquil than Scilly. There is little traffic, and country lanes and cliff-top paths provide excellent walking.

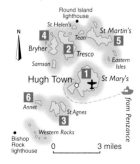

Aerial view of St Mary's.

BIRDS

Scilly has a good selection of breeding seabirds, but is best known for migrants. Every October over 1000 twitchers arrive on St Mary's, the largest island, for a feast of rarities. Although the arrival of birds is dependent on weather, American birds are annual in October. When fast-moving depressions cross the Atlantic from America, small falls can occur. If the weather has an easterly or southerly influence, vagrants from Europe and Asia can be expected. Scarce drift migrants such as Red-breasted Flycatcher and Yellow-browed Warbler are annual at this time.

When a rarity is found, the news is broadcast over CB radio, and this ensures that everyone on the islands can be watching the bird within minutes of its discovery. If the rarity is on an island other than St Mary's, the boatmen ferry bird-watchers across. At times, as hundreds of bird-watchers pour on to an island, the event can resemble an Army exercise.

If bird-watching in crowds is not for you, migrants can be enjoyed in solitude in spring and in early autumn. From late March through to May, and aside from the commoner summer visitors, rarities such as Golden Oriole and Hoopoe are annual. During summer, the main interest is the breeding seabirds. August and particularly September are excellent months for migrants: large falls can be experienced and there is a good chance of rarities.

OTHER ANIMALS

The surrounding seas are rich in marine life. Grey Seals and porpoises are seen regularly in summer. On land, the mammal speciality is the Scilly Shrew. Migrant butterflies and moths include Clouded Yellows and Hummingbird Hawk Moths, and, more rarely, Monarch butterflies from America.

FLOWERS

The mild, frost-free climate allows many introduced plants to thrive, and many early growing flowers are grown commercially in the small fields.

SITE GUIDE

1

St Mary's

A number of small nature reserves and sites worthy of particular attention are detailed below.

■ **THE LOWER MOORS NATURE TRAIL** is reached by taking the main road out of Hugh Town. Boardwalks lead through scrub and reeds. In spring, a variety of migrant warblers might be expected; Blackcaps, and Sedge, Reed, and Willow Warblers remain to breed. Occasional vagrant herons have been recorded at this time. During autumn, the small scrape may attract passage waders such as Greenshank. It is overlooked by two hides and is excellent for observing Water Rail, Snipe and Jack Snipe, the latter annual in October.

■ **HIGHER MOORS AND PORTHELLICK** is another small nature reserve, the main interest being Porthellick Pool, viewable from two small hides. Various species of duck visit, with Mallard and Teal breeding. Waders are attracted to the limited amount of mud exposed when water-levels are low. In autumn, Snipe, Water Rail and Jack Snipe are likely. Along the Higher Moors Trail, look out for the giant tufts of Tussock-sedge and Royal Fern.

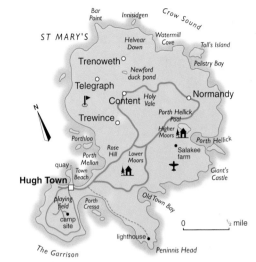

Jack Snipe can give close views at Lower Moors and Porthellick.

■ **HOLY VALE TRAIL** is an extension of the Higher Moors Trail, and is reached by crossing the road. The ivy-clad elms are some of the tallest trees on Scilly. In spring, you may be lucky enough to hear the flutey song of a Golden Oriole. During autumn, Yellow-browed Warblers, Red-breasted Flycatchers and Firecrests favour these trees.

■ **THE AIRPORT AND GOLF COURSE** can be excellent in autumn, regularly attracting rare pipits such as Tawny and Richard's, and waders such as Dotterel. During September, both sites should be checked for Buff-breasted Sandpiper, an American vagrant that is almost annual.

■ **PORTHLOO BEACH,** just north of Hugh Town,

The Red-breasted Flycatcher is an annual drift migrant in October.

attracts waders. In autumn and winter, a flock of Sanderling reside, here, and there are often Dunlin, Grey Plover and Bar-tailed Godwit. The cliff and boulder beach at the northern end can be good for passerine migrants such as Black Redstart, Redstart, warblers and flycatchers.

■ **THE GARRISON** offers a short circular walk, ideal before breakfast or after dinner if you are staying in Hugh Town. The sheltered eastern side is best for passerine migrants. In autumn, look out for Red-breasted Flycatcher, Yellow-browed Warbler and Firecrest, and, on the short turf, Snow and Lapland Buntings. During the summer, check the sea for terns, and in autumn for divers. The interior of The Garrison should not be ignored as the plentiful cover here regularly shelters interesting birds.

■ **PENINNIS HEAD** offers another short walk close to Hugh Town. The fields along the head are attractive to larks, buntings, pipits and

wagtails. In spring, look for Ring Ouzels and Wheatears. The short turf at the end of the head is favoured by Lapland and Snow Buntings in autumn.

2

Tresco

■ **THE GREAT POOL** is centre of attraction on the island. Fringed by reeds for much of its length, the open shore attracts a few waders. The pool is the best site in Scilly for ducks. Gadwall, Teal and Mallard are resident, while Garganey are regular in spring. Two hides, one at the western end and one half-way along the north shore, ensure good coverage. The bushes bordering the path along the north shore attract migrant warblers. In autumn, large numbers of Goldcrests are likely, and Spotted Crakes are regular. The adjoining fields attract

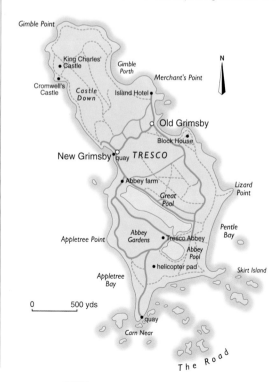

the end of the quay, and following the path along the coast. Numbers of birds present depend on the water-level, but if it is low then a few waders may be encountered in late summer and autumn.

■ **PERIGLIS BEACH** is behind the Big Pool and favoured by waders. Rarities here have included American Lesser Golden Plover, Baird's Sandpiper and Britain's first Semi-palmated Plover.

Twitchers on the quay at St Agnes.

Abbey Gardens, Tresco.

pipits, larks and buntings. The southern side of the Great Pool is dominated by firs and pines that prove unproductive for birds.

■ **THE ABBEY POOL,** nearby, is a favoured haunt for waders, and is regularly visited by gulls.

■ **ABBEY GARDENS**, home to a variety of temperate and subtropical plants, are not particularly good for birds, but are worth a look.

The northern end of Tresco is covered in pine and Rhododendron, and by an expanse of heathland. If time allows, the north is worth exploring as there is plenty of habitat for migrants and it is often neglected by bird-watchers in favour of the Great Pool.

3

St Agnes

St Agnes is the most westerly inhabited of the islands. The following sites are worthy of attention.

■ **THE BIG POOL** can be reached by turning right at

The old lighthouse, St Agnes.

■ **THE OLD PARSONAGE GARDEN** is close to the lighthouse. The shelter available ensures that a variety of warblers, chats and flycatchers are attracted to the garden when migrants are about. Many rare warblers have been recorded, and during easterly winds in autumn Pallas's Warbler is a distinct possibility here. View from the path.

■ **WINGLETANG DOWN**, the southern tip of St Agnes, is best reached along Barnaby Lane, which is bordered by hedgerows and is an excellent site for warblers and Firecrests in autumn. This is also a favoured site for Cuckoos in spring. From the end of the lane, you can take a path down through the gorse on Wingletang, past the Giant's Punchbowl (a perched boulder). Paths also skirt off to the right and left. Whichever way you choose, you will reach Horse Point, which is the best place on the island for sea-watching.

■ **COVEAN** is a sheltered cove on the eastern side of the island. Migrants are attracted to the plentiful cover and shelter here.

■ **GUGH**, attached to St Agnes by a sand bar that is exposed at low tide, is worth exploring if time and tides permit. Remember to ask the boatman what time you need to be off Gugh to avoid being stranded.

4
Bryher

When the tide is out during spring tides, Bryher can be reached on foot by a sand causeway from Tresco, its near neighbour (consult the locals for advice). Bryher is often neglected by bird-watchers, but the island receives its fair share of migrants and rarities. The pool on the western side of the island is worth checking first of all. It attracts waders, though the water-level is often quite high. Stinking Porth, the bay on the seaward side of the pool, can be good for waders, but it collects masses of washed-up seaweed, so is often a bit smelly. For passerines, concentrate on the sheltered parts of the

island. In stormy weather, the aptly named Hell Bay can be spectacular when huge Atlantic rollers crash against the rocks.

5
St Martin's

This large island is difficult to cover in a day. One of the best areas is close to the quay at Higher Town. On the north side of the cricket pitch is a pool that is worth watching to see what comes down to drink, and close by towards Higher Town are areas of willow scrub and elms.

6
Annet and Western Rocks

Annet has nesting seabirds that include Puffins, British Storm-petrels and Manx Shearwaters. Landing is forbidden, but regular boat trips around Annet, the Western Rocks and Bishop Rock lighthouse leave St Mary's during the summer. An evening cruise is best as Manx Shearwaters gather off the northern end of Annet before coming ashore to their nesting burrows after dark. British Storm-petrels are much harder to see, but they may be encountered if you are lucky.

BIRDS THROUGH THE SEASONS
ALL YEAR: Cormorant, Shag, Grey Heron, Mallard, Teal, Gadwall, feral Canada Geese (Tresco), Mute Swan, Kestrel, Oystercatcher,

Ringed Plover, Lesser Black-backed Gull, Great Black-backed Gull, Herring Gull, Skylark, Rock Pipit and Stonechat. Woodpeckers and owls are absent, as are a number of other species found commonly on the mainland.

SPRING: Passage waders include Green Sandpiper, Greenshank, Bar-tailed Godwit, Turnstone, Dunlin, Redshank, Curlew, Whimbrel, and Grey and Golden Plover. Summer migrants include Garganey, Cuckoo, Swift, hirundines, Spotted Flycatcher, Ring Ouzel, Wheatear, Whinchat, White and Yellow Wagtails, Grasshopper Warbler, Wood Warbler, and most of the commoner warblers. Rarities that appear almost annually include Hoopoe, Golden Oriole and Woodchat Shrike.

SUMMER: Breeding seabirds include Manx Shearwater, British Storm-petrel, Fulmar, Kittiwake, Common Tern, Puffin, Guillemot and Razorbill. A few species of warbler breed. Passage waders start to appear.

AUTUMN: Seabirds possible in early autumn (often seen on the boat crossing from Penzance) include Manx, Balearic, Sooty, Great and Cory's Shearwaters, British Storm-petrel, Gannet, Arctic, Great, Pomarine and Long-tailed Skuas, and terns. Peregrine is occasional. Additional species to those listed under spring include Water Rail, Spotted Crake, Jack Snipe, Buff-breasted Sandpiper (September), Dotterel, Spotted Redshank, Grey Phalarope, Pied Flycatcher,

Red-breasted Flycatcher, Redstart, Black Redstart, Yellow-browed, Icterine, Melodious and Barred Warblers, Firecrest, Goldcrest, Tawny and Richard's Pipits, Rose-coloured Starling, Red-backed Shrike, and Snow, Lapland and Little Buntings. October always produces surprises, with European, Asian and American vagrants. The most commonly recorded American landbird vagrant is Red-eyed Vireo.

Red-eyed Vireo.

WINTER: Great Northern Diver, Shoveler, Pochard, Wigeon, Tufted Duck, occasionally Scaup, Pintail, Goldeneye and seaduck. Greenland White-fronted Geese are the most frequently recorded goose. Whooper Swans are occasional. Merlin, Water Rail, Purple Sandpiper, Sanderling, Short-eared and Long-eared Owls are possible. Redwings and Fieldfares can arrive in big numbers if the weather is bad on the mainland.

ACCESS: Most visitors stay on St Mary's, where there is plenty of accommodation. An excellent network of lanes and paths throughout the

islands offer easy walking. The main 'off islands' can all be reached by boat from St Mary's, these leaving from the quay mid-morning and early afternoon.

Scilly can be reached by the following means.

By sea: on the MV *Scillonian*. This is a 2½-hour journey, which can be excellent for seabirds. Further details and sailing times from the Isles of Scilly Steamship Co, Penzance Quay, Penzance. Tel: 01736 62009.

By helicopter: with British International Helicopters from Penzance heliport. Although this is not the cheapest option, it is the most reliable in rough weather. For further information, Tel: 01736 64296.

By aircraft: from Land's End Airport, St Just, with Skybus. For further information, Tel: 01736 787017.

DISABLED ACCESS: None for wheelchair users other than the lanes, which are quiet and have little traffic.

OTHER ATTRACTIONS

THE ISLANDS make an excellent base for a family holiday if you enjoy deserted, long sandy beaches and coastal walks. The Abbey Gardens on Tresco are a popular attraction. On St Agnes, the Turks Head pub close to the quay does an excellent Cornish pasty, while there are some delicious cream teas on offer throughout the islands. Scilly offers beautiful scenery and the chance to get away from it all.

LAND'S END encompasses some of Cornwall's top birding spots, notably a string of sheltered valleys open to the sea. The peninsula is of most interest in spring and autumn for migrants and passing seabirds.

The valleys have patches of scrub and gardens, some with trees and dense cover. In autumn, they are a popular site for birders *en route* to Scilly. Land's End itself is plagued by tourists during summer; however, the few bushes here are worth checking in autumn.

BIRDS

During spring, a good variety of summer migrants can be encountered, though numbers are low. Seabird passage is light in spring, with the chance of Pomarine Skuas in May and often small parties of Whimbrel. Rarities usually involve European species that have overshot their summer breeding grounds, such as Hoopoe and, more rarely, Woodchat Shrike.

Summer, although quiet on land, can prove productive for seabirds. By late July and during August, there is the chance of seeing a Cory's Shearwater. They fly with distinctive, bowed wings and can be seen daily if the weather conditions are right. From early August, numbers and diversity of seabirds increase. Balearic and Manx Shearwaters are joined by Great and Arctic Skuas and a variety of auks. Later in the month, the chance of a Great Shearwater increases. Sea-watching is best in strong south-easterly to south-

westerly winds when visibility is poor.

Passerine migrants start to appear in August, with chats, flycatchers and the commoner warblers evident. In easterly winds, Wryneck, Barred Warbler, Yellow-browed Warbler and Red-breasted Flycatcher may occur, along with the more likely Firecrests and Black Redstarts. Goldcrests and Robins can be numerous. The valleys are best known for the American vagrants that have been found. These have included Yellow-throated Vireo, American Redstart and Chimney

Swift. In winter, a lingering Firecrest may be encountered, while Merlins are regularly seen dashing along hedgerows and over moorland.

SITE GUIDE

1

Porthgwarra

Porthgwarra is the most south-westerly valley on the British mainland, and it has a reputation for attracting rare birds. From the car park, take the main path to the cliff top;

Aerial view along the north coast from Land's End.

various paths lead across the moorland. For passerine migrants, pay particular attention to the gardens and scrub in the bottom of the valley.

Gwennap Head is the best point on Land's End for sea-watching. Birds often pass close to the Runnelstone Buoy a mile offshore and so a telescope is essential. If the day is sunny, then light can be a problem from mid-morning as most birds will appear as silhouettes. An early start or a visit in the late afternoon is recommended in such conditions.

 Access: Leave Penzance for Land's End on the A30. Turn off on to the B3283 to St Buryan. Drive through the village and on past the junction with the B3315, heading towards Sennen. Where the road turns sharply to the right, turn off left down a narrow lane to the car park at the bottom of the valley.

2
Land's End Airfield

The airfield attracts a few waders such as Ruff, Whimbrel and Golden Plover, while Buff-breasted Sandpiper and Dotterel are possible in autumn.

 Access: *See* map.

3
Nanquidno

This is a sheltered valley east of St Just Airfield. The copse of trees near the head of the valley is productive for warblers and flycatchers.

 Access: From the A30, turn off on to the B3306 to St Just. At the northern end of the airfield, take the minor road on the left to Nanquidno Valley. Park at the top and walk down.

4
Cot Valley

There are two small parking areas, one by the sea and one near the head of the valley. Park in the latter and take the path off to the left. This takes you along a stream past gardens and large Sycamores, and is one of the most productive areas. Alternatively, you can walk along the centre of the valley to the sea. American vagrants are almost annual in autumn.

 Access: From the centre of St Just take the road signed to Cape Cornwall, then turn left down a minor road sign-posted to Cot Valley. There is a youth hostel in the valley.

5

Kenidjack

This valley has less cover than some of the other valleys in the area and attracts fewer birds. However, rarities regularly appear in autumn. Tin was once mined here, and remnants of that industry are still evident today.

 ACCESS: From the centre of St Just, take the B3306 towards St Ives. After approximately 2 miles, turn left at the bottom of a steep hill. Drive for another 2 miles before parking.

6

Pendeen Watch

In recent years this has proved to be a good sea-watching point, especially for the larger shearwaters during seabird movements. Birds can be quite distant compared to the more popular St Ives and Porthgwarra, but larger numbers have been recorded here on occasions. *See* St Ives (Site 5) for details of the ideal conditions.

 ACCESS: North of St Just on the B3306, take the minor road on the left in the village of Pendeen, signposted to the lighthouse.

BIRDS THROUGH THE SEASONS

ALL YEAR: Shag, Sparrowhawk, Kestrel, Buzzard, Little Owl, Rock

Melodious Warbler.

Pipit, Stonechat and Raven. SPRING: Offshore: Manx Shearwater, Gannet, divers, Fulmar, Kittiwake, Common Scoter, Sandwich Tern, Common Tern, Whimbrel and Pomarine Skua. Passerine migrants include Ring Ouzel and various warblers and chats. Rarities may include Hoopoe, Serin or, more rarely, Woodchat Shrike. SUMMER: Offshore: Manx Shearwater and, from the end of July, possibly Cory's Shearwater.
AUTUMN: Offshore from August: British Storm-petrel, Gannet, Great, Sooty and Balearic Shearwaters, and Pomarine, Arctic and Great Skua. Passerine migrants in August include all the commoner warblers, chats and flycatchers, including Pied Flycatcher and a good chance of Melodious Warbler. Rarities later in autumn include Red-breasted Flycatcher, Yellow-browed Warbler, Icterine Warbler, Barred Warbler, Wryneck and, annually, American and Asian vagrants. In late autumn, Black Redstart, Firecrest and

flocks of thrushes, buntings and finches occur. WINTER: Hen Harrier, Peregrine and Merlin. Occasional wintering Chiffchaff, Blackcap, Firecrest and Black Redstart.

 ACCESS: *See* under site guide.

DISABLED ACCESS: Wheelchair access is possible to a very limited extent in all the valleys. St Just Airfield can be watched from a vehicle.

OTHER ATTRACTIONS

THE LAND'S END peninsula has some beautiful coves, while the picturesque fishing village of Mousehole lies south of Penzance. Not to be missed is the Minack open-air theatre, an amphitheatre overlooking the sea where performances are conducted regularly during summer. At Land's End there is a tourist complex with exhibitions. Tin-mining was once prevalent in the villages along the north coast, and relics of the industry can still be seen.

THIS SMALL wetland reserve opposite St Michael's Mount is conveniently situated close to Penzance. The reedbed is the largest in Cornwall, and pools and scrub complete the 130-acre site.

🐦 BIRDS

Breeding species include Cetti's Warbler and Grey Heron. A few dabbling ducks and passage waders use the pools. Large numbers of starlings and hirundines roost in the reedbed, which attracts Sparrowhawks and the occasional Peregrine.

Marazion is probably the most reliable site in Britain for seeing the rare Aquatic Warbler. From early August to mid-September, the birds are regularly recorded along the edge of the rushes. Another regular in autumn is the Spotted Crake, which occasionally shows itself on the edge of a pool.

A short walk can be taken along the eastern boundary of the reserve, and to the west a raised road junction gives views across a pool which is frequented by ducks.

Opposite the reserve is Mount's Bay. The sandy shoreline attracts waders. Offshore, in winter, Great Northern Divers and Slavonian Grebes are regular visitors, as are various seaducks. The gatherings of gulls along the beach should be checked for Mediterranean, Ring-billed, Glaucous and Iceland Gull.

BIRDS THROUGH THE SEASONS

ALL YEAR: Cormorant, Shag, Grey Heron, Sparrowhawk, Cetti's Warbler and Reed Bunting.
SPRING: Early migrants include hirundines, Wheatear and possible Garganey. Sandwich Terns offshore. From mid-April, a variety of summer migrants pass through.

SUMMER: Cetti's, Reed and Sedge Warblers breed.
AUTUMN: A few passage waders include Green and possibly Wood Sandpiper. Aquatic Warblers from early August. Spotted Crake from late August. Starlings and hirundines in to roost.
WINTER: Teal, Shoveler, Gadwall, Pochard, Tufted Duck and Water Rail on pools. Offshore: Great Northern Diver, Slavonian Grebe, Eider, Common Scoter and possibly Long-tailed Duck. On the beach: waders and rarer gulls.

The rare Aquatic Warbler is an annual visitor in autumn.

🢂 ACCESS:
Take the A30 from Penzance towards Hayle, turning off for St Michael's Mount. Pass over the railway and then turn left.

♿ DISABLED ACCESS:
There is no wheelchair access on to the reserve. However, the pool by the road junction and the bay can both be viewed from the road.

OTHER ATTRACTIONS

SEE UNDER Land's End (Site 2).

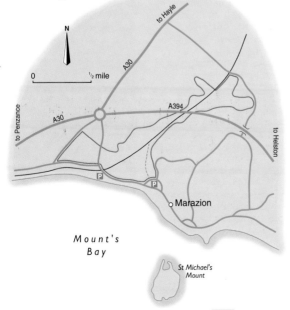

THERE ARE three main areas worth exploring. The main estuary is best viewed from the Old Quay House Inn car park, where there is a hide. Copperhouse Creek is a muddy tidal channel close to Hayle town, and is of most interest for gulls. The third site is Carnsew Pool, a partially tidal pool that is worth checking for waders, ducks and the occasional diver or Slavonian Grebe.

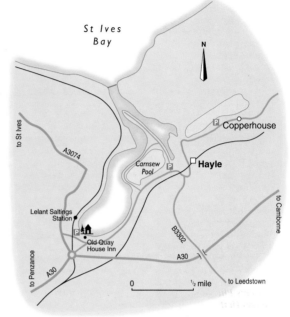

BIRDS

The estuary is best in autumn and winter for wildfowl and waders, and has a reputation for attracting rare American waders. Past sightings have included Least Sandpiper, Wilson's Phalarope and White-rumped Sandpiper.

Numbers of wintering birds are relatively low, with a few hundred waders – mainly Dunlin, Curlew and Lapwing. Wigeon are the most numerous duck. The Hayle has a resident rarity, Little Egrets, and at Copperhouse Creek at least one Ring-billed Gull is likely from late summer through the winter, and will often come if bread is offered in the car park.

BIRDS THROUGH
THE SEASONS

ALL YEAR: Grey Heron, Little Egret, Ring-billed Gull and Oystercatcher.

SPRING: Sandwich Tern, Whimbrel, Little Ringed Plover, and possibly Wood Sandpiper and Black Tern.

SUMMER: Shelduck breed.

AUTUMN: Little Stint, Curlew Sandpiper, Ruff, Wood Sandpiper, Green Sandpiper, Spotted Redshank, Greenshank, Common Sandpiper and wintering waders (see below). American rarities are annual. Large numbers of gulls, with Ring-billed and possible Little and Mediterranean Gulls.

WINTER: Great Northern Diver, often a few Brent Geese. Regular wildfowl include Wigeon, Teal, Gadwall and Tufted Duck. Peregrines are regular. Waders include Curlew, Bar-tailed Godwit, Dunlin, Ringed Plover, Grey Plover, Golden Plover, Lapwing, Knot, Dunlin, Redshank, Turnstone and Snipe.

ACCESS: To reach the Old Quay House Inn car park, leave the A30 at the head of the estuary, just before the Hayle bypass. Parking in the pub car park is allowed outside of pub opening hours. There is a RSPB hide here too.

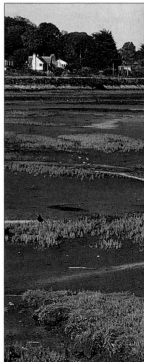

Hayle Estuary.

Wilson's Phalarope is one of a number of American waders that have been recorded on the estuary.

Incidentally, the pub is worth a visit for a meal and a pint. Carnsew Pool is reached by taking the road along the east side of the estuary a short distance from the pub, and then entering along a path by some industrial units. Copperhouse Creek is further along the east side as you enter Hayle town.

DISABLED ACCESS: This is excellent, with good viewing from a wheelchair from both the Old Quay House Inn car park and Copperhouse Creek.

OTHER ATTRACTIONS

SEE UNDER Land's End and St Ives (Sites 2 and 5).

ST IVES is widely acclaimed as Britain's premier sea-watching site. To witness the impressive movements of seabirds that do occur in some autumns, the weather has to be right. Between late August and November, the best days are when the winds blow west-north-west to northerly, preferably after gale-force south-westerly winds associated with an Atlantic depression that has moved across from the south-west. In these perfect conditions, passage can be spectacular, with thousands of birds coming through every hour. The place to watch from is the coast-guard look-out on St Ives island above the town. Birds are pushed into the bay and then struggle out again, often flying close to the assembled bird-watchers.

In such conditions, the weather can be diabolical, so don't forget your waterproofs.

 BIRDS
During north-westerly winds in September, thousands of Gannets and Kittiwakes are likely, along with Sabine's Gulls and Leach's Storm-petrels (two St Ives' specialities). Even in light winds, passage can be good in spring and autumn, but the winds do need to be from the right direction. A sewage outfall in the bay attracts British Storm-petrels, gulls and terns.

During winter, the bay is a good site for seaduck and divers. Great Northern Divers are joined later in the winter by a few Black-throated Divers. Following gales during autumn and occasionally in winter, the bay may shelter a Grey Phalarope.

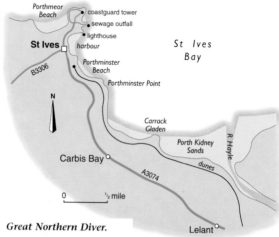

Great Northern Diver.

BIRDS THROUGH THE SEASONS
AUTUMN: Great Northern Diver, Black-throated Diver and, rarely, Red-throated Diver, Manx Shearwater, Balearic Shearwater, Sooty Shearwater, Great Shearwater and, rarely, Cory's Shearwater, British Storm-petrel, Leach's Storm-petrel, Arctic Skua, Great Skua, Pomarine Skua, Long-tailed Skua, possible Sabine's Gull (recorded here more than anywhere else in Britain). In late autumn, Grey Phalarope, large numbers of Razorbills and Guillemots, and a few Little Auks. During early autumn, various terns and Whimbrel pass.
WINTER: In the bay: Great Northern and Black-throated Divers, Slavonian Grebe, Eider, Common Scoter and a few gulls, plus a chance of Grey Phalarope after there have been gales.

ACCESS: Drive through the town of St Ives to its northern end and the car park. From the car park, walk to the top of St Ives island and watch from the coastguard look-out. The sewer outfall can be seen from both the car park and the island.

DISABLED ACCESS: The bay is viewable from a wheelchair in a number of places.

OTHER ATTRACTIONS

ST IVES, a picturesque fishing port, is well known for its attraction to artists and sculptors.

Nestled among moorland, this shallow reservoir is one of the most productive for birds in Cornwall.

The reservoir can be viewed from the road, and there are two hides at its southern end. Alternatively, a 6-mile walk around the reservoir will take around 3½ hours to complete.

BIRDS

Waders are attracted to the reservoir's wide, muddy margins in autumn. In winter, Teal and Wigeon outnumber the Mallard, Gadwall and few diving duck.

Stithians is at its best in autumn when waders are most numerous. Green Sandpipers can number 20 or more, and are joined by numerous Wood and Common Sandpipers. Greenshanks reach double figures, as can Ruff, Little Stints and Curlew Sandpipers.

Rarities are discovered regularly. The large number of Golden Plover that remain to winter often conceal an American Lesser Golden Plover. Pectoral Sandpiper is almost annual; past records reveal Lesser Yellowlegs, Semi-palmated Sandpiper and Wilson's Phalarope, to name a few.

BIRDS THROUGH THE SEASONS

ALL YEAR: Little Grebe and Coot.
SPRING: A few waders pass through, though they rarely linger.
SUMMER: By mid-July, Green, Wood and Common Sandpipers start to appear.
AUTUMN: Passage waders include Dunlin, Ringed Plover, Little Ringed Plover, Little Stint, Curlew Sandpiper, Ruff, Greenshank, Golden Plover, Lapwing and American vagrants. Little Gull and Black Tern are possible.

WINTER: Wigeon, Teal, Mallard, Gadwall, Pochard, Tufted Duck, Goldeneye, Peregrine, Merlin, Golden Plover, Lapwing, Snipe and Ruff.

Lapwings can be abundant in autumn and winter.

ACCESS: From
Redruth, take the A393 and then the B3297 before turning off left along the lanes for the reservoir. The southern end, good for ducks, has two hides, and can be viewed from the road. The northern end, best for waders, is also crossed by a road near the Golden Lion pub.

DISABLED ACCESS:
The reservoir can be viewed from both of the causeways described above, either from a car or a wheelchair.

OTHER ATTRACTIONS

WEST OF Helston at Gweek is a seal sanctuary which rehabilitates sick and injured seals, and which has an exhibition centre and aquarium. At Wendron, north of Helston, Cornish mining history can be explored at the Poldark tin-mine.

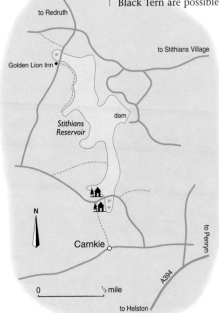

to Redruth

to Stithians Village

Golden Lion Inn

Stithians Reservoir

dam

N

Carnkie

to Penryn

A394

0   ½ mile

to Helston

LUNDY IS owned by the National Trust and lies 10 miles off the Devon coast, where the Atlantic Ocean meets the Bristol Channel. This island measures 3½ miles long by half a mile wide, and is dominated by cliffs. The boggy moorland on its top is 330 feet above the sea. Steep cliffs with deep gullies characterise the north and west while, along the east side, gentler slopes are cloaked in Rhododendron. In the south-east of the island is a small village and a wooded valley that is most attractive to passerine migrants. A bird observatory operated here from 1947 to 1973.

BIRDS

Lundy is derived from the Norse *Lun-dey,* meaning 'Puffin Island'. Sadly, the Puffins have declined to a state where although a few still breed, they are more likely to be seen offshore. A few other species of seabird breed, notably gulls, but it is the migrant birds that

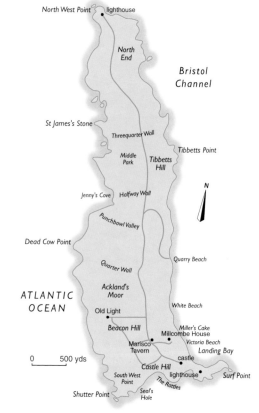

Lesser Black-backed Gulls breed on Lundy.

During summer, a few pairs of auks breed, along with larger numbers of gulls. Features of the summer are large rafts of Manx Shearwaters that congregate offshore. The majority of these birds are thought to be from the large breeding colonies on the Pembrokeshire islands, but a few do come ashore at night.

Autumn rarely witnesses large numbers of migrants, but a good variety filters through in August and September. Millcombe Valley is the place to look, while the moorland attracts a few wagtails, larks and

attract most visitors. A good variety of summer migrants pass through in spring, and a few rarities are always recorded, such as a small trip of Dotterel or a Hoopoe. Good numbers of the commoner warblers and chats can be expected in spring; these are best looked for in the wooded Millcombe Valley.

Spotted Flycatchers can be searched for in the Millcombe Valley in spring and autumn.

pipits, notably Meadow Pipit. A sprinkling of rarities may include a Melodious Warbler or Pectoral Sandpiper. Lundy has recorded some impressive American vagrants – for example, Veery and Yellow-billed Cuckoo. The most remarkable vagrant of all turned up in spring 1990 and returned the following year: an Ancient Murrelet, which should have been in the Pacific Ocean!

A blackboard at the Marisco Tavern details interesting bird sightings.

OTHER ANIMALS
Lundy lies within a Marine Nature Reserve, and there is even an underwater nature trail for divers. Basking Sharks are seen annually in these waters, while Grey Seals are easily seen around the coast. On land, the Lundy Cabbage grows, found nowhere else and the sole host to two endemic beetles. The

cabbage can be found near Millcombe House and in one or two other sites. Sika Deer, wild goats, Soay Sheep and Lundy ponies all graze on the island.

BIRDS THROUGH THE SEASONS
ALL YEAR: Shag, Oystercatcher, Herring Gull, often Peregrine for much of the year, Rock Pipit, Raven. SPRING: Manx Shearwaters appear in March. A few Whimbrel pass from April. Early migrants include Merlin, Wheatear, Black Redstart, Firecrest, Chiffchaff, hirundines. From mid-April, Yellow Wagtail, Ring Ouzel, Pied Flycatcher, Whinchat, Redstart, all commoner warblers, and the chance of rarities such as Hoopoe, Golden Oriole and, regularly, Dotterel. SUMMER: Manx Shearwater offshore and British Storm-petrels possible on boat crossing. Puffin (very few offshore), Guillemot,

Razorbill, Kittiwake, Fulmar, Great Black-backed Gull, Lesser Black-backed Gull, Herring Gull, Lapwing and Curlew all breed. AUTUMN: Warblers, flycatchers, chats, pipits and wagtails on passage. Movements of thrushes and finches in late autumn. Rarities occur. WINTER: Merlin, Golden Plover, Snipe, Purple Sandpiper and Water Rail.

ACCESS: Day cruises to Lundy are possible throughout the year, departing from Bideford, and on some dates from Ilfracombe or Clovelly. There is plentiful accommodation on the island. For sailing times, bookings and accommodation details, Tel: 01237 470422 or write to Lundy Sales Office, The Quay, Bideford, North Devon EX39 2LY.

DISABLED ACCESS: Neither Lundy nor the boat have special facilities for the disabled. However, a Landrover is available to meet the ship to transport passengers who require assistance as the hill from the quay is steep.

OTHER ATTRACTIONS

THE ISLAND has its own brewery, the ale from which can be sampled at the Marisco Tavern, which acts as the centre of island life. There are guided walks and lots of history to explore. Events are detailed on the board at the tavern. The seas around Lundy offer excellent diving, with over 200 wrecks and bountiful marine life.

PERCHED ON the edge of Dartmoor, Yarner Wood's 370 acres is of prime interest for the western woodland specialities: Redstart, Wood Warbler and Pied Flycatcher. Yarner was declared a National Nature Reserve in 1952, one of the first in Britain. Sessile Oak and birch woodland covers most of the reserve, with a small area of conifers and heath.

There are two walks: one is a nature trail which takes around an hour to complete and is 1½ miles long; the other is a longer woodland walk, is 3 miles long and takes about 2 hours to complete. A visit in May or June is recommended. The reserve's centre is an abandoned oak coppice. The bark was used for tanning leather, and the wood used for charcoal burning. The charcoal was fuel for smelting ore in the copper and tin mines of the south west.

BIRDS
The 40–50 pairs of Pied Flycatcher mostly breed in nesting boxes. From early May, the distinctive trill of the Wood Warbler rings out through the wood, while a flash of red may give away the more secretive Redstart. A variety of other woodland birds breed. The resident Lesser Spotted Woodpeckers are best looked for in late winter when the trees are bare; the birds' soft drumming tells you their whereabouts.

OTHER ANIMALS
The wood supports Dormice, Badgers and Roe Deer. Butterflies are well represented by Purple and Green Hairstreak, Pearl Bordered, Silver Washed and the rare High Brown Fritillary, Holly Blue and White Admiral.

BIRDS THROUGH THE SEASONS
ALL YEAR: Sparrowhawk, Buzzard, Lesser Spotted, Great Spotted and Green Woodpeckers, Tawny Owl, Marsh Tit, Nuthatch and Grey Wagtail.
SPRING AND SUMMER: Mandarin ducks visit the streams regularly. Tree Pipit, Wood Warbler, Whitethroat, Blackcap, Redstart, Spotted Flycatcher, Pied Flycatcher.
AUTUMN AND WINTER: Woodcock, Redpoll, Siskin.

Yarner Wood.

ACCESS: From Bovey Tracey, take the B3344 to Manaton. After approximately 2 miles, the road turns sharply right; the reserve is on the left. Drive past the warden's cottage to the car park.

The reserve is open from 8.30am to 8pm or dusk, whichever is sooner.

DISABLED ACCESS: None, other than the immediate vicinity of the car park, although this situation may change. Contact the warden, Yarner Wood NNR, Bovey Tracey, Newton Abbot, Devon TQ13 9LJ.

OTHER ATTRACTIONS

THE DARTMOOR National Park interpretative centre, is based at Parke House, where there is also a rare breeds farm. Just off the A38 at Buckfastleigh is Buckfast Abbey, an active monastery. Buckfast Butterfly farm, and the Dart Valley Railway, are further attractions.

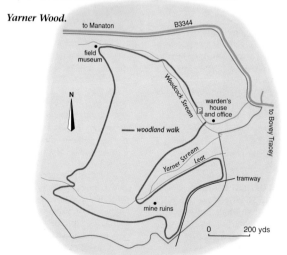

Dawlish Warren Local Nature Reserve is a sand-dune spit at the mouth of the Exe Estuary. A few small pools and scrub lie within the dunes. The reserve is bordered by a golf course on the estuary side and by a wide sandy beach.

🦆 BIRDS

Bird-watching is at its best in autumn and winter. Estuarine wildfowl and waders throng the mudflats, while offshore, seaduck, divers and grebes congregate. This is one of the most reliable sites in Britain for Slavonian Grebes, with the species regularly reaching double figures. Within the estuary an impressive high-tide wader roost attracts a variety of shorebirds, especially Oyster-catchers. A hide overlooks the roost.

Passage migrants start to appear in March, the first arrivals being Wheatears and Sandwich Terns. A good variety of summer migrants pass through in April and May, and again in the autumn. Rarities appear in both seasons.

🌸 FLOWERS

Over 450 species of flowering plant have been recorded, including the Warren Crocus found nowhere else on the British mainland. More conspicuous in June are the Californian Tree Lupins. Orchids include Southern Marsh Orchid and Autumn Lady's Tresses Orchid occur in autumn.

BIRDS THROUGH THE SEASONS

ALL YEAR: Shag, Eider (non-breeding birds), Red-breasted Merganser, Oystercatcher, Ringed Plover, Dunlin and Reed Bunting.

SPRING: Arctic Skua, Sandwich Tern, Little Tern, Common Tern, Black Tern, Hobby, Whimbrel, Common Sandpiper, Wheatear, Cuckoo, commoner warblers and the chance of a rarity.

SUMMER: Sandwich and Common Terns, Cuckoo, Reed Warbler, Sedge Warbler, Whitethroat, Willow Warbler, Chiffchaff and Blackcap.

AUTUMN: Peregrine, Merlin, Little Stint, Curlew Sandpiper, Ruff, Whimbrel, Spotted Redshank, Redshank, Greenshank, Green Sandpiper and arrival of wintering waders (listed below). Arctic Skua and terns in the bay.

WINTER: Red-throated Diver, Great Northern Diver, Slavonian, Great Crested and Little Grebes, Brent Geese, Shelduck, Wigeon, Teal, Common Scoter, Goldeneye, possible Long-tailed Duck and Velvet Scoter, Red-breasted Merganser, Peregrine, Merlin, Short-eared Owl, Avocet, Grey Plover, Turnstone, Dunlin, Knot, Sanderling, Redshank, Greenshank, Green Sandpiper, Curlew, Black-tailed and Bar-tailed Godwits, possible Mediterranean Gull, Short-eared Owl, Chiffchaff and occasional Snow Buntings.

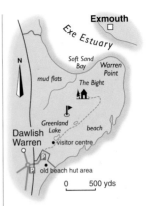

Look for Slavonian Grebes offshore in winter.

▶️ ACCESS:

From the A379 Dawlish–Exeter road, turn off to Dawlish Warren. Turn into the car park by Lee Cliff Holiday Park and proceed under the railway bridge, parking at the far end away from the amusements. A gate here leads to the reserve.

♿ DISABLED ACCESS:

None, other than wheelchair access in the vicinity of the visitor centre, but this does not allow the estuary to be viewed. Other sites on the Exe can be viewed from roads.

OTHER ATTRACTIONS

THE SEASIDE resorts of Dawlish, Teignmouth and Torbay are near by.

***Slapton Ley, looking
towards Torcross.***

SLAPTON LEY is 1½ miles long
and the largest of a series of
freshwater pools separated
from the sea by a shingle
bank. Fringed with reeds
and scrub, its sheltered bays
attract wildfowl in winter.
The other attraction is the
wide variety of summer
migrants that pass through
in spring and autumn.

BIRDS
Slapton Ley is a
delightful place at any time
of year. Breeding birds
include Cirl Buntings that
are local to the ley, Cetti's
Warbler, and hordes of Sedge
and Reed Warblers. In
winter, the wildfowl are
mainly Pochard and Tufted
Ducks outnumbering the
scattered Goldeneye. Off-
shore, seaduck, divers and
grebes reside in Start Bay.
To the south of Slapton
Ley is Beesands Ley.
Beesands is much smaller,
but as it has the same type
of habitats and attracts
similar birds it is always
worth a look if time permits.

OTHER ANIMALS
The field study centre
in Slapton village is
responsible for managing
the ley as a nature reserve.
The reserve is famed for its
abundant animal wildlife.
Otters are occasionally seen
from Slapton Bridge, and the
Jersey Tiger Moth is another
local speciality, restricted to
the south coast of Devon.

FLOWERS
The reserve's plant life
includes rarities such as
Strap-wort, which grows on
the shingle bank and is
found nowhere else in
Britain.

BIRDS THROUGH
THE SEASONS
ALL YEAR: Great Crested
Grebe, Grey Heron, Mallard,
Gadwall, Sparrowhawk,
Kestrel, Buzzard, Water Rail,
Cetti's Warbler, Stonechat,
Cirl Bunting and Reed
Bunting.
SPRING: Garganey and Marsh
Harriers are regular. Early
Wheatears on the shingle
bank. From mid-April, terns
and Whimbrel. Yellow
Wagtail, hirundines

and warblers.
SUMMER: Manx Shearwaters
occur regularly in Start Bay.
Breeding summer visitors
include Reed and Sedge
Warblers. Large numbers of
Swifts gather to feed over
the ley.
AUTUMN: Sandwich,
Common and occasional
Black Terns and Little Gulls.
Common Sandpiper,
Greenshank and large
numbers of hirundines
(especially Swallows) roost.
Hobby are sometimes
attracted to the roosts. A
good variety of warblers
and chats.
WINTER: Offshore: Great
Northern Diver, Slavonian
Grebe, Common Scoter,
Eider, Shag and Cormorant.
On the ley: Gadwall,
Wigeon, Teal, Shoveler,
Tufted Duck, Pochard,
Goldeneye, and occasional
Smew and Goosander.
Firecrest and Chiffchaff
often winter in the
surrounding scrub.

ACCESS: The ley lies
alongside the A379
south of Dartmouth. There
is a public hide in the car

park by the tank monument in Torcross. A second hide is located on the opposite bank, reached from the A379 as it climbs away from the lake.

Ireland Bay, good for wildfowl, can be reached by taking the trail opposite the ringing hut (*see* map). To follow other trails, a permit is needed from the field centre.

Beesands Ley is south of Torcross.

DISABLED ACCESS: Much of the ley can be seen from the road and car parks. The public hide in Torcross allows wheelchair access.

OTHER ATTRACTIONS

DELIGHTFUL DARTMOUTH, with its strong shipping links, is home to the Butterwalk Museum. The miniature railway at Kingsbridge is ideal for kids. See also Yarner Wood (Site 8).

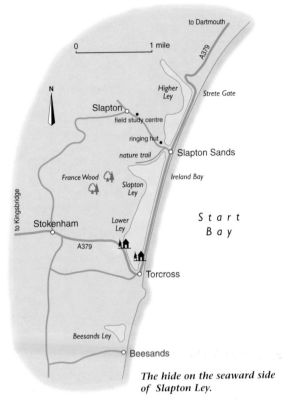

The hide on the seaward side of Slapton Ley.

PRAWLE POINT, reached along narrow lanes bordered by high hedges, lies south of Kingsbridge. It is the southernmost point in Devon, and so is an excellent sea-watching site and migration watch-point.

🦆 BIRDS

A major attraction is resident Cirl Bunting; Prawle is one of the most reliable sites for seeing this species. Search the hedgerows and woodland edges as the birds can often be located close to the car park or along the

to mid-May, chats, flycatchers and warblers move through. Willow Warblers can be particularly abundant. In May there is a good chance of a migrant raptor such as a Honey Buzzard. During onshore winds, seabird and wader passage can be interesting. Whimbrels pass in small flocks, and there are often a few terns and skuas. Manx Shearwaters pass daily at this time.

The summer can be quiet. Cirl Buntings become difficult to find, and one of

Shearwater, the latter most likely in September.

Passerine migrants are numerous in autumn, with August and September witnessing the biggest movements. The sheltered coves along the cliffs are the best places to search, and October can be a good month for rarities. American vagrants have included Black and White Warbler and Chestnut-sided Warbler. Almost annual are Red-breasted Flycatcher and Yellow-browed Warbler, while vagrants from further

lane. In winter they flock and often associate with other species feeding along field edges.

Spring brings a variety of passerine migrants. Wheatears and Chiffchaffs are first, and from mid-April

the most prominent residents is the Stonechat. By late summer, seabirds will be moving. During gales associated with poor visibility, sea-watching can be productive for skuas, Gannets and Sooty

east have been recorded. In winter, the occasional Chiffchaff or Firecrest may be discovered, while offshore, Gannets, auks and divers pass.

On arrival at Prawle during a spring or autumn

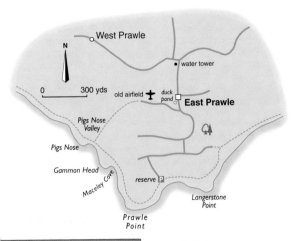

Prawle Point.

sheltered coves along the cliff for migrants. After passing Langerstone Point you will reach Prawle Wood, its edges attracting warblers and flycatchers. You can then walk back along the lane to complete a circular route.

To the west of Prawle Point is Pigs Nose Valley. A stream runs through the centre of the valley, which has plenty of cover for migrants. A circular walk can take in the valley, starting in the car park.

BIRDS THROUGH THE SEASONS

ALL YEAR: Sparrowhawk, Buzzard, Little Owl, Rock Pipit, Stonechat, Cirl Bunting, Tree Sparrow and Raven.
SPRING: Offshore: Manx Shearwater, Fulmar, divers, Eider, Common Scoter, Red-breasted Merganser, Whimbrel, Bar-tailed Godwit, Sandwich Tern, and Great, Arctic and Pomarine Skua (late April to early May). In early spring, Black Redstart, Wheatear, Chiffchaff, Firecrest and

Goldcrest. From mid-April, Willow Warbler, Wood Warbler, Blackcap, Garden Warbler, Whitethroat, Lesser Whitethroat, Reed Warbler, Sedge Warbler, Grasshopper Warbler, Cuckoo, Redstart, Spotted Flycatcher, Tree Pipit, Whinchat, Turtle Dove and Hobby. Rarities may include a Hoopoe or Serin.
SUMMER: Manx Shearwater, Balearic Shearwater, Gannet and Fulmar.
AUTUMN: Balearic Shearwater, Sooty Shearwater and skuas in the right conditions. From August, Wheatear, Whinchat, Redstart, Yellow Wagtail, Tree Pipit, various warblers, and Pied and Spotted Flycatchers. Late autumn, hirundines, Meadow Pipit, Chiffchaff, Firecrest, Black Redstart, often Yellow-browed Warbler and Red-breasted Flycatcher. American vagrants possible in October.
WINTER: Offshore: Great Northern Diver, Common Scoter, Gannet, Kittiwake and auks. Peregrine and Purple Sandpiper. Overwintering birds may include Chiffchaff, Firecrest or Black Redstart, finch and thrush flocks.

 ACCESS: From Kingsbridge, take the A379 before turning off down minor roads for East Prawle village. Drive through the village and down a cul-de-sac to the National Trust car park.

DISABLED ACCESS: None.

OTHER ATTRACTIONS

SEE UNDER Slapton Ley (Site 10).

visit, check the car park area thoroughly first as this can be one of the most productive sites. From the car park you can take the cliff path either to the east or to the west. If you head east, check the gullies and

ALTHOUGH A shadow of its former self due to modern drainage and the peat industry, the Somerset Levels are still of major importance for birds.

Winter flooding is necessary to keep the vitality of life on the levels, but this only occurs in scattered pockets, many of which are nature reserves. Perhaps the best known of these is the reserve at West Sedgemoor, established by the RSPB in 1978.

BIRDS
The Icelandic population of Whimbrel uses the levels for a refuelling stop on its spring migration. However, in years when the ground is dry, Whimbrel are recorded less on the levels and in higher numbers on the coast. Black-tailed Godwits have nested, but are sporadic. Lapwings, Redshanks, Snipe and Curlew all breed. Quail are heard most years, while Yellow Wagtails and

Whinchats both nest. One of the highlights of a day's bird-watching on the levels is an encounter with Barn Owls, a species that is widespread and often seen hunting during the daytime in winter.

A number of roads criss-cross the levels, allowing large areas to be covered. This helps in locating birds that congregate in the best feeding areas, often dictated by the amount of flooding. Bewick's Swans, Teal, Wigeon, Golden Plover, Dunlin and often a few Ruff all use these floods in winter.

OTHER ANIMALS
Roe Deer are common. Hares are widespread, but the most elusive mammal is the Otter, which occurs at just a few sites.

FLOWERS
The levels support an abundance of insect and aquatic life, while the meadows are rich in flowers.

West Sedgemoor
RSPB Reserve

West Sedgemoor Reserve extends up on to a steep escarpment that is cloaked in deciduous woodland. A short walk leads from the car park to a hide which overlooks one of the largest heronries in Britain. A good cross-section of woodland birds is present, including Willow Tit, a species that is scarce in Somerset.

A steep walk from the car park down to the wetland gives good panoramic views. From the hide on the edge of the moor, distant views of wintering wildfowl are often possible. Hen Harrier, Short-eared Owl, Peregrine and Merlin are

West Sedgemoor.

regular in winter. In spring and summer, this is a good reserve for chancing upon a hobby.

The wet grassland covers 1300 acres and is managed in a traditional way, with haymaking and grazing during the summer, followed by flooding in winter. Roe Deer are often seen grazing on the grassland.

ACCESS: The car park is signposted from the A378, 1 mile east of Fivehead. The heronry hide is closed during February to allow the birds to settle in. Visitors are asked not to venture out on to the moor so as not to disturb breeding and wintering birds.

DISABLED ACCESS: The heronry hide is accessible to wheelchair users; otherwise access for the disabled is difficult.

2

Shapwick Heath & Westhay Moor

Both sites lie in the former heart of the peat industry in north Somerset. The Somerset Levels are divided into sections, segregated by low ridges. Shapwick and Westhay lie to the north of such a ridge, the Polden Hills, in an area drained by the Brue and Axe rivers.

Shapwick is an excellent site for Barn Owls, which are best looked for at dusk although they may be encountered at any time during the day. Grasshopper

Warbler and Cetti's Warbler both breed. Alders provide food for Siskins and Redpolls.

Shapwick Heath is one of the few remaining examples of a raised bog,

Roe Buck.

albeit much encroached upon by commercial peat digging. Shapwick is a National Nature Reserve, and supports a rich variety of plants, including Marsh Fern and Marsh Orchid. Insect life also abounds, with many rare species present. Roe Deer are common, and are best observed at dawn or dusk, when they often come out on to the exposed peat workings. Of the other mammals, Otters may still survive here, but you are much more likely to encounter a Mink.

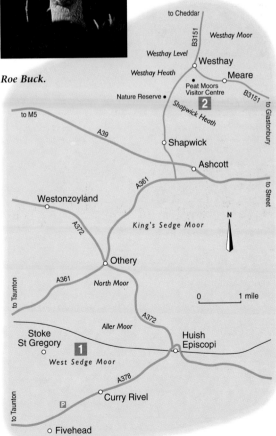

Barn Owls can often be seen hunting out on the Levels in daylight.

SPRING: Garganey, Redshank, Snipe, Lapwing and Curlew breed. Whimbrel on passage, Black-tailed Godwits often attempt to breed. Yellow Wagtail and Whinchat breed on the grassland. Woodland species include a few pairs of Nightingales. A few Nightjars, Redstarts, Tree Pipits and Grasshopper Warblers on Shapwick Heath. The heronry at West Sedgemoor is best viewed before leaves emerge on the trees.

SUMMER: Apart from the breeding species mentioned above, Hobby is likely. Warm summer evenings may produce calling Quail. The heronry is deserted by late June.

AUTUMN: Green Sandpiper on suitable pools.

WINTER: Bewick's Swan, Wigeon, Pintail, Teal, Shoveler, Hen Harrier, Merlin, Peregrine, Short-eared Owl, Ruff and occasional Jack Snipe.

Westhay Moor is an example of what can be made of an area when peat extraction has ended. The numerous reed-fringed pools are attractive to Garganey, and Marsh Harriers breed locally. The latter can be encountered quartering the surrounding fields and reedbeds. A hide at Westhay overlooks a series of pools, which attract wildfowl in winter. As the peat industry gradually winds down, so more land is being left for nature. Various plots have been bought by conservation bodies, thereby giving this area great promise for the future.

ACCESS: Shapwick Heath is a permit-only reserve, but most of the interesting birds can be seen from the road or from the numerous tracks. Shapwick village lies off the A39 which leads to Bridgwater. The B3151 should be followed to the heath, which lies between Shapwick and the village of Westhay. The best place for bird-watching is the area just south of the main drain.

Westhay Moor lies just off the B3151. The droves can all be walked, and some are accessible by car.

DISABLED ACCESS: Wheelchair access is not possible off the roads. Much of the area can be worked from a vehicle.

BIRDS THROUGH THE SEASONS

ALL YEAR: Little Grebe, Grey Heron, Mute Swan, Water Rail, Sparrowhawk, Buzzard, Kestrel, Lapwing, Snipe, Redshank, Curlew, Tawny Owl, Little Owl, Barn Owl, Kingfisher, Lesser Spotted, Great Spotted and Green Woodpeckers, Cetti's Warbler, Willow Tit, Corn Bunting and Reed Bunting.

OTHER ATTRACTIONS

THERE ARE a number of attractions close to West Sedgemoor, including Exmoor National Park. Crinkley Bottom at Cricket St Thomas is Britain's first television theme park, and has attractions for all the family.

Close to Westhay and Shapwick is New Road Farm, with a variety of farm breeds and wild animals. Between Shapwick and Westhay is the Peat Moors Visitor Centre, giving a fascinating insight into the history of the area.

THE VAST mudflats of Bridgwater Bay form a National Nature Reserve. The Parrett and Brue rivers, and the Huntspill Canal all drain into the estuary, which is bordered on its eastern side by the resort of Burnham-on-Sea.

BIRDS
Bridgwater Bay is the most important moulting site for Shelducks in Britain, with over 2000 congregating in late summer. Another prominent species is the Whimbrel; in spring,

Over 2000 Shelduck congregate to moult in Bridgwater Bay in late summer.

View from Stert towards Burnham-on-Sea.

large numbers stop off here and on the nearby Somerset Levels while *en route* to Iceland. In years when the levels provide good feeding, the birds mostly just roost in the bay.

Waders are the main attraction, with various species passing through on passage and in large wintering concentrations. In winter, Dunlin can reach a population of 15,000, with lesser numbers of all the typical estuarine species. Black-tailed Godwits of Icelandic origin are a feature throughout much of winter, while luck is needed to find the handful of Spotted Redshanks. Due to the vast expanse of mud, it is imperative to visit as close to high tide as possible, otherwise many of the birds are just dots in the distance. Ideally, an hour before high tide and two hours after allows the best viewing, as birds are pushed up close and can also be watched at high-tide roosts.

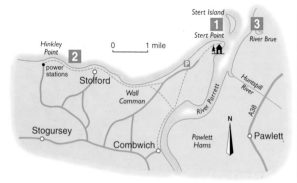

Raptors patrol the shore and fields. There are few sites more spectacular than a Merlin or Peregrine stooping into a flock of wheeling waders. As spring arrives, so the wader numbers fluctuate, with various species passing through. Yellow Wagtails occur in small flocks in the fields, while fence posts should be checked for Wheatears and Whinchats.

A few waders remain through the summer. By early July, return migration has commenced, with the arrival of a few Whimbrel, Curlew and Black-tailed Godwits. By August, Curlew Sandpipers, Spotted Redshanks and Little Stints mingle with the commoner species. The fields abound with Yellow Wagtails. The small reedbeds attract Reed and Sedge Warblers, and have also produced Aquatic Warblers usually trapped by ringers, implying that this species is probably an annual passage migrant in autumn.

During autumn and early winter, strong westerly or north-westerly winds can sometimes blow seabirds into the bay. Manx Shear-waters, skuas, and British and Leach's Storm-petrels are often then recorded.

SITE GUIDE

1

Stert and Fenning Islands

Stert and Fenning islands, on the south side of the bay opposite Burnham-on-Sea, have some of the most productive sites. The River Parrett to the south and the bay to the north sandwich a few fields grazed by cattle, and at Fenning Island there are a few small pools and hides. Along the shore, a thin strip of reeds has attracted Aquatic Warblers in autumn. A circular walk can be taken out along the shore to the hides and back along a track between the fields. The fields are attractive to Yellow Wagtails and Wheatears, and are often quartered in winter by Hen Harriers and Short-eared Owls. Merlins and Peregrines are also regular.

The pools at Fenning Island attract very few birds, although the occasional rarity such as Wilson's Phalarope has been seen. The hides are best visited around high tide. Waders fly about in restless flocks before roosting out on the island, or on the Spartina on the banks of the River Parrett.

Hides at Stert.

ACCESS: From Bridgwater, take the A39 towards Minehead, turning right at Cannington for signs to Combwich and Hinkley Point. After Combwich, turn right to Otterhampton, turning right again after a mile, along a cul-de-sac to Steart village. Park in the car park on the left, and proceed to the hides.

DISABLED ACCESS: None.

Stolford and Hinkley Point

Just behind the shingle-banked shoreline at Stolford are a few seasonal shallow pools, and behind these are grazed fields. In winter, Golden Plover use the fields, as do hunting raptors. The mud does not extend as far at low tide here as it does off Stert, so waders can often be seen closer too. Occasional Snow and Lapland Buntings occur along the grass and shingle foreshore. During spring, Wheatears can be encountered along the sea wall that leads to Hinkley from Stolford. A warm-water outflow from the power station attracts a few gulls and terns. The rocks have resident Rock Pipits and, often in winter, a Black Redstart.

ACCESS: A track runs from Steart along the coast to Stolford. This can be driven along with care. Otherwise, park at Stolford and walk along the track towards Steart or to Hinkley Power Station.

DISABLED ACCESS: Bird-watching is possible from a car along the track that runs between Stolford and Steart; however, this is very limited.

3

Burnham-on-Sea and River Brue

At the mouth of the River Brue, a small wader roost can be watched from the southern end of the Burnham-on-Sea promenade. A path leads along the Brue from the promenade. During autumn gales, the promenade can be a good place to watch for seabirds that are blown into the bay.

ACCESS: Drive on to the Burnham-on-Sea promenade and park at the southern end.

DISABLED ACCESS: Viewing from a wheelchair is possible.

BIRDS THROUGH THE SEASONS
ALL YEAR: Cormorant, Grey Heron, Shelduck, Oystercatcher and Rock Pipit (Hinkley).
SPRING: All the winter waders, and Whimbrel and Greenshank. Common and Arctic Tern (early May), Arctic Skua, Wheatear, Whinchat, Yellow Wagtail, White Wagtail, Swallow and Sand Martin.
SUMMER: Moulting Shelduck peak, Yellow Wagtail breed.

Waders start to return by early July.
AUTUMN: During gales, seabirds blown into the bay may include Manx Shearwater, Fulmar, Leach's and British Storm-petrels, and skuas. Passage waders (in addition to those listed under winter) include Curlew Sandpiper, Little Stint and Greenshank. Passerines include Yellow Wagtail, Wheatear, Whinchat, Reed and Sedge Warbler and Black Redstart.
WINTER: Wigeon, Teal, Mallard, Hen Harrier, Peregrine, Merlin, Short-eared Owl, Golden Plover, Grey Plover, Ringed Plover, Lapwing, Knot, Snipe, Bar-tailed and Black-tailed Godwits, Curlew, Redshank, Spotted Redshank (scarce), Turnstone and Dunlin. Occasional Snow and Lapland Buntings.

 ACCESS: *See* under site guide.

DISABLED ACCESS: Very poor, with little scope for decent bird-watching if you are confined to a wheelchair.

OTHER ATTRACTIONS

THE MENDIP Hills are close by, encompassing such attractions as Cheddar Gorge and the caves at Wookey Hole. Nearby Glastonbury, a place of pilgrimage and steeped in history, has the small cathedral city of Wells as a neighbour. Burnham-on-Sea and Weston-Super-Mare, just up the road in Avon, are both holiday resorts and have all the usual family attractions and provide plentiful accommodation.

NESTLING AT the base of the Mendip Hills and lying just 8 miles south of Bristol is Chew Valley Lake, a popular recreational centre for fishing, sailing and bird-watching.

🦆 BIRDS

Since the lake's completion in 1956, over 250 species have been recorded. Large numbers of wildfowl winter, including a flock of Ruddy Ducks that can exceed 1000 birds. Some of these ducks, a native of North America, escaped from nearby Slimbridge, which led to the species breeding in 1960. They then spread to the West Midlands, now their breeding stronghold.

Bristol Water Company designated the southern end of the lake at Herriot's Bridge a nature reserve in 1969. This is where you tend to find large numbers of birds, safe from the disturbance created by sailing activities. Ruddy Ducks favour this end, as do Goosanders. The causeway at Herriot's Bridge is a good vantage point for bird-watching from a car.

There are four hides that require a permit, and one open hide on the Bittern Trail that does not. This trail offers the opportunity to see a cross-section of woodland birds. Kingfishers are a common sight, and various waders and ducks can be observed from the hide. Denny Island, opposite, is used for breeding by Shoveler, Pochard, Tufted and Ruddy Ducks.

Chew is renowned throughout Europe as a trout fishery. With the stocking of thousands of fish each year, there is never any shortage of food for the occasional visiting Osprey. Little Gulls and Black Terns are frequent visitors during late summer, and rarities in autumn can include the occasional Grey Phalarope. Anything is possible, as the past occurrences of Killdeer and Greater Sand Plover prove.

BIRDS THROUGH THE SEASONS

ALL YEAR: Great Crested Grebe, Little Grebe, Cormorant, Grey Heron, Canada Goose, Mallard, Shoveler, Pochard, Tufted Duck, Ruddy Duck, Sparrowhawk, Buzzard, Little Owl, Kingfisher, Grey Wagtail, Reed Bunting.

SPRING: Passage waders include Common Sandpiper, Dunlin, Ruff and Whimbrel. Common Scoter and Garganey are possible from March. Hobby, Marsh Harrier and Osprey from late April. Common, Arctic and Black Terns and Little Gulls. Passerines include Yellow Wagtails, Wheatears and Whinchats.

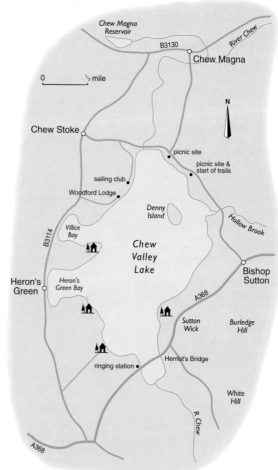

The colourful Ruddy Duck is a native of North America, and is a resident breeder and winter visitor to Chew.

SUMMER: Breeding birds include Ruddy Duck, Gadwall, Pochard, Tufted Duck, Shoveler. Cuckoo and Sedge and Reed Warbler. Hobby is regular.

AUTUMN: Black-necked Grebe, Osprey, Black Tern and various other terns, and Little Gull. A variety of passage waders attracted to the wide muddy margins start to appear by early July, including Little Ringed and Ringed Plover, Curlew Sandpiper, Dunlin, Black-tailed Godwit, Spotted Redshank, Green and Common Sandpiper, Wood Sandpiper, Little Stint, Greenshank and Ruff. Rare waders have included Buff-breasted Sandpiper, Pectoral Sandpiper, Wilson's Phalarope and Long-billed Dowitcher.

WINTER: Wintering birds include all the commoner dabbling ducks, with Shoveler, Wigeon and Teal in large numbers. Goosander and Goldeneye have increased their wintering populations in recent years. Ruddy Ducks can number over 1000. Red-breasted Merganser, Smew and Long-tailed Duck are regular. A large gull roost may include the odd Mediterranean, Glaucous or Iceland Gull. Other irregular visitors include Bearded Tit and wintering Chiffchaff and Firecrest. Golden Plover flocks, if not on the exposed mud, can be located on the surrounding farmland, Ruff often linger into winter.

ACCESS: Roadside viewing is possible from various points around the lake. The best sites for this are at Herriot's Bridge at the southern end on the A368, and at Heron's Green on the eastern side on the B3114. To access the hides a permit is required, obtainable by post from Woodford Lodge, Chew Stoke, Bristol BS18 8XH, or by calling at the lodge from Monday to Friday, 8.45am to 4.45pm, and at weekends during the trout-fishing season (April to October).

You can reach the Bittern and Grebe trails (for which there are information leaflets available) by parking in the top north-east car park, off Denney Road. Here, there are also refreshments and an information display. Parking is also possible at the start of the trails in the next car park to the south.

DISABLED ACCESS: Wheelchair access is possible from the information centre off Denney Road, and around the Grebe Trail which is on a hard-standing surface. Viewing is possible from the car at both Herriot's Bridge and Heron's Green.

OTHER ATTRACTIONS

*S*EE BRIDGWATER Bay (Site 13).

THESE TWO wetland reserves lie close to each other in Weymouth. Although they differ markedly in habitat, there is much interchange of birds between the two. Lodmoor is primarily a flooded grazing marsh with muddy scrapes, pools and small areas of reeds. Radipole is composed of reed beds with pools and scrub, and lies in the heart of Weymouth.

BIRDS
Cetti's Warblers and Bearded Tits are characteristic of both reserves throughout the year. During winter, both areas attract a variety of wildfowl, although Wigeon,

Radipole Lake.

Cetti's Warblers are secretive residents on both reserves.

OTHER ANIMALS
Mammals are scarce, with Fox being the most regular. Roe Deer are occasionally seen at Lodmoor. Due to the reserves' positions on the coast, migrant butterflies such as Clouded Yellows and Painted Ladies are regular, as are a number of migrant moths.

FLOWERS
The numerous Buddleia attract butterflies as outlined above.

often abundant on Lodmoor, are scarce at Radipole. Gulls are a year-round feature and are one of the commoner species. Rarities such as Glaucous, Iceland, Ring-billed and, regularly, Mediterranean Gulls are seen among the loafing flocks in autumn and winter.

Both reserves attract a good variety of migrants.

Lodmoor is much more attractive to waders, particularly in autumn when a good selection is likely, although numbers are never high. Radipole is more attractive to passerines, particularly to large numbers of warblers. Radipole's reedbeds are used in autumn by roosting Swallows and Yellow Wagtails, which in turn often attract a migrant Hobby.

BIRDS THROUGH THE SEASONS
ALL YEAR: Little and Great Crested Grebes, Grey Heron, Gadwall, Water Rail, Kingfisher, Cetti's Warbler, Bearded Tit, Reed Bunting.
SPRING: Garganey are annual. Hobby, Common Tern, Little Tern, Black Tern, Green Sandpiper, Common Sandpiper, Little Ringed Plover, Ruff, Black-tailed

Radipole Lake Information Centre.

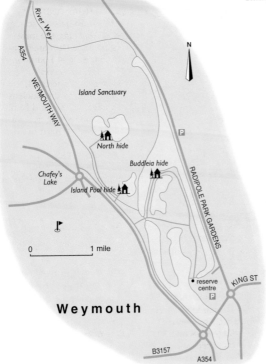

Weymouth

and Bar-tailed Godwits, Whimbrel, Spotted Redshank, Greenshank, Cuckoo, Swifts, hirundines, Yellow Wagtail, Water Pipit (Lodmoor), Reed, Sedge, and Grasshopper Warblers and Nightingale (Radipole). There is a chance of a rarity. SUMMER: Lesser Whitethroat, and Reed, Sedge and Grasshopper Warblers all breed. Yellow Wagtail (Lodmoor) and gulls. AUTUMN: Garganey, Hobby, Spotted Crake (annual at Radipole), Little Ringed Plover, Little Stint, Curlew Sandpiper, Ruff, Wood, Green and Common Sandpipers, Spotted Redshank, Greenshank, Whimbrel, Bar-tailed and Black-tailed Godwits, Mediterranean Gull, Little Gull, terns, Swifts, hirundines, Yellow Wagtails (large roost at Radipole), and Sedge and Reed Warblers.

WINTER: Bittern (Radipole), Teal, Pochard, Tufted Duck, Shoveler, Scaup, occasional Goldeneye, Wigeon (Lodmoor), occasional Merlin, Peregrine, Snipe, occasional Jack Snipe, Lapwing and Mediterranean Gull. Glaucous, Iceland, Ring-billed and Little Gulls are annual. Often over-wintering Blackcap, Chiffchaff and Firecrest.

ACCESS: Radipole Lake is reached from the centre of Weymouth, the reserve lying just north of the King's Roundabout. Park close to the reserve centre in the far right-hand corner of the Swannery car park. The reserve centre is open from 9am to 5pm daily. Car parking is in the long-stay car park, but RSPB members can obtain concessionary tickets for this from the reserve centre on arrival.

Lodmoor is just east of Weymouth town on the A353 coast road. There are car parks at either end of the reserve.

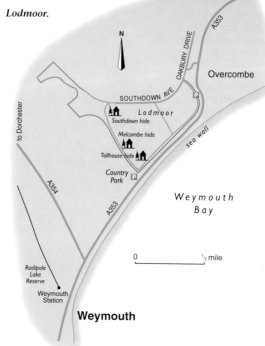

Lodmoor.

DISABLED ACCESS: This is excellent on both reserves. Firm, even paths lead to the hides, all of which are accessible to wheelchairs.

OTHER ATTRACTIONS

WEYMOUTH is a popular seaside resort, and so has the usual attractions for the family.

JUTTING 6 miles out into the English Channel from Weymouth is Portland Bill, renowned as a migration watch-point. Portland is attached to the mainland by Chesil Beach, which is a shingle bank running away to the west. Behind the beach at Ferry Bridge is an area of brackish water known as The Fleet, and to the east of the beach lies Portland Harbour. The harbour and Fleet are both excellent bird-watching sites.

Portland is a limestone massif, tallest on its northern flank, and gently sloping down to Portland Bill and the sea, where the cliffs are only a few yards high. Much of the isle is quarried and built upon. However, south of Southwell to the Bill there are fields with hedgerows, small copses and overgrown quarries, all providing ideal cover for migrants.

View towards Chesil Beach and Weymouth.

SITE GUIDE

1

Portland Bill

A bird observatory has operated here since 1955, based in the old lighthouse.

There is no wader habitat, and so the main interest lies in passerine migrants and sea-watching.

Migrants start to filter through in March and gradually build up in number. Between mid-April and May is the best time to visit for the widest variety

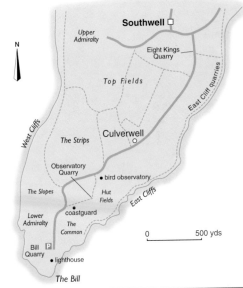

of species. Early mornings are best as many migrants rarely linger, often moving on shortly after day-break. However, some diurnal migrants, such as hirundines and raptors, will arrive later in the day, having set off from across the other side of the Channel at dawn. Southerly and particularly south-

Sea-watching at Portland.

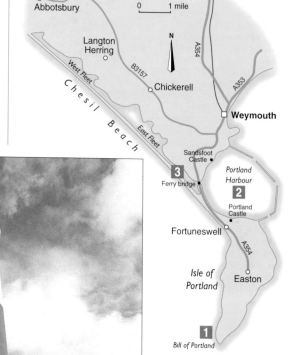

easterly winds are best for migrants and the chance of rarities. Typical overshoots from the Continent recorded annually include Hoopoe and Serins, though the latter are usually seen or heard just flying over.

Offshore, movements up the Channel commence in March, involving divers, auks and Common Scoters. From April, Manx Shearwaters, Bar-tailed Godwits, Whimbrels, terns and skuas pass. From late April to mid-May, Pomarine Skuas are the main attraction. Sea-watching in autumn is much less reliable and more prone to the weather. Onshore south-westerly to south-easterly winds during periods of unsettled weather are best. In autumn, there is the added possibility of Sooty and Balearic Shearwaters, and an outside chance of Grey Phalarope, petrels and perhaps Sabine's Gulls.

Autumn migrants include the same species as are seen in spring, but in larger numbers and with the increased likelihood of species such as Pied Flycatcher. The same winds as in spring are best for rarities. Migrants often linger for days at a time in autumn, so the necessity of a well-timed visit is less important.

Within the observatory recording area on the Bill cover is fairly limited, so any patch of bushes deserves attention. The observatory garden can be particularly rewarding, as can the overgrown quarry to the south and the cover in the vicinity of the coastguard cottages. A circular walk can be taken up on to the Top Fields and back down via Culverwell, an often productive patch of scrub. The common land leading down to the new lighthouse is attractive to pipits and Wheatears, but can get very disturbed by day-trippers at weekends.

ACCESS: Take the A354 south from Weymouth. Portland Bill is well signposted from Weston or from Southwell.

Accommodation is available at Portland Bird Observatory by advance booking. Further details from Portland Bird Observatory, Old Lower Light, Portland Bill, Dorset DT5 2JT.

DISABLED ACCESS: For wheelchair users access is very limited, and is confined to the lighthouse and the area around the coastguard cottages.

2

Portland Harbour

Between November and March, the harbour, primarily a winter site, attracts divers, grebes and seaduck. At times all three species of diver may be seen, as well as Black-necked, Slavonian and Red-necked Grebes. Red-breasted Mergansers are numerous, with often in excess of 300 present. Long-tailed Ducks, Velvet and Common Scoters, Eider and various auks are regular in small numbers in most winters. The harbour is best on a calm day as birds can be quite distant. Sands-foot Castle in Weymouth is the best vantage point for viewing the northern side. The west side can be viewed from alongside the A354, and at Ferry Bridge.

Migrant Chiffchaffs start to appear by late March.

ACCESS: Sandsfoot Castle is reached off the A354. Heading towards Portland, from Weymouth turn down Old Castle Road, which leads off on a sharp right-hand bend.

DISABLED ACCESS: Viewing from a wheelchair is easiest from Ferry Bridge.

3

Ferry Bridge and The Fleet

The Fleet is a brackish lagoon that enters Portland Harbour at Ferry Bridge. At its western end is Abbotsbury, with its famous swannery where Mute Swans have bred for more than 900 years. Protected from the sea by the 18-mile long Chesil Beach, The Fleet attracts a variety of wildfowl and waders. Brent Geese, Wigeon and Coot can be found in large numbers in winter, along with a variety

Scaup are regular in winter.

of other wildfowl. A good selection of waders winter, while in spring and autumn rarities are regular, particularly Kentish Plover, which often favour the mud at Ferry Bridge.

 ACCESS: Access to much of Chesil Beach is restricted to avoid disturbance to breeding and wintering birds.

Ferry Bridge and the eastern end of The Fleet is reached on the A354 road to Portland.

The Fleet near Langton Herring can be good for waders and wildfowl, and can be viewed from the Dorset Coast Path. This can be reached from paths leading down to The Fleet between Chickerell and Langton Herring.

Abbotsbury Swannery is well signposted off the B3157 at Abbotsbury, and is open from mid-May to the end of September.

DISABLED ACCESS: Restricted to Ferry Bridge and sea-watching from Portland Bill.

BIRDS THROUGH THE SEASONS

ALL YEAR: Fulmar, Great Crested Grebe, Grey Heron, Mute Swan, Cormorant, Shag, Kittiwake, Rock Pipit. SPRING: Offshore: Manx Shearwaters, divers, Gannet, Common Scoter, Arctic Skua, Great Skua, Pomarine Skua (late April to mid-May), terns, Whimbrel, Bar-tailed Godwit, Little Gull and Kittiwake. Migrant waders on The Fleet: Greenshank, Common Sandpiper and, annually, Kentish Plover. Passerine migrants at Portland Bill, from March onwards: Black Redstart, Ring Ouzel, Wheatear, Chiffchaff, Firecrest. From mid-April: various species of warbler, Tree Pipit, Yellow Wagtail, Whinchat, hirundines, Cuckoo, Turtle Dove, Spotted Flycatcher, Hoopoe and Serin are annual. Merlins in April and Hobbies in May. Quail in late spring. SUMMER: A few seabirds breed on the West Cliffs at Portland, and on summer evenings Manx Shearwaters can be seen offshore. On Chesil Beach, breeding Little and Common Terns. AUTUMN: Offshore, in the right conditions: Manx Shearwater, Balearic Shearwater, chance of Sooty Shearwater, British and Leach's Storm-petrel, Common Scoter, skuas, terns and gulls. Passage waders on The Fleet. At Portland Bill from August: migrants as in spring, plus Pied Flycatcher. Annual rarities may include Wryneck, Melodious and Icterine Warblers, and Tawny and Richard's Pipits. WINTER: Offshore: Gannet, Kittiwake, Common Scoter, Great Skua, auks. Purple Sandpiper on the rocks at Portland Bill. In harbour: Great Northern Diver, Black-throated Diver, more rarely Red-throated Diver, Great Crested, Black-necked, Red-necked and Slavonian Grebes, Eider, Red-breasted Merganser and, regularly, scoters, Long-tailed Ducks, auks. On The Fleet: Wigeon, Teal, Gadwall, Pintail, Shoveler, Pochard, Tufted Duck, Scaup, Goldeneye, Merlin, Peregrine, Dunlin, Knot, Greenshank, Curlew, Bar-tailed Godwit, Ringed Plover, Lapwing and Sanderling.

 ACCESS: *See* under site guide.

DISABLED ACCESS: *See* under site guide.

OTHER ATTRACTIONS

WEST OF Weymouth is Abbotsbury, with a swannery, large subtropical gardens and one of England's largest tithe barns. *See also* Radipole Lake and Lodmoor (Site 15).

POOLE HARBOUR, west of Bournemouth, is a popular resort. Although urban development has swallowed up its northern and eastern shorelines, extensive heaths still exist along the south and western shores. These heaths protect some of Britain's most endangered wildlife. Brownsea, in the middle of the harbour, is the largest island and has a superb nature reserve with a varied birdlife.

 BIRDS

The Dorset heaths are home to the Dartford Warbler, a resident which was almost wiped out in the hard winter of 1962/63, when just two pairs remained at Arne. In harsh winters the population suffers, yet the heaths of Studland and Arne are probably the easiest sites in Britain to see this species. The birds can be difficult to locate; during spring listen for their scratchy song. During the summer at dusk, another sound fills the air:

that of the Nightjar emitting a repetitive churr. Nightjars can be found on the heaths, often where there are scattered trees.

In Poole Harbour, wildfowl, grebes and waders are numerous in winter. A sprinkling of passerine migrants can be expected in both spring and autumn, but much more pronounced is the passage of waders, particularly evident on Brownsea Island.

OTHER ANIMALS

The heaths support some of our rarest plants and animals. All six species of reptile native to Britain occur. On warm summer days, look out for the localised Sand Lizards and Smooth Snake. At Arne, Palmate Newts inhabit some of the pools. These same pools attract a number of species of dragonfly and damselfly. The star butterfly is the Silver-studded Blue, while over 800 species of moth have been recorded at Arne alone. Mammals

include both Roe and Sika deer, the latter are on Brownsea Island along with Red Squirrels.

SITE GUIDE

1

Arne RSPB Reserve

This picturesque reserve of 1300 acres allows fine views of the harbour. Heathland, valley bogs, mixed woodland and saltmarsh ensure a diverse list of birds is likely on a typical visit. The reserve's star attraction are

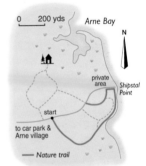

Trail through Arne RSPB Reserve.

17

Dartford Warbler.

2

Studland National Nature Reserve

The heaths on this reserve, like those at Arne, support Dartford Warblers and Nightjar. However, Studland is one of the best sites in the harbour for observing wildfowl and waders in winter. The peninsula has a large freshwater lake called Little Sea, where all the commoner diving and dabbling duck can be seen. Out in the harbour and in Studland Bay, Slavonian and

the Dartford Warblers, which can be seen throughout the year but which are most prominent in early spring.

A hide overlooks the saltmarsh which, during winter, allows views of wildfowl and waders, most notably Black-tailed Godwits. During spring, passage waders such as Whimbrels, Spotted Redshanks and Greenshanks appear. An hour or two before high tide is best, ensuring the waders are pushed close to the hide.

A circular walk can be taken around the reserve, allowing all the major habitats to be visited.

ACCESS: Drive to Arne village, where there is an RSPB car park. Take the public footpath past the church and farm to Shipstal. Where you enter the reserve, turn right for a circular route (leaflets available).

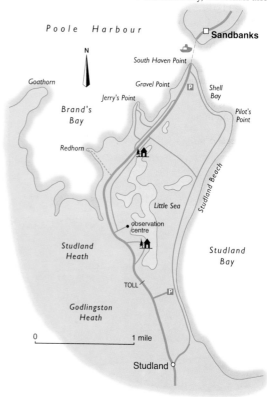

Black-necked Grebes are likely, along with large numbers of Red-breasted Mergansers. Brand's Bay is attractive to estuarine wildfowl and waders, and is favoured by Brent Geese. Studland has a long list of rarities to its name, and hardly a year goes by without it attracting something special.

To get the most out of a visit, aim to arrive about two hours before high tide. Waders roost in Studland and Shell bays. You should note that during summer, especially during school holidays, Studland can become crowded with holidaymakers.

 ACCESS: Take the B3351 to Studland village, and then take a toll road to the peninsula. Alternatively, a ferry can be taken from Sandbanks on the eastern side of the harbour to Studland on the west.

There is an observation centre and hides.

Brownsea Island.

DISABLED ACCESS: Wheelchair access is possible but limited.

3

Brownsea Island

The island is owned by the National Trust, although a brackish lagoon, freshwater lakes and woodland in the north-east of the island are leased to the Dorset Trust for Nature Conservation, which manages this area as a nature reserve. This is the most interesting site for birds on Brownsea. Hides look out on to the lagoon, this hosting a flock of Avocets in winter, along with a good selection of estuarine wildfowl and waders. In autumn, migrant waders include large numbers of Spotted Redshanks and Greenshanks, two Brownsea specialities.

Breeding birds include Sandwich and Common Terns on artificial islands, and there is a reasonably sized heronry. Wood Warblers occur in the woods, as do Golden Pheasants.

Brownsea has many visitors at weekends and during midsummer, and so a visit early or later in the day is best at these times.

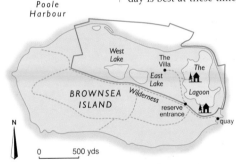

Poole Harbour

ACCESS: Boats run from Poole Quay and Sandbanks every half-hour from 10am to 5pm (6pm in July and August). There is a National Trust landing fee not applicable to members. Note that parking in Sandbanks can be almost impossible on hot weekends in the height of summer. The island is open from 1 April to 30 September.

Sika Deer are found on Brownsea Island.

Non-members of the Dorset Trust for Nature Conservation are given access to the lagoon and hides on Mondays, Wednesdays, Fridays and Saturdays from 10.30am to 1pm from April to June and September. In July and August there are guided tours at 2.45pm on Tuesdays, Thursdays and at weekends. Meet at the gate to the reserve.

 DISABLED ACCESS: This is good once you are on the island as most tracks and the hides around the lagoon are accessible to wheelchairs. The ferries readily transport wheelchair-bound passengers, although this can be a little tricky.

BIRDS THROUGH THE SEASONS

ALL YEAR: Little Grebe, Grey Heron, Mute Swan, Little Egret, feral Canada Goose, Tufted Duck, Golden Pheasant (Brownsea), Black-tailed Godwit, Water Rail, Stonechat, Dartford Warbler, Redpoll and Reed Bunting.

SPRING: Passage waders include Whimbrel, Common Sandpiper, Greenshank, Spotted Redshank and wintering waders. Sandwich, Common, Arctic and Little Terns in harbour. Arriving summer migrants.

SUMMER: Sandwich and Common Terns breed (Brownsea). On heaths: Nightjar and Hobby. Wood Warblers and Crossbills on Brownsea. Returning waders such as Avocets (Brownsea) and Black-tailed Godwits.

AUTUMN: Passage waders include those listed under winter, plus Whimbrel, Avocet, Spotted Redshank, Greenshank, Common Sandpiper, Little Stint, Curlew Sandpiper, Ruff, and occasional Green and Wood Sandpiper on Brownsea. Terns, including occasional Black Tern, and Little Gull. Firecrest, Pied Flycatcher and Black Redstart are among the commoner migrants.

WINTER: In the harbour: divers, Great Crested, Slavonian and Black-necked Grebes, Brent Geese, Wigeon, scoters, Red-breasted Mergansers and Long-tailed Ducks. On Little Sea (Studland): Gadwall, Pintail, Pochard, Tufted Duck, Goldeneye and Scaup. Merlin, Peregrine, Hen Harrier on heaths. Waders include Curlew, Knot, Bar-tailed and Black-tailed Godwits, Sanderling, Dunlin, Oystercatcher, Ringed Plover, Avocet, a few Spotted Redshank, Grey Plover and Turnstone. Occasional Great Grey Shrike on the heaths.

ACCESS: *See* under site guide.

DISABLED ACCESS: *See* under site guide.

OTHER ATTRACTIONS

THE RESORTS of Bournemouth and Poole are close by, and Studland has some beautiful beaches. *See also* Durlston Country Park (Site 18).

ESTABLISHED IN 1973 as Dorset's first country park, Durlston is one of the county's bird-watching hot spots. During spring and autumn, migrants can be both abundant and varied.

Sited within the Purbeck Heritage Coast, Durlston has much to offer in terms of scenery, from sheer limestone cliffs to views of the Isle of Wight. Various trails pass through woodland and downland. Hedgerows and scrub provide tired migrants with cover, while the cliffs attract nesting seabirds.

From the park centre, a circular route can be taken; The Globe is a good starting point. Installed in 1887 and weighing 40 tons, The Globe is made of Portland stone mined from local quarries. The stone was taken to London to be sculpted, before being returned in segments and assembled. The Globe acts as a reminder of the Victorians' quest for travel and science.

The Globe at Durlston.

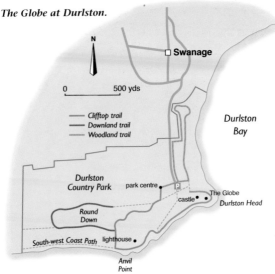

BIRDS

Walking west from The Globe along the cliff path, you come to a view-point from which nesting seabirds can be seen. This viewpoint also serves as an excellent sea-watching site.

From Anvil Point Lighthouse, a dry, scrub-filled valley backed by downland runs north, acting as a shelter for tired migrants. Looking for birds here is difficult due to the dense cover. Honeysuckle and Old Man's Beard drape the Hawthorn and Elder bushes.

The traditional hedged farming landscape behind

DURLSTON COUNTRY PARK 18

the downland provides further shelter and feeding areas for birds. Blackcaps, Whinchats and Redstarts are particularly fond of these hedgerows.

 OTHER ANIMALS AND FLOWERS
The downland supports a variety of flowers and insects. Early Spider and Pyramidal Orchids can both be found. Vivid Blue Milkwort carpets the ground in spring. Butterflies include Adonis and Chalk Hill Blue, while the Wall Brown is attracted to the small, stony quarries. A visit in July or August gives a good chance of seeing the highly localised Lulworth Skipper.

Back at the visitor centre, a circular route can be taken through the woodland to the east. Butterflies such as the Speckled Wood can be seen in the woodland glades. Along the cliff edge, hunting Sparrowhawks are regular.

BIRDS THROUGH THE SEASONS
SPRING: Migrants include Wheatear, Whinchat, Pied Flycatcher, Tree Pipit, Redstart and all the commoner warblers. Sea passage can be excellent, with scoter and divers moving in March, and skuas, terns and wildfowl in April. On the cliffs by March, Shags, Fulmars, Kittiwakes, Guillemots and Razorbills are all breeding, forming one of the largest seabird colonies in southern England. Spring rarities have included Golden Oriole, Honey Buzzard, Bee-eater, Hoopoe and Red-footed Falcon.
SUMMER: The sea-bird cliffs are busy up until early July.

Manx Shearwaters are often seen offshore on evenings during June and July.
AUTUMN: From August, returning migrants start to build in numbers. Chats, Wheatears and Yellow Wagtails are common. Hobby can occur. September can be exceptional for scarce migrants such as Wryneck, Tawny Pipit and Melodious Warbler. Sea-watching can be good in stormy weather. October often produces an exciting rarity or two; Pallas's Warbler and Isabelline Shrike have both occurred. Winter visitors such as Brambling, Fieldfare and Redwing arrive. Offshore, Little Gull, Little Auk and Leach's Storm-petrel are all possible.
WINTER: During November, north-easterly winds can produce movements of seaduck such as Velvet Scoter and Long-tailed Duck. November has produced Durlston's most famous rarity from America, a Brown Thrasher. December and January can produce divers and grebes offshore, while winter visitors may include Black

Fulmars nest on the cliffs.

Redstart or Firecrest. By February, the seabirds are returning to their nesting ledges on the cliffs.

ACCESS: Well signposted from the centre of Swanage, and there are no access restrictions. The park is only a 15-minute walk from the town, so is accessible by train or bus.

DISABLED ACCESS: Wheelchair access is possible, although there are some steep slopes to negotiate. Otherwise, the paths are even and well-maintained.

OTHER ATTRACTIONS

THE HOLIDAY town of Swanage has all the typical seaside attractions. Close by is historic Corfe Castle, one of Britain's most spectacular ruins, and dating back to medieval times. Bovington Camp Tank Museum near Wareham is also near by.

CORNWALL

Camel Estuary

Most bird interest is concentrated in the upper reaches of the estuary at Amble Marshes. A good variety of waders winter and come through on passage, during which time terns of various species occur on the estuary. Take the A39 north out of Wadebridge and then take the B3314 to the left. Park at Trewornan Bridge and view the marshes before proceeding through the gate just before the bridge. Then go along a footpath, following a hedge until you reach the hide.

Drift Reservoir

The reservoir lies just west of Penzance, and is easily reached off the A30. A rare wader or gull is found during most autumns, along with a handful of the commoner passage waders. A few duck winter.

Fal Estuary

Close to Falmouth, the Fal Estuary has a number of interesting tidal creeks which attract wildfowl and waders in winter and on passage. Out in the deeper water of the Carrick Roads in winter, Great Northern Divers and Slavonian Grebes are regular, along with other seaduck. It is best viewed from Pencarrow Point on the west side near Mylor. The most accessible site for viewing waders in autumn and winter is at Tresillian, a narrow tree-lined tidal river. Leave Truro north on the A39, turning off to Pencalenick. Park and walk downstream along the river.

The Lizard

Surprisingly little visited by bird-watchers, The Lizard is the southernmost point on the British mainland. Migrants and rarities are the main attractions in spring and autumn. The coves around Lizard Point and any suitable habitat around Lizard are worth checking.

Drift Reservoir.

DEVON

Aylesbeare Common
RSPB Reserve

A heathland reserve of 540 acres. Dartford Warbler, Nightjar, Stonechat, Tree Pipit and Grasshopper Warbler all breed. The common is rich in insect life, and there is a trail that starts opposite the car park. From Newton Poppleford, take the A3052 Lyme Regis–Exeter road. The reserve is 1 mile along here on the right.

Chapel Wood
RSPB Reserve

A small, 15-acre woodland reserve with a varied birdlife. All three species of woodpecker, Redstarts, Pied Flycatchers, Buzzards and Dippers occur. The reserve is 10 miles from Barnstaple and is approached off the A361 north of Knowle. Visiting is by appointment only. Write, enclosing an SAE, to the Honorary Warden, Cyril Manning, 8 Chichester Park, Woolacombe, Devon EX34 7BZ.

Exe Estuary
RSPB Reserves

At the head of the Exe Estuary are two RSPB reserves. A good variety of estuarine wildfowl and waders can be seen on both reserves in winter. On the marshes at Exminster, Lapwings and Redshanks

breed, while Cetti's Warblers inhabit the ditches. Exminster Marshes are reached off the A379 Exeter–Dawlish road, by turning east down Swan's Nest Lane close to Exminster village. Park in the car park just beyond the pub. Bowling Green Marsh, on the opposite side of the estuary, is south-east of Topsham village. The reserve can be reached by foot-ferry from Exminster Marshes, or, alternatively, by driving through Topsham to Bowling Green Road, from which the marshes can be viewed from a hide.

Great Haldon Forest

This large conifer forest, on an 850-foot high ridge, is best known as a raptor watch-point. Honey Buzzards are the local speciality, with sightings possible from late spring through to the summer. Goshawks are regularly seen, along with Hobbies and Buzzards. Many migrant raptors have been seen from here, particularly during May. Other birds of interest include Nightjars, Redstarts, Whinchats and Tree Pipits. There are some

Christchurch Harbour viewed from Hengistbury Head.

excellent butterfly walks where Grizzled Skipper, Wood White and High Brown Fritillary may be encountered. From Exeter, take the A38 towards Plymouth. The road climbs a steep hill; turn off left near the crest just before the racecourse. Follow this road round and under the A38 towards Dunchideock. The viewpoint is along this road on the left and is signposted 'Raptor Watchpoint'. Late May and June are best for Honey Buzzards. Goshawks can be seen throughout the year, but are most active in early spring.

DORSET

Christchurch Harbour

Christchurch Harbour attracts a wide selection of estuarine wildfowl and waders in winter. During spring and autumn, passage waders are best viewed at Stanpit Marsh. The southern side of the harbour is dominated by Hengistbury Head. The head can be excellent for migrants in both passage periods, and in autumn regularly attracts scarcer species as well as the occasional rarity.

Stanpit Marsh is reached by taking Stanpit Lane off the A3059 to Mudeford. Just past the Ship in Distress pub, park in the recreation ground car park and walk to the harbour. Hengistbury Head is reached along roads from Southbourne. Park in

the car park at the head and proceed along the various paths. Disabled access is good at this latter site.

Garston Wood
RSPB Reserve

Garston Wood is an ancient coppiced woodland of Hazel, Field Maple and Ash on the chalk downs of Cranborne Chase. Nightingales and a good selection of woodland birds can be seen. In May, Bluebells and Wood Anemones cover the woodland floor. Butterflies include Silver-washed Fritillary. Roe Deer and Dormice are also present. The reserve is reached off the A354 Salisbury–Blandford Forum road by taking the B3081 east off a roundabout, and then taking a minor road to Broad Chalke. The reserve is on the left-hand side.

SOMERSET

Cheddar Reservoir

This circular reservoir, at the foot of the Mendips, supports good numbers of wildfowl in autumn and winter, and on occasions has seaduck. A few passerine migrants, mainly wagtails and chats, might be expected in spring. In autumn, depending on the water-levels, there are likely to be a few waders. After severe gales, storm-blown Grey Phalaropes or a more unusual gull are possible.

Exmoor National Park

This vast area can be bleak and birdless in winter. In

Cheddar Reservoir.

spring and summer, however, a good range of specialised species can be encountered. The oak woodlands support Pied Flycatchers, Redstarts and Wood Warblers, while the moorland attracts Ring Ouzels, Tree Pipits and Whinchats. Anywhere with suitable habitat is worth exploring.

The Quantock Hills

These hills support the same range of birds as are found on Exmoor, but due to the smaller area they are more easily worked. Various roads allow access, and the areas around Holford Green and Quantoxhead in particular are worth checking.

SOUTH-EAST ENGLAND

of Little Egrets, with up to 150 birds regularly roosting in one particular site.

These south-coast counties not only act as a gateway to and from Europe for migrant birds, but they also offer some vital wintering sites for estuarine wildfowl and waders. The woodland and heath habitats of the New Forest support such sought-after species as Dartford Warbler, Woodlark and Nightjar.

The region has a variety of mammals, with most woodland areas supporting Roe and Fallow Deer. Badgers are common, as are several species of bat. Otters are now making a comeback through successful reintroduction schemes, and reptiles are well represented, with national rarities such as the Smooth Snake and Sand Lizard. A visit to Rye Harbour or Dungeness may reveal the Marsh Frog, a vociferous amphibian introduced from Eastern Europe.

Beachy Head at dawn.

LONDON **32**

33

31 **29** **30**

28

27 **26**

35

34

SOUTHAMPTON

19

20 PORTSMOUTH

21

22

BRIGHTON

25

24

23

The Redwing is a common winter visitor.

Kent, Surrey, Sussex and Hampshire offer some of the best birding in Britain. The close proximity of the Continent and the mild, dry climate mean that many summer migrants and residents such as the Dartford Warbler find the South-east favourable. Because there are just 21 miles of sea between Kent and France, this is one of the first counties to welcome new colonists, such as Cetti's Warbler, to Britain. In the last few years the south-coast estuaries have played host to increasing numbers

DUE TO its rich diversity of habitats, including ancient woodlands, heathland and bogs, the New Forest supports some of Britain's rarest breeding birds. Although thousands of people visit the region, the resulting disturbance is fortunately largely restricted to the environs of the car parks, leaving much of the forest in relative quiet.

William I decreed the New Forest a royal hunting reserve specifically for deer, and several hundred deer of four different species are still to be found, although they are shy and difficult to spot. In more recent times, Sika have spread from Beaulieu. Other grazing animals include the famous ponies and a few cattle and pigs, all commoners' animals.

BIRDS
The forest is managed by the Forestry Commission and there are a few commercial conifer plantations that attract some interesting breeding birds, notably Siskin, Crossbill and the elusive Firecrest. The broad-leaved woodland is dominated by Beech and oak, some trees dating back over 300 years. Here both Redstarts and Wood Warblers can be found in summer. Where woodland borders the heath, both Nightjars and Tree Pipits are found.

The heaths are the Dartford Warbler's stronghold. Susceptible to the vagaries of our weather, the entire population of this species can be almost wiped out in harsh winters, yet it invariably recovers after a few years. Woodlarks are best looked for on the open heaths, especially in newly burnt areas and along the edges of woodlands, and they can often be found feeding on the closely cropped forest lawns. In winter, Hen Harriers hunt over the heaths.

Raptors are a big attraction in summer; the aerial antics of the Hobby can be enjoyed as they dash after dragonflies. Honey Buzzards are highly localised and are best searched for by scanning the skies regularly on warm, sunny days; in early summer you may be lucky enough to find a pair displaying. Goshawks breed but are very elusive; they are best looked for on sunny days in late winter or early spring when they display. Montagu's Harriers occasionally nest in the forest, and so are always worth keeping a look out for.

OTHER ANIMALS
The woodlands and bogs are rich in insect life, the most notable species being Britain's only cicada, the New Forest Cicada. Reptiles include the Smooth Snake and the Sand Lizard.

Although the New Forest is one of the richest wildlife sites in the British Isles, discovering its secrets is not easy and much time can be wasted searching aimlessly for birds. However, there are specific sites that are particularly good, and these are listed below.

SITE GUIDE

1

Ashley Walk & Hampton Ridge

This ridge in the north-west of the forest passes through open heath and gorse favoured by Dartford Warbler, Stonechat and Whinchat. Pitts Wood Inclosure has Hawfinch (best looked for in winter), Tree Pipit, Redstart and Wood Warbler. The Ashley

The New Forest supports rare breeding birds such as the Dartford Warbler.

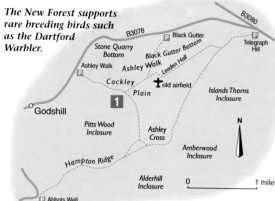

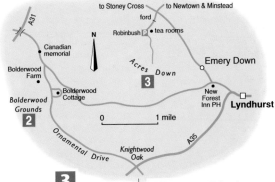

The Fallow is one of four species of deer found in the forest.

Walk area attracts Hen Harriers in winter.

 ACCESS:
See map.

 DISABLED ACCESS:
None.

Bolderwood Grounds

This area of ornamental, mixed conifer and broad-leaved woodland has traditionally been the best place to search for Firecrests. This was their first recorded breeding site in Britain, in 1962. Firecrests sing high up in the conifers and can be frustratingly difficult to locate. Look out, too, for Crossbill and Hawfinch.

 ACCESS: Any spot along the Ornamental Drive where there is suitable habitat may produce birds. *See map.*

 DISABLED ACCESS:
None.

Acres Down

North-west of Lyndhurst, this ridge overlooks large stretches of woodland and is a good viewpoint from which to search for raptors. Hobby, Sparrowhawk and Buzzard are commonly seen. Goshawk are occasional, and although this used to be a reliable site for Honey Buzzard, sightings have become more sporadic. Nightjars frequent the heath below the ridge in summer.

 ACCESS: Take the minor road that runs between Emery Down and the A31. If travelling from Emery Down, take the turning on the left after 2 miles marked 'no through road' opposite the turning for Newtown and Minstead. Follow this road to the end, past the tea rooms and along the gravel track to a car park on the left. Walk up on to the ridge from here.

 DISABLED ACCESS:
None.

The New Forest in winter.

4

Beaulieu Road Station

This site encompasses woodland, bog and heath, and is one of the most productive within the forest for seeing the main specialities: Dartford Warbler, Tree Pipit, Nightjar, Woodlark and Hobby. The woodlands hold the typical New Forest species, while the bogs support breeding Curlew, Snipe, Redshank and Teal. Crossbills are often found in the pines around the car park, and this is one of the most reliable sites for wintering Great Grey Shrike. During summer, Honey Buzzard and Goshawk are occasionally seen.

Woodlarks are best looked for in the more open areas.

ACCESS: From Lyndhurst take the B3056 to Beaulieu Road Station. Just before the railway bridge is a car park by some pines. Park here and explore the area, keeping to the tracks. Alternatively, carry on past the station and park in the Pig Bush car park.

DISABLED ACCESS: A limited amount of exploration is possible from a wheelchair.

BIRDS THROUGH THE SEASONS

ALL YEAR: Mandarin, Mallard, Teal, Goshawk, Sparrowhawk, Kestrel, Buzzard, Snipe, Woodcock, Kingfisher, Lesser Spotted, Green and Great Spotted Woodpeckers, Woodlark, Grey Wagtail, Stonechat, Siskin, Redpoll, Crossbill, Hawfinch and the usual woodland residents. Both Woodlark and Dartford Warbler can be elusive and in many areas absent in winter.

SPRING: Occasional rarities have included Red-footed Falcon (many records) and Roller.

SUMMER: Summer visitors that breed include Shelduck, Honey Buzzard, Hobby, Curlew, Redshank, Turtle Dove, Nightjar, Tree Pipit, Nightingale, Redstart, Whinchat, Wheatear, Grasshopper Warbler, Wood Warbler and Firecrest.

AUTUMN: Occasional passage migrants and rarities.

WINTER: A few Wigeon use some of the pools. Hen Harrier, occasional Merlin, Peregrine, Short-eared Owl, and Great Grey Shrike. Often a few Bramblings.

ACCESS: Access to the sites listed is straight-forward from the A31.

DISABLED ACCESS: This is difficult as access to most sites in the forest is by foot along un-even tracks. However, there are certain areas with tracks ideal for wheelchair access, though these sites may be disturbed and not neces-sarily productive for birds.

OTHER ATTRACTIONS

THE NEW Forest is an ideal destination for a family trip. Apart from its diverse natural history, there are a number of attractions ranging from the National Motor Museum at Beaulieu to pony-trekking. Many of the attractions are sign-posted from Lyndhurst, where further information is available.

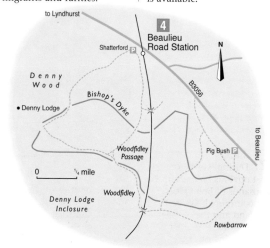

FARLINGTON MARSHES jut into Langstone Harbour and cover 300 acres of rough grassland, reed-fringed lagoons and scrub. They are a haven for birds throughout the year. The marshes are managed by the Hampshire Wildlife Trust, while much of the inter-tidal mud and islands on the eastern side of the harbour are under the auspices of the RSPB.

The marshes are protected by a sea wall, which was erected in 1773 by the lord of the manor of Farlington. This sea wall provides an ideal path for viewing the harbour and the marshes. A circular walk will take approximately 90 minutes.

reserve, allowing excellent photographic opportunities. The other typical estuarine wildfowl and waders are present in winter. At high tide, large concentrations of waders roost on the harbour islands and within the sea wall. Dunlin are abundant, along with Knot and both Bar-tailed and Black-tailed Godwits. The harbour is the premier wintering site for Black-necked Grebes in Britain and there are often more than 30. The best place to look for them is in the north-east corner.

During spring and autumn, the marshes are a superb site for migrants. Early Wheatears and Sand

May. Garganey are annual visitors to the reed-fringed lagoon. This is a good place to look for scarce waders in both spring and autumn, and there is always a chance of Wood Sandpiper or Little Stint, with Spotted Redshank and Whimbrel more regular. Rarities are often found.

❀ FLOWERS
On the grasslands, look out for Yellow Rattle, a semi-parasitic plant with seed heads that rattle when the hay is cut. The grasslands have numerous ant hills, a feature that identifies the area as old-established grazing land.

Rough grazing marsh at Farlington Marshes reserve.

🦆 BIRDS
During winter, the most obvious birds are the thousands of Brent Geese that commute between the grassland and the harbour. They are often very tame when grazing on the

Martins return in March, and are soon followed by the first Sandwich Terns before a flood of birds arrives during April and

BIRDS THROUGH THE SEASONS
ALL YEAR: Cormorant, Grey Heron, Water Rail, Shelduck, Oystercatcher, Ringed

Black-necked Grebe.

Plover, Redshank, and Reed Bunting. Little Egrets have started to appear throughout the year, but it remains to be seen whether this species becomes a permanent fixture along the south coast.

SPRING: Summer migrants include Garganey, Hobby, and occasionally Osprey. Migrant waders include Wood Sandpiper, Curlew Sandpiper, Common Sandpiper, Green Sandpiper, Ruff, Little Stint, Avocet, Greenshank, Spotted Redshank, Whimbrel, Little Ringed Plover, Black-tailed Godwit and Bar-tailed Godwit. Sandwich Terns arrive at the end of March. Black Terns and Little Gulls are regular in the harbour. Wheatears and Sand Martins first appear in March, followed in April and May by Cuckoo, Yellow Wagtail, Whinchat, Ring Ouzel, Firecrest, Pied Flycatcher, various warblers and often a rarity.

SUMMER: A few non-breeding waders occur in the harbour. Common and Little Terns breed in large colonies on the islands. Yellow Wagtail, Sedge and also Reed Warbler breed.

AUTUMN: As listed for spring, with the added likelihood of a rare wader such as Temminck's Stint or, in bad weather, a Grey Phalarope. Black Redstart are possible.

Rarities may include a Spotted Crake or Wryneck.

WINTER: Divers occasionally occur in the harbour. Black-necked Grebe and a few Slavonian Grebes, Little Grebe, Great Crested Grebe, Brent Goose, Wigeon, Teal, Pintail, Shoveler, Goldeneye, Red-breasted Merganser, often Long-tailed Duck, occasional Gadwall, Eider and Common Scoter. Grey Plover, Dunlin, Knot, Curlew, Bar-tailed Godwit, Black-tailed Godwit, Green Sandpiper and a few Greenshank. Peregrine, Merlin, Hen Harrier, Short-eared Owl and sometimes a few Long-eared Owls roost through the winter. Mediterranean Gulls are regular. A few Bearded Tits roost in the reeds. Twite are on the saltmarsh in some years, and also sporadic are

Snow and Lapland Buntings.

ACCESS: On approaching Portsmouth on the A27 from the east, turn off on to the roundabout that leads on to the A2030. There is an entrance from this roundabout to a car park.

DISABLED ACCESS: This is very limited although some viewing of the harbour is possible from a vehicle.

OTHER ATTRACTIONS

THE PORTSMOUTH area is rich in naval history and there are some famous exhibits including HMS *Victory* and the *Mary Rose*. The D-Day Museum outside the naval base is worth a visit.

Map labels

to Petersfield
to London
Havant Station
B2149
A3
Havant
B2150
A27
to Chichester
to Fareham
Farlington Marshes
N
The Point
to Portsmouth
A2030
Langstone Harbour
0   1 mile

PAGHAM HARBOUR, one of a series of estuaries along the south coast, is small enough to explore fully in a day, and yet it supports an excellent variety of estuarine birds. The harbour has an interesting history and was nearly lost to land reclamation in the latter half of the last century. Pagham was designated a Local Nature Reserve in 1964 and was later given Ramsar site status because of its importance for wintering wildfowl and waders.

BIRDS

During the autumn, there are few better places for watching passage waders at close quarters than at the Siddlesham Ferry Pool, opposite the visitor centre. It is best viewed in the early morning as the sun will be against you by afternoon. Waders roost on the pool at high tide.

During low tide in winter, the tidal creeks resound to the calls of Redshank, Curlew and Oystercatcher. In autumn and winter, the gorse bushes bordering the path along the western side of the harbour are home to a few Stonechats and, occasionally, a Dartford Warbler. Brent Geese are the most conspicuous winter inhabitants, their numbers varying from year to year, and with the January peak ranging from 2500 to 4500. Ruff winter on the Ferry Pool and in the damp fields at Church Norton.

The woodlands around Church Norton attract over-wintering Firecrest and Chiffchaff. All three species of woodpecker occur, and the fainter, slower drum of the Lesser Spotted Wood-pecker should be listened for in early spring. Near by, an area of reedbeds known as the Severals attracts Bearded Tits in winter. The beach in front of The Severals gives the best vantage point for observing passing birds, and grebes and duck offshore.

Pagham Lagoon, on the northern side of the harbour, is best visited during winter because heavy disturbance in summer deters birds from lingering. Red-breasted Mergansers are regular, as in some winters are Smew.

Near by is Selsey Bill, which once had a bird observatory. Today, there is very little habitat for migrants due to urban encroachment. However, this is still an excellent sea-watching site, particularly in spring when Pomarine Skuas can be expected in the first half of May.

OTHER ANIMALS

Around 20 species of mammal are recorded annually on the reserve.

FLOWERS

Over 340 species of flowering plant include the rare Childing Pink found on the shingle ridges.

BIRDS THROUGH THE SEASONS

ALL YEAR: Grey Heron, Sparrowhawk, Shelduck, Oystercatcher, Redshank, Ringed Plover, Little Owl, Barn Owl at Siddlesham Ferry, Green, Great Spotted and Lesser Spotted Wood-pecker, Reed Bunting and Corn Bunting. Little Egrets have recently taken up residence locally and can regularly be seen in the harbour.

SPRING: Wheatear, Sandwich Tern and Sand Martin start to appear in March. Common and Little Terns arrive in April. Whimbrel, Greenshank, Wood Sandpiper, Spotted Redshank, Curlew Sandpiper and Bar-tailed Godwit pass through in small numbers. Offshore, flocks of Scoter and divers will be moving. Willow Warbler, Blackcap, Lesser Whitethroat, Whitethroat, Yellow Wagtail

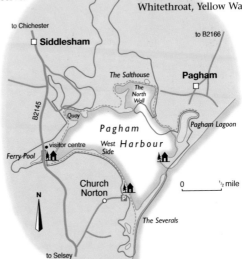

and hirundines. Hobby from May onwards. The Ferry Pool occasionally attracts a Garganey. You may encounter a migrant Osprey, though they rarely linger in spring. Scoter, divers, grebes, terns, skuas and wildfowl pass Selsey Bill.

SUMMER: Returning waders by July. Hobbies are regular. Little, Common and Sandwich Terns fish close to the harbour mouth, while the former breed on the spit. Shelduck numbers start to reduce as they depart for the German coast to moult. Reed Warbler, Sedge Warbler and Lesser Whitethroat breed. Lapwing and Redshank will both have young in the vicinity of the Ferry Pool.

AUTUMN: By August, migration is in full swing with waders building in numbers on the Ferry Pool. Curlew Sandpiper, Little Stint, Little Ringed Plover, Black-tailed Godwit, Spotted Redshank, Greenshank and Ruff should all be seen. There is always a good chance of a rarity here. Passerine migrants in the Church Norton area may include Whinchat, Pied Flycatcher, Redstart, Firecrest and Wryneck. Black Tern and Little Gull in the harbour and on the Ferry Pool.

WINTER: Slavonian Grebe on the sea off Church Norton and sometimes in the harbour, especially in November. Great Crested Grebe, Little Grebe. Brent Geese start arriving in September and peak in January. Wigeon, Pintail, Teal, Goldeneye, Eider, Red-breasted Merganser and occasional Smew. Hen Harrier, Merlin, Peregrine and Short-eared Owl. Water

Mudflats and saltmarsh, Pagham Harbour.

Rail are heard more often than they are seen at The Severals and Ferry Pool. Waders include Grey and Golden Plover, Knot, Dunlin, Ruff, Snipe, Black-tailed Godwit. Sanderling, Bar-tailed Godwit and Avocet are recorded in small numbers. Stonechat, Chiffchaff, Firecrest, Rock Pipit and occasional Twite.

ACCESS: From the A27 Chichester bypass, take the B2145 signposted to Selsey. Approximately half a mile south of Siddlesham village, park in the reserve car park on the left. From here, you can walk north along the Siddlesham Ferry nature trail (leaflets available at visitor centre).

Alternatively, once you have viewed the Ferry Pool, take the path on the west side of the harbour to Church Norton, which can also be reached by car by carrying on along the B2145 from the visitor centre. After 1½ miles take the left turn on a right-hand bend signposted to Church Norton. Follow the lane to the end and park in the car park by the church (often full at weekends). The harbour is then just a

short walk away. Once you have reached the harbour, turn left for the hide or right to the beach.

To reach Pagham Lagoon, take the left-hand fork (B2166) signposted to Pagham shortly after joining the B2145 from the A27. Follow signs to Pagham village; the road running west out of the village past the church will take you to a car park by the harbour mouth. Pagham Lagoon and the harbour can be viewed from here. Selsey Bill is reached along the B2145.

DISABLED ACCESS: The Siddlesham Ferry nature trail that leads off from the visitor centre is ideal for wheelchair users. The Ferry Pool can also be viewed easily from a wheelchair. Pagham Lagoon and access to the harbour from the car park at Church Norton are possible with a wheelchair, though at these localities a little assistance may be necessary.

OTHER ATTRACTIONS

THE HISTORIC cathedral city of Chichester is close by.

PULBOROUGH BROOKS, in the picturesque Arum Valley in West Sussex, opened in August 1993. It has since become one of the RSPB's most popular reserves – no fewer than 100,000 RSPB members live less than two hours' drive away.

The attraction here is the 420 acres of flood meadows that have been reclaimed from intensive agriculture. Drainage works and river improvements caused the breeding and wintering birds of the brooks to decline dramatically. This trend has now been reversed so that today the

Flood meadows, Pulborough.

reserve is one of the most impressive wetlands in the South-east. Waterfowl have been quick to return to meadows that were once famous for their wintering flocks.

From the Upperton's Barn Visitor Centre, a path leads down to the heart of the reserve. A circular route that takes about three hours is recommended.

Adjoining the Upperton's Barn Centre is a popular tea room, providing a welcome retreat on a chilly winter's day.

BIRDS

From Nettley's Hide, a view out across the flooded meadows in winter will produce a variety of wildfowl. The Hanger Watchpoint is a good place to linger as birds that were hidden from view among

Upperton's Barn Visitor Centre.

the sedge from the hide can be spotted from here, although a telescope is desirable. Looking across the valley towards the River Arun, the town of Pulborough nestles on the adjacent hillside.

OTHER ANIMALS
Over 9 miles of ditches dissect the brooks, harbouring Grass Snakes and a variety of interesting plants including Flowering Rush and Frogbit. Mammals include Roe and Fallow Deer. The speciality of the area is the rare Club-tailed Dragonfly, which is found on the adjacent River Arun.

BIRDS THROUGH THE SEASONS
SPRING: Breeding birds have included Lapwing, Redshank, Snipe, Yellow Wagtail, Teal, Shoveler, Garganey, Gadwall, Mandarin, Woodcock, Little Owl and Barn Owl. Waders pass through on passage.
SUMMER: Apart from the wetland breeding birds, summer visitors include Nightingale, Nightjar and Turtle Dove.
AUTUMN: Passage migrants

include Wheatear, Whinchat, Stonechat, Redstart and Ringed Plover.
WINTER: Undoubtedly the most exciting period. Wildfowl include Wigeon, Gadwall, Teal, Mallard, Pintail, Shoveler, White-fronted Goose and Bewick's Swan. Also possible are Peregrine, Merlin, Sparrowhawk and Barn Owl.

ACCESS: The nearest town is Pulborough, 2 miles away. The reserve is well signposted from the A29. For small groups, it may be possible for collection from Pulborough railway station. Contact the centre before your planned visit. Tel: 01798 875851.

The nature reserve is open from 9am to sunset daily except Christmas Day.
Upperton's Barn Visitor Centre and tea rooms are open from 10am to 5pm.

DISABLED ACCESS:
Motorised wheelchairs are available (contact the reserve in advance). Two

hides are accessible to wheelchairs. A strong pusher is recommended. Disabled visitors should note that the paths are bumpy in places.

OTHER ATTRACTIONS

THIS AREA of Sussex has many attractive villages to explore. The historic town of Arundel and its castle lie just a few miles away towards the sea, and boating can also be enjoyed here on Swan Lake opposite the Wildfowl & Wetlands Trust. The latter has a wide variety of captive wildfowl in pleasant grounds. A number of hides look out on to reed-fringed pools and a scrape. Wild birds attracted to these habitats include Kingfisher, Water Rail, Snipe and Green Sandpiper, while Spotted Crakes are occasionally seen in autumn. Increasing numbers of wildfowl (including occasional Bewick's Swans) fly into the reserve in winter.

THE SHEER, white cliffs of Beachy Head rise to a dizzying 500 feet.

BIRDS

The area is excellent for passage migrants in both spring and autumn, although many just pass straight overhead. The first few hours after sunrise invariably see most movement. This site is the main departure point in autumn for Sylvia Warblers. In August, the bushes come alive with the 'tac' calls of Whitethroats, Lesser Whitethroats, Garden Warblers and Blackcaps.

The Hoopoe is an annual spring visitor.

Sea-watching can be productive, especially in spring. In late April, an impressive movement of waders takes place offshore; numbers of Bar-tailed Godwits are particularly notable. Sea-watching is generally best in strong, southerly or south-easterly gales.

Birling Gap is one of the best spring sea-watching points in the South-east, and is also an excellent spot for migrants. Other sites providing cover include

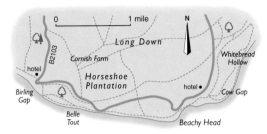

Belle Tout Wood and Whitebread Hollow. Various areas of scrub just back from the cliffs often shelter birds, and the ploughed fields can be good for viewing larks, pipits and wagtails.

Beachy Head has an interesting flora of downland plants.

OTHER ANIMALS

Resident butterflies include Chalkhill Blue, Adonis Blue, Brown Argus and Marbled White; migrants include Painted Lady and Clouded Yellow.

BIRDS THROUGH THE SEASONS

ALL YEAR: Sparrowhawk, Kestrel, Green Woodpecker, Stonechat, Yellowhammer and Corn Bunting.
SPRING: Offshore are Red-throated Diver, Black-throated Diver, Fulmar, Gannet, Brent Goose, Common and Velvet Scoter, Red-breasted Merganser, Eider, Bar-tailed Godwit, Whimbrel, Pomarine, Arctic and Great Skuas, terns and gulls. A variety of warblers, chats, flycatchers and wagtails include Nightingale, Grasshopper Warbler, Redstart, Pied Flycatcher, Wheatear, Whinchat and often Ring Ouzel. Hoopoe and Serin are annual.
SUMMER: Breeding birds include Whitethroat, Lesser Whitethroat, Nightingale and Grasshopper Warbler.

AUTUMN: Skuas and the occasional shearwater offshore. Many passerines, mainly pipits, finches and wagtails, pass overhead for the first couple of hours after sunrise. Large numbers of Sylvia Warblers in August. Other migrants include Ring Ouzel, Redstart, Wryneck, Tree Pipit, Yellow Wagtail, Firecrest and Pied Flycatcher. Large numbers of martins and swallows gather in late autumn. Winter thrushes and finches arrive, and often big flocks of Woodpigeon congregate and depart for the Continent. Among the more regularly recorded rarities are Tawny Pipit, Pallas's and Yellow-browed Warbler, Melodious Warbler and Red-backed Shrike.
WINTER: Just the residents and a few birds offshore, especially in hard weather when wildfowl and waders may be on the move.

ACCESS: The B2103 runs in a loop from the A259; a number of car parks allow access.

DISABLED ACCESS: None.

OTHER ATTRACTIONS

BEACHY HEAD is, in itself, a popular beauty spot, offering cliff-top walks and picnic areas. The resort of Eastbourne is close by.

THE RYE Harbour Local Nature Reserve is a large shingle beach that was once the sea-bed. Look back towards the town of Rye to see the old coastline.

 BIRDS
A circular walk starting at the car park will take at least half a day to complete. Follow the path along the Rother and you soon come to a hide overlooking a muddy scrape that attracts a variety of passage waders. Walk on and you eventually reach the tern pool, overlooked by two hides.

The main bird interest is centred here, with the surrounding shingle being used by breeding Little and Common Terns. Further back are a series of pits that all hold birds, so if time allows they are worth checking.

During winter, a variety of wildfowl use the pits, and at high tide waders come in to roost. Numbers are never great but the variety is good. In spring and autumn, passage waders, Garganey and often small groups of Black Terns and Little Gulls occur. Passerine migrants include Wheatears and flocks of Yellow Wagtails in spring. During autumn, large flocks of hirundines often congregate before departing across the Channel.

Pett Level, a lagoon just behind the sea wall west of Rye, can be excellent in autumn for passage waders and has attracted rarities.

 OTHER ANIMALS
The reserve has an impressive list of moths obtained by regular trapping. You may notice the croaking of Marsh Frogs, an introduced species common in ditches and pools.

FLOWERS
Rye Harbour has much to interest the botanist: more than 300 species of flowering plant have been recorded, and the shingle in late May and June exhibits a colourful display of Yellow-horned Poppies, Sea Pea and Sea Kale.

BIRDS THROUGH THE SEASONS

ALL YEAR: Cormorant, Little Grebe, Great Crested Grebe, Grey Heron, Mute Swan, Mallard, Teal, Gadwall, Shoveler, Pochard, Tufted Duck, Common Scoter, Ruddy Duck, Kestrel, Sparrowhawk, Grey Partridge, Oystercatcher, Ringed Plover, Turnstone, Redshank, Barn Owl, Tree Sparrow, Reed Bunting and Corn Bunting.

SPRING: Garganey and Hobby. Passage waders include Ruff, Black-tailed Godwit, Bar-tailed Godwit, Whimbrel, Spotted Redshank, Greenshank, Green Sandpiper, Common Sandpiper, plus occasional Kentish Plover and Temminck's Stint. Little Gull, Black Tern, Sandwich Tern, often Roseate Tern, Yellow Wagtail, Redstart, Whinchat, Stonechat and the chance of a rarity.

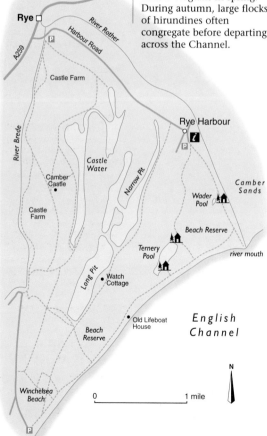

The shingle expanse of the nature reserve was once the sea-bed.
(Right) Little Gulls visit the Tern pool in spring and autumn.

SUMMER: Breeding birds include Little Tern and Common Tern. Sandwich Tern sometimes attempt to breed. A few pairs of Mediterranean Gull breed, Avocets have recently started to summer and attempt to breed, and Turtle Dove, Cuckoo, Wheatear, Yellow Wagtail and Blue-headed Wagtails are annual breeding birds.
AUTUMN: As for spring, with the addition of Gannet, Little Ringed Plover, Knot, Sanderling, Little Stint, Curlew Sandpiper, Black Redstart and rarities.
WINTER: Offshore are Red-throated Diver, Brent Goose, Eider, Common Scoter and Guillemot. On the pits, the rarer grebes and Long-tailed Duck and Smew occasionally occur. Regulars include Wigeon, Pintail, Scaup and Goldeneye. Hunting over the shingle are Merlin and often Peregrine, Hen Harrier and Short-eared Owl. Waders include Golden Plover, Grey Plover, Knot, Dunlin, Jack Snipe on the wader pool, Curlew, Kingfisher and Rock Pipit.

ACCESS: Leave Rye westwards on the A259, turning left to Rye Harbour on the town's outskirts. Follow this road to the end to a car park. From here, take the path alongside the river to the reserve.

To reach Pett Level, continue westwards along the A259 from Rye, turning left at the signs for Winchelsea Beach. The lagoons are on the right of this coast road.

DISABLED ACCESS: There is wheelchair access to the Colin Green Memorial Hide, which overlooks the wader scrape and shingle beach beyond. The main path around the seaward side of the reserve is a narrow tarmac road closed to vehicular access, and so is ideal for wheelchairs. For disabled visitors not confined to wheelchairs but who find walking difficult, vehicular access may be granted by the warden before a visit. Contact the warden at 2 Watch Cottages, Nook Beach, Winchelsea, East Sussex TN36 4LU. Tel: 01797 223862.

OTHER ATTRACTIONS

THE NARROW, cobbled streets of Rye have great character and much of historical interest. There are several notable pubs.

DUNGENESS, REFERRED to affectionately as 'Dunge' by Kent bird-watchers, is the best example of a cuspate shingle foreland in Europe, or in layman's terms a huge shingle spit. The landscape is dominated by Dungeness Nuclear Power Station, but it also boasts an RSPB reserve and a bird observatory. Gravel pits and areas of scrub add to the value of the area for birds.

BIRDS
In winter, the pits attract an interesting array of wildfowl, including a regular flock of Smew. During spring and autumn their margins often attract a few passage waders. Islands provide safe breeding areas for gulls, terns and a few wildfowl.

Due to its position close to the Continent, Dungeness is a superb migration watch-point, and in the right weather conditions notable falls of passerine migrants occur. At any season there is something to see. This is Kent's prime sea-watching location. In early May, Dungeness is the most reliable site on the south coast for seeing passing flocks of Pomarine Skuas.

OTHER ANIMALS
Interesting resident insects are often joined by vagrant dragonflies and damselflies, and by migrant butterflies such as Painted Lady and Clouded Yellow, which can be numerous. Great-crested Newts live in some of the pits, along with noisy Marsh Frogs.

FLOWERS
Due to the rarity of this shingle habitat, Dungeness is important for a specialised flora.

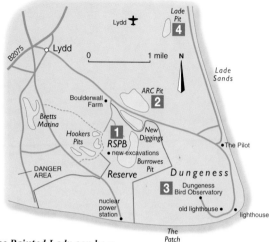

The Painted Lady can be a common migrant in summer.

SITE GUIDE

1

RSPB Reserve

This was the society's first reserve, established in 1931 to protect shingle-nesting birds. However, these nesting colonies were decimated by foxes and were heavily disturbed by human visitors. Ironically,

it was gravel extraction that attracted the birds back, the islands in the gravel pits providing secure nesting sites. Today, Dungeness boasts one of the most important seabird colonies in the South, with a major colony of Sandwich and Common Terns and large numbers of Black-headed Gulls. A few pairs of the attractive Mediterranean Gull breed among the Black-headed Gull colonies,

but picking out the individual 'Meds' among the hundreds of Black-headed can be difficult.

The pits attract wildfowl that include Smew, Goosander and Ruddy Duck, and often Red-necked and Black-necked Grebe. Very few waders occur, preferring the ARC Pit close by, where there is more mud. Hookers Pits, just outside the reserve but accessible from the reserve's western boundary, attract a few wildfowl; the surrounding fields are a good place to find wintering Ruff and Golden Plover.

The reserve has five hides and a centre with a large observation area. A circular walk can be taken round the reserve.

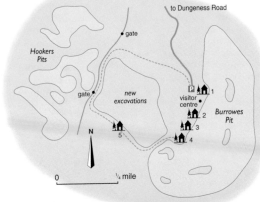

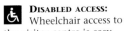 **Access:** The reserve is approximately 1½ miles from the Lydd roundabout on the Dungeness road. Turn right down the track at Boulderwall Farm.

○ Open daily (except Tuesdays) from 9am until sunset.

& **DISABLED ACCESS:** Wheelchair access to the visitor centre is easy, and many birds can be seen from here. Wheelchair access is also possible to a number of other hides.

2

ARC Pit

This pit is opposite the RSPB reserve, and is one of the oldest and largest on the spit, attracting wildfowl,

Aerial view of the Dungeness Peninsula.

waders and gulls. During winter, Smew favour the pit, along with Ruddy Duck. There is often also a diver or rare grebe present. Bewick's Swans that feed out on Romney Marsh sometimes come in to roost. New diggings opposite can be just as productive for wildfowl in winter. Both pits can only be seen from the road, and are ideal for viewing from a car. However, the road is extremely busy with traffic travelling to and from the power station, so care is essential.

Bird Observatory Area

The observatory is in the shadow of the power station. Here, the area of scrub known as the trapping area, the 'moat' surrounding the observatory and the bushes around the old lighthouse are the most productive sites in which to search for migrants. The right weather is needed for large numbers of birds in spring. The best conditions are winds with a southerly influence, coupled with clear weather to the south but with a belt of rain or low cloud over Dungeness to hamper progress north. In clear weather, birds often fly straight over the area. Wheatears, Chiffchaffs and Ring Ouzels appear during March, signalling the onset of spring migration. Large numbers of Willow Warbler pass through in April before the most exciting period in

early May when the flood of migrants includes chats, flycatchers, warblers and, regularly, rarities such as Golden Oriole.

By late July migrants have started to reappear. The variety of migrants increases through August and migration continues in to October with the arrival of thrushes and finches, as well as late-departing summer visitors. When the wind is easterly, rarities such as Wryneck, Icterine Warbler, Tawny Pipit and Red-backed Shrike might be encountered.

Sea-watching is best from the coastguard tower or from the sea-watching hide on the beach (key from observatory). Spring passage offshore involves a variety of species, on some days hundreds and sometimes thousands of scoters may be moving. Brent Geese, Gannets, gulls, terns, wildfowl and waders can often be seen passing by. During summer and autumn, The Patch , the warm-water outflow from the power station, attracts terns and gulls. Autumn passage is not so impressive, though occasional shearwaters, Leach's Storm-Petrels and rarities such as Sabine's Gull are possible in strong winds.

 ACCESS: Park next to the old lighthouse or by the observatory. There are a number of paths through the trapping area. To view The Patch, walk along the front of the power station and observe it from the beach. Hostel-type accommodation is available at the observatory. Contact David Walker,

Dungeness Bird Observatory, Dungeness, Romney Marsh, Kent TN29 9NA. Tel: (01797) 321309.

 DISABLED ACCESS: None.

4

Lade

Along the eastern side of the spit is Lade Sands. At low tide, large areas of sandflats are exposed, attracting a small but varied collection of waders. The main species in winter are Sanderling, Dunlin, Bar-tailed Godwit, Oystercatcher and Grey Plover. The car park at Greatstone is worth checking for Mediterranean Gull which, if present, can be enticed to come close by surrendering a chip or two from the excellent fish and chip shop near by. Lade Pit should be checked for wildfowl and grebes in winter.

 ACCESS: *See* map.

 DISABLED ACCESS: None other than the viewing of gulls at Greatstone car park.

BIRDS THROUGH THE SEASONS
ALL YEAR: Great Crested Grebe, feral Greylag and Canada Geese, Tufted Duck, Pochard, Shoveler, Gadwall, Ringed Plover, Oystercatcher, Red-legged Partridge, Black-headed Gull, Kestrel, Black Redstart (sometimes breeds around the power station), Yellowhammer and Corn Bunting.
SPRING: Offshore: passage of divers, scoters, Garganey

Red-legged Partridge is a common resident.

(March), Eider, Red-breasted Merganser, waders, terns, gulls, auks, skuas (including Pomarine Skua in early May), migrant warblers and chats in the trapping area. SUMMER: Breeding birds include Common Gull (a few pairs), Black-headed Gull, Mediterranean Gull, Sandwich Tern, Common Tern, Wheatear, Reed Warbler and Sedge Warbler. Lingering non-breeders include Roseate Tern and often Little Gull. Returning migrants include Cuckoo and Yellow Wagtail. AUTUMN: Offshore: possibility of Leach's Storm-petrel, Manx Shearwater and Sooty Shearwater. Gannet, skuas, gulls, auks and terns pass. Migrants in the trapping area include Black Redstart, Redstart, Whinchat, Pied Flycatcher, Ring Ouzel, Goldcrest,

The few pairs of breeding Mediterranean Gulls can be difficult to locate among the Black-headed Gull colonies.

Firecrest, often Wryneck and Red-backed Shrike. Around the pit margins, passage waders may include Wood Sandpiper, Green Sandpiper, Greenshank and Little Stint. Finches and thrushes in late autumn. WINTER: Offshore: Slavonian Grebe, Red-throated Diver and Common Scoter. On pits: Red-necked and

sometimes Black-necked Grebe, Teal, Goldeneye, Smew, Goosander, Ruddy Duck and sometimes Bewick's Swan on the ARC. On the fields of Dengemarsh and RSPB reserve: Hen Harrier, Merlin, Ruff, Golden Plover, Lapwing and Grey Plover. In bushes: sometimes Chiffchaff, Firecrest, Stonechat and Woodcock. Glaucous Gulls are regular.

 ACCESS: *See* site guide and map.

 DISABLED ACCESS: In general, very limited for wheelchair users due to shingle terrain. *See* site guide.

OTHER ATTRACTIONS

DURING THE summer, the old lighthouse is open, allowing those who have a head for heights spectacular views across the peninsula. A narrow-gauge steam railway runs from the café on the point to Hythe, and is a popular attraction for families.

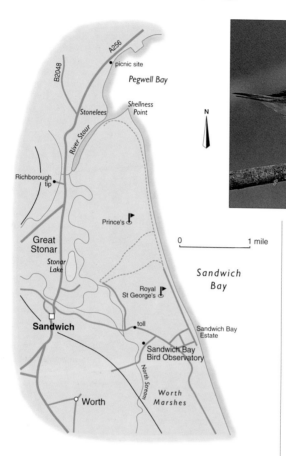

Pallas's Warbler.

Snow and Lapland Buntings. The former can exceed 100 in some years, and are often seen along the beach towards Shellness Point or on the short turf of the golf courses. Hen Harrier, Short-Eared Owl and Merlin hunt over the meadows and saltings.

Near by, Pegwell Bay attracts waders in small numbers throughout the year, and Kentish Plovers also occur annually. This species takes its name from a specimen collected here. A few wildfowl overwinter, including Brent Geese.

If time allows during a winter trip, it is worth visiting both Stonar Lake and Richborough tip. The lake has regularly held wrecked Little Auks and rare grebes, while the tip may have a wintering Glaucous Gull.

TO THE south of Ramsgate lies Sandwich Bay, an area best known for its migrants. A bird observatory was established in 1961 and, both here and at nearby Pegwell Bay, various conservation bodies are involved in protecting saltmarsh, sand-dune, meadow and mudflat habitats. The Sandwich Bay Estate has mature gardens and areas of scrub, while adjacent to the coastal strip are two of the country's top golf courses, Royal St George's and Prince's. Towards Shellness Point a wader scrape has recently been constructed; it has much potential, but access to the scrape is restricted to permit-holders.

BIRDS
A variety of migrants occur in spring, although numbers depend on the weather. Autumn can be particularly exciting, especially in easterly winds when rarities such as Pallas's Warbler are regular among the commoner migrant warblers, chats and flycatchers. As autumn merges into winter, finches and thrushes arrive, along with winter visitors such as

OTHER ANIMALS
Migrant butterflies include Clouded Yellow.

FLOWERS
Sandwich Bay has an interesting flora that includes the Sharp Rush,

Parasitic Bedstraw and Carrot Broomrape. Orchids are abundant and include, among the nine species present, Pyramidal, Southern Marsh and the rare Lizard Orchid.

BIRDS THROUGH THE SEASONS

ALL YEAR: Kestrel, Oystercatcher, Ringed Plover, Redshank, Meadow Pipit, Reed Bunting, Corn Bunting, Yellowhammer. SPRING: Migrants include Black Redstart, Wheatear, Whinchat, Ring Ouzel, various warblers and rarities such as the Golden Oriole. In Pegwell Bay, a few waders may include a Kentish Plover and, in the bay and offshore, Sandwich Tern. SUMMER: Breeding birds include Shelduck, a small colony of Little Terns, Cuckoo and Yellow

Wagtail. Non-breeders include Sandwich Tern, occasional Quail and Mediterranean Gull. AUTUMN: Migrant warblers, chats and flycatchers include Redstart and Pied Flycatcher. In easterly winds, regulars such as Firecrest can be joined by large numbers of Goldcrests, plus rarities such as Icterine Warbler and Wryneck. In late autumn, Pallas's and Yellow-browed Warbler are possible, with influxes of finches and thrushes. In Pegwell Bay and on the wader scrape, passage waders such as Green and Wood Sandpiper, Spotted Redshank and Greenshank may be anticipated. WINTER: Red-throated Diver offshore, and Teal, Wigeon and Brent Goose in Pegwell Bay. Over the saltings and

fields: Hen Harrier, Short-eared Owl and Merlin. Waders include Golden Plover, Grey Plover, Dunlin, Sanderling and Bar-tailed Godwit. Twite, Snow Bunting, Lapland Bunting, and Stonechat.

 ACCESS: *See* map for directions to sites. There are a number of options for walks. In winter, a walk along the shore to the point may be rewarding, while in spring and autumn attention may be better focused on the areas of scrub within the Sandwich Bay Estate. To enter the estate and reach the observatory by car, you must pass through a toll. This can be avoided by arriving before 8am, or parking outside and walking in. Hostel-type accommodation is available at the observatory; booking and details from the warden, Sandwich Bay Bird Observatory, Old Downs Farm, Guildford Road, Sandwich Bay, Sandwich, Kent CT13 9PF. Tel: 01304 617341.

DISABLED ACCESS: None at Sandwich Bay other than access around the roads on the estate. At Pegwell Bay much can be seen from a vehicle.

OTHER ATTRACTIONS

SANDWICH IS one of Kent's most attractive towns. Historically fascinating, its narrow streets are full of character.

Wintering Snow Bunting feed along the beach and on the short turf of the golf course.

BLEAN WOODS, close to Canterbury, is one of Britain's largest ancient forests. Oak woodland and Sweet Chestnut coppice predominate.

BIRDS
Blean Woods RSPB reserve is best visited in spring and in early summer when an excellent range of woodland birds can be found. Nightingales are particularly common. Wood Warbler and Redstart usually breed; both are scarce elsewhere in Kent. One of the best ways to experience the forest is to arrive for the dawn chorus in May. At first, just Nightingales sing, joined at dawn by birds such as Blackbird and Song Thrush, before gradually the whole forest comes alive.

OTHER ANIMALS
The woods are an important site for the Heath Fritillary butterfly, which is on the wing in June and July. The fritillary

Blean Woods.

caterpillars feed on Cow-wheat, a plant that favours newly coppiced areas.

BIRDS THROUGH THE SEASONS
ALL YEAR: Sparrowhawk, Kestrel, Tawny Owl, Woodcock, Lesser Spotted, Great Spotted and Green Woodpeckers, Marsh Tit, Willow Tit, Nuthatch, Treecreeper, Hawfinch.
SPRING AND SUMMER: Hobby, Nightjar, Tree Pipit, Turtle Dove, Nightingale, Redstart, Wood Warbler, Willow Warbler, Blackcap, Garden

Map showing Blean, RSPB Reserve, A290 to Canterbury, Dog & Bear pub, Rough Common, access for eastbound traffic only, A2 to Canterbury, Harbledown, to Whitstable, to Faversham & M2, to Dover. Scale 0 – ½ mile. N.

Warbler and, occasionally, Crossbill.
WINTER: Siskin, Redpoll and Goldcrest.

ACCESS:
If approaching Canterbury from the west on the A2, take the first turning to Canterbury and then the second turning on the left to Rough Common. The reserve is signposted on the left along this road.

There are three trails that allow access into the heart of the forest. Each gives the opportunity of a circular walk, and takes between 30 minutes and 2 hours to complete.

DISABLED ACCESS:
Wheelchair access is good on one of the paths for a reasonable distance. In general, the paths are fairly even, and the walks not particularly strenuous.

OTHER ATTRACTIONS

THE CATHEDRAL city of Canterbury, with its varied attractions, is close by.

The Lampen Wall provides a good vantage point from which to watch.

STODMARSH NATIONAL Nature Reserve lies in the Stour Valley, north-east of Canterbury, and was once known as Stud-marsh because Augustinian monks bred horses on the marshes. Extensive reedbeds and areas of open water border the Lampen Wall, a flood defence that provides an excellent vantage over the area. Further along the wall, where the path follows the River Stour, there are flood meadows overlooked by a hide.

A number of walks can be enjoyed at Stodmarsh. Boardwalks lead through areas of Alder carr and scrub. A walk along the Lampen Wall will lead to Grove Ferry, where there is a pleasant pub that is ideal for lunch before the walk back in the afternoon.

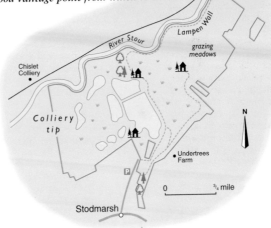

BIRDS
The reedbeds were formed after subsidence occurred at the nearby Chislet Colliery, which opened at the turn of the century. These reedbeds support Bearded Tits throughout the year. Bitterns have bred but are sporadic, as is the Savi's Warbler, which was once an annual breeder here. Stodmarsh was the English stronghold of the Cetti's Warbler when this species first started colonising the area in the early 1970s. Sadly, by 1988 the entire population had been wiped out by a series of hard winters. Occasional birds have since reappeared, although it remains to be seen whether successful recolonisation will occur.

Grasshopper Warblers breed in most years, but the most numerous summer

Great Grey Shrikes occasionally winter.

visitors are Reed and Sedge Warblers. Garganey are best seen in early spring before they disappear off into the reeds to breed. On warm summer evenings, the Lampen Wall is a good place from which to watch hunting Hobbies, these congregating to feed on insects and hirundines.

During winter, duck, particularly Shoveler, use the main lagoon, and on the flooded meadows wildfowl are joined by a few wintering waders. Marsh Harrier and Hen Harrier roost in the reeds, and so can often be seen at dusk. In some years, Great Grey Shrikes winter, though this species is less regular than it once was. Close to the car park, areas of Alder scrub have roving tit flocks in winter; these flocks often include an overwintering Chiffchaff. Throughout the year, the stands of mature Alder are a good place to

look for the secretive Lesser Spotted Woodpecker. Success is most likely in February and March, when they start to drum.

OTHER ANIMALS

Stodmarsh has an interesting range of aquatic plants along its ditches, the latter inhabited by Water Shrews, Water Voles and Grass Snakes. The meadows have a varied flora; the occasional Hare can be seen in summer, while bats often hunt over the Lampen Wall. Look out for the Noctule, a large, narrow-winged bat that pursues high-flying insects.

BIRDS THROUGH THE SEASONS

ALL YEAR: Great Crested Grebe, Little Grebe, Cormorant, feral Greylag and Canada Geese, Gadwall, Teal, Shoveler, Pochard, Tufted Duck, Water Rail, Snipe,

Redshank, Sparrowhawk, Kingfisher, Lesser Spotted Woodpecker, Bearded Tit and Reed Bunting.

SPRING: Garganey, Hobby, often Osprey, and a few waders on the meadows. Black Tern, Cuckoo, Sand Martin, Yellow Wagtail, Grasshopper Warbler, possibly Savi's and Cetti's Warblers, Reed Warbler and Sedge Warbler.

SUMMER: Common Tern breed on the rafts in the main lagoon. Hobbies are regular.

AUTUMN: A few migrant terns and waders. Hirundines can roost in large numbers in the reedbed.

WINTER: Wintering wildfowl include Wigeon, often a few Bewick's Swan and, in some years, small flocks of Bean or Pink-footed Geese. Hen Harriers roost with the occasional Marsh Harrier. Bittern are occasional. Water Pipit and Green Sandpiper occur on the meadows. Great Grey Shrikes often appear in late autumn, but do not always stay through the winter. Corn Buntings arrive at dusk to roost in the reedbed.

ACCESS: Leave Canterbury on the A257 to Sandwich; after 1½ miles turn left for the village of Stodmarsh. In the village, take the track on the left immediately after the Red Lion pub to the car park.

DISABLED ACCESS: Good for wheelchair users.

OTHER ATTRACTIONS

CANTERBURY IS close by.

BRITAIN'S LARGEST heronry of over 200 pairs is found within a small woodland on this hill. Areas of Oak and dense hawthorn thickets characterise this RSPB reserve.

BIRDS
Apart from the Grey Herons in spring and summer, breeding birds include Nightingales, various warblers, Turtle Doves and both Great and Lesser Spotted Woodpeckers.

During winter, the wood hosts large roosts of Woodpigeons, thrushes and finches. They arrive at dusk, and provide prey for the Long-eared Owls that roost among the hawthorns during the day. Merlins and Sparrowhawks also take advantage of this food source.

OTHER ANIMALS
During the summer, White-letter Hairstreak butterflies should be looked for in the Elm scrub and around brambles. Badgers thrive on the reserve, and can be seen at dusk.

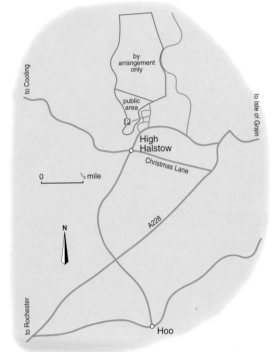

BIRDS THROUGH THE SEASONS
ALL YEAR: Long-eared Owl, Tawny Owl, Great Spotted Woodpecker, Lesser Spotted Woodpecker and Treecreeper.

SPRING AND SUMMER: The Grey Herons nest early and will be on eggs by mid-March. Breeding summer visitors include Turtle Dove, Nightingale, Chiffchaff, Willow Warbler, Whitethroats, Lesser Whitethroat, Garden Warbler and Blackcap. There is a large rookery.

AUTUMN AND WINTER: Roosts of Woodpigeons, thrushes and finches. Long-eared Owls, Sparrowhawk and Merlin. Goldcrest and roving tit flocks.

Access: From the A228 Isle of Grain–Rochester road, take one of the minor roads to High Halstow. The reserve is on the edge of the village and is well signposted.

 DISABLED ACCESS: None.

During winter thousands of birds roost in the wood.

The Isle of Sheppey, encompassing the North Kent marshes, is of international importance as many species of waterfowl use it for both breeding and wintering. The extensive mudflats, and floods provided by both the Swale NNR and neighbouring Elmley, are a vital refuelling stop for thousands of waders migrating to and from their more northerly breeding grounds. A variety of raptors can be found throughout the year, making this one of the top spots in the country for birds of prey.

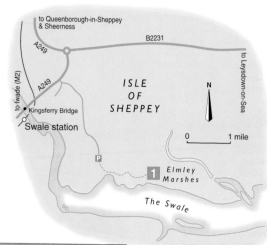

The Swale Estuary.

wildfowl bred among the meadows. In 1975, the RSPB set about re-creating a substantial wetland, and this has been achieved with dramatic effect. In some winters over 20,000 Wigeon use the reserve, along with a host of other ducks. White-fronted Geese are regular on the grazing marsh, and waders often occur in their thousands at high tide, having been pushed off the mudflats of the Swale. Raptors such as Peregrine hunt over the area, and are often the cause of panic when clouds of birds rise into the air.

During spring and autumn, migrant waders abound, with Temminck's Stint annual in May. During autumn, Curlew Sandpipers and Little Stints are often joined by a rarity. Black-tailed Godwits occur throughout the year, including a regular summering flock and a few pairs that breed. Another recent breeding colonist is the Avocet.

OTHER ANIMALS
The rare Ground Lackey moth occurs in summer; in early summer the caterpillars build silken tents among the saltmarsh. Another rarity, the Essex Skipper butterfly, occurs on the Swale reserve; this species is confined to coastal areas of South-East England. Slow-worms and Common Lizards can be seen basking on the sea wall during summer, while Marsh Frogs are common in the network of dykes on the Swale reserve.

SITE GUIDE

Elmley Marshes
RSPB Reserve

Rough pasture, reed-fringed ditches and the flood, an area of flooded grazing land, attract a wide variety of wildfowl and waders at all seasons. Before the RSPB established this reserve, just a handful of waders and

From the reserve car park there is a 1½-mile walk along a raised bank to the flood. As you walk, scan the fields in winter for harriers, Short-eared Owl, Merlin and Peregrine, and at dusk throughout the year for Barn Owl. Lapland Buntings may be encountered flying overhead or on the marsh. Three hides overlook the flood, while a further two hides overlook the Swale. Grebes and sea duck can often be seen from these hides at high tide, while wildfowl and waders are always visible at low tide. The furthest hide (at Spitend) entails a further 1½-mile walk.

ACCESS: The RSPB reserve is reached along a rough track on the right about a mile from the Kingsferry Bridge. The hides are a 1½-mile walk from the car park.

Open daily, except Tuesday, from 9am to dusk.

DISABLED ACCESS: No access for wheelchairs. For the partially disabled and those unable to walk far, the warden may grant permission for a vehicle to be driven down to the flood.

2

Capel Fleet

This is an excellent site from which to see a variety of raptors in winter, and from January to March over 1000 White-fronted Geese may use the surrounding fields.

Short-eared Owl, Merlin, Peregrine, Hen Harrier and Marsh Harrier are likely on a typical visit. Towards dusk, Barn Owl is a possibility. This is one of the best sites in Britain for Rough-legged Buzzards, though only in invasion years. During the summer, Marsh Harriers breed close by and can often be seen hunting. Montagu's Harrier often occur in autumn and have bred in the past.

Apart from the wintering flock of White-fronted Geese, a few Bewick's Swans are joined by flocks of Golden Plovers and Lapwings; look for overwintering Ruff in the dampest fields.

ACCESS: After crossing the Kingsferry Bridge, and after the turning for Elmley, turn right at the roundabout on to the B2231 to Eastchurch. About 1½ miles after Eastchurch, take a turning on the right (Harty Ferry Road). Drive to the bottom of the hill to the sharp left-hand bend; you can pull in here and scan the area.

DISABLED ACCESS: This is good as all bird-watching is done from the road, a vehicle making the ideal hide.

3

Warden Point

Rising to 100 feet, the unstable clay cliffs of Warden Point have behind them areas of bramble, scrub and gardens. In autumn, during north-easterly winds, migrants such as Pied Flycatcher, Redstart and Firecrest occur regularly, and sometimes a rarity such as Yellow-browed Warbler.

ACCESS: Take the left turn in Eastchurch signposted to Warden Point, then take the first right, parking near the cliffs. Any areas of cover are worth checking.

DISABLED ACCESS: None.

4

The Swale NNR and Shellness

Tucked away in the far south-east corner of the Isle of Sheppey is the Swale National Nature Reserve, Kent's best-kept secret. Walking at a leisurely pace, it will take a full day to complete the circular route, taking in all six hides and then returning to the Shellness spit.

Saltmarsh, grazing marsh, creeks and mudflats make up the 620 acres of the reserve, opened in October 1991. Funding provided by the Council to the European Community has assisted the large-scale bunding scheme. These bunds (earth banks), which are a major topo-graphical feature of the reserve, enable rotational flooding of the grazing marsh to take place. A borehole allows extra water to be pumped on to the reserve when required. The floods are allowed to dry out in summer, thus enabling plant and invertebrate life to survive.

During the winter, large numbers of Brent Geese use the floods and surrounding fields. In recent years the occasional Red-breasted Goose, a vagrant from eastern Europe, has been found among the flocks. Wigeon usually occur in large numbers, along with a variety of waders. Short-eared Owl and Hen Harrier hunt over the adjacent saltmarsh and over the floods and fields, while Marsh Harrier,

North Kent marshes.

Peregrine and Merlin are regular visitors. The reserve is starting to attract a range of species similar to those at Elmley, and during passage periods the same species of wader occur.

Shellness is a spit composed almost entirely of shells and sand washed up from the cockle beds off Whitstable. In winter, Snow Buntings are one of the attractions; they favour the area beyond the block-house. In some years, the surrounding saltmarsh has wintering Twite. Large numbers of Knot roost on the spit, accompanied by smaller flocks of the other typical estuarine waders. These can all be watched as they feed on the surrounding mud at low

Red-breasted Goose among Brent Geese.

tide. In the mouth of the Swale, a variety of sea duck, grebes and often divers can be expected, notably Eider, Red-breasted Merganser and Common Scoter. Long-tailed Duck, Velvet Scoter and Slavonian Grebe are rare but regular.

In the autumn, Shellness is a good sea-watching location, but you need a north-westerly wind to push the birds into the mouth of the Swale. Great and Arctic, and more rarely Pomarine Skuas are joined by Manx Shearwaters and a few Leach's Storm-petrels. Look out, too, for Sabine's Gull, with the possibility of Little Auks from late October.

Shellness is composed of sand and shells.

 ACCESS: Once on the Isle of Sheppey, follow signs to Leysdown on the B2231. Drive through Leysdown and along the sea wall, pass Muswell Manor and enter a private road. This road is deeply pot-holed, and extreme care should be taken. The road leads to a small car park and the start of the reserve. A 2-mile circular walk around the reserve is recommended.

The reserve is open from dawn to dusk every day of the year. The privacy of the residents at the hamlet on Shellness should be respected. Sea-watching is best from the point by the corner of the hamlet.

DISABLED ACCESS: None.

BIRDS THROUGH THE SEASONS

ALL YEAR: Little Grebe, Cormorant, Greylag Goose (feral), Shelduck, Gadwall, Teal, Mallard, Shoveler, Eider (non-breeding birds), Marsh Harrier, Kestrel, Sparrowhawk, Oystercatcher, Ringed Plover, Snipe, Redshank, Barn Owl, Meadow Pipit, Corn Bunting.

SPRING: Passage waders include Black-tailed Godwit, Whimbrel, Little and Temminck's Stint, Greenshank, Spotted Redshank and Wood Sandpiper. Garganey are annual on passage and breed. Wheatear and Yellow Wagtail.

SUMMER: Returning waders by late June include Green Sandpiper, Curlew Sand-

There are six well-placed hides on the Swale NNR.

piper, Dunlin and Spotted Redshank. Marsh Harriers breed. Breeding wildfowl include Pintail (occasional), Wigeon, Gadwall and Shoveler. Breeding waders include Black-tailed Godwit and Avocet. Common and Little Tern breed on the flood. Yellow Wagtail, Sedge and Reed Warblers on the marsh.

AUTUMN: Wader passage peaks at the end of July. Curlew Sandpiper, Little Stint and Spotted Redshank can be expected. In north-westerly gales sea-watching from Shellness may produce Leach's and British Storm-petrels, Manx Shearwater, all four species of skua, Little Auk and various gulls, including Little and Sabine's. Passerine migrants may include Pied Flycatcher and Firecrest. Montagu's

Harrier are possible in early autumn.

WINTER: Large numbers of Wigeon, Teal, Shoveler, Pintail, Brent Geese and smaller numbers of White-fronted Geese build to a peak from January to March. On the Swale estuary, seaduck include Eider, Red-breasted Merganser, Common Scoter. Long-tailed Duck, Goldeneye and Velvet Scoter are regularly recorded. Raptors include Peregrine, Merlin, Hen Harrier, Marsh Harrier, Short-eared Owl and Barn Owl, with Rough-legged Buzzard in some years. All the common estuarine waders are present. Passerine specialities include Twite (absent in some winters), Snow Buntings, Lapland Buntings and, in some winters, Shorelark.

 ACCESS:
See site guide.

DISABLED ACCESS:
See site guide.

OTHER ATTRACTIONS

THE ISLE of Sheppey has little to offer the family other than its bird-watching locations.

CLIFFE POOLS are located on the south shore of the River Thames near Rochester, and support important wintering populations of waders. They act as a vital refuelling area for migrant waders, especially in autumn. A series of pools, some shallow and muddy, others much deeper with water all year round, are the main feature. The site is bordered by the Thames and by large expanses of rough grazing land. A chalk cliff, with areas of thick hawthorn at its base, skirts along the eastern side, and behind the cliff are two deep quarry pits that are also attractive to diving duck.

The site is owned by Blue Circle, which has drawn up a management plan with the RSPB and English Nature to safeguard the area.

BIRDS

Numbers of birds and viewing conditions are dependent on water-levels in the shallow lagoons

Cliffe Pools are one of the south-east's premier sites for watching waders in autumn.

lying directly west of the Black Barn. In autumn, these pools attract large numbers of Curlew Sandpipers, Little Stints, Wood Sandpipers and Ruffs. Black-tailed Godwits, Grey Plover, Dunlin, Spotted Redshanks and Greenshank are some of the other species that occur in impressive numbers on passage. Rarities in autumn are frequent, with past records of up to three Broad-billed Sandpipers

few terns, Wheatears and Yellow Wagtails.

 OTHER ANIMALS
The dykes and lagoons support a diverse range of water beetles and flies, while the scarce Emerald Damselfly is one of the local specialities. The lagoons also hold the curiously named Opossum Shrimp, a highly localised species. Stoats can often be seen around the Rabbit warrens.

BIRDS THROUGH THE SEASONS
ALL YEAR: Little Grebe, Great Crested Grebe, Grey Heron, Shelduck, Gadwall, Teal, Shoveler, Pochard, Tufted Duck, Red-legged Partridge, Water Rail, Oystercatcher, Ringed Plover, Dunlin, Snipe, Little Owl, Barn Owl, Reed Bunting, Corn Bunting.
SPRING: Garganey, Whimbrel, Black-tailed Godwit, Greenshank, Ruff, Yellow Wagtail, Wheatear and Whinchat.
SUMMER: Breeding birds include Garganey, Avocet, and Common Tern.
AUTUMN: By late July, waders are returning: Curlew Sandpiper, Little Stint, often Temminck's Stint, Ruff, Spotted Redshank, Greenshank, Grey Plover, Avocet, Green Sandpiper, Wood Sandpiper, Dunlin, Black-tailed Godwit and Curlew; rarities are annual.

On the Thames, skuas are possible. Little Gulls are regular on the pools.
WINTER: Occasional Black-necked Grebe and Slavonian Grebe, Wigeon, Pintail, Goldeneye, occasional Smew, Avocet, Grey Plover, Golden Plover, Curlew, Black-tailed Godwit, Short-eared Owl, Long-eared Owl, Hen Harrier, Merlin, Sparrowhawk, Fieldfare and Redwing.

 ACCESS: Take the B2000 to Cliffe village, and drive through it until you reach a sharp right-hand bend. Go straight on down this track past the farm to the pools. To view the waders, park by the Black Barn and take the path immediately west between Radar Pool and the series of muddy lagoons. Take care to limit disturbance, and do not leave the paths. All the pools, including the quarry pits, attract birds. *See* map.

DISABLED ACCESS:
A limited amount can be seen from a vehicle, including the Radar Pool and Alpha Pool.

OTHER ATTRACTIONS

C HATHAM'S FAMOUS naval dockyard is where Nelson's HMS *Victory* was built, and there is now a museum here. Fort Amherst, the only surviving Napoleonic fort, is also in Chatham and has a visitor centre. Nearby Rochester has some interesting historical sites.

Up to 5000 Dunlin winter at Cliffe.

together, Stilt Sandpiper and Buff-breasted Sandpiper. Return wader passage is in full swing by the end of July, and continues through the autumn.

During winter, up to 5000 Dunlin are joined by Avocets and a good selection of estuarine waders. Wigeon, Pintail, Teal and Gadwall all use the pools. Black-necked and Slavonian Grebes both occur regularly in the winter, while hard weather on the Continent often brings Smew. In the scrub below the chalk cliff, a few Long-eared Owls roost; they can sometimes be seen hunting at dusk under the floodlights of the oil depot. Short-eared Owls hunt over the rough ground and marshes, along with Hen Harrier and Merlin. Both Little Owl and Barn Owl breed and can be seen year-round. During spring, waders pass through on passage, as do Garganey, a

To the north-east of London, straddling the River Lee, are over 100 areas of open water, reservoirs and lakes.

BIRDS
The area attracts large numbers of wintering wild-fowl, including the rarer sawbills such as Smew and Goosander. In recent winters Bitterns have been annual, attracting bird-watchers from all over the

During winter Bitterns are seen daily from the Waverley Hide in the River Lee Country Park.

South-East. Kingfishers are encountered throughout the year along the valley.

OTHER ANIMALS
The park is rich in wildlife, and Water Shrews, Harvest Mice and introduced Otters thrive. Cornhill Meadows is one of the top sites in the British Isles for dragonflies and damselflies, attracting over 20 species including the Ruddy Darter and Emerald Damselfly.

pairs of herons and a recently formed Cormorant breeding colony. Tufted Duck gather to moult in late summer, and are joined in winter by Pochard and Shoveler. The reservoirs are of most interest in winter during hard weather when wildfowl numbers swell and more interesting species then occur.

ACCESS: Managed by Thames Water; permits are required to visit. Tel: 0181 8081527.

SITE GUIDE

1

Walthamstow Reservoirs

Constructed between 1866 and 1903, this complex of ten basins has a number of wooded islands that are a safe haven for over 100

2

King George V Reservoirs

Opened in 1913, these two large basins, separated by a causeway, are a popular site for bird-watchers living in this part of London. Passage migrants can be abundant, with pipits, wagtails and Wheatears attracted to their grassy banks. Around the concrete aprons, migrant waders rarely linger for long but a good variety are recorded annually. Terns, hirundines and swifts hawk over the water in summer, while, in winter Goosander and Goldeneye join the commoner diving and dabbling ducks. At dusk, up to 25,000 gulls arrive to roost.

 ACCESS: As for Walthamstow.

3
River Lee Country Park

Numerous paths provide easy walking. The site is one of the best along the valley for a wide range of birds. The Hall Marsh Scrape, with its three hides, has breeding birds such as Little Ringed Plover.

The Fishers Green area attracts not only water-birds but also a good selection of woodland species. Kingfishers are regular along the river here and are frequently seen perched in front of the Waverley Hide. In winter, this hide has become the place in Britain for close-up views of Bitterns. Up to three Bitterns often fish the tiny reedbed within a few feet of a packed hide of bird-watchers.

In winter, the Holyfield Lake attracts Smew, Goldeneye and Goosander. Grasshopper Warbler breed close by. Large numbers of Great Crested Grebes nest throughout the Fishers Green area, along with

scarcer species such as Ruddy Duck, Gadwall and Shoveler.

 ACCESS: There are a number of access points along the B194. For the Waverley Hide turn off the B194, on a sharp bend to Fishers Green car park (after Fishers Green Lane if travelling north). From the car park walk across the bridge over the river and turn right.

DISABLED ACCESS: Wheelchair access within the park is generally very good, especially within the River Lee Country Park. Facilities are being improved continually. To gain current access information, Tel: 01992 713838.

4
Rye Meads and Rye House Marsh
RSPB Reserve

These two adjacent sites support a typical cross-section of birds found in the valley. Both reserves consist of marsh and meadow, and are important sites within the valley for breeding wildfowl. There are six hides on the RSPB reserve, three of which are good for specific species. One hide overlooks a Sand Martin colony, another a bank used by breeding Kingfishers, and the third overlooks rafts used by breeding Common Tern.

Rye Meads is an SSSI managed by the Herts and Middlesex Wildlife Trust. In winter, both Bittern and Water Rail occur, and often

Water Pipits can be found on the meadows.

 ACCESS: *See* map.

DISABLED ACCESS: There is limited access on the RSPB reserve. The Ashby Hide, close to the car park, is accessible to wheelchairs, as is an adapted room under the North Hide, although assistance may be needed in the latter.

5
Amwell Quarry Nature Reserve

A range of breeding birds includes Little Ringed Plover and Grasshopper Warbler, along with a variety of wildfowl. During winter, most species of duck are well represented here – in particular Shoveler and Gadwall.

ACCESS: No access on to the site; but views are possible from the Amwell walkway.

BIRDS THROUGH THE SEASONS
ALL YEAR: Great Crested Grebe, Little Grebe, Grey Heron, Cormorant, Mallard, Gadwall, Shoveler, Tufted Duck, Pochard, Ruddy Duck, Sparrowhawk, Kestrel, Snipe, Redshank, lapwing, green, Great Spotted and Lesser Spotted Woodpecker, Kingfisher, Goldfinch and Reed Bunting.
SPRING: A few passage waders pass through. Black

Tern, Yellow Wagtail and Wheatear.

SUMMER: Breeding birds include Shelduck, Little Ringed Plover, Common Tern, Grasshopper Warbler, Sedge Warbler, Reed Warbler, Garden Warbler, Lesser Whitethroat, Whitethroat, Blackcap, Willow Warbler, Chiffchaff and Spotted Flycatcher.

AUTUMN: Passage waders, wagtails, pipits and finches. Migrant terns.

Kingfishers are found throughout the valley.

WINTER: Large numbers of dabbling and diving ducks swell the resident populations. Goldeneye, Goosander, Smew, Teal, Wigeon and Pintail. Also Bittern, Long-eared Owl, Water Pipit, Jack Snipe, Siskin and Redpoll.

ACCESS: The Lee Valley Park extends from Tottenham north along the River Lee to Ware. *See* map and the site guide above.

DISABLED ACCESS: *See* site guide.

OTHER ATTRACTIONS

THE LEE Valley Park is a major recreational area for all residents of north-east London. The park is a mosaic of nature reserves, waterways and sites of historical interest, and there are numerous sporting and general leisure facilities available to members of the public. More information can be obtained from the park authority at the address given above within the site guide.

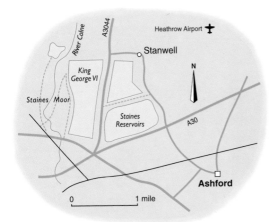

STAINES RESERVOIR lies close to Heathrow Airport and can be a noisy place for birdwatching, yet, below the low-flying jets, a multitude of birds thrive.

BIRDS

Wildfowl winter in large numbers, while many migrants can be seen during spring and autumn. The causeway separating the two basins acts as a meeting place for local birders as this is the most accessible reservoir in west London.

During winter, Tufted Duck and Pochard are most numerous, with lesser numbers of other species such as Goosander and Goldeneye. During spring and autumn, a few waders are joined by flocks of Black Terns and Little Gulls. Wheatears, Yellow Wagtails and Whinchats occur around the margins and along the causeway. A speciality of the site is the late-summer congregation of Black-necked Grebes. They start to appear in late July and sometimes stay into winter, though August through to October is the peak time.

The basins are drained every few years, leaving vast expanses of mud.

During these periods, wader watching can be excellent, and often Little Ringed Plover and, sometimes, Ringed Plover are induced to breed.

BIRDS THROUGH THE SEASONS

SPRING: Terns include Black Tern, Little Gull, Little Ringed Plover, Ringed Plover, Common Sandpiper, Dunlin and a variety of other passage waders. Wheatear and Yellow Wagtail.

SUMMER: Black-necked Grebes arrive in late July, remaining into late autumn and often through winter.

AUTUMN: Passage waders and terns similar to those in spring, but there are greater numbers and they are more prone to linger.

WINTER: Great Crested Grebe, Little Grebe, Pochard, Tufted Duck, Goldeneye, Goosander and a few dabbling duck. Black Redstart occasionally winter.

ACCESS: Take the A3044 north of Staines. Park on the verge along this road opposite the access path to the causeway. There are no access restrictions.

OTHER ATTRACTIONS

THORPE PARK: A popular theme park near Chertsey providing a fun-filled day out for all the family.

WINDSOR: Windsor Castle, surrounded by Windsor Great Park, is the world's largest inhabited castle.

Common Sandpipers feed along the waters edge during spring and autumn.

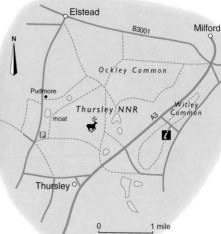

May and June are the best months to visit Thursley Common.

THE NATIONAL Nature Reserve of Thursley Common is primarily a lowland heath with areas of bog, pine forest and small stands of Birch.

 BIRDS
Dartford Warbler, Woodlark, Nightjar and Hobby are the breeding specialities of the heath, while the pine woods support a breeding population of Redstarts.

During the winter months, both Merlin and Hen Harrier may be encountered, while in some years a Great Grey Shrike may be present. Crossbills can occur throughout the year, though in some years none are recorded.

For many breeding species, an early morning or dusk visit is recommended in May or June. During winter Thursley can seem a lifeless place, and the few birds that are present are invariably difficult to find.

OTHER ANIMALS
The large Marsh Grasshopper and White-faced Darter are two nationally rare invertebrates

that occur in the damp areas. In the dry areas of heath there are both Smooth Snake and Sand Lizard, while uncommon butterflies such as the Grayling and Silver-studded Blue thrive.

 FLOWERS
Thursley is an important reserve for some rare insects, and for heath and bog plants. The mires have Bog Bean and Lesser Bladderwort, while the surrounding wetter heath is characterised by Purple Moor Grass. Southern Marsh Orchids thrive alongside two species of sundew and the colourful Bog Asphodel.

BIRDS THROUGH THE SEASONS
SPRING AND SUMMER: Breeding birds include Little Grebe, Hobby, Curlew, Snipe, Redshank, Woodcock, Cuckoo, Nightjar, Tree Pipit, Woodlark, Nightingale, Redstart, Dartford Warbler, Grasshopper Warbler and, in some years, Crossbill.
AUTUMN AND WINTER: Hen Harrier, Merlin, possible

Great Grey Shrike and Crossbills.

 ACCESS: From the A3, take the B3001 to Elstead. Once in the village, turn left at the village green just past the Woolpack pub. The Moat car park at Thursley is a mile further along on the left. *See* map for walks.

DISABLED ACCESS: None.

OTHER ATTRACTIONS

CLANDON PARK: Close to Loseley House; an 18th-century building, home to the museum of the Queen's Royal Surrey Regiment.

GUILDFORD: A cathedral city with a good shopping centre and an array of historical sites.

LOSELEY HOUSE: This Elizabethan mansion contains fine panelling, tapestries and contemporary furniture. It is north-east of Thursley, close to Shalford.

NESTLING BELOW the Greensand ridge just south of Sevenoaks is Bough Beech Reservoir. It was completed in 1969 and has been used intensively by bird-watchers ever since. The reservoir is surrounded by woodlands, hedgerows and fields, so a good variety of woodland species can be seen, as well as wildfowl, waders and passage migrants on the reservoir itself. Over 230 species have been recorded.

A concrete-banked causeway segregates the main reservoir from the North Lake, a man-made lake on which the water-levels are regulated during autumn for the benefit of the birds. The reservoir has a big rise and fall, water being pumped from the nearby River Eden in winter. The level starts to drop from late spring as water is used, and by the summer there are wide, muddy margins that are attractive to waders.

Aerial view of Bough Beech Reservoir.

🦆 BIRDS

A good variety of dabbling and diving duck winter. In spring, passage migrants include Whimbrels and other waders, Wheatears, Yellow Wagtails, Black Terns and Osprey. These birds rarely stop for long, and the best time to see them is shortly after dawn.

Little Ringed Plovers arrive in March. They were once a annual breeding bird on the concrete apron, but are now sporadic in their nesting attempts. By late July the autumn passage of waders is underway, with individuals often lingering for a few days. Throughout

Little Ringed Plovers sometimes breed on the concrete apron of the causeway.

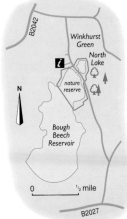

August, Common and Green Sandpipers are joined by Greenshank and Snipe. Other species, such as Wood Sandpiper, Ruff and Little Stint, are near annual. The North Lake attracts most waders, allowing excellent views from the causeway. The occasional Black Terns and Little Gulls are often overshadowed by an Osprey or two, for Bough Beech is one of the best sites in southern England to see this species. Individuals often stay for days and even weeks.

Access is restricted to the causeway, which is the best place for observing Ospreys and all the other birds that occur. The northern end of the reservoir on either side of the causeway is a reserve owned by the Kent Trust for Nature Conservation.

BIRDS THROUGH THE SEASONS

ALL YEAR: Great Crested Grebe, feral Greylag and Canada Geese, Mallard, Grey Heron, Sparrowhawk, Kestrel, Little Owl, Kingfisher, Green, Great and Lesser Spotted Woodpeckers, Nuthatch, Treecreeper, Grey Wagtail, Marsh and Willow Tit, and Reed Bunting.
SPRING: Passage waders and terns pass through, usually shortly after dawn, but rarely stop. Likely species include Curlew, Whimbrel, Dunlin, Ringed Plover, Common Sandpiper, Common Tern, Black Tern, Wheatears and Yellow Wagtails. Little Ringed Plovers arrive in March.
SUMMER: Breeding birds include Shelduck, Little Ringed Plover, Cuckoo, Reed Warbler, Chiffchaff, Willow Warbler, Blackcap, Garden Warbler,

Whitethroat, Lesser Whitethroat and Spotted Flycatcher. Hobbies are regular.
AUTUMN: Passage waders on the North Lake, Green Sandpiper, Common Sandpiper, Greenshank, often Dunlin, Ringed Plover, occasional Little Stint, Wood Sandpiper and Ruff. Osprey, Black Tern, Common Tern, and occasional Little Gull and Arctic Tern all linger. Passerine migrants include

Knole Park in winter.

Wheatear, Yellow Wagtail and Whinchat.
WINTER: Wigeon, Gadwall, Shoveler, occasional Pintail, Tufted Duck, Pochard, Teal, Mandarin, Goldeneye, Goosander, Snipe, Green Sandpiper, Fieldfare and Redwing. Gulls roost in winter. In periods of hard weather, the rarer grebes, divers, Bewick's Swans and various waders may be expected.

ACCESS: From Sevenoaks, take the B2042; the reservoir can be

seen from this road at Ide Hill. Drive down the hill and take the turning on the left signed to Bough Beech Reservoir.

A converted oast house acts as the reserve centre and is open at weekends from April to October.

DISABLED ACCESS: Viewing from a wheelchair from the pavement on the causeway is possible as sections of the hedge have been cut back.

OTHER ATTRACTIONS

CHARTWELL: Chartwell, south of Westerham, was Sir Winston Churchill's home. It is full of memorabilia and atmosphere, and is well worth a visit.

KNOLE: Managed by the National Trust, this stately home lies within Knole Park. The park has Fallow, Sika and Red Deer, as well as a good bird population. In summer, Tree Pipit, Redstart, Stonechat and Woodlark breed. There are a number of access points.

HAMPSHIRE

Keyhaven Marshes

This area of marsh, pools and inter-tidal mudflats south of Lymington has a year-round appeal for the bird-watcher. In winter, a wide variety of waders and wildfowl can be seen, including a few Ruff and Spotted Redshank, usually on the pools behind the sea wall. In spring and autumn, migrant waders and passerines should be searched for and, from Hurst Beach, sea-watching can be productive. Sandwich, Common and Little Terns breed. Near by, Pennington Marshes attract a similar range of species. Both sites are best reached along the Solent Way footpath from Keyhaven Harbour.

Titchfield Haven

This reserve is situated south-east of Southampton, just behind the shore bordering the Solent. It comprises marsh, scrub, reeds and pools, and attracts migrant waders and passerines. In winter, a good selection of birds can be seen, these often including wintering Bittern and small numbers of Bearded Tits. Cetti's Warblers breed. Access is on Fridays, Saturdays and Sundays by permit only, obtained in advance from the naturalist ranger, Haven Cottage, Hill Head, Fareham, Hampshire PO4 3JT.

THE ISLE OF WIGHT

Bembridge

The harbour and foreshore attract a variety of waders in winter at low tide. The pools behind the harbour, and Bembridge Pond bordering the east side of the harbour, support wintering duck. It can be worthwhile sea-watching from Foreland, the headland in Bembridge, while Black Rock Ledge, the southern shore of the headland, often has a few wintering Purple Sandpipers. The Bembridge area regularly attracts migrants in spring and autumn.

The Needles and Alum Bay

The Needles and Alum Bay, perhaps the most famous landmark on the island, attract a variety of summer migrants in spring and autumn. The cliffs provide nesting sites for Fulmar, Guillemot and a few Shags and Razorbills.

Newtown Estuary

This is the most important estuary for birds on the island. Large numbers of Brent Geese, along with a variety of ducks and waders, occur in winter. Waders occur on passage, although not in any great numbers. The estuary can be particularly good in hard weather in winter. If here just before high tide, then watch from the East Hide in the south-east corner known as the Main Marsh. Otherwise, at high tide good numbers of birds may be on the scrape north of Marsh Farm House, which is itself north of Newtown village.

St Catherine's Point

Lying at the southernmost tip of the Isle of Wight is the island's top migration watchpoint, attracting the typical range of summer migrants experienced by other south-coast headlands. Sea-watching can be good in April and May, and again from August onwards. Strong onshore winds or gales are ideal. The point is south of Niton.

Yar Estuary

Easily reached on foot from Yarmouth Harbour with a footpath running down the eastern side along the dismantled railway and sea wall to Freshwater Bridge. During winter, a good variety of estuarine wildfowl and waders are present, including a few overwintering Spotted Redshanks. In spring and autumn, expect passage waders and a few passerine migrants.

KENT

Bedgebury Pinetum

This collection of pines, one of the best in Europe, is a roost site in winter for Chaffinch, Hawfinch and Brambling. In irruption years it often also has good numbers of Crossbills. The birds roost in Cypress trees about half a mile south-east of the entrance, across the other side of a steep-sided valley. The hour before dusk is best. The car park is along the B2079 Goudhurst–Flimwell road. Bewl Bridge Reservoir is near by. The southern arm, a nature reserve, is usually best for winter wildfowl.

Nor Marsh & Motney Hill
RSPB Reserve

Sited in the Medway Estuary, Nor Marsh has breeding Common Terns, while in winter the whole area attracts ducks and waders, and often one of the rarer grebes. In spring and autumn, passage waders include Whimbrels and Black-tailed Godwits, as well as a few passerine migrants in the country park. Nor Marsh can be viewed from Horrid Hill, reached from the Riverside Country Park off the B2004 east of Gillingham. Motney Hill can be covered from the sea wall by parking in the car park along Motney Hill Road, also off the B2004 and just east of the country park.

Thanet

Although this headland is heavily built up, the few green patches and coastal strip around Margate attract good numbers of passerine migrants and often some exciting rarities. There are two main birding areas. The first, Northdown Park, has a resident population of Ring-necked Parakeets. The large Sycamores and the rose garden attract Pied Flycatcher, Firecrest and an array of warblers in spring. In autumn, Yellow-browed Warblers are annual, and there is often a Red-breasted Flycatcher or even Pallas's Warbler during easterly winds. Large numbers of Goldcrests and thrushes sometimes occur.

To the north of Northdown Park is Foreness Point. This is the most reliable site in Kent for Purple Sandpipers, these are found on the rocks below the cliffs. The point can produce some excellent sea-watching, and during spring and autumn passerine migrants should be searched for along the cliff tops. The area between Foreness Point and North Foreland should be explored, and is reached off the B2052. Northdown Park is nestled between the B2052 and B2051.

Tudeley Woods
RSPB Reserve

This attractive woodland reserve has a diverse range of resident and migrant breeding birds, including Tree Pipits and Hawfinches.

Seven species of orchid may be found. Leave Tonbridge on the A21 to Hastings, then just before a garage take the minor road signed to Capel. The reserve car park is a short drive along here.

SUSSEX

Fore Wood
RSPB Reserve

This coppiced woodland, on the outskirts of Crowhurst, accessed off the A2100 Battle–Hastings road (park at the village hall and walk up the road), has a fine array of woodland birds, including Lesser Spotted Woodpecker, Spotted Flycatcher, Nightingale and Hawfinch.

Thorney Island and Pilsey Island
RSPB Reserve

Thorney Island, on the edge of Chichester Harbour, is an excellent site for wintering wildfowl and waders, and for passage migrants. Pilsey Island RSPB reserve, off the tip of Thorney Island, has the largest wader roost in Chichester Harbour and can be viewed from the sea wall. The southern tip of the island is an army base, but the island can be walked around and Pilsey Island viewed by gaining entry through the security gates. Park along the road on Thorney Island, taking one of the paths out to the sea wall.

W A L E S

WALES HAS a diverse landscape, from scenic estuaries to the rugged mountains of Snowdonia. Over half its land area lies 500 feet above sea-level, these uplands supporting specialist bird communities. During the summer, the high tops are inhabited by Ring Ouzels and Wheatears, while the rivers and streams support Dippers and Grey Wagtails. Most special are the hanging oak wood-lands, characteristic of mid-Wales. The oaks that grow here are not the large, Pedunculate Oaks common in lowland Britain, but Sessile Oaks, often stunted because of the terrain. The birds that typify this habitat are Pied Flycatcher, Wood Warbler, Redstart, Buzzard and Red Kite.

of Ramsey and Bardsey are also Chough strongholds. To the south of Ramsey lie the islands of Skomer and Skokholm, famed for their colonies of Manx Shearwater.

Off the west coast of Wales, Harbour Porpoises are common, while whales and Basking Shark are occasional. Grey Seals use some of the islands to pup. The woodlands are home to Polecats, Badgers and a few Red Squirrels, while many of the rivers have resident Otters, although these are rarely seen.

Dinas (right) and Gwenffrwd RSPB reserves, Dyfed.

Wood Warbler in song

The skies over mid-Wales are the domain of the Red Kite. Persecuted almost to extinction, this was their last refuge before adequate protection allowed the population to recover to the 100-plus pairs that are found today.

The Chough is another Welsh speciality. This acrobatic member of the crow family can be encountered south from Anglesey, to the beautiful Pembroke coast. The islands

43
41
42
40
39
38
37
36

SWANSEA

NEWPORT

CARDIFF

ADMINISTERED BY Glamorgan County Council as a Local Nature Reserve, Kenfig's sand dunes and freshwater pool extend for 1200 acres. There is an information centre and two hides that overlook the pool.

BIRDS

Several hundred wildfowl winter in the area, while a few species remain to breed. Migrants are likely in spring and autumn. Kenfig has attracted some impressive rarities – for instance, Pied-billed Grebe, Surf Scoter and, near by,

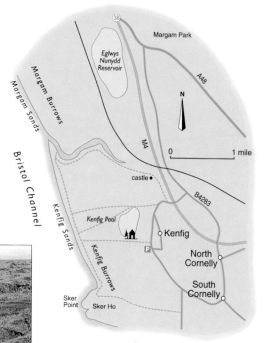

Kenfig NNR.

Britain's first Little Whimbrel.

Sker Point, reached by taking any of the paths that lead down to the sea through the dunes, can be a good sea-watching site in autumn. Manx Shearwaters are present offshore from July, while in bad weather petrels and skuas are possible.

FLOWERS

Over 500 species of flowering plants have been recorded on the reserve.

BIRDS THROUGH THE SEASONS

ALL YEAR: Great Crested Grebe, Mute Swan, Mallard, Tufted Duck, Shoveler, Sparrowhawk, Kestrel, Oystercatcher, Ringed Plover, Lapwing, Snipe, Redshank and often Cetti's Warbler.

SPRING: Migrants include Sandwich Tern, occasional Garganey, Whimbrel, Cuckoo, Sand Martin and Wheatear.

SUMMER: Breeding birds include Reed, Sedge and Grasshopper Warblers. Swifts often gather to feed over the pool.

AUTUMN: Manx Shearwater offshore. In rough weather there is a chance of skuas and petrels. A few migrants are likely.

WINTER: Occasional family groups of Whooper Swans and, more rarely, Bewick's Swans. Bitterns sometimes winter. Wildfowl include Shelduck, Pochard, Wigeon, Gadwall, Goldeneye, occasionally Long-tailed Duck, Goosander, Smew and seaduck. Merlin and Short-eared Owl are annual. Water Rail around the pool.

Waders on the beach include Sanderling, Dunlin, Turnstone and Curlew. Offshore, occasional divers and grebes.

ACCESS:
Leave the M4 at junction 37 and travel south on the A4229. Then take the B4283 through Cornelly, turning left over the motorway to the reserve car park.

DISABLED ACCESS:
None.

OTHER ATTRACTIONS

NORTH-EAST of Bridgend is the attractive village of Coity, with its superb medieval church. North of Pyle is Margam Castle and park. Fallow Deer roam the park, which contains sculptures and an adventure playground.

THE ISLANDS of Skokholm, Skomer, Grassholm and Ramsey, although close to each other, differ markedly in their birds, with Skomer and Skokholm, the two closest neighbours, being the most similar.

BIRDS

Seabirds are one of the main attractions. Grassholm is impressive for its Gannet colony, while Skomer and Skokholm offer one of the most dramatic bird-watching experiences in Britain. On most nights during the summer, thousands of Manx Shearwaters come ashore to visit their nesting burrows. And on moonless nights, when the greatest numbers of birds arrive, the islands reverberate to their cries.

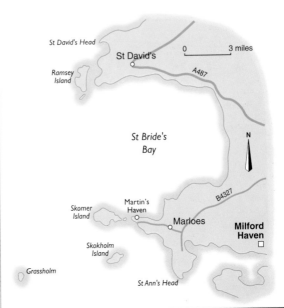

SITE GUIDE

1

Grassholm

Owned by the RSPB, this flat-topped basalt island lies 8 miles off the Pembrokeshire coast. Over 30,000 pairs of Gannets nest on the island's 22 acres. A few Guillemots, Razorbills, Shags, Kittiwakes, Herring Gulls and Great Black-backed Gulls also breed.

ACCESS: Landing on the island is only possible in the calmest of weather, but it is not necessary to land in order to enjoy the breeding colony. Circumnavigations of the island leave from Martin's Haven west of Marloes. The Dale Sailing Company runs these trips and can be contacted on Tel: 01646

601636. Alternatively, further information can be obtained from the RSPB's Welsh Regional Office, Tel: 01686 626678.

2

Skokholm

Measuring just 250 acres, Skokholm is bordered by red sandstone cliffs. Due to their lack of suitable ledges, these cliffs host only a few

Skokholm bird observatory.

pairs of Razorbills and Guillemots, and no Kittiwakes. However, this shortfall in cliff-nesting birds is made up by an abundance of Puffins and over 40,000 pairs of Manx Shearwaters. Another night-time visitor, the British Storm-petrel, may number 7000 pairs. They nest on the boulder beaches and within the dry-stone walls close to the observatory,

Broad Sound

N

Little Bay
North Haven
The Stack
North Pond
The Neck
Mad Bay
bird observatory
The Knoll
South Haven
SKOKHOLM
Hog Bay
The Head
lighthouse
Crab Bay
Franks Point
0   ½ mile

The loo wall on Skokholm!
(Below) View along cliffs to the lighthouse.

from which they can be heard singing at night. Lesser Black-backed Gulls breed among the Bluebells that carpet the island in May. Choughs and Peregrines regularly visit, yet rarely nest.

Some of the more numerous passage migrants are Sedge Warblers, Willow Warblers, Wheatears, Whinchats and hirundines. A variety of waders pass through in spring and autumn. Rarities have included Black-browed Albatross and Britain's second White-throated Robin. It is a tradition on Skokholm for the finder of a new bird to paint it on the loo wall.

The fauna suffers from being nibbled by Rabbits. Introduced around 1280, the Rabbits were harvested to provide a considerable revenue. Nowadays, in late summer the population peaks at 15,000, providing a feast for Great Black-backed Gulls. The only other mammal is the House Mouse, while Slow Worms are the only reptiles.

Skokholm was put on the ornithological map by Ronald Lockley. Lockley arrived on the island as a young man in 1927 with the intention of farming and fishing to make a living. This was later abandoned in favour of ornithological research and a writing career. In 1933, Lockley constructed Britain's first Heligoland trap and, in doing so, established the first bird observatory in Britain. Lockley's many books make fascinating reading.

The bird observatory is based in the old farm buildings, and is run by the Dyfed Wildlife Trust.

ACCESS: Full-board accommodation for up to 15 visitors is available from mid-March to mid-September. Booking enquiries and further information from the Dyfed Wildlife Trust, 7 Market Street, Haverfordwest, Dyfed DA61 1NF. Tel: 01437 765462.

3

Skomer

Skomer has larger numbers of cliff-nesting seabirds than Skokholm. Guillemots and Razorbills are neighbours to Kittiwakes and large numbers of Fulmars. Around 6000 pairs of Puffins breed. The 120,000 pairs of Manx Shearwaters are most impressive.

Due to the presence of the Skomer Vole, an endemic variety of Bank Vole, at least two pairs of Short-eared Owls breed. Peregrines, Ravens and Choughs nest on the cliffs, and regularly commute to and from the mainland. A variety of passage migrants occurs, along with an annual selection of rarities.

The island is popular with day-trippers. However, as with Skokholm, the most dramatic events take place at night when the Manx Shearwaters come ashore. For this reason an overnight stay is recommended. Skomer also has around 1000 pairs of British Storm-petrels.

A visit in May or June is best for the seabirds. The Wick (on the southern side) is a good spot for seeing cliff-nesting birds.

 ACCESS: Skomer is administered by the Dyfed Wildlife Trust and is open daily except Mondays (with the exception of bank holidays) from Easter or the beginning of April, whichever is sooner, to mid-September, weather permitting. Boats leave from Martin's Haven from 10am.

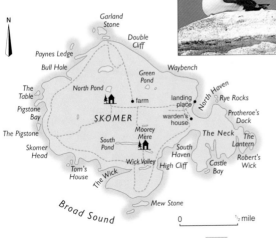

Puffins entertain visitors to Skomer in summer (above).

The weather vane of a Manx Shearwater shares its roof-top vantage point with a Lesser Black-backed Gull.

Contact the Dale Sailing Company, Tel: 01646 601636. There is a landing fee. Overnight accommodation is available. For more information, contact the Dyfed Wildlife Trust (*see* Skokholm).

Ramsey Island viewed from the Pembrokeshire coast.

4

Ramsey Island

Owned by the RSPB, Ramsey Island lies less than a mile off the coast near St David's. The island's 600 acres comprise maritime heath in the south and fields bordered by traditional Pembrokeshire banks in the north.

Ramsey is a stronghold of the Chough. A few Kittiwakes, Razorbills and Guillemots nest on the cliffs. Other breeding birds include Lapwing and Wheatear. From late August to mid-November, Grey Seals come ashore to pup and can be seen hauled up on the beaches and in caves.

ACCESS: The island is open daily except Tuesdays from April to October, weather permitting. Visitor numbers are limited to 40 a day. Boats depart from April to mid-July from St Justinian's Lifeboat Station, west of St David's, at 10am, returning at 3.30pm, with an extra sailing at 11am from mid-July to the end of August. There is also a 1½-hour cruise around the island daily at 11am and 2pm. To check sailing times and for further information on boats, Tel: 01437 720285.

BIRDS THROUGH THE SEASONS
ALL YEAR: Cormorant, Shag, Mallard, Buzzard, Kestrel, Peregrine, Pheasant, Oystercatcher, Turnstone, Herring Gull, Great Black-backed Gull, Little Owl, Short-eared Owl, Rock Pipit, Chough, Raven and Reed Bunting.
SPRING: Manx Shearwaters return in early March. British Storm-petrels return in late April. Lesser Black-backed Gulls arrive on Skokholm and Skomer to breed. Most other seabirds return in late March but,

depending on weather, come and go before settling down to breed. Passage migrants include chats, flycatchers and warblers in small numbers. Passage waders include Whimbrel and Common Sandpiper.
SUMMER: Guillemots and Razorbills start incubating at the beginning of May and have deserted the cliffs by the end of July. Puffins are best seen from June onwards, once they are feeding their young. Breeding birds include Curlew, Lapwing, Sedge Warbler, Whitethroat and Wheatear. Ducks such as Shoveler and Mallard often attempt to breed on the island's ponds; Pintail have bred successfully on Skomer.
AUTUMN: A variety of waders and passerines pass through. Sea-watching may be productive in rough weather.
WINTER: A few divers around the coasts. Merlin and a small number of wildfowl. Fulmars return in January.

ACCESS: *See* entries under site guide.

 DISABLED ACCESS: This is not practical on any of the islands.

OTHER ATTRACTIONS

THE PEMBROKESHIRE coast offers some of the finest coastal scenery in Britain, and has numerous cliff-top walks. Choughs are likely to be encountered along the cliffs. St David's, with city status yet the size of a village, has a fascinating cathedral and 13th-century bishop's palace to explore.

THESE TWO scenic reserves in mid-Wales straddle the River Tywi and its tributaries. The Dinas is the smaller and most accessible, being a steeply sided knoll covered in oak woodland and surrounded by fast-flowing rivers and streams.

BIRDS

During summer, the trills of Wood Warblers ring out from the hillside at Dinas. Both Redstarts and Pied Flycatchers should be seen, and the latter can number over 100 pairs, with nearly all of them using nest boxes. Further on along the trail the river rushes over an impressive cataract.

At Dinas, when not under the cover of the trees, scan the skies for Buzzards, Ravens and Red Kites. Kites do not breed on the Dinas reserve, but appear regularly overhead in summer.

OTHER ANIMALS

Other wildlife to look out for includes the beautiful Demoiselle Damselfly, a small blue-winged damselfly. In midsummer, look for Purple Hairstreak butterflies high up in the treetops of the oak wood. Polecats and Otters are resident. The rivers hold Brown Trout, as well as migrant Salmon and Sea Trout.

The neighbouring Gwenffrwd Reserve supports the same species of birds, but is much larger and offers an attractive 4-mile walk.

BIRDS THROUGH THE SEASONS

ALL YEAR: Sparrowhawk, Buzzard, Kestrel, Peregrine, Kingfisher, Grey Wagtail, Dipper, Nuthatch, Green, Great Spotted and Lesser Spotted Woodpeckers.
SPRING AND SUMMER: Red Kites overhead. Woodcock breed. Summer migrants from May onwards include Cuckoo, Tree Pipit, Redstart, Wood Warbler, Garden Warbler, Blackcap, Chiffchaff, Willow Warbler and Pied Flycatcher in the woodland. Along the streams and rivers: Goosander, Common Sandpiper and Sand Martin. Above the trees and on the moorland: Wheatear, Whinchat, Ring Ouzel and a few Red Grouse.
AUTUMN: By mid-July, after breeding, the birds in the woodland are difficult to see.
WINTER: *See* All year.

ACCESS: The reserves lie in the central Welsh hills along the Tywi Valley north of Llandovery (*see* map). The Dinas Reserve is open daily throughout the year. A visitor centre opens from 10am to 5pm from Easter to August. The circular walk takes two hours, but the path can be slippery in wet weather. If planning to take the 4-mile trail through the Gwenffrwd Reserve, then report to the visitor centre at Dinas first for directions.

Llyn Brianne
Llyn Brianne Dam
to Lampeter
Gwenffrwd
Dinas
church
N
Towy Bridge Inn
0   1 mile
River Tywi
Rhandirmwyn
to Cilycwm & Llandovery
to Llandovery

Boardwalk at Dinas.

DISABLED ACCESS: None.

OTHER ATTRACTIONS

THIS IS one of the most scenic areas in Wales. Just to the south lie the Brecon Beacons, offering a range of outdoor activities, walks and family attractions.

MID-WALES is recognised as the best region in the British Isles for seeing Red Kites, one of our most enigmatic birds of prey. Grid references are provided for the following sites, all of which offer excellent opportunities to see kites. With the exception of Tregaron, the sites

There is an information centre with live pictures and recorded footage of kites and other wildlife.

♿ DISABLED ACCESS: This is the best site for the disabled to view kites in winter. Hides are accessible to wheelchairs.

2

Llanwrtyd Wells, Dol y Coed Park

Grid reference SN 874468. Lies west of Dinas; one to

have been organised by the Kite Country Project. For more information on seeing Red Kites in Wales, you can contact the Kite Country Project at Bryn Aderyn, The Bank, Newtown, Powys SY16 2AB.

Red Kite.

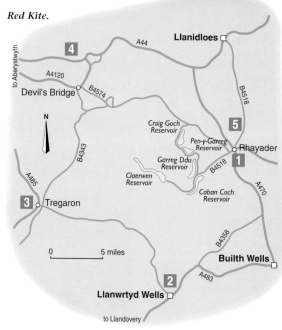

SITE GUIDE

1

Gigrin Farm, Rhayader, Powys

Grid reference SN 990678. Meat is put out for kites between 2 and 3.30pm daily from November to Easter. During 1995–6, over 50 kites were recorded daily viewable from a hide.

four kites are attracted daily between 12.30 and 1pm. They feed in a small field overlooked by a hide. Enquire at the town's information centre (SN 879467). In spring and early summer, live pictures of kite nests can be watched in the information centre.

3

Tregaron

Grid reference SN 661579. The Tregaron area is a good place to see kites throughout the year. During winter, a local lady attracts over 60 kites daily by putting out food in the late afternoon.

River through the Dinas RSPB reserve.

There are no hides, and parking can be difficult. The site is south of town near the hamlet of Llanio on the hump of an old Roman fort.

4

Nant yr Arian Forest Centre

Grid reference SN 718813. Run jointly by the Forest Enterprise and the Kite Country Project. The centre is open from Easter to September. From the tearoom there are superb views along the Melindwr Valley, along which kites

hunt. Live pictures from local kite and other raptors' nests are transmitted in the auditorium.

5

Gilfach Farm Wildlife Reserve

Grid reference SN 966717. Although Red Kites are seen here, the main attractions are the other species typical of mid-Wales. The Kite Country Project has supplied nest-box cameras that give an insight into the secret lives of species such as the Pied Flycatcher and Redstart.

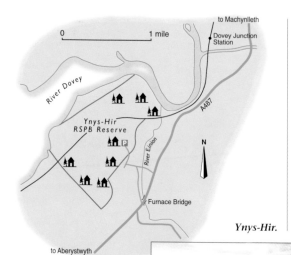

Ynys-Hir.

Red-breasted Merganser and Common Sandpiper along the river.

AUTUMN: A few passage waders.

WINTER: Greenland White-fronted Geese, Wigeon, Teal, Goldeneye, Hen Harrier, Merlin, Peregrine, Grey Plover, Golden Plover, Dunlin and Curlew.

ACCESS: Open daily from 9am to dusk. Reached by turning off the A487 Aberystwyth–Machynlleth road in Eglwysfach.

YNYS-HIR, OVERLOOKING the picturesque Dovey Estuary, encompasses saltmarsh, freshwater marsh, bracken-covered hillsides and oak woodland among its 1000 acres. The name Ynys-Hir means 'Long Island', and it is likely that the wooded ridge was once surrounded by marsh. A nature trail takes the visitor through the reserve's habitats to hides overlooking freshwater marshes and the estuary.

 BIRDS
In winter, a small population of Greenland White-fronted Geese, along with other wildfowl and waders, uses the estuary. Wood Warbler, Redstart and Pied Flycatcher all nest in the oak woods.

OTHER ANIMALS
Badger, Stoat, Weasel, Otter and Polecat are all resident. Butterflies include Dark-green, Pearl-bordered and Marsh Fritillary, while the Purple Hairstreak flies in July, favouring the oak canopy.

 FLOWERS
A small peat bog crossed by a boardwalk has Bog Asphodels, Bog Rosemary, Heath Spotted Orchids and three species of sundew.

BIRDS THROUGH THE SEASONS
ALL YEAR: Grey Heron, Mallard, Water Rail, Buzzard, Kestrel, Sparrowhawk, Redshank, Tawny Owl, Kingfisher, Great Spotted Woodpecker, Lesser Spotted Woodpecker, Raven and Reed Bunting.
SPRING: Passage waders include Whimbrel. Summer migrants arrive.
SUMMER: Approximately 68 species breed, including Redstart, Pied Flycatcher, Wood Warbler, Grasshopper Warbler, Sedge Warbler, and

 DISABLED ACCESS:
By arrangement with the warden, cars with disabled occupants can be driven to the Ynys Eidiol Estuary hide, which is suitable for wheelchair users with a strong pusher. Contact Dick Squires, Cae'r Berllan, Eglwysfach, Machynlleth, Powys SY20 8TA. Tel: 01654 781265.

OTHER ATTRACTIONS

SNOWDONIA NATIONAL Park is close by. Northwards along the coast is Fairbourne, offering a butterfly safari and a narrow-gauge railway which passes through some impressive Welsh scenery.

BARDSEY LIES 2 miles off the southern tip of the Lleyn Peninsula. Once a place of pilgrimage, it is said that 20,000 saints lie buried here.

Bardsey is home to an active bird observatory that provides accommodation, and there are also a few renovated cottages available for weekly rent. Sheep are farmed on the island, which comprises 120 small fields, areas of bracken and scrub, boulder beaches and low cliffs. When viewed from the mainland, a 550-foot mountain shields most of the island.

BIRDS THROUGH THE SEASONS
ALL YEAR: Kestrel, Peregrine, Chough and Raven.
SPRING: Passage migrants include Ring Ouzel, Black Redstart, Wheatear, Redstart, hirundines, flycatchers and warblers.
SUMMER: Breeding seabirds include Manx Shearwater, Lesser Black-backed Gull, Kittiwake, Razorbill and Guillemot.

Peregrines breed on Bardsey's cliffs.

AUTUMN: A variety of migrants are likely, including a smattering of rarities. Offshore, seabird passage in September may involve terns, skuas and shearwaters. In late autumn, influxes of thrushes, buntings and pipits are possible.
WINTER: *See* All year.

ACCESS: Bardsey is owned by the Bardsey Island Trust. Self-catering houses, run by the trust, are available to rent. Bookings and more information from, the Trust Officer, Stabal Hen, Tyddyn Du, Criccieth, Gwynedd LL52 OLY. The bird observatory allows a maximum of 12 visitors. For further information and bookings, write to Mrs Alicia Normand, 46 Maudlin Drive, Teignmouth, Devon TQ14 8SB.

DISABLED ACCESS: None.

BIRDS
Migrant birds can be attracted to the lighthouse beacon at night, which over the years has proved fatal to many. Rarities have included some outstanding American vagrants, and the most important breeding birds are Choughs. A few seabirds nest on the island, notably Manx Shearwaters.

OTHER ANIMALS
Mammals are represented by House and Wood Mice, Common Shrews and Rabbits. Palmate Newts are the only amphibians present.

THIS EXTENSIVE 18,000-acre reserve lies in the Berwyn Hills. Central to the reserve is a 5-mile long reservoir surrounded by fir, pine and oak woods and by heather and grass moorland. The reservoir was formed in 1891 after the construction of an impressive dam.

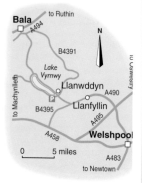

BIRDS

The lake supports a few wildfowl, including up to 40 Goosander, some of which remain to breed. A few passage waders linger along the muddy shoreline in autumn, but it is the breeding birds that hold the most interest. The oak woods have Redstarts, Pied Flycatchers and Wood Warblers, while Crossbills and Siskins are found in the conifers and pines. The moorlands attract breeding raptors, Curlew and Ring Ouzel.

OTHER ANIMALS

Badgers, Red Squirrels and Polecats inhabit the forests. Butterflies include Pearl-bordered and Silver-washed Fritillaries and Green Hairstreak.

Lake Vyrnwy is popular with visitors in summer, so early mornings in late spring are perhaps the optimum time for a visit. A number of nature trails and sites worth exploring are detailed below.

SITE GUIDE

1

Craig Garth-Bwlch Nature Trail

This 3-mile walk takes two hours and starts at the visitor centre at the southern end of the lake. The path leads through Sessile Oak wood and birch plantations, home to Redstart, Pied Flycatcher and Wood Warbler. On the open higher ground, look out for breeding Whinchats. The trail is covered by a leaflet available at the visitor centre.

2

The Grwn-oer Nature Trail

This trail (leaflet available) also starts at the visitor centre at the southern end of the lake; it takes approximately 1 hour to complete the 1½-mile walk. The typical oak wood species can all be seen.

3

Rhiwargor Island Nature Trail

At the northern end of the lake is a 2-mile trail, visiting a variety of habitats, and taking 1½ hours to complete. The Sessile Oak woods have the typical species. Where the path crosses the river,

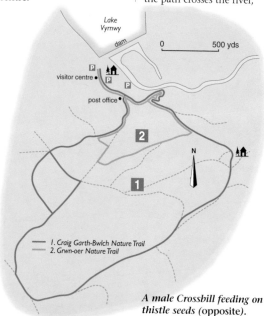

A male Crossbill feeding on thistle seeds (opposite).

look for Goosanders, Dippers and Grey Wagtails. An RSPB hide on the island overlooks a pool that is attractive to herons and the odd Teal and Kingfisher. Otters are occasionally seen here.

Moorland

Two minor roads leave the lake at its northern end, passing out on to moorland. Either road will provide the opportunity to look for the typical moorland birds of the area.

BIRDS THROUGH THE SEASONS

ALL YEAR: Great Crested Grebe, Grey Heron, Teal, Mallard, Goosander, Sparrowhawk, Buzzard, Kestrel, Peregrine, Long-eared Owl, Great Spotted and Green Woodpeckers, Kingfisher, Grey Wagtail, Dipper, Crossbill, Siskin, Redpoll, Goldcrest, Coal Tit, Treecreeper and Raven.

SPRING AND SUMMER: Breeding birds include Goosander, Hen Harrier, Merlin, Short-eared Owl, Golden Plover, Curlew, Lapwing, Woodcock, Common Sandpiper,

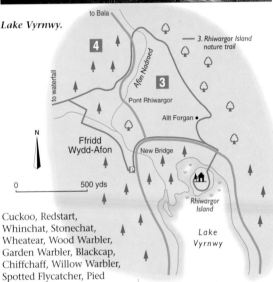

Lake Vyrnwy.

Cuckoo, Redstart, Whinchat, Stonechat, Wheatear, Wood Warbler, Garden Warbler, Blackcap, Chiffchaff, Willow Warbler, Spotted Flycatcher, Pied Flycatcher and Ring Ouzel.

AUTUMN AND WINTER: A few wildfowl include Goldeneye, Goosanders, Wigeon, Tufted Duck and Pochard.

ACCESS: The reserve lies south of Bala in the Berwyn Hills. *See* map and site guide above.

DISABLED ACCESS: This is good. A road runs around the lake perimeter and some parts of the trails are accessible to wheelchairs. The hide on the Rhiwargor Island is accessible to wheelchairs.

OTHER ATTRACTIONS

AT THE dam end of the reservoir are gift shops, a tea room and a picnic site. The walks are ideal for a family.

SOUTH STACK RSPB Reserve is on the northern tip of Holy Island, attached to the coast of Anglesey by a causeway. The cliffs are the reserve's main feature, used by breeding seabirds, Choughs and Peregrines. Behind the cliffs, maritime heath, a habitat now rare in Britain, is of great botanical interest.

There are a number of paths, but the best bird-watching is to be had from Ellin's Tower and the lighthouse area.

Seabirds are present on the cliffs from April to July.

BIRDS

Choughs are often prominent, and best looked for in the vicinity of Ellin's Tower, the RSPB visitor centre. During the breeding season, closed-circuit TV cameras beam live pictures of nesting seabirds to a monitor in Ellin's Tower, allowing visitors an opportunity to witness life on the cliff face. The other

Ellin's Tower.

prominent building here is the lighthouse perched on a lump of rock at the base of the cliffs, built in 1809.

OTHER ANIMALS

Silver-studded Blue butterflies are found on the heath, as are Adders.

FLOWERS

The reserve is home to the Spotted Rock-rose, a rare plant that grows in a few small colonies near Ellin's Tower. In June, Heath-spotted Orchids flower on the mountain. Other flowers to look out for are Pale Heath Violets and Spathulate Fleawort.

Holyhead Bay

North Stack

Holyhead Mountain

South Stack
• lighthouse
• Ellin's Tower
visitor P
centre

HOLY ISLAND

Holyhead
Holyhead Station

to Bangor
A5
B4545

to Trearddur Bay & Four Mile Bridge

N

Penrhyn Mawr

B4545

0   1 mile

BIRDS THROUGH THE SEASONS

ALL YEAR: Buzzard, Peregrine, Stonechat, Chough, Raven.

SPRING: A few migrants, including Wheatears. Seabirds arrive back on the cliffs by April, but do not usually settle until early May.

SUMMER: Breeding seabirds include Fulmar, Shag, Guillemot, Razorbill, Puffin, Herring Gull and Kittiwake. Whitethroats nest on the heath.

AUTUMN: Seabird passage may include skuas, terns and shearwaters, notably passing Manx Shearwaters from July. A few migrants.

WINTER: Merlins and sometimes Hen Harriers present.

Stonechat (right).
South Stack lighthouse.

Access: From Holyhead on Anglesey, head towards Holyhead Mountain. The reserve is well signposted.

Disabled access: Ellin's Tower is accessible by wheelchair only with difficulty. Car access by arrangement.

OTHER ATTRACTIONS

THE ISLE of Man, Ireland and Snowdon can all be seen from Holyhead Mountain on a clear day.

Just across the Menai Straits from Anglesey is the historic town of Caernarfon, with its imposing castle. The impressive Snowdonia National Park is close by (*see* page 110).

CLWYD

Point of Ayr
RSPB Reserve

At the mouth of the Dee Estuary, this shingle spit and surrounding saltmarsh and mudflats form primarily a winter site. Thousands of estuarine wildfowl and waders winter on the Dee, with the Point of Ayr providing a good vantage point. The spit attracts Snow Buntings, Twites and occasional Shorelarks. In late summer, large numbers of terns gather off the point. Leave the A548 2 miles east of Prestatyn to Talacre (Station Road). A public hide can be reached along the sea wall by heading south.

DYFED

Cors Caron

Close to Tregaron, this bog is protected as a National Nature Reserve and supports around 40 breeding species that include Red Grouse, Tree Pipit, Redstart and Grasshopper Warbler. In winter, Hen Harriers are sometimes joined by hunting Red Kites. A public hide can be reached by leaving Tregaron north on the B4343, and parking just north of Maesllyn Lake.

Pengelli Forest

Owned by the Dyfed Wildlife Trust, this is the largest block of ancient woodland left in south-west Wales. A good range of resident woodland species are supplemented by Redstarts, Wood Warblers and Pied Flycatchers. The White-letter Hairstreak butterfly is found on the reserve. From the A487 Cardigan–Fishguard road, just east of Felindre Farchog, proceed along the unclassified road at the foot of the hill. Paths lead from the access gate.

Strumble Head

Strumble is one of the top sea-watching sites on the British coast, and is best visited from August through to October. A variety of skuas, shearwaters, petrels, terns and gulls pass annually. The best weather conditions are gale-force south-westerly winds, veering westerly or north-westerly. The head is reached by taking an unclassified road from Fishguard Harbour, signed to Strumble Head. Watching is possible from the car (ideal for the disabled), but most bird-watchers congregate in the wartime bunker below.

GLAMORGAN

Cwm Clydach
RSPB Reserve

Oak woodland borders the River Clydach, with Heather and Bracken covering the

upper slopes. Summer visitors include Redstart, Pied Flycatcher and Wood Warbler. Residents include all three species of woodpecker, Dipper and Grey Wagtail, while Buzzards, Sparrowhawks and Ravens also breed. Both Purple Hairstreak and Silver-washed Fritillary butterflies are present. From junction 45 of the M4, drive north along the A4067, turning off left to Clydach. The reserve car park lies 2 miles north of the village, at the New Inn pub.

Gower Peninsula

There are three main sites worth exploring: the Burry Inlet, Oxwich Bay and Worms Head. Burry Inlet, an area of saltmarsh and mudflats, is of most interest during winter for estuarine wildfowl and waders. There are various access points from the B4295. From Crofty, a minor road off to the right follows the saltings, rejoining the B4295 at Llanrhidian. From Llanrhidian, drive to Cwm Ivy, just before Llanmadoc. A footpath from Cwm Ivy leads out on to Whiteford Burrows, a large dune system owned by the National Trust, and Berges Island within the National Nature Reserve, where there is a hide.

Oxwich Bay is a National Nature Reserve on the south shore of the peninsula. In winter, there

A recently fledged Buzzard (opposite).

are wildfowl and waders with the occasional diver close inshore. Waders and terns occur on passage. The reeds and freshwater marsh are attractive to breeding wildfowl, and to summer migrants such as Reed and Sedge Warbler. There is an information centre and footpaths on the seaward side of Oxwich village.

Worms Head, a long rocky peninsula, is only accessible at low tide. Kittiwakes and a few Razorbills, Guillemots and Shags breed. In strong south-westerly winds during autumn, skuas and shearwaters are also possible. Drive to the end of the B4247 in Rhossili village, and then proceed to the head from here.

GWYNEDD

Cemlyn Lagoon

Lying on the north coast of Anglesey, this brackish lagoon is separated from the sea by a shingle beach and is best visited in summer for its breeding terns. Numbers fluctuate annually, with Common, Arctic, Sandwich and Roseate Terns present. In autumn, a variety of passage waders can be expected. During winter, a few wildfowl use the lagoon and bay. From the A5025 at Tregele, take the unclassified road signed to the lagoon.

Conwy
RSPB Reserve

This new reserve borders the Conwy Estuary and is still very much in the development stage, both in terms of habitat for birds and visitor facilities. Two pools attract a variety of

The Grey Wagtail favours fast-flowing rivers.

wildfowl and waders throughout the year, and Little Ringed Plovers breed. Mammals of interest include Noctule Bats and Short-tailed Voles. The reserve is reached by leaving the A55 where it crosses the A470 and then following signs.

Mawddach Valley
RSPB Reserve

Two separate RSPB reserves border this beautiful estuary in the south of Snowdonia. The Arthog Bog Reserve is on the south side of the estuary and has a trail accessible to wheelchair users. Turn off the A493 to Morfa Mawddach station, where cars can be parked. Breeding birds include Grasshopper Warbler and Whitethroat.

The Coed Garth Gell Reserve, on the northern side, is an oak and birch woodland above a river. Pied Flycatchers, Wood Warblers, Buzzards, Ravens, Lesser Spotted Woodpeckers, Dippers and Grey Wagtails all breed. Park in the lay-by on the A496 opposite the Borthwnog Hall Hotel at the head of the estuary, and walk up the public footpath.

Newborough Warren

In the south-west of Anglesey, this area encompasses the Cefni Estuary, conifer plantations, dune slacks and Malltraeth Pool. The latter is featured in many of Charles Tunnicliffe's paintings of wildfowl and waders. The whole area is rich in bird-life, with estuarine wildfowl and waders in winter that include a flock of Pintail

A flock of Pintail winter at Newborough Warren.

and, regularly, Whooper Swans. The Malltraeth Pool attracts passage waders. The A4080 passes the pool south of Malltraeth; continue along this road for various access points into the area.

Snowdonia

Birds are difficult to find within this vast area. The high tops in summer are home to Ring Ouzels and Wheatears. Choughs, Peregrines and Buzzards should be scanned for. Dippers and Grey Wagtails inhabit the streams and rivers.

Valley Lakes
RSPB Reserve

Llyn Penrhyn, a large freshwater lake, is the main feature of this 150-acre reserve in north-west Anglesey. A variety of wildfowl breed, with much larger numbers wintering. The surrounding reed-

fringed pools and grassland are hunted over in winter by Hen Harriers and Short-eared Owls. The reserve car park is 2 miles south-east of Valley village, reached on minor roads from the A5.

POWYS

Dyffryn Wood
RSPB Reserve

A 76-acre oak woodland in the upper reaches of the Wye Valley, just south of Rhayader. The typical Welsh oak wood species are found here, including Redstart, Pied Flycatcher, Wood Warbler and Buzzards. The streams support Dippers and Grey Wagtails, while it is always worth glancing skyward regularly for Peregrine and Red Kite. For a circular walk, park in the lay-by at the north end of the wood by the A470, just south of Rhayader.

THE MIDLANDS

THE MIDLANDS may lack a coastline, but this is well compensated for by some of the best reservoirs for birds in the country. Sites such as Rutland Water eclipse many coastal reserves for variety and excitement. Although reservoirs dominate the bird-watching scene, there are some interesting woodlands supporting western specialities such as the Pied Flycatcher.

The north Midlands are bordered by the Peak District, an area of outstanding natural beauty, while the southern boundary is graced by the gentle limestone hills of the Cotswolds. In between is the conurbation of Birmingham. Yet even among this urban sprawl there are places for birds.

Wintering wildfowl are a major attraction. Many of the reservoirs support nationally and, in some cases internationally important numbers of birds.

The Tawny Owl is one of three species of resident owl at Coombes Valley.

For the wildfowl enthusiast, Slimbridge is hard to beat. Bordering the Severn Estuary in the south-west, Slimbridge is the home of the Wildfowl and Wetlands Trust. With its extensive facilities, excellent winter bird-watching and its collection of captive wildfowl, Slimbridge is the most popular site within the region.

THIS RESERVE covers 740 acres within the ancient Forest of Dean. The woodland is a mix of oak, beech, birch, Holly, Rowan and conifers, among which there is a rocky stream and woodland pool.

There are two walks through the reserve, one of 1 mile, and the second of 2 miles. Hides overlook glades and the pool.

BIRDS

The typical western oak wood species of Wood Warbler, Pied Flycatcher and Redstart nest, and the latter two species readily use nest boxes. Nagshead is a good site for seeing common woodland birds. The elusive Hawfinch breeds, although these are more often heard than seen, giving their presence away by a loud 'tik' call. Hawfinches have a fondness for Hornbeam fruit, which attracts flocks in winter.

By early May all the summer visitors will have arrived. Search the open areas for Tree Pipits, Whinchats and Grasshopper Warblers, remembering to keep an eye out overhead for soaring Buzzards and the chance of a Hobby.

OTHER ANIMALS

Mammals include a few Fallow Deer and Dormice.

FLOWERS

A visit in autumn will find the woodlands quiet, but there are still birds to be found. The autumn colours can be spectacular, Sweet Chestnut, beech and birch adding yellows and golds to the browns of oaks and the greens of the conifers.

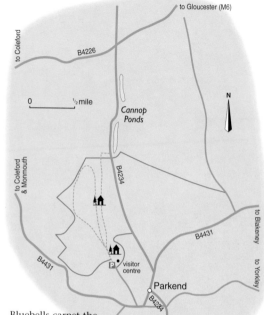

Bluebells carpet the woodland floor in spring, and Foxgloves grow along the rides, which attract White Admiral and Silver-washed Fritillary butterflies.

BIRDS THROUGH THE SEASONS

ALL YEAR: Sparrowhawk, Buzzard, Woodcock, Tawny Owl, Lesser Spotted, Great Spotted and Green Woodpecker, Grey Wagtail, Nuthatch, Treecreeper, Goldcrest, Marsh, Willow and Long-tailed Tit, Redpoll, Siskin, Crossbill, Hawfinch.
SPRING AND SUMMER: Hobby, Turtle Dove, Nightjar (churring at dusk in open areas), Cuckoo, Tree Pipit, Whinchat, Redstart, Wood, Willow, Garden and Grasshopper Warblers, Chiffchaff, Blackcap, Whitethroat, and Spotted and Pied Flycatchers.
AUTUMN AND WINTER: Parties of tits, maybe with Lesser Spotted Woodpecker, Treecreeper and Nuthatch. Fieldfares and Redwings. Woods can be quiet, with many birds moving away.

ACCESS

ACCESS: The reserve is reached off the B4431 Parkend–Coleford road, just west of Parkend village. Take the track up through the wood to the car park. A visitor centre is open from mid-April to August at weekends. There is a board at the entrance detailing the latest sightings.

OTHER ATTRACTIONS

Numerous picnic sites and walks can be enjoyed within the Forest of Dean. One of the best trails is at Symonds Yat, which overlooks a gorge of the River Wye and has breeding Peregrines. The site is wardened during the breeding season.

Bewick's Swans on Swan Lake.

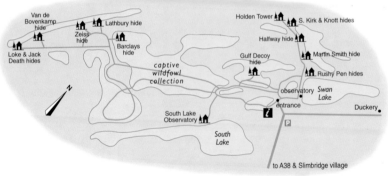

Van de Bovenkamp hide
Lathbury hide
Zeiss hide
Loke & Jack Death hides
Barclays hide
captive wildfowl collection
Holden Tower
S. Kirk & Knott hides
Halfway hide
Gulf Decoy hide
Martin Smith hide
Rushy Pen hides
observatory
Swan Lake
entrance
Duckery
South Lake Observatory
South Lake
to A38 & Slimbridge village

SLIMBRIDGE WILDFOWL and Wetlands Trust, situated on the upper reaches of the River Severn, is the most important site for wintering White-fronted Geese in Britain. The Geese prompted a visit by Peter Scott in December 1945. Among a flock of White-fronts he found a Lesser White-fronted Goose, only the third occurrence in Britain at the time. Scott had realised the need for an organisation that would protect wildfowl and the wetlands they depend on. That visit prompted him to set up the Wildfowl and Wetlands Trust (WWT) a short while later. Slimbridge became the headquarters of the WWT, and now has the largest collection of captive wildfowl in the world.

BIRDS

Hundreds of Bewick's Swans winter. Many can be seen on Swan Lake during the day. However, the majority feed out on the fields, arriving towards dusk on Rushy Pen and Swan Lake. After dark they can be watched under floodlight from the comfort of a heated observatory.

Over 4000 White-fronted Geese are usually present by midwinter. As in 1945, the occasional Lesser White-fronted Goose is found among them. Red-breasted Geese have turned up on a number of occasions, but more usual are stragglers such as Pink-footed, Brent, Barnacle or Bean Geese. The most abundant ducks are Pochard, Wigeon, Teal, Shoveler, Gadwall and Mallard. Pintail number around 200, many of which join the captive birds among the pens, attracted by the food on offer. Other opportunists include Water Rails, along with hundreds of Moorhens and Collared Doves.

The marshes are the haunt of Peregrine, Merlin and the occasional Short-eared Owl, although the latter is more likely on passage than in winter. Wintering Lapwing, Golden Plover and Dunlin are found in large flocks out on the fields and saltmarsh. A few Ruff may winter but are more likely on passage. Terns, a few Little Gulls and passerines such as Wheatear, Yellow Wagtail and Whinchat are all annual in spring and autumn. In early spring, Garganey appear, but diligent searching among the Teal is needed to locate this species in autumn.

A number of hides overlook the saltmarsh and fields. The Dumbles is one of the more attractive areas favoured by geese and by roosting waders at high tide. Two hides and the heated Peng Observatory look out on to Swan Lake and Rushy Pen, where the birds are fed. The Bewick's Swans can be watched from Peng Observatory, enjoying their evening feed under floodlight on Swan Lake.

Further facilities at Slimbridge include a tropical house, shop, restaurant, visitor centre and exhibition area. Winter is the ideal time to visit, not just for the wintering wildfowl but for the captive birds that will be in their best plumage.

BIRDS THROUGH THE SEASONS

ALL YEAR: Little Grebe, Mute Swan, Gadwall, Mallard, Tufted Duck, Sparrowhawk, Kestrel, Moorhen, Collared Dove, Lapwing, Redshank, Little Owl, Kingfisher, Chaffinch, Reed Bunting. SPRING: Wintering wildfowl depart in March. Occasional Garganey and Marsh Harrier. Regular passage birds include Whimbrel, Black-tailed Godwit, Greenshank, Black, Common and Arctic Terns, Little Gull, Wheatear, Whinchat and Yellow Wagtail. SUMMER: Breeding birds include Great Crested Grebe, Redshank, Yellow Wagtail, Reed Warbler and, recently, Little Ringed Plover and Oystercatcher. AUTUMN: Bewick's Swans and White-fronted Geese start to return at the end of October. Peregrine, Merlin, Hobby, Black, Little and Common Terns and occasional Little Gulls. Passage waders in small numbers include Ringed Plover, Knot, Bar-tailed and Black-tailed Godwits, Dunlin, Grey Plover, Ruff, Spotted Redshank, Greenshank, Green, Wood and Common Sandpipers and Curlew Sandpiper. Gathering of gulls may include Yellow-legged Herring and Mediterranean Gulls. WINTER: Bewick's Swan, occasional Whooper Swan, White-fronted Goose and regularly other species, which may include Brent, Pink-footed, Bean, Barnacle or vagrant Lesser White-front or Red-breasted Goose, Wigeon, Gadwall, Teal, Pintail, Mallard, Shoveler, Tufted Duck, Pochard, Peregrine, Merlin, occasional Short-eared Owl, Water Rail, Dunlin, Redshank, Curlew, Golden Plover, Snipe, occasional Jack Snipe, Ruff and Little Stint.

ACCESS: Slimbridge is well signposted off the M5. Drive through the village of Slimbridge, crossing the canal to reach the car park. The centre is open daily from 9.30am to 4pm in winter and until 5pm in summer. Admission is free for members of the WWT. Special events are held throughout the year. During winter, the swans can be watched under floodlight. Contact the trust for details at the Wildfowl and Wetlands Trust, Slimbridge, Gloucestershire. GL2 7BT. Tel: 01453 890333.

DISABLED ACCESS: There are excellent facilities for wheelchair users, with most of the hides accessible and good paths throughout.

OTHER ATTRACTIONS

SLIMBRIDGE IS an ideal destination for a family day out. The captive birds are particularly popular with children, who can hand-feed many of the geese and ducks.

THE COTSWOLD Water Park has been created over the past 70 years by gravel extraction. Over 100 lakes now exist, bordering the edge of the Cotswolds in the upper Thames Valley. They are a major recreational resource, offering a range of watersports, walks, picnic sites and an excellent location for bird-watching.

The older pits have a well-developed vegetation of trees, bankside cover and aquatic plants, while other more recent excavations are more barren. Hedgerows, ditches and woodlands add variety. Such a varied habitat ensures that a wide range of woodland and wetland species may be seen during a typical visit.

There are two distinct sections to the park. Around 70 pits make up the western end, while around 35 pits make up the eastern end. Bird-watching is good in many areas, and a large number of the lakes can be viewed from footpaths and the roadside. There are nature reserves and a few hides. The two walks detailed in the site guide are merely suggestions for a visit, and are likely to produce a good cross-section of the park's birds at any season.

BIRDS

Wintering wildfowl abound, with Pochard and Coot most numerous, followed by Wigeon, Teal, Mallard and Tufted Duck. Goldeneye, Shoveler and Gadwall are dotted around the various pits, and Pintail, Ruddy Duck and Goosander are regular visitors. Occasional visitors, particularly in cold weather, include Smew, and the chance of a seaduck, diver or one of the rarer grebes.

The park lies on a migration flyway, with birds using the Thames corridor. This results in a wide variety of migrants in both spring and autumn. Migrants linger for longer in autumn, with species such as Black Tern often staying for a few days, as do many of the waders. Passerine migrants include Wheatears and Yellow Wagtails in early spring, followed by a flood of birds in late April. Great Crested and Little Grebes, and a few species of wader and wildfowl breed with varying success.

Little Grebes nest on the more vegetated lakes.

SITE GUIDE

1

Bird-watching Walk 1
(Western end)

This walk starts at the nature reserve car park in Spratsgate Lane, off Spine Road, and takes around two hours to complete. A hide opposite the car park overlooks Lake 34, which has a variety of waterbirds at most times of the year. It is worth checking the recent-sightings book in the hide, and collecting the leaflet describing this walk in detail. During winter, wildfowl should include Wigeon, Gadwall, Shoveler, Teal, Goldeneye, Ruddy Duck and a good chance of Goosander and Red-crested Pochard. Smew favour Pit 41, which is one of the top wildfowl sites within the park, while the Alders along the river are

favoured by Redpolls and Siskins. During summer, keep an eye out for Hobbies.

ACCESS:
See map.

2

Bird-watching Walk 2
(Western end)

This route begins at Neigh Bridge car park and takes about three hours to complete at a leisurely pace. Similar species to those encountered on Walk 1 should be expected. This walk goes past Pit 41 as mentioned in Site Guide 1 Kingfishers may appear anywhere, and look out for Great Spotted Woodpeckers in the wooded areas. Lake 77 is always worth a good scan for waders, particularly Green Sandpiper.

ACCESS:
See map.

BIRDS THROUGH THE SEASONS

ALL YEAR: Great Crested Grebe, Little Grebe, Grey Heron, feral Canada and Greylag Geese, Mute Swan, Mallard, Tufted Duck, Red-crested Pochard, Coot, Sparrowhawk, Kestrel, Lapwing, Redshank, Kingfisher, Green and Great Spotted Woodpeckers, Grey Wagtail and Reed Bunting.
SPRING: Garganey are annual. Common, Black and occasional Arctic Terns, Little Gull (scarce), Little Ringed and Ringed Plovers, Curlew, Whimbrel, Green and Common Sandpipers, Dunlin, Oystercatcher, Turnstone, Greenshank, Ruff, Wheatear, Whinchat, Yellow Wagtail, Sand Martin, Swallow, House Martin, Swift, warblers. Chance of Osprey, an estuarine wader and rarities.
SUMMER: Breeding species include Hobby, Lapwing, Redshank, Ringed and Little Ringed Plovers, Common Tern, Cuckoo, Sand Martin, Nightingale, Sedge and

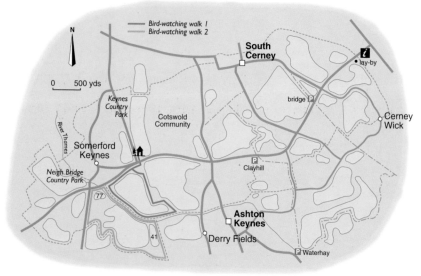

Green Sandpipers are regular in small numbers. (Left) Nightingale.

section, *see* below for directions to the Whelford Pools reserve.

DISABLED ACCESS: Many of the pits can be viewed from a vehicle. There is wheelchair access to a hide at Keynes Country Park. Wheelchair access is also possible at a hide at the Gloucestershire Wildlife Trust reserve at Whelford Pools near Fairford, reached off the A417 east of Cirencester by taking the minor road to Whelford.

OTHER ATTRACTIONS

THE PARK is a popular recreational centre. Watersports, walks, picnic sites, cycle routes, horse riding, golf and fishing can all be enjoyed.

Reed Warbler, Lesser Whitethroat, Whitethroat, Blackcap, Garden Warbler, Chiffchaff, Willow Warbler, Spotted Flycatcher and Yellow Wagtail.
AUTUMN: As for spring, plus the chance of Wood Sandpiper, Curlew Sandpiper, Little Stint and Spotted Redshank.
WINTER: Chance of a diver or one of the rarer grebes. Other irregular visitors include Smew, White-fronted Goose, Bewick's Swan and Peregrine.

Regulars include Cormorant, Teal, Gadwall, Wigeon, Pintail, Shoveler, Pochard, Ruddy Duck, Goldeneye, Goosander, Water Rail, Golden Plover, Snipe, Jack Snipe, Green Sandpiper and Dunlin. The gull roost may include a rarer species, Siskin and Redpoll.

ACCESS: The western end of the water park is easily reached off the A419 Swindon–Cirencester road. For the eastern

THIS LARGE Staffordshire reservoir is fed by the River Blithe and by Tad Brook, both entering at its northern end. A causeway carrying the Rugeley–Uttoxeter road splits Blithfield in half. The southern section has a dam, while the northern end is more interesting for birds, mainly due to the lack of sailing and a more varied habitat. There are conifer plantations and areas of deciduous woodland, while the gently sloping banks attract waders.

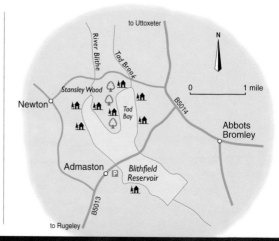

Access is by permit. There are a number of hides erected around the northern end. The causeway allows views across both sides, and although adequate for a quick visit it is very limiting.

🦆 BIRDS

Wintering wildfowl are the main interest. Wigeon graze the banks along the southern section. Mallard and Teal are also abundant, and there are a few Pintail Shoveler and Gadwall. Of

Smew are occasional visitors in winter.

the diving duck, Tufted Duck and Pochard are sparse. Goosanders and Goldeneye can exceed 50. Male Goldeneyes can often be watched displaying in early spring. Common Scoter may appear, often from late spring through to early autumn. Scaup, Long-tailed Ducks, divers and the rarer grebes are occasional winter visitors. The gull roost regularly attracts Iceland and Glaucous Gulls, both of which are more reliable in late winter.

Spring and autumn passage involves waders, terns and passerines such as Yellow Wagtail and Wheat-ear. Few migrants stay for long in spring, and waders are scarce. In autumn, wader numbers are greater, attracted by more mud.

BIRDS THROUGH THE SEASONS

ALL YEAR: Great Crested Grebe, Little Grebe, Cormorant, Grey Heron, Mute Swan, feral Canada Goose, Mallard, Tufted Duck, Sparrowhawk, Kestrel, Coot, Lapwing, Little and Tawny Owls, Kingfisher, Great Spotted, Lesser Spotted and Green Woodpeckers, Treecreeper, Nuthatch and tits.

SPRING: Occasional Garganey and Common Scoter, Shelduck, Hobby, Osprey, Oystercatcher, Little Ringed Plover, Ringed Plover, Dunlin, Curlew, Redshank, Greenshank, and Green and Common Sandpiper. Occasional visiting waders include both Bar-tailed and Black-tailed Godwits, Whimbrel and Grey Plover, Sanderling, Turnstone, Little Gull, Black, Common and Arctic Tern, occasional Sandwich and Little Tern, Swift, hirundines, Wheatear, Whinchat, Yellow Wagtail.

SUMMER: Resident breeding birds and breeding warblers.

Goldeneye drakes can be watched displaying in spring.

AUTUMN: As for spring, plus arrival of wintering wildfowl. Additional passage waders may include Knot, Curlew and Wood Sandpipers, Ruff, Snipe, Black-tailed Godwit and Spotted Redshank. Rock Pipits are regular in late autumn.

WINTER: Occasional visits by divers, rarer grebes, parties of Bewick's Swan, White-fronted Goose, Scaup, Common Scoter, Smew, Hen Harrier, Merlin and Peregrine. Regulars include Wigeon, Gadwall, Teal, Shoveler, Pochard, Goldeneye, Goosander, Ruddy Duck, Golden Plover, Snipe, Redshank, Green Sandpiper, Grey Wagtail, Fieldfare and Redwings. Within the gull roost, there is a chance of Iceland and Glaucous Gull.

ACCESS: The reservoir lies on the B5013 Rugeley–Uttoxeter road. There are parking areas at either end of the causeway. Access permits can be obtained from the West Midlands Bird Club, Miss M Surman, 6 Lloyd Square, 12 Niall Close, Edgbaston, Birmingham B15 3LX.

DISABLED ACCESS: Restricted to the causeway; viewing is possible from a car at either end.

OTHER ATTRACTIONS

THE WOODS and heaths of Cannock Chase, just west of Rugeley, offer numerous walks and picnic sites.

OAK WOODLAND covers much of this steep-sided valley. The Coombes Brook cuts its way through the valley floor, and bracken-covered slopes and a small area of pasture add to the habitat.

A nature trail has an accompanying leaflet. Some paths are steep and can be slippery, so good footwear is recommended. In addition to two hides, there is an information centre.

BIRDS
Residents include all three species of woodpecker, which are best located in early spring when they are most vocal and drum.

Sparrowhawks are regularly seen, in contrast to the elusive Long-eared Owl. Look for Grey Wagtail, Dipper and Kingfisher along the stream and on the pool, which is overlooked by a hide.

Pied Flycatchers use nest boxes, and can often be seen from an elevated hide. In the more open areas, Tree Pipits breed. In spring, they perform a display flight, singing as they drop to the ground like a parachute.

OTHER ANIMALS
An interesting array of insects includes over 1200 species of beetle and 24 species of butterfly. Badgers are common, while the flora includes Greater Butterfly, Common Spotted and Early Purple Orchids.

BIRDS THROUGH THE SEASONS
ALL YEAR: Grey Heron, Sparrowhawk, Woodcock, Little Owl, Tawny Owl, Long-eared Owl, Kingfisher, Great Spotted, Lesser Spotted and Green Woodpeckers, Grey Wagtail, Dipper, Nuthatch, Treecreeper, Goldcrest, tits and Redpoll.
SPRING AND SUMMER: Cuckoo, Tree Pipit, Pied and Spotted Flycatchers, Redstart, Wood Warbler and commoner warblers.
AUTUMN AND WINTER: The woodland can be quiet. Roving tit flocks, Fieldfares and Redwings, along with the residents, are the main interest.

ACCESS: Coombes Valley is 3 miles south-east of Leek. Turn off the A523 to Apesford; the reserve is 1 mile further on.

OTHER ATTRACTIONS

THE PEAK District is popular with walkers. A good variety of upland birds are possible, and include Black and Red Grouse, Ring Ouzel and Twite. The town of Buxton has nine thermal springs, opposite which is a grand crescent, a very good example of Regency architecture. To the east of Buxton lies Chatsworth House, a Palladian mansion built between 1687 and 1707, with a deer park and gardens designed by Capability Brown.

Two further sites are worth visiting. Churnet Valley is an RSPB reserve with similar species, while Swallow Moss is mostly moorland (*See* Additional Sites).

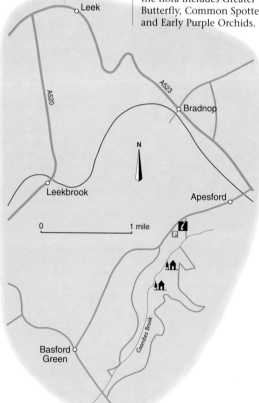

DRAYCOTE WATER is a storage reservoir, filled by pump from the River Leam. Severn Trent Water manages the site and allows bird-watching by permit. The reservoir is embanked in many parts, with a road allowing access by car around its perimeter. Some sheltered bays have a little waterside vegetation, but there is little mud for waders. Toft Bay has a small marsh overlooked by a hide and is the most attractive site for birds.

BIRDS

Draycote is at its best for wildfowl between October and March. A few hundred Wigeon graze the banks, along with Mallard and lesser numbers of Teal. Tufted Duck, Pochard and Goldeneye are the most numerous diving ducks. Wildfowl numbers vary depending on the weather. Cold snaps regularly produce sawbills such as Smew, Goosander and, occasionally, Red-breasted Merganser. Seaduck are annual in winter, with Scaup and Long-tailed Duck being most likely. Divers appear annually; Great-northern Diver is the most frequent, and will often stay for a few weeks.

A main feature of winter is the large gull roost. Tens of thousands of Black-headed Gulls are joined by a few thousand Common Gulls and lesser numbers of the larger species. Diligent searching may lead to the discovery of an Iceland or Glaucous Gull and, less regularly, a Mediterranean Gull or Kittiwake. The latter are most likely after gales. Draycote has a reputation for producing seabirds such

as a skua or Leach's Storm-petrel after autumn gales.

Wader passage is poor, especially in spring when there is often an absence of suitable feeding areas. In autumn, a trickle of species passes through. Most regular are Dunlin, Common Sandpiper, and Ringed and Little Ringed Plovers. Terns drop in on passage, Arctic Terns outnumbering Common Terns in spring, and the reverse in autumn.

BIRDS THROUGH THE SEASONS

ALL YEAR: Grey Heron, Mallard, Tufted Duck, Sparrowhawk, Kestrel, Green, Great Spotted and Lesser Spotted Woodpeckers, and Reed Bunting.

SPRING: Passage waders include Oystercatcher, Little Ringed Plover, Ringed Plover, Dunlin, Redshank and Common Sandpiper. Annually recorded but scarce species include Grey

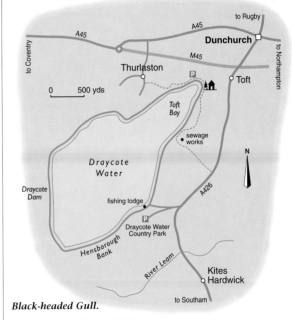

Black-headed Gull.

Plover, Knot, Sanderling, Bar-tailed Godwit, Whimbrel, Curlew, Greenshank and Turnstone. Others include Arctic and a few Common Terns, occasional parties of Black Terns and Little Gulls, Swifts, hirundines, Wheatear, Whinchat, and Yellow and White Wagtails. Rare but annual visitors include Common Scoter, Sheduck and Kittiwake.

SUMMER: Breeding birds include Mallard, Tufted Duck, Cuckoo, Sedge and Reed Warblers, Blackcap, Whitethroat and Lesser Whitethroat.

AUTUMN: As for spring, but with Common Terns more abundant than Arctic. Waders are more likely but in low numbers, and include Little Stint, Ruff, Spotted Redshank, Redshank, Greenshank and

Pintail, Shoveler, Mallard, Pochard, Tufted Duck, Goldeneye, Smew (scarce), Goosander, occasional Red-breasted Merganser, Lapwing, Dunlin, Snipe, Green Sandpiper and Ruff (scarce). Rock Pipit is a scarce visitor. Large gull roost, mainly Black-headed Gulls, smaller numbers of other species. The roost annually attracts Kittiwake, and Mediterranean, Iceland and

are required and can be obtained from the fishing lodge, or by calling Tel: 01788 812018. The shore can be reached without a permit through the Hensborough Hill Country Park, accessed from the main entrance.

DISABLED ACCESS: This is good, as Toft Bay and a number of other viewpoints around the

Draycote has an impressive winter gull roost.

Green Sandpiper. After gales, Kittiwake and the chance of a seabird. Hobby in early autumn.

WINTER: Little and Great Crested Grebes, Great Northern is most frequent diver, rare grebes are annual, Cormorant, Wigeon, Gadwall, Teal, occasional

Glaucous Gull. Occasional Bewick's Swan and small parties of geese visit.

ACCESS: The reservoir is accessed off the A426 Rugby–Southam road, just south of the M45.

In foul weather, bird-watching is possible from the car and there is a parking area at Toft Bay close to the hide. Permits

reservoir can be worked from either a car or a wheelchair.

OTHER ATTRACTIONS

COVENTRY, TO the north-west, has a cathedral which is regarded as an outstanding example of modern-day architecture.

A CAUSEWAY cuts the reservoir in two, with the northern end forming a nature reserve administered by the Northamptonshire Wildlife Trust. The banks at this end are bordered in places by reeds and rushes, behind which are conifers and deciduous woodland.

The entire reservoir can be walked around, but the northern half is by far the more productive and has two hides. Good views can be enjoyed from the causeway, and for a short visit this viewpoint is adequate.

BIRDS

Winter brings a good selection of wildfowl. Pitsford is a regular wintering site for Goosanders, often with over 40 present. Smew are occasional visitors, as are some of the seaducks, divers and rarer grebes. Wigeon, Teal, Mallard, Pochard and Tufted Duck are numerous, with fewer Pintail, Shoveler, Gadwall and Goldeneye. Mediterranean, Iceland and Glaucous Gulls are discovered annually within the gull roost.

During spring and autumn, typical passage migrants include a good selection of waders, though numbers and variety are likely to be sparse in spring

The northern half of Pitsford is a nature reserve.

A508

Scaldwell

Walgrave

Scaldwell Bay

Walgrave Bay

Brixworth

Holcot Bay

causeway

fishing lodge

Holcot

P

P

dam

reservoir car park

Pitsford Reservoir

N

Pitsford

0   1 mile

to Northampton

if water-levels are high. Terns and Little Gulls, the occasional Osprey, Garganey and passerine migrants such as Wheatear, Yellow Wagtail and Rock Pipit all show.

At any time of year a reasonable variety of woodland birds may be encountered, although Pitsford is best visited between August and mid-May for winter birds and migrants.

Godwit, Green and Common Sandpipers, Redshank, Spotted Redshank, Greenshank, Dunlin, Black, Common and Arctic Terns, hirundines, Swift, Wheatear, Whinchat, Grey Wagtail, Yellow Wagtail, Rock Pipit and arrival of summer migrants.
SUMMER: A few wildfowl breed, and there is a good variety of breeding warblers.

Goldeneye, Goosander, Shelduck, feral Greylag and Canada Geese, Mute Swan, Lapwing, Golden Plover, Snipe, Dunlin, Kingfisher, Fieldfare, Redwing, Grey Wagtail, Redpoll and Siskin. Gulls may include a rarity within the roost such as Mediterranean, Glaucous or Iceland Gull.

ACCESS: Pitsford is reached off the A508 north of Northampton. If travelling north, turn off right at Brixworth for Holcot. This road turns into the causeway. Paths lead from the causeway around both halves. A permit is needed for the northern half and the hides, and can be obtained from the fishing office at the eastern end of the causeway. Alternatively, write to: Pitsford Warden, Lings House, Billing Lings, Northampton NN3 4BE. Tel: 01604 405285.

DISABLED ACCESS: Good views possible from the causeway if using a vehicle or wheelchair.

Redshank are among a number of passage waders that feed along the reservoir's margins in autumn.

BIRDS THROUGH THE SEASONS

ALL YEAR: Great Crested Grebe, Mallard, Gadwall, Tufted Duck, Shoveler, Coot, woodpeckers and common woodland birds.
SPRING: Occasional Black-necked Grebe, Garganey, Common Scoter and Osprey. Regular passage migrants include Hobby, Oystercatcher, Lapwing, Ringed Plover, Little Ringed Plover, Snipe, Curlew, Whimbrel, Black-tailed

AUTUMN: As for spring, plus Wood Sandpiper, Little Stint, Curlew Sandpiper and Ruff.
WINTER: Occasional visits by divers and rarer grebes, chance of Long-tailed Duck, Red-breasted Merganser, Smew, Scaup, Bewick's Swan, White-fronted Goose, Peregrine or other raptor. Regulars include Little Grebe, Cormorant, Grey Heron, Mallard, Teal, Gadwall, Wigeon, Pintail, Shoveler, Tufted Duck, Pochard, Ruddy Duck,

OTHER ATTRACTIONS

THE WATERWAYS MUSEUM is to the south of Northampton, alongside the Grand Union Canal, and is reached off the A508. Holdenby House Gardens are to the north-west of Northampton, reached off the A428 and A50. Within the grounds are a falconry centre and rare breeds farm. This was once the largest house in Elizabethan England and it has some impressive gardens. Open Tuesdays to Fridays and on Sundays from Easter to the end of September.

RUTLAND WATER was created in the 1970s, and is one of the largest man-made reservoirs in Europe. At its western end, a nature reserve run by the Leicestershire and Rutland Trust for Nature Conservation encompasses 9 miles of shoreline. Within the reserve are extensive areas of open water, lagoons, marsh, reedbeds, meadows and woodland.

While there are interesting pockets around the reservoir that attract birds, it is best to concentrate your efforts within the reserve where the greatest variety and number occur. There are two parts to the reserve. The Lyndon Reserve has a visitor centre, hides and a nature trail, while the Egleton Reserve is the more interesting site, with 11 hides and a bird-watching centre, complete with heated viewing gallery. This reserve is home to the British Bird-watching Fair, held in August.

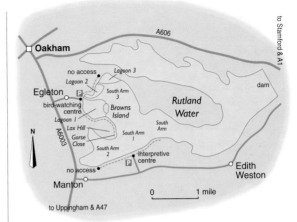

BIRDS

Rutland has developed into a wetland of international importance. During winter, average peak waterfowl counts regularly exceed 10,000 birds. Most numerous are Coot, Mallard, Wigeon, Gadwall, Teal and Tufted Duck. Flocks of Goosander often share the reservoir with their sawbill cousins, Red-breasted Merganser and Smew. Seaduck such as Long-tailed Duck, Scaup and Common Scoter are regular visitors. Each winter, divers and the rarer grebes visit, sometimes staying for days or weeks. White-fronted and the occasional Pink-footed Goose drop in from time to time, often joining the feral flocks of Greylag and Canada Geese.

As spring arrives, wildfowl start to disperse just as the first summer migrants appear. Sand Martin, Wheatear and Chiffchaff are some of the early arrivals. By mid-April, each day brings new and exciting birds for the year. Flocks of terns and Little Gulls may hawk over the water for just a few hours before moving on. Passage waders of a wide range of species come and go, while the surrounding scrub and woodland are full of song. Ospreys, Hobbies and Marsh Harriers are frequent visitors at this time, and within the lagoons Garganey and Black-necked Grebes may appear.

By late May, passage has died away. Breeding birds are well advanced with the business of rearing a family. Various species of duck breed

Black-necked Grebe in summer plumage.

and, on the dried mud, both Ringed and Little Ringed Plovers nest. June is the quietest month, though there is always something of interest. By July, waders are reappearing and, by August, returning migrants include Ospreys and terns. Black-necked Grebes are likely and wildfowl arrive to moult. Hobbies hunt over the lagoons, while, along the shoreline in August and September, around 20 species of wader are possible.

BIRDS THROUGH THE SEASONS

ALL YEAR: Great Crested Grebe, Little Grebe, Cormorant, Grey Heron, Mallard, Teal, Gadwall, Shoveler, Tufted Duck, Ruddy Duck, feral Greylag and Canada Geese, Mute Swan, Kestrel, Sparrowhawk, Lapwing, Redshank, Barn Owl, Kingfisher, Great Spotted, Lesser Spotted and Green Woodpeckers, Marsh and Willow Tit, Treecreeper, Corn Bunting, Reed Bunting and Tree Sparrow.
SPRING: Garganey, Marsh Harrier, Osprey, Hobby, Oystercatcher, Ringed, Little Ringed, Grey and Golden Plovers, Turnstone, Curlew, Whimbrel, Black and Bar-tailed Godwits, Green, Wood and Common Sandpipers, Redshank, Spotted Redshank, Greenshank, Knot, Little Stint, Dunlin, Curlew Sandpiper, Sanderling, Ruff, Snipe, Black, Common and Arctic Terns, Turtle Dove, Swift, hirundines, Wheatear, Whinchat and Yellow Wagtail.
SUMMER: Breeding wildfowl, plus Oystercatcher, Little Ringed and Ringed Plover, Common Tern, Hobby,

Nightingale, Grasshopper, Reed, Sedge, Garden and Willow Warblers, Chiffchaff, Blackcap, Whitethroat, Lesser Whitethroat, Spotted Flycatcher, Yellow Wagtail.
AUTUMN: Return of wildfowl in numbers, as for winter. Black-necked Grebe, Common Scoter, Jack Snipe and same birds as for spring.
WINTER: Divers and rarer grebes, Wigeon, Pintail, Scaup, Pochard, Goldeneye, Goosander, Shelduck, chance of Smew, Red-breasted Merganser, Long-tailed Duck and scoter, occasional White-fronted and Pink-footed Geese, and visits by Whooper and Bewick's Swans. Visiting raptors include Hen Harrier, Peregrine, Merlin and Short-eared Owl, though all are very scarce. Occasionally a Bittern may winter. Lapwing, Golden Plover, Snipe, Redshank, Dunlin, Ruff and Water Rail. Good chance of other waders. Various gulls roost and may include Iceland, Glaucous, Mediterranean and Yellow-legged Herring Gulls. Fieldfare, Redwing, Grey Wagtail, Meadow Pipit, Redpoll and Siskin.

ACCESS: Rutland Water lies just west of Stamford, and is easily reached off the A1.

The Lyndon Reserve is on the south-west shore between Manton and Edith Weston. It is open at weekends only during the winter, and from Good Friday to the end of October it is also open on Tuesdays, Wednesdays, Thursdays and Fridays between 10am and 4pm. A small entrance fee is charged.

The Egleton Reserve is clearly signposted off the A6003 south of Oakham, and is reached from the village of Egleton. The reserve is open daily from 9am to 5pm except on Christmas Day and Boxing Day. Permits for access to the hides are available from the bird-watching centre.

Whitethroats breed in the scrub bordering the reservoir.

DISABLED ACCESS: A wheelchair is available at the bird-watching centre, and toilets are accessible to the disabled. Some hides on both reserves are accessible to wheelchairs.

OTHER ATTRACTIONS

THE TOWN of Oakham is close by. Rutland Water offers many recreational activities, from trout fishing to windsurfing. There are also picnic areas, adventure playgrounds and bicycles for hire.

THIS WATER-supply reservoir was created in the mid-1960s and is owned by Anglian Water. There are almost 10 miles of shoreline, bordered by fields, woodlands and a concrete dam. Grafham Water is of most interest for its wintering wildfowl.

Much of the open water is heavily disturbed by sailing and fishing. However, the western side is a nature reserve administered by the Cambridgeshire Wildlife Trust. Within the reserve, two arms of the reservoir are out of bounds to water-users and so attract good concentrations of duck. A path runs from the Mander Park, where there is a wildlife cabin from which recent sightings and information can be gleaned. There are four hides within the reserve, all reached along the nature trail.

One of the best ways to cover ground at Grafham is to cycle, as a cycle route runs around the perimeter and bicycles can be hired on site.

Grafham Water has almost 10 miles of shoreline.

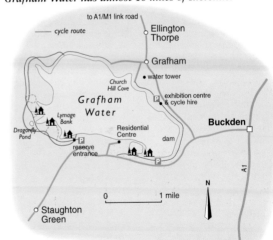

🦆 BIRDS

Many birds commute between Grafham and neighbouring gravel pits, most notably Goosanders, which are often absent during the day before re-appearing in late afternoon to roost at the dam end. Most abundant are Coots, Great Crested Grebes, Tufted Ducks, Wigeon, Teal, Mallard and Cormorants. Lesser numbers of Pochard, Shoveler, Gadwall and Goldeneye can all be seen on a typical winter visit. More unusual visitors include Smew, divers and the rarer grebes, especially in cold weather. Seaduck such as Common Scoter and Scaup are recorded annually. A gull roost often attracts Glaucous and Iceland Gulls.

Terns and waders are the main interest in spring and autumn. Wader numbers are never high, but a good variety are seen. Terns include Black and Common, and Arctic Terns frequently in spring. Little Gulls drop in at both seasons. During autumn, Mute Swans arrive to moult and, although numbers are much lower than they once were, there are signs of an increase, with recent counts exceeding 50. One or two pairs of Grasshopper Warbler usually breed, as do a small population of Nightingales. A heronry has recently been established.

OTHER ANIMALS
Other wildlife of interest includes Purple Hairstreak butterflies, Great Crested Newts and Muntjac Deer.

FLOWERS
Plants to look out for include Golden and Marsh Docks, and Hairy Buttercup.

BIRDS THROUGH THE SEASONS
ALL YEAR: Great Crested Grebe, Grey Heron, Mallard, Tufted Duck, Coot, Sparrowhawk, Kestrel, Goldcrest, Willow Tit, Nuthatch and Treecreeper.
SPRING: Osprey, Hobby, Little Ringed and Ringed Plovers, Common and Green Sandpipers, Dunlin, Whimbrel, Curlew, Oystercatcher, Turnstone, Lapwing, Greenshank, Redshank and the chance of a more unusual wader, Arctic, Common and Black Terns, Little Gull, Yellow Wagtail, Wheatear, Whinchat, Swift, hirundines, arrival of breeding summer migrants.
SUMMER: Breeding birds include Shelduck, Gadwall, Little Ringed Plover, Cuckoo, Grasshopper Warbler, Nightingale, Lesser Whitethroat, Whitethroat, Chiffchaff, Willow Warbler, Blackcap, Garden Warbler and Spotted Flycatcher. Common Tern and Hobby are frequent.
AUTUMN: As for spring, plus the chance of a Little Stint, Curlew Sandpiper, Knot, Ruff, Black-tailed Godwit, Spotted Redshank or Wood Sandpiper.
WINTER: Occasional diver and rarer grebe, Little

The Little Stint is annual in autumn.

Grebe, Wigeon, Gadwall, Teal, Pintail (scarce), Shoveler, Pochard, Goldeneye, Goosander, occasional visits by Smew, Scaup and Common Scoter, Golden Plover, Lapwing, Snipe, Dunlin, Siskin, Redpoll.

ACCESS: Grafham Water is just off the A1. Mander Park and the start of the nature trail are reached along the southern shore, as are two public hides in the south-east corner (*see* map).
The wildlife cabin is open at weekends and often during mid-week.

DISABLED ACCESS:
At Mander Park, the wildlife garden and the first two hides on the reserve are accessible to wheelchairs, as is one of the public hides in the south-east corner.

OTHER ATTRACTIONS

GRAFHAM OFFERS a good family day out. There are walks, cycling on safe paths around the reservoir, and adventure playgrounds for the children. Sporting opportunities include sailing, windsurfing and trout fishing. The exhibition centre is worth a visit, and has a café.
Just to the east are a series of gravel pits along the Great Ouse River at Little Paxton, just north of St Neots and east of the A1. Many of the birds that use Grafham commute to these pits, so the site is well worth a visit if time permits.

LYING JUST 4 miles from Birmingham city centre, this 25-acre reserve forms part of the Sandwell Valley Country Park. Rough grassland, marsh, pools and thickets ensure good bird-watching throughout the year.

There are four hides overlooking a pool, marsh and a wader scrape. One of the main aims of the reserve is to educate the public, and hence it has a very good information centre.

Sandwell Valley has good paths, ideal for the disabled.

BIRDS
A few wildfowl winter in addition to Water Rail, Snipe and often Jack Snipe. Spring and autumn bring a variety of migrants ranging from waders to warblers. Most of the common warblers breed, along with Little and Great Crested Grebes. Kingfishers are resident and are seen regularly. In winter, the hawthorn bushes attract hordes of Fieldfares and Redwings.

BIRDS THROUGH THE SEASONS
ALL YEAR: Great Crested and Little Grebes, feral Canada Goose, Mallard, Tufted Duck, Coot, Moorhen, Sparrowhawk, Kestrel, Snipe, Woodcock, Tawny Owl, Kingfisher, Willow Tit and common woodland birds.

SPRING: A few passage waders may include Ringed and Little Ringed Plovers, Green and Common Sandpipers, Greenshank, Curlew and Dunlin. Chance of terns and Hobbies. Regular passerine migrants include hirundines, Swift, Wheatear, Whinchat, Yellow Wagtail and Reed and Sedge Warblers. Arrival of breeding birds.
SUMMER: Breeding birds include Mallard, Tufted Duck, Coot, Moorhen, Little Ringed Plover, Lapwing, Snipe, Sedge, Reed and Willow Warblers, Chiffchaff, Blackcap, Whitethroat and Lesser Whitethroat. Common Terns appear over the pools.
AUTUMN: As for spring.
WINTER: Grey Heron, Mute Swan, Wigeon, Gadwall, Teal, Shoveler, Pochard, Goldeneye, Ruddy Duck, Water Rail, occasional Jack Snipe, Green Sandpiper, Stonechat, occasional Long-eared Owl, Fieldfare and Redwing.

ACCESS: Reached off the M6 at junction 7 (*see* map for directions). The information centre is open from 9am to 5pm Mondays to Thursdays, and from 10am to 5pm at weekends. It is closed on Fridays.

DISABLED ACCESS: Wheelchair access to hides on good paths.

OTHER ATTRACTIONS

THE BIRMINGHAM Nature Centre is a zoo, nature trail and museum. It is open daily from March to October and at weekends through the winter; admission is free. The centre is on the A441 Pershore Road opposite BBC Pebble Mill.

BEDFORDSHIRE

The Lodge
RSPB Reserve

The Lodge is the headquarters of the RSPB. Adjoining the Victorian mansion and associated buildings used by the society is a reserve popular with members. Woodland, a lake and a remnant of heath attract a good selection of birds. Tree Pipits, woodpeckers and warblers breed, and

Kingfisher, Grey Heron and Sparrowhawk all visit occasionally. A small colony of Natterjack Toads and Muntjac Deer add interest. There are paths through the reserve and gardens. Of the two hides, one is accessible to wheelchairs, and there is a shop, picnic area and toilets. The reserve and gardens are open daily from 9am to sunset or 9pm, whichever is earlier. From Sandy, drive for 1 mile on the B1042 towards Potton. The reserve is signposted.

BUCKINGHAM-SHIRE

Church Wood
RSPB Reserve

Situated within the Chilterns, this small woodland reserve hosts a good variety of resident woodland birds. Butterflies include White Admiral and Purple Hairstreak, while Muntjac Deer are regular visitors. The reserve is reached along a private track

Upton Warren's pools are attractive to wildfowl in winter.

Chestnut and Maple coppices. A wide variety of resident and summer migrants breed, including Nightingale, Lesser Whitethroat and all three species of woodpecker. The rides are used by White Admiral butterflies. Bluebells carpet the woodland floor in spring. Cowslips, Early Purple Orchids and Tintern Spurge, a rarity found in ancient woodlands, all thrive. The Hazel coppice is favoured by Dormice. A hide overlooking a pond is accessible to wheelchairs. The reserve is 3 miles west of Gloucester, just east of Churcham, and is entered off the A40 Ross-on-Wye–Gloucester road.

HEREFORD AND WORCESTER

Upton Warren

A reserve of the Worcester-shire Wildlife Trust. A permit is required, obtainable from the trust. Hides look out on to pools attractive to wildfowl in winter. Passage migrants include terns, waders and various passerines, and a number of rarities have been found in recent years. From the M5 at junction 5, take the A38 towards Bromsgrove. In Upton Warren, turn right down the lane by the AA phone, shortly after passing the Swan pub.

HERTFORDSHIRE

Tring Reservoirs

This series of reservoirs, constructed in the 19th century, attracts a variety of passage migrants in spring and autumn, along with an interesting variety of wintering wildfowl. The reservoirs lie just west of Aylesbury and north-west of Tring.

LEICESTERSHIRE

Eyebrook Reservoir

Wintering wildfowl and passage waders are the main attractions at Eyebrook. In hard weather, sawbills, divers and the rarer grebes may appear. Autumn is best for waders, when large areas of mud can attract a good variety. Eyebrook is south of Uppingham and to the west of the A6003. Much of the reservoir can be seen from the surrounding roads.

NORTHAMPTON-SHIRE

Thrapston Gravel Pits

Goosanders and a variety of other wildfowl winter. In summer, look for Little Ringed Plovers and

beside the pond and beyond a pub in Hedgerley village, which is south of the M40 near junction 2.

GLOUCESTER-SHIRE

Highnam Woods
RSPB Reserve

An ancient woodland of oak and Ash with Sweet

Snipe.

Common Terns. Passage migrants occur in spring and autumn. Reached off the A605 along a footpath that leads from a lay-by north of Thrapston.

STAFFORDSHIRE

Belvide Reservoir

Wildfowl are the prime interest. A variety of species breed, moult and winter. The gull roost regularly holds Glaucous and Iceland Gulls in late winter. A good variety of passage migrants can be expected in spring and autumn. Unfortunately, access is by permit only, obtainable from the West Midlands Bird Club. Contact Miss M Surman, 6 Lloyd Square, 12 Niall Close, Edgbaston, Birmingham B15

3LX. Belvide lies alongside the A5 Cannock–Telford road, just east of the A41.

Chasewater

This Midlands reservoir has a reputation for attracting Iceland and Glaucous Gulls to its large winter gull roost. Wintering wildfowl include Goldeneye and occasional Goosanders. Passage migrants can be searched for in spring and autumn, though wader numbers vary depending on the water-level. The reservoir is just north of Birmingham, reached off the A5 at Brownhills.

Churnet Valley Woods
RSPB Reserve

South of Coombes Valley RSPB Reserve, these woodlands within the

Churnet Valley support the same species, such as Redstart, Wood Warbler and Pied Flycatcher. White Letter Hairstreak butterflies will be on the wing from July. There are circular walks from the country park car park. Reached down a minor road from Consall village, which is east of the A522 Leek–Cheadle road.

Swallow Moss

Black Grouse are the main attraction. They can be seen throughout the year, but during spring males can be watched lekking in front of a hide that has been converted from a stone barn. During winter, Hen Harriers and Merlins are frequent visitors. Turn off the B5053 at Warslow (east of Leek) on to a minor road heading north-west. Go straight over the crossroads; Swallow Moss is on the right, near Fernyford Farm.

EAST ANGLIA

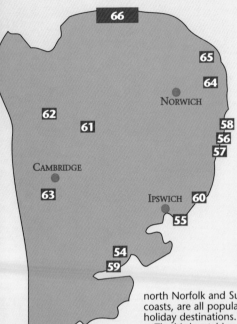

66
65
64
NORWICH
62
61
58
56
57
CAMBRIDGE
63
IPSWICH **60**
55
54
59

Failure of the berry crop in their native Scandinavia can lead to the arrival of Waxwings on the east coast during winter.

EAST ANGLIA stretches from the Wash to the Thames Estuary and bulges into the North Sea. Much of the region is relatively flat, with the land rarely rising above 290 feet, yet the landscape has a beauty of its own. The Norfolk Broads, and the north Norfolk and Suffolk coasts, are all popular holiday destinations.

The bird-watching is often said to be the best and most varied on offer in the British Isles. Habitats range from reedbeds, supporting Bitterns and Marsh Harriers, to the sandy heaths of the Brecklands, the stronghold of the Stone Curlew. In winter, the coastline, particularly around the Wash, attracts huge numbers of wildfowl and waders. Spring and autumn provide endless excitement as migrants bring with them the inevitable rarities. Few places can match the Norfolk coast during autumn for the variety of birds. In spring, over 100 species can be seen in a day at a number of sites, perhaps most notably at Minsmere in Suffolk, one of the RSPB's most popular reserves.

East Anglia's wildlife extends to more than birds. Otters have been re-introduced at many sites. The Muntjac Deer is widespread, in contrast to the Chinese Water Deer which remains localised, mainly within the Norfolk Broads area. Perhaps the most popular attraction off the Norfolk coast are the Common and Grey Seals.

Grey Herons are common throughout the region.

ABBERTON RESERVOIR was formed by the flooding of a shallow valley in 1941, and is the largest stretch of fresh water in Essex. Its close proximity to the coast, 4 miles away (*see* map for Site 59), encourages an average of over 20,000 waterfowl to use the reservoir in winter.

There are two trails that lead from the visitor centre. One is a small nature trail that visits the Scott and Wainwright hides, while the other more productive route is the Peninsular Nature Trail, which visits three hides and is just over a mile long.

BIRDS

Wigeon and Teal are most numerous, followed by Coot, Tufted Duck, Pochard and Mallard. Abberton is one of the main inland wintering sites for Goldeneye. Small flocks of Goosander are much scarcer but usually present, and Smew are regular. These generally only reach double figures when harsh weather on the Continent causes an influx here. During most winters, occasional divers and the rarer grebes appear.

A good variety of passage waders are recorded annually. During late summer, Common Sandpipers can be numerous. Scarcer species such as Wood Sandpiper and Little Stint are regular. Concentrations of Mute Swan, Gadwall, Shoveler, Pochard and Tufted Duck arrive in autumn to moult. In spring and autumn, a variety of terns and passerine migrants pass through.

Common Terns nest on a raft viewable from hides near the information centre, while tree-nesting Cormorants can be viewed from the Layer Breton causeway.

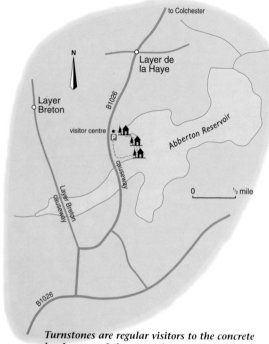

Turnstones are regular visitors to the concrete banks around the reservoir.

BIRDS THROUGH THE SEASONS

ALL YEAR: Great Crested Grebe, Grey Heron, Cormorant, Tufted Duck,

Cormorant.

Black-tailed Godwit, Spotted Redshank, Redshank, Greenshank, Curlew, and Green, Wood and Common Sandpipers. Annual in varying numbers are Red-crested Pochard, Osprey, Black Tern and Little Gull. Flocks of Yellow Wagtails are a feature in August. Hirundines and Swifts hunt over the water.

WINTER: Divers (most commonly Red-throated), Black-necked Grebe (most likely of rarer grebes), Little Grebe, Bewick's Swan, Wigeon, Teal, Pintail, Pochard, Goldeneye, Smew, Goosander, Golden Plover, Dunlin and Snipe.

Gadwall, Shoveler, Mallard, Ruddy Duck and Coot.

SPRING: Many of the wintering duck will be present in April. Passage migrants include Garganey, Osprey (rarely linger), Little Ringed Plover, Dunlin, Turnstone, Common Sandpiper, Whimbrel, Redshank, Curlew, various species of tern (including flocks of Black Terns), Little Gull and Yellow Wagtail.

SUMMER: Breeding Cormorants, Common Terns and wildfowl. Returning passage waders by late July. Breeding passerines include Sedge and Willow Warblers, Nightingale, Whitethroat, Lesser Whitethroat, Turtle Dove, Great Spotted Woodpecker and Reed and Corn Buntings.

AUTUMN: Moulting wildfowl include Mute Swan, Gadwall, Shoveler, Tufted Duck and Pochard. Passage waders include Ringed Plover, Little Ringed Plover, Dunlin, Little Stint, Curlew Sandpiper, Ruff,

reach a causeway that allows viewing on either side. A second causeway near Layer Breton is reached by continuing for a further mile and turning right. The visitor centre is open daily except Mondays from 9am to 5pm. The hides are all reached from here, and a permit is required for the Peninsula Nature Trail.

DISABLED ACCESS: The causeways and Wainwright and Scott hides at the visitor centre allow viewing from a wheelchair.

Goldfinch.

ACCESS: There is a visitor centre and hides near Layer-de-la-Haye. From Colchester, take the B1026 south. The visitor centre is on the left, approximately 1 mile past Layer-de-la-Haye. Continue for a further half-mile to

OTHER ATTRACTIONS

COLCHESTER, NEAR by, claims to be the oldest town in England. North-east of Colchester is Flatford Mill, depicted in John Constable's painting *The Hay Wain*, and used as a field studies centre. Upstream is Bridge Cottage, another of Constable's subjects.

Curlew Sandpipers and Little Stints are just three of perhaps 20 species of wader that may be present.

You will notice that the hides are named after famous Suffolk bird-watchers. Although all are now deceased, they were in their time, great contributors to the county's ornithology.

Mention must be made of the outstanding Fagbury Cliff, accessed from the reserve car park and well signposted. This rarity hot spot has hosted some

Wood Sandpiper.

TRIMLEY IS a Suffolk Wildlife Trust reserve, and represents what can be done with farmland which is of little wildlife value. Arable land has been transformed back into the freshwater marsh and meadows it was many years ago.

The Trimley story started in late 1984 when Felixstowe Docks made an application to extend further up the River Orwell. A consortium of conservation bodies strongly opposed the development in a fight which lasted three years and, although development of some of the Orwell's mudflats did take place, £250,000 was made available to establish a nature reserve. The first stage of transformation to wetland occurred in the winter of 1989/90, and so Trimley Marshes Reserve was born.

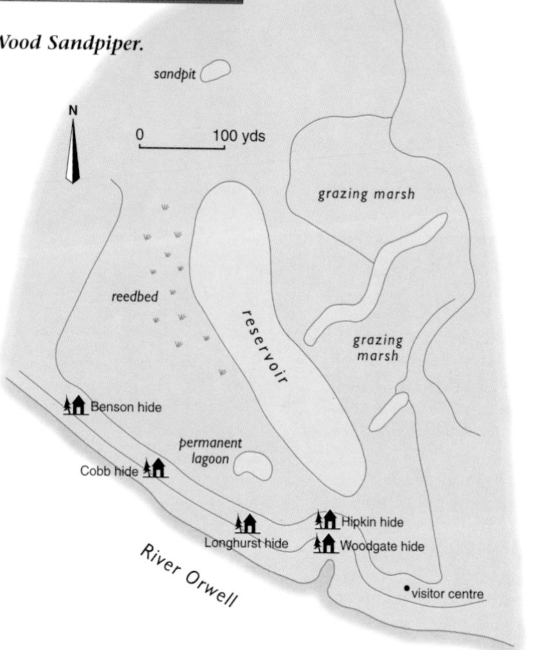

BIRDS

The long walk from the car park to the reserve passes through some rather uninteresting arable land. From the embankment

of the River Orwell, waders in autumn and winter will include Knot, Dunlin, Curlew and Grey Plover, all roosting on the saltmarsh. From the hides in spring and autumn, an excellent variety of passage waders can be viewed. In May, Ruffs have been observed lekking. In autumn, Wood Sandpipers,

outstanding birds, and an intensive ringing programme ensures that few slip through the net. The reason for this site's success is its proximity to the lights of Felixstowe Dock, these attracting passing migrants. Landguard Point and its observatory are also close by (*see* Additional Sites).

Map labels: sandpit, grazing marsh, reedbed, reservoir, grazing marsh, Benson hide, permanent lagoon, Cobb hide, Hipkin hide, Longhurst hide, Woodgate hide, visitor centre, River Orwell, 0 100 yds, N

BIRDS THROUGH THE SEASONS

ALL YEAR: Gadwall, Shoveler, Redshank, Sparrowhawk and Corn Bunting.

SPRING: Garganey, Ruff (often lek), Little Ringed Plover, Ringed Plover, Little Stint, Temminck's Stint (scarce), Curlew Sandpiper, Whimbrel, Greenshank, and Green, Common and Wood Sandpipers.

SUMMER: Breeding species include Shelduck, Avocet and Common Tern. Little Tern attempt to breed.

AUTUMN: Passage waders include the same species as in spring but in much greater abundance. In addition, Spotted Redshank and returning wintering estuarine species.

WINTER: Peregrine, Merlin, Brent Goose, Wigeon, Pintail, Teal, Snipe,

Trimley Marshes Reserve.

Redshank, Knot, Dunlin, Black-tailed Godwit, Curlew and Grey Plover.

Access: Open throughout the year. The visitor centre, manned by volunteers, is open on Mondays, Wednesdays, Saturdays and Sundays from 10am to 4pm. Various displays give an insight into the history and development of the reserve.

Groups are welcome to visit, and should contact the Suffolk Wildlife Trust office, Tel: 01473 890089. Mick Wright, the warden, can take groups by bus to the reserve.

Trimley is signposted off the A45, but from the car park there is approximately a 2-mile walk to the reserve.

Access can also be made from Levington Creek.

Walk past Levington Marina, which incidentally often hosts a Mediterranean Gull during the winter months, and view Trimley Lake, a regular haunt for the rarer grebes. Follow the sea wall round to the reserve. This is roughly the same distance as walking from the reserve car park.

DISABLED ACCESS: By contacting the Suffolk Wildlife Trust office (Tel: 01473 890089) prior to your visit, disabled access can be arranged. Disabled viewing areas exist in the hides.

OTHER ATTRACTIONS

FELIXSTOWE IS a popular seaside resort. Ipswich is the county town of Suffolk, and is a major shopping centre.

WALBERSWICK NATIONAL
Nature Reserve covers 1500
acres. Within the reserve lie
Westwood Marshes, the
largest commercial reedbed
in Britain, extending inland
for 2 miles. Scrub and small
pockets of trees grow on
the periphery, with
heathland, arable
farmland and the Blyth
Estuary close by.

Walberswick has an
excellent network of paths,
and to explore the area
fully would take a few days.

***Marsh Harriers breed
within the reedbed.***

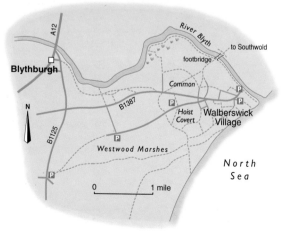

Various circular walks can
be taken, but as some of
the paths can be very
muddy in winter good
footwear is recommended.

 BIRDS
Over 100 species can
be seen in a day in May,
reflecting the importance of
the area for breeding and
migrant birds. The reedbed
specialities of Bearded Tit,
Marsh Harrier and Bittern
breed. Bitterns are
occasionally seen in flight,
otherwise they give their
presence away by
booming in spring. In

winter, the reedbeds at
Westwood Marshes are used
as a roosting site for harriers
and Short-eared Owls, which
are best looked for from late
afternoon to dusk.

The heaths form part of
the remnants of the Suffolk
Sandlings, which before
widespread development
extended almost to
Ipswich. They attract
breeding Nightjars, Tree
Pipits and Woodlarks, and
occasionally Great Grey
Shrike in winter. The
woodlands support a good
selection of birds, and are
most productive in spring
once the summer visitors
have arrived.

At Blythburgh, the River
Blyth forms an inner
estuary attractive to
migrant and wintering
waders and wildfowl.
Spotted Redshanks winter
occasionally along the river,
while Avocets have started
to winter in increasing
numbers. Along its lower
reaches, the river is
embanked and bordered by
damp meadows that are
grazed by Wigeon, Teal
and occasionally by
Bewick's Swans.

OTHER ANIMALS
The marshes have a
rich insect life that includes
the wainscots, rare moths
whose caterpillars feed on
reed stems.

FLOWERS
The reeds are
harvested on a rotational
basis to be used for
thatching, this regular
harvest ensuring the vitality
of the reedbed.

**BIRDS THROUGH
THE SEASONS**
See under Minsmere
(Site 57).

Walberswick.
(Left) Redshank are common along the River Blyth and on the tidal creeks.

Westwood Lodge to view the marshes.

To explore the Blyth Estuary, take the path in Blythburgh by the White Hart pub, or alternatively approach from the B1387.

 DISABLED ACCESS: None.

OTHER ATTRACTIONS

WALBERSWICK IS a village full of Suffolk charm. There are tearooms and an excellent pub, The Bell, which serves good food and the local Adnams beer, brewed in nearby Southwold just across the Blyth. Beer is still delivered here by horse-drawn carriage.

ACCESS: The Westwood Marshes can be entered from the B1125 along a boardwalk through marshy woodland, before reaching the reedbed. Alternative access is from the car park at Hoist Covert, which also starts in woodland, or from Walberswick village. To view the roosting raptors and perhaps chance upon a Barn Owl, proceed along the minor road that forks off to the left when leaving the village, and park 1½ miles further on at

MINSMERE HAS long been the RSPB's flagship reserve, attracting tens of thousands of visitors each year. The reason for its popularity is quite simply the rich array of birdlife to be found on the 2000-acre reserve. Over 100 species breed, while double that number are recorded annually. Reedbeds, mixed woodland, heath and a scrape are the main habitats, protected

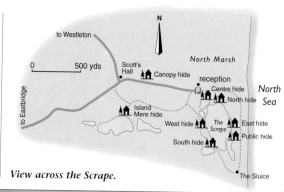

View across the Scrape.

from the sea by a shingle beach. This part of the coast was reclaimed marshland until World War II, when it was deliberately flooded for coastal defence. The RSPB secured a lease on the land in 1949, and so the reserve has developed to become one of the finest in Europe.

The paths at Minsmere allow easy walking. A number of hides overlook the Scrape and reedbeds, and there is a canopy hide in the woodland. Minsmere

has recently undergone a facelift, with improvements to the Scrape and hides, and the construction of a new visitor centre.

🦆 BIRDS

The Scrape, a coastal lagoon, is not only attractive to breeding Avocets, but to a wide range of wildfowl and waders throughout the year. Terns nest on the artificial islands, while in spring and autumn the surrounding mud provides food for a

variety of migrant waders. The reedbeds support Bearded Tits, Marsh Harriers, Bitterns and various warblers, many of which can be seen from the Island Mere Hide.

Minsmere's heathland supports Nightjars and Woodlarks, while the neighbouring mixed woodlands are home to all three species of wood-pecker, and in summer are filled with Nightingale song.

OTHER ANIMALS
In 1985 Otters were introduced; the best chance of a sighting is from Island Mere Hide towards dusk. Red Deer are present but rarely seen, spending the day in the woods and coming down to the reedbed at night. The small Muntjac Deer also occurs in the woodland. Between mid-June and mid-August, look out for the Silver-studded Blue butterfly on the heaths.

BIRDS THROUGH THE SEASONS
ALL YEAR: Little Grebe, Great Crested Grebe, Bittern, Gadwall, Teal, Shoveler, Pochard, Tufted Duck, Marsh Harrier, Sparrowhawk, Water Rail, Snipe, Redshank, Ringed Plover, Lapwing, Woodcock, Kingfisher, Green, Great Spotted and Lesser Spotted Woodpeckers, Cetti's Warbler (very scarce), Bearded Tit, Stonechat, Marsh Tit, Willow Tit, Siskin, Redpoll and various other woodland species.
SPRING: Garganey, Shelduck, Hobby, Whimbrel, Green Sandpiper, Wood Sandpiper, Common Sandpiper, Spotted Redshank, Greenshank, Ruff, Avocet, Black-tailed and Bar-tailed Godwits, and commoner waders present in winter. Little Gull, Black Tern, Little Tern, Common Tern, Sandwich Tern, Ring Ouzel, Wheatear, Whinchat, Black Redstart, Redstart, Firecrest, and warblers including breeding species listed below. Most likely rarities are Spoonbill, Purple Heron, Osprey, Hoopoe and Red-backed Shrike.
SUMMER: Breeding species include Avocet, Little Tern, Common Tern, Sandwich Tern (often present through summer), Nightjar, Woodlark, Nightingale, Grasshopper Warbler, Savi's Warbler (very rare), Reed Warbler, Sedge Warbler, Garden Warbler, Blackcap, Whitethroat, Lesser Whitethroat, Spotted Flycatcher, Tree Pipit, Yellow Wagtail, Redstart and Sand Martin (there is a breeding colony near the reserve centre).
AUTUMN: Same birds as in spring, plus Little Stint, Curlew Sandpiper, Arctic Skua offshore, Wryneck and other drift migrants that may include Barred or Icterine Warbler. Rarities are annual.
WINTER: Offshore: Gannet, Shag, Cormorant, Red-throated Diver, grebes and seaduck, including Eider, Red-breasted Merganser, Common Scoter and Goldeneye, and passing Brent Geese.
Pintail, Wigeon, Shelduck, Scaup, White-fronted Goose (a few appear annually), Bewick's Swan, Buzzard (rare), Rough-legged Buzzards appear during invasion years, Hen Harrier, Peregrine, Merlin, Dunlin, Knot, Grey Plover, Golden Plover, Oystercatcher, Avocet (wintering on the Blyth), Curlew, Bar-tailed and Black-tailed Godwits, occasionally a few Ruff and Spotted Redshank, Short-eared Owl, Water Pipit, Shorelarks in some winters, Twite, Snow Bunting and occasionally Great Grey Shrike.

Hide at Minsmere.

ACCESS: The reserve is open daily from 9am except Tuesdays. There is a public hide overlooking the Scrape. This is reached along the beach from the National Trust car park at Dunwich Cliffs, and is always open.
The reserve is well signposted from Westleton village.

DISABLED ACCESS: There is wheelchair access to most of the reserve and hides.

OTHER ATTRACTIONS

THE AREA offers a number of coastal and heathland walks. Aldeburgh, to the south, is a quiet, attractive town which has been made famous by its annual music festival, held each June.

Gulls are a feature of the broad in autumn and winter. It is worth searching through the flocks for Mediterranean Gulls, which are annual. Wildfowl may include seaduck after winter storms. Offshore, Brent Geese often pass, and the sea is always worth scanning for divers, grebes and ducks. From the pits at Benacre, north towards Kessingland, there are often Snow Buntings and, in some years, Shorelarks.

Curlew Sandpiper are regularly present in Autumn.

NORTH OF Southwold, a series of pits and broads stretches to Kessingland. By far the most interesting section of this coast for birds runs between Covehithe's church and the gravel pits at Benacre.

In between is Benacre Broad, separated from the sea by a low-lying beach. This brackish broad is fringed partly with reeds and deciduous woodland. A public hide overlooks the broad. To the north and south are low sandy cliffs, constantly being eroded by the sea.

BIRDS

Benacre is best in autumn and winter for migrants and wintering birds. The limited amount of mud attracts a few passage waders in autumn. Migrant passerines can be abundant, and are best looked for in the scrub around the gravel pits at Benacre. Typical species in autumn include Pied Flycatcher, Redstart and rarer drift migrants such as Wryneck or Barred Warbler.

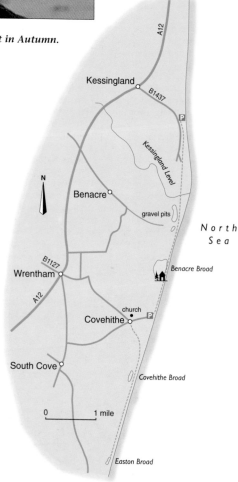

This stretch of coast offers some excellent walking in attractive scenery throughout the year. Summer, however, can be quiet for birds. Easterly or southeasterly winds in spring and autumn are best for migrants, and for the chance of rarities. Covehithe and Easton broads, to the south of Covehithe's church, are worth visiting if time permits.

BIRDS THROUGH THE SEASONS

ALL YEAR: Great Crested Grebe, Gadwall, Tufted Duck and Sparrowhawk.
SPRING: Waders and wildfowl moving offshore. Hobby, Sandwich Tern, Wheatear, Firecrest and warblers.
SUMMER: Sand Martins nest along the cliffs. Marsh Harriers usually attempt to breed.
AUTUMN: Offshore: Gannet and migrating terns. Passage waders include Little Stint, often Curlew Sandpiper, Ruff, Spotted Redshank, Green and Common Sandpipers, and the commoner species. Little Gulls are regular, passerine migrants include Redstart, Pied Flycatcher, Whinchat, Wheatear, Yellow Wagtail and various species of warbler. Scarce drift migrants may include Wryneck, Icterine and Barred Warblers.
WINTER: Offshore: Red-throated Diver, Cormorant, Shag, Brent Goose, Wigeon, Common and Velvet Scoter (rare), Red-breasted Merganser and Long-tailed Duck (rare). On the broad: Teal, Pochard, Scaup, Goldeneye and occasionally Goosander and Smew. Hen Harriers hunt over the reeds and, on occasions, Marsh Harriers. Of the rarer gulls, Mediterranean Gull is the most likely. Snow Buntings and occasionally Shorelarks occur north of the pits.

 ACCESS: Turn off the A12 in Wrentham, and follow the lane to Covehithe. Pass the ruined church and park at the end. From here, walk north along the cliff top. Alternatively, you can walk south from Kessingland, or turn off the A12 to Benacre and walk along a footpath that leads to the pits.

DISABLED ACCESS: None.

OTHER ATTRACTIONS

A T KESSINGLAND is the Suffolk Wildlife and Rare Breeds Park, which also boasts a miniature railway. At Bungay, the Otter Trust has a collection of Otters in grounds bordering the River Waveney. The trust is closed in winter.

Pits at Benacre.

Old Hall Marshes were purchased by the RSPB in 1985 and comprise the largest area of coastal grazing marsh remaining in Essex. Small reedbeds, tidal creeks, saltmarsh and the islands of Great and Little Cob add variety.

To cover the area thoroughly by walking along the sea walls, a whole day is desirable. Outside the reserve, much of the marshland towards Tollesbury is good for birds, especially in winter. Various footpaths cut across the area, and if you are equipped with a good OS map, much ground can be covered.

BIRDS

When walking along the sea walls in winter, it is often difficult to imagine a colder, more desolate place, but the bird-watching is excellent. Twite feed on the saltmarsh, while large flocks of Brent Geese, Wigeon and Teal feed out on the marshes. Estuarine waders roost on the grazing marsh when not feeding in the tidal areas. At high tide there are often Goldeneyes and Red-breasted Mergansers, plus occasional Long-tailed Ducks, divers and grebes along the creeks.

A good variety of passage waders come through in spring and autumn. Breeding birds on the islands include Common Terns, while on the marsh are Yellow Wagtails. The typical grassland nesting waders such as Redshank, Lapwing and Snipe are also present.

BIRDS THROUGH THE SEASONS

ALL YEAR: Lapwing, Redshank, Snipe, Barn Owl, Corn Bunting and Reed Bunting.

SPRING: Marsh Harrier, Avocet, Ringed Plover, Whimbrel, Common Tern, Wheatear, Whinchat and Yellow Wagtail.

SUMMER: Breeding birds include Shelduck, Shoveler, Pochard, Common Tern, Bearded Tit, Yellow Wagtail and Corn Bunting. Marsh Harriers may be present.

AUTUMN: A variety of passage waders may include stints, sandpipers and godwits among the commoner estuarine species arriving for the winter. Other migrants include Yellow Wagtail, Wheatear and Whinchat.

WINTER: Great Crested Grebe, Slavonian Grebe (scarce), Cormorant, Bewick's Swan, White-fronted Goose, Brent Goose, Shelduck, Wigeon, Teal, Goldeneye, Eider, Red-breasted Merganser, occasional Long-tailed Duck, Hen Harrier, Merlin, Peregrine (scarce), Grey Plover, Dunlin, Bar-tailed Godwit, Curlew, Redshank, Short-eared Owl and Twite.

ACCESS:

The reserve is south-east of Tiptree. In the village of Tolleshunt D'Arcy, take Chapel Road and follow it for 1 mile, taking Old Hall Lane, which is the second turning on the left. The car park is reached through Old Hall Farm. To visit the reserve, a car-parking permit is required. Send an SAE to the RSPB, East Anglia Office, Stalham House, 65 Thorpe Road, Norwich, Norfolk NR1 1UD.

DISABLED ACCESS:
None.

to Colchester

Abberton Reservoir

N

0 ——— 1 mile

B1026

to Tiptree & A12

Salcott

Old Hall Lane

P

Tolleshunt D'Arcy

B1023

Tollesbury

OTHER ATTRACTIONS

ABBERTON RESERVOIR (Site 54) is close by and is worth combining with Old Hall Marshes.

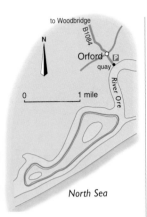

 to Woodbridge

N

 Orford

quay

River Ore

0   1 mile

North Sea

HAVERGATE ISLAND, an RSPB reserve, lies downstream of Orford, where the River Alde changes to the River Ore and splits in two. The 9-mile shingle spit of Orford Ness protects Havergate from the sea. The island is surrounded by an embankment, within which is a series of pools overlooked by hides.

BIRDS

Before the War, Havergate was used as grazing land for sheep and cattle. During a military exercise in 1940, one of the sluices was hit by a shell, causing sea water to flood the island. Brackish conditions resulted, attracting Avocets to breed in 1947, for the first time in Britain since the mid-19th century. (Coincidentally, they first bred at Minsmere in the same year.) Havergate now has the largest breeding colony in Britain, with almost 100 pairs and with good numbers wintering. Sandwich and Common Terns also nest. Outside the breeding season, a good variety of passage and wintering wildfowl and waders can be enjoyed, particularly in autumn.

OTHER ANIMALS

One of the insect specialities is Roesel's Bush Cricket, a rarity that favours saltmarsh and moist grassland.

FLOWERS

The surrounding shingle banks and Orford Ness have an interesting flora. In the saltmarsh are Sea Lavender and Sea Purslane, while the shingle ridges have various stonecrops and Yellow Vetch.

BIRDS THROUGH THE SEASONS

ALL YEAR: Avocet, Ringed Plover, Oystercatcher and Redshank.
SPRING: A few passage waders, lingering winter visitors and arriving breeding birds.
SUMMER: Breeding birds include Shelduck, Redshank, Oystercatcher, Ringed Plover, Sandwich Tern, Common Tern, Little Tern (regularly visits lagoons), Black-headed Gull and Short-eared Owl.
AUTUMN: Passage waders include Greenshank, Ruff, Curlew Sandpiper, Little Stint, Black-tailed Godwit and the commoner estuarine waders listed under winter.
WINTER: Occasionally a few Bewick's Swans and White-fronted Geese visit. Wigeon, Teal, Shoveler, Gadwall, Pintail, Goldeneye, Red-breasted Merganser, Short-eared Owl, Hen Harrier, Grey Plover, Curlew, Dunlin, Knot and Bar-tailed Godwit.

 ACCESS: By special permit only. Boat trips are run from Orford Quay to the island from April to August on the

Avocet.

first and third Saturdays and Sundays of each month, leaving at 10.30 and 11.30am, and from September to March on the first Saturday and Sunday of each month.

Write, enclosing an SAE for tickets, to John Partridge, Warden, 30 Mundays Lane, Orford, Woodbridge, Suffolk IP12 2LX.

 DISABLED ACCESS: None.

OTHER ATTRACTIONS

ORFORD'S CASTLE was built in 1165 by Henry II, and has a unique 18-sided keep giving views across the River Alde. It can be seen from Havergate Reserve.

STRADDLING THE counties of Suffolk and Norfolk, and intruding just into Cambridgeshire is the Breckland. Thetford is regarded as the heart of the 'Brecks', which are characterised by grassy heaths, pine belts and conifer plantations.

 BIRDS
The Brecks are of most interest in spring and summer, when nationally rare species such as Stone Curlews, Goshawks and Woodlarks can be found. Stone Curlews are easier to see here than anywhere else, and not only nest on the grassy heaths but on open farmland too. Many of the plantations support Crossbills and a few pairs of Long-eared Owls. The expanses of clear fell and young plantations are attractive to Woodlarks, Nightjars and Tree Pipits. A watchful eye should always be kept on the sky for the chance of a Goshawk. They are best looked for in early spring when they display above the trees. One of the most elusive of the Brecklands birds is the introduced Golden Pheasant, a beautiful exotic.

 OTHER ANIMALS
Red, Roe, Fallow and Muntjac Deer inhabit the forests, and there is an ongoing project to reinstate Red Squirrels in Thetford Forest. The most important mammal is the Rabbit. They ensure the grassy heaths remain tightly cropped and thus attractive to Stone Curlews and Wheatears.

FLOWERS
Many of the heaths support nationally rare plants and insects.

SITE GUIDE

Weeting Heath

Weeting Heath National Nature Reserve is the most accessible site in England for observing Stone Curlews without the danger of disturbance. The Stone Curlews return in mid-March, and can be viewed from hides. Wheatears nest in disused Rabbit burrows, while the pine belt often harbours Crossbills.

The reserve has some interesting plants, such as Spiked Speedwell, Spring Beauty, Broad-leaved Helleborine, Breckland Mugwort and Spanish Catchfly. Butterflies include Grayling, Grizzled Skipper, Brown Argus and Essex Skipper.

ACCESS: Open from April to August. Leave Brandon north on the A1065, turning off left to Weeting on to the B1106.

Once in the village, turn left at the green by a phone box, towards Hockwold. The reserve entrance is a further mile along this road on the left.

 DISABLED ACCESS: None to the hides.

2

Mayday Farm Forest Trail

Mayday Farm is one of the more reliable sites for seeing Goshawks in spring, as they soar and display over the plantations. Woodlarks,

Goshawk.

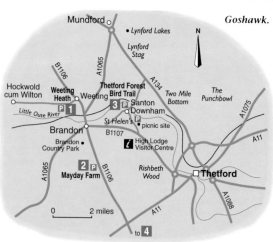

Nightjars and Tree Pipits all breed in the more open areas, while Crossbills and Golden Pheasants inhabit the forests. Occasionally, Great Grey Shrikes winter here. The trails are clearly marked, and under no circumstances should you stray from them.

 ACCESS: On foot along forest tracks and paths. Leave Brandon south on the B1106; the entrance is approximately 1 mile past the Brandon Country Park entrance on the right. Drive down into the dip and park, proceed along the main track to the large clear fell. Watch for Goshawks from here. Nearby Brandon Country Park is a good spot for Golden Pheasants.

 DISABLED ACCESS: Wheelchair access is possible along to the clear fell.

3

Thetford Forest Bird Trail (Santon Downham)

A 3½-mile long trail which can be shortened if necessary, starts near the village of Santon Downham at the site where Red-backed Shrikes last bred in the Brecks in 1988. The trail leads through all the forest habitats. Woodlarks, Nightjars and Tree Pipits breed in the clear fell. The plantations support Golden Pheasants, Crossbills and the occasional Firecrest. An excellent leaflet describing the trail is available.

 ACCESS: The trail is waymarked by orange posts and starts at St Helens picnic site. This is reached by crossing the river on the southern edge of the village and taking the first turning on the right.

 DISABLED ACCESS: Parts of the trail are accessible by wheelchair. For further information, contact Forest Enterprise, Santon Downham, Brandon, Suffolk IP27 0TJ. Tel: 01842 810271.

4

Cavenham Heath

Cavenham Heath National Nature Reserve is one of the finest remaining Breckland heaths, with areas of heather, fen and woodland. During summer, Nightjars, Woodlarks, Grasshopper Warblers and Whinchats can all be found here. Hawfinches inhabit the woodlands, but they can be difficult to locate.

 ACCESS: Leave Bury St Edmunds north on the A1101. At Icklingham, take a minor road on the left after a church on the left. There is a car park at Temple Bridge on the River Lark.

BIRDS THROUGH THE SEASONS

ALL YEAR: Goshawk (highly localised), Sparrowhawk, Golden Pheasant, Woodcock, Barn Owl (scarce), Long-eared Owl (scarce), Great Spotted, Lesser Spotted and Green Woodpeckers, Crossbill and Hawfinch.

Golden Pheasants have become naturalised in the area.

SPRING AND SUMMER: Stone Curlew from mid-March, Ringed Plover, Curlew, Nightjar, Tree Pipit, Woodlark, Nightingale, Redstart, Whinchat, Wheatear, Grasshopper Warbler, Garden Warbler, Blackcap, Whitethroat, Firecrest (scarce), Spotted Flycatcher and occasional Red-backed Shrike (used to breed).
AUTUMN AND WINTER: Hen Harrier, occasional Great Grey Shrike, Redpoll, Siskin and Brambling.

 ACCESS: See site guide above.

 DISABLED ACCESS: See site guide above.

OTHER ATTRACTIONS

GRIMES GRAVES, just north of Brandon, are 4000-year-old neolithic flint mines. Wheatears breed here. The Thetford House Museum has displays on local history and the natural history of the Brecks. The whole Breckland area provides enjoyable forest walking, and there are numerous picnic sites.

TRAVELLING TO the Ouse Washes across the Fens, you pass through a landscape dominated by intensive agriculture. This was once one of the largest wetlands in Europe. Frequent fogs and damp meant life was hard for those who eked out a living in the isolated communities on the islands of higher ground.

In the early 17th century a local landowner, the Earl of Bedford, commissioned

during medieval times. Because of their importance to wildlife, over 70 per cent of the washes are now owned by conservation organisations. Tens of thousands of birds use the Ouse Washes to escape from the cold of Europe and Northern Asia. The two reserves featured below are particularly well suited to seeing large numbers of birds, with excellent facilities for the visitor.

SITE GUIDE

1

Welney Wildfowl and Wetlands Trust Reserve

Winter is the best time to visit as there are spectacular numbers of wildfowl

a Dutchman, Cornelius Vermuyden, to tame the winter floods. Vermuyden created a half-mile strip of flood meadows that runs for some 22 miles, bordered by the Old and New Bedford Rivers and embankments. The idea of this strip was to straighten the meanders of the Great Ouse River, and so channel the winter flood water, leaving the surrounding lower, rich agricultural land dry.

These flood meadows are representative of how the Fens would have looked

A winter dusk on the Ouse Washes.

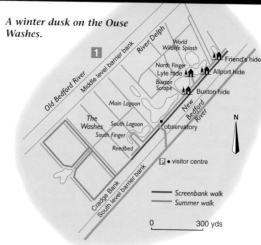

The observatory and swans at Welney.

present. In recent years Welney has become famous for its wild swans, which congregate in their hundreds in front of the hides. Welney has the largest herd of Whooper Swans in England. These Whoopers breed in Iceland and can number 600. This is the species you are most likely to see during the day. The washes also support the largest concentration of wintering Bewick's Swan in Europe. Breeding on the Siberian Arctic tundra, this, our smallest swan, makes a 2500-mile journey to winter at Welney. Bewick's can be encountered in large flocks feeding in the surrounding fields, their white plumage ensuring that they are easily seen against the dark, peaty earth.

Both Whooper and Bewick's Swans stay in family groups, as swan cygnets learn the migration route from their parents. The swans are fed at certain times during the day. They are not dependent on this food, but it does attract them to the front of the hides where ring

numbers and bill patterns can be studied.

After dark during the winter, wildfowl can be watched under floodlights in front of the heated observatory, the perfect way to end a winter's day on the washes.

Out on the meadows, there are some interesting plants, while butterflies and dragonflies abound. During the summer, you can take a 2½-mile walk across the meadows. Reed and Sedge Warblers and Yellow Wagtails are common at this time.

ACCESS: From the A10 near Littleport, turn off at a roundabout on to the A1101 towards Wisbech.

This road eventually runs alongside the New Bedford River, where it turns sharply left over a bridge. Carry straight on for 1 mile to the reserve. Open daily from 10am to 5pm. There is a charge for non-members.

DISABLED ACCESS: The main heated observatory and both Buxton and Lyle hides are accessible by wheelchair.

2

Ouse Washes
RSPB Reserve

Purchased by the RSPB in 1964, this was the first section of the washes to gain protection by a conservation organisation. Breeding Black-tailed Godwits, discovered in 1952, drew attention to the area. Until the mid-1970s, the Ouse Washes were the principal British breeding site for this species, with over 90 per cent of the population here. However, this population declined

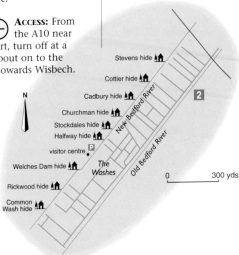

Stevens hide
Cottier hide
Cadbury hide
Churchman hide
Stockdales hide
Halfway hide
visitor centre
Welches Dam hide
Rickwood hide
Common Wash hide

N

New Bedford River
Old Bedford River
The Washes

2

0   300 yds

markedly from over 60 pairs to less than 20 pairs in the 1980s, owing to a succession of deep spring floods. Numbers remain low, with breeding success sporadic.

The other breeding wader for which the washes are famous is the Ruff. The Ruff is at the western tip of its breeding range in Britain, with generally fewer than six pairs breeding in the country in any one year. Ruff lek in late April, the males gathering on a ridge of slightly higher ground on the marsh. They display their varied coloured ruffs, energetically jumping and strutting to entice a female. Lekking reaches a peak soon after sunrise, and is a fascinating ritual to observe.

Breeding wildfowl include Garganey, best looked for in early spring. Gadwall, Shoveler, Pochard, Tufted Duck and Shelduck all nest, as occasionally does a pair of Pintail. Black Terns are recorded on passage in spring and have bred. In autumn you can expect passage waders such as Wood Sandpiper.

The washes can be spectacular in winter. The birds are further away than at Welney but can be abundant, with Wigeon and Teal in their thousands. The washes can support over 30,000 Wigeon, evidence of this site's status as the most important wetland for wintering wildfowl in Britain. Hen Harriers, Short-eared Owls, Merlins and the occasional Peregrine hunt along the embankments and across the floods.

A number of hides stretch for over 3 miles along the embankment bordering the Old Bedford River. There are some rare plants on the reserve, including Fringed Water Lily along the drains. Mammals include Water Shrew and Harvest Mouse, and Otters have recently been reintroduced.

 ACCESS: The reserve is east of Chatteris, and is signposted from the village of Manea.

 DISABLED ACCESS: Welches Dam and Stevens hides are accessible by wheelchair, although it is likely to be a struggle without assistance.

Sedge Warbler and Yellow Wagtails.

AUTUMN: From July, passage waders include Little Stint, Ruff, Black-tailed Godwit, Spotted Redshank, Green-shank, Green and Wood Sandpiper.

WINTER: Whooper, Bewick's and Mute Swans, Shelduck, Wigeon, Teal, Pintail, Ruddy Duck, Hen Harrier, Merlin, often Peregrine, Golden Plover, Short-eared Owl, Scaup, Goldeneye, Smew and Goosander more likely in cold weather.

 ACCESS: *See* site guide above.

BIRDS THROUGH THE SEASONS
ALL YEAR: Little Grebe, Great Crested Grebe, Gadwall, Mallard, Shoveler, Tufted Duck, Pochard, Lapwing, Redshank, Snipe, Barn Owl and Kingfisher.
SPRING: Arrival of breeding birds, which may include Black-tailed Godwit and Ruff. Passage species include Ruff, Black Tern, Little Gull and often Marsh Harrier.
SUMMER: Marsh Harriers are often present. Annual breeders include Garganey, Shelduck, Reed Warbler,

The Washes are the main wintering site for Whooper Swans in England.

 DISABLED ACCESS: *See* site guide above.

OTHER ATTRACTIONS

ELY, TO the south, sits on a hill once surrounded by marsh. The exquisite Norman cathedral was built in 1083, and houses a stained-glass museum and exhibition on stained-glass window construction.

FOWLMERE WAS once a large lake until silting created the reedbed it is today. Local villagers used to harvest the reeds for thatch, and watercress was grown commercially from 1890 to 1982 using pure water from the site's springs. Remains of the cress beds can still be seen.

Fowlmere is a delightful reserve to visit at any time of year. There are hides and a thatched observation tower that overlooks the reedbed. A circular walk, exploring the reserve fully, will take half a day.

BIRDS

Surrounded by the intensive agriculture of the Fens, Fowlmere is an oasis for birds, attracting a good variety of marsh and woodland species. In spring and summer, hordes of Reed and Sedge Warblers sing from the tops of reed stems, while Grasshopper Warblers reel. Bearded Tit, Marsh Harrier and Bittern are absent as breeding birds, but it is hoped that these species will be attracted before too long with the help of ongoing RSPB management. The latter two species already occur here. In winter, the berry-laden hawthorn bushes prove irresistible to Fieldfares and Redwings.

OTHER ANIMALS

Mammals include Muntjac Deer and Pygmy and Water Shrews. There are many aquatic insects, too, notably Great Diving Beetle and Water Stick Insect. Local villagers used to collect medicinal leeches from the mere to send to hospitals.

FLOWERS

Cowslips and Bee Orchids grow on the outcrops of chalk that are found on the reserve.

BIRDS THROUGH THE SEASONS

ALL YEAR: Little Grebe, Water Rail, Kingfisher (regular visitor), Sparrowhawk and Reed Bunting.

SPRING AND SUMMER: Turtle Dove, Sedge Warbler, Reed Warbler, Grasshopper Warbler, Willow Warbler, Chiffchaff, Blackcap, Lesser Whitethroat, Whitethroat and Spotted Flycatcher.

AUTUMN AND WINTER: A few wildfowl. Green Sandpiper, Redwing, Fieldfare, Siskin and Redpoll. Corn Buntings roost in the reedbed. Hen Harrier, Marsh Harrier and Bittern have made occasional visits.

ACCESS:

If approaching from the village of Fowlmere to the east, take the left-hand fork out of the village. The reserve is reached along a lane on the left by a cemetery.

DISABLED ACCESS:

A boardwalk allows wheelchair access for a short way through the reedbed, and one hide is accessible.

OTHER ATTRACTIONS

THE HISTORIC city of Cambridge has a variety of attractions. Just off the M11 at junction 10 is the Duxford's military air museum.

Fowlmere in winter.

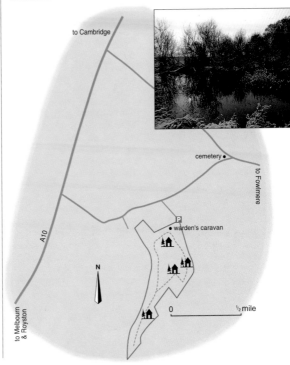

LYING IN the Yare Valley east of Norwich, the RSPB reserve of Strumpshaw Fen has all the main broadland habitats, from open water, reedbeds and carr to rough grazing marshes. Near by, the grazing marshes at Buckenham are the only regular wintering site for Bean Geese in Britain.

Wagtails to breed, are important for the few hundred Bean Geese that arrive in November, and which are best seen in December and January. These geese are of the western race *fabalis* and originate in central Sweden. Only occasionally are there influxes of the eastern *rossicus*

Bean Geese are best searched for in December and January.

A visit in May/June or in winter is likely to be most productive. A circular walk can be taken around the main part of the reserve, and there are a number of hides along the way.

race, usually associated with hard weather on the Continent. A hide on Buckenham Marshes assists in viewing the Geese, which are sometimes joined by a few White-fronted Geese.

BIRDS
The reedbeds support Bearded Tits, Marsh Harriers and sometimes Bitterns. It is hoped Bitterns may be encouraged to breed regularly. Cetti's Warblers favour the carr, but are more often heard than seen. A variety of wildfowl include Garganey, which nest in some years.

The grazing marshes, apart from attracting a few species of waders and Yellow

OTHER ANIMALS
The reserve is particularly good for seeing Swallowtail butterflies in June. The introduced Chinese Water Deer, although very shy, can sometimes be spotted from one of the hides.

FLOWERS
The fen has a rich flora, with many typical broadland species present.

BIRDS THROUGH THE SEASONS
ALL YEAR: Little Grebe, Great Crested Grebe, Grey Heron, Gadwall, Shoveler, Pochard, Tufted Duck, Water Rail, Snipe, Lapwing, Redshank, Kingfisher, Green, Great Spotted and Lesser Spotted Woodpeckers, Cetti's Warbler, Bearded Tit, Marsh Tit, Willow Tit, Nuthatch, Treecreeper, Reed Bunting.

SPRING AND SUMMER: Garganey, Marsh Harrier, Yellow Wagtail, Grasshopper Warbler, Reed Warbler, Sedge Warbler, Garden Warbler, Blackcap, Chiffchaff, Willow Warbler, Whitethroat, Lesser Whitethroat, Cuckoo and Spotted Flycatcher.

AUTUMN AND WINTER: Bean Geese, often a few White-fronted Geese and Wigeon (all on Buckenham Marshes), Teal, Pintail, Goldeneye, Ruddy Duck, Hen Harrier, Merlin, occasional Peregrine, Golden Plover, Short-eared Owl, occasional Great Grey

Shrike, Fieldfare, Redwing, Redpoll and Siskin.

ACCESS: From Norwich, take the A47 towards Great Yarmouth and turn off to Brundall. Pass through Brundall and under the railway bridge, then take the minor road named Low Road off to the right. After approximately half a mile, park in the car park by the railway line.

For the geese on Buckenham Marshes, take the minor roads to Buckenham station, cross over the railway line and follow the track down to the river. Then turn left and follow the river to the hide.

OTHER ATTRACTIONS

NEAR BY, Norwich boasts one of the best-preserved cathedrals in England. Great Yarmouth offers many of the usual seaside resort attractions for all the family.

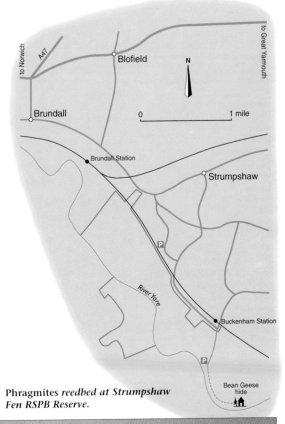

Phragmites *reedbed at Strumpshaw Fen RSPB Reserve.*

HICKLING IS the largest of the Norfolk Broads and just 3 miles from the coast. The broad was formed by man in the 12th and 13th centuries, when peat was excavated, leaving a shallow depression.

Vast areas of reeds surround open water, and wader scrapes have been created by the Norfolk Wildlife Trust. Surrounding the broad are areas of grazing marsh and woodlands.

BIRDS

The reedbeds come alive in spring to the songs of Reed and Sedge Warblers, while the distinctive 'ping, ping' call of the Bearded Tit is the best way of locating this species. Two of the rarer reedbed inhabitants are Marsh Harrier and Bittern. The best chance of seeing the Bittern at Hickling is when it is in flight; otherwise listen for its distinctive booming call which can carry a considerable distance.

From midsummer, when the reedbeds fall silent, attention turns to the more open areas where wildfowl begin to gather; by mid-winter a few thousand duck will have arrived. The muddy scrapes in spring and autumn are favoured by a good variety of passage waders, with Temminck's Stint being annual in May and often appearing in autumn too. During passage periods, Little Gulls and Black Terns hawk over the water, along with large numbers of hirundines and Swifts.

OTHER ANIMALS

One of Hickling's best-known inhabitants is the Swallowtail butterfly, on the wing between June and August. Water Shrew and Chinese Water Deer are two of the more interesting mammals, though both are rarely seen.

SITE GUIDE

Norfolk Wildlife Trust Reserve

This site has a number of trails of varying length leading through different habitats and to the broad itself. Boardwalks take you through reedbeds, good for Bearded Tits. A number of hides overlook small reed-fringed pools. The reserve is a good site for Swallowtail butterflies.

The trust runs boat trips out to distant hides which overlook Rushhill's and Coot Swim scrapes. There are few better ways of experiencing Hickling and its wildlife than taking the 2½-hour trip, which is by traditional reed-lighter boat. The scrapes attract a good variety of passage waders, including Temminck's Stints, Wood Sandpipers and Ruff.

ACCESS: From the A149, turn off to Hickling. In Hickling Green, take Stubb Road by the Greyhound pub. The reserve is well signposted from here. There is a charge for non-trust members. The visitor centre is open from 10am to 5pm from April to October, and from 10am to 4pm from November to March.

Boats for the water trail leave the Pleasure Boat Inn at Staithe, which is easily reached from Hickling Green. Boats depart at 10am and 2pm from May to September on Tuesdays, Wednesdays and Thursdays, and in June, July and August on Mondays and Fridays.

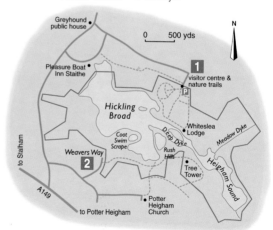

The boats are limited to 12 people and must be booked in advance. Tel: (01692) 598276 or book in person at the visitor centre on the reserve.

The Spoonbill is an almost annual visitor in spring.

When rarities turn up on the scrapes, a ferry service to and from the hides is usually operated.

 DISABLED ACCESS: Restricted to the boardwalks for wheelchair users. The disabled are accommodated on the boats for the water trail.

2

Weavers Way

Reached from Potter Heigham's church, this path runs alongside the reedbed. For a circular walk, turn right at the reedbed; you will eventually return to the church via farmland and a lane. Allow two to three hours to complete this route. This is another good site for Swallowtail butterflies.

ACCESS: Park at Potter Heigham's church, and take the lane down the left-hand side to a sharp left-hand turn. A footpath leads off along the edge of the field to a wood and the reserve boundary.

 DISABLED ACCESS: None.

BIRDS THROUGH THE SEASONS

ALL YEAR: Little Grebe, Great Crested Grebe, Bittern, Grey Heron, Gadwall, Shoveler, Pochard, Tufted Duck, Marsh Harrier, Sparrowhawk, Water Rail, Snipe, Barn Owl, Kingfisher, Green, Great Spotted and Lesser Spotted Woodpeckers, Cetti's Warbler (scarce) and Bearded Tit.
SPRING: Garganey, Osprey (rarely linger), Spoonbills are a rare but almost annual visitor, Hobby, Avocet, Ringed Plover, Little Stint, Temminck's Stint, Ruff, Black-tailed Godwit, Green, Common and Wood Sandpiper, Redshank, Spotted Redshank, Greenshank, Dunlin, Black Tern, Common Tern, Little Gull, Cuckoo, Yellow Wagtail, Whinchat and arrival of breeding warblers.
SUMMER: Breeding birds include Garganey, Grasshopper Warbler, Savi's Warbler (very scarce, absent in some years), Reed Warbler, Sedge Warbler, Blackcap, Willow Warbler and Chiffchaff.
AUTUMN: As for spring.
WINTER: Whooper Swan, Wigeon, Teal, Pintail, Scaup, Goldeneye, Hen Harrier, Short-eared Owl, Merlin, Ringed Plover, Golden Plover, Dunlin and occasional Great Grey Shrike.

 ACCESS: *See* site guide above.

DISABLED ACCESS: *See* site guide above.

OTHER ATTRACTIONS

T HE BROADS are popular with tourists in summer, many of them hiring pleasure boats to tour the waterways. Near Ranworth, north of the A47, is the Broadland Conservation Centre, open from April to October. The centre has a nature trail and displays on the history and natural history of the Broads.

Holme-next-the-Sea **5** **4** Thornham Titchwell A149
Overy Staithe A149 **3**
Blakeney Point **2**
Cley-next-the-Sea **1**
Burnham Market **Wells-next-the-Sea** Blakeney Salthouse
The Wash □ **Hunstanton**
Docking
0 _____ 3 miles
N
to Cromer
6 Snettisham
to King's Lynn   to Fakenham   to Fakenham
A148

A STRING of reserves lies along the north Norfolk coast, an area of outstanding natural beauty. Much of the coastline has a wild feel to it, with wide sandy beaches stretching to the horizon and backed by sand dunes, pine plantations and grazing marsh. There are reedbeds and brackish pools with wader scrapes, saltmarshes, heaths and the Wash, a vast area of mudflats. Such a diversity of habitats and its geographical position, acting as landfall for many migrants arriving from across the North Sea, make North Norfolk the bird-watching capital of Britain.

BIRDS
During winter, thousands of Pink-footed Geese arrive to graze on the coastal marshes and farm-land. These geese are joined by wintering raptors and a diverse range of wildfowl and waders. Snettisham plays host to a wildlife spectacular, when, as the tide sweeps across the Wash, tens of thousands of waders – mostly Knots – take to the air and descend on to the reserve to roost.

Offshore, there is always something of interest, with divers, grebes and seaduck located at traditional sites along the coast. The

beaches are a favoured haunt of Snow Buntings and Shorelarks. One of the more exotic visitors to this stretch of coast is the Waxwing, which in some years arrives in flocks from Scandinavia to adorn roadside berry bushes.

In spring and autumn, migrants abound and there are always rarities to seek out. When the weather has an easterly influence, drift migrants may include Bluethroats, Wrynecks and Red-backed Shrikes. In both seasons, wader hot spots such as Cley Marshes and Titchwell have a good selection of birds on offer. However, it is in autumn that the coast is at its best. Between August and October, scarce migrants are annual. These include Icterine, Barred and Yellow-browed Warblers, Red-breasted Flycatcher and Dotterel.

The reedbeds and wader scrapes become the breeding grounds in summer for Marsh Harriers, Bearded Tits, Avocets and the elusive Bittern. Most impressive are the large tern colonies on Blakeney Point and Scolt Head Island. Bird-watching is never dull along the north Norfolk coast, at whatever time of year you choose to visit.

Shorelark.

SITE GUIDE

Cley and Salthouse

The attractive village of Cley-next-the-Sea, complete with windmill, has been a bird-watching mecca for many years. Before the advent of the information services we enjoy today, news of rare birds nationally as well as locally was collated in Cley village at Nancy's Café, and before that at The George, where bird-watchers could find out 'what was about'. The East Bank on Cley Marshes was the place for meeting fellow bird-watchers. Times have changed, yet Cley still remains a focal point, and arguably can enjoy the title of 'Top British Bird Spot' on mainland Britain.

Cley Marshes Reserve, owned by the Norfolk Wildlife Trust (NWT), is the main attraction. The marsh was acquired in 1926 by Dr Sydney Long with the help of a number of donors, and led to the formation of the NWT. Hides overlook reedbeds, grazing marsh and wader scrapes.

BIRDS

Cley Marshes is probably the best place in the country for viewing passage waders. Temminck's Stints are annual in May, and in most years the rarer Kentish Plover is recorded from April onwards. Spotted Redshanks, Wood Sandpipers and Little Stints are just a few of a large supporting cast in spring. Return wader passage resumes in mid-July, when birds gather in much larger numbers than are seen in spring. Common, Green and Wood Sandpipers can be numerous in early autumn. By August, Curlew Sandpipers, Little Stints, Spotted Redshanks, Greenshanks, Ruffs and various other species grace the scrapes, and passage continues into October.

Sea-watching is most productive in autumn, particularly in north to north-westerly gales when skuas, terns, gulls, petrels and shearwaters can occur. Later in the year, gales may offer the chance of Little Auk.

During easterly winds, drift migrants can be expected, perhaps a Bluethroat in spring or an Icterine Warbler in autumn. Cley annually hosts some outstanding rarities. Wherever there is cover, it is worth checking for migrant passerines, but Walsey Hills is one of the more productive sites. Rare breeding birds include Avocets on the scrapes, and, in the reedbeds, Marsh Harriers and Bitterns. Garganey are an annual sight in spring.

Wander along the East Bank in spring and you have a good chance of hearing the foghorn-like booming of the Bittern, or the reeling of a Grasshopper Warbler. The East Bank is also a good spot for Bearded Tits and for abundant Reed and Sedge Warblers. Black Terns visit in May, as do Little Gulls, a few of which may remain throughout the summer.

Wildfowl dominate the winter scene, with flocks of Wigeon and Brent Geese grazing the marshes, these

Cley windmill.

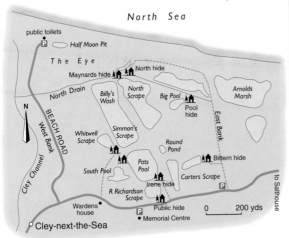

quartered by Hen Harriers and Short-eared Owls. Offshore, the Red-throated is the most likely diver, along with a few seaduck such as Red-breasted Merganser and Eider.

April/May and August/September are four of the best months, though a visit at any time will provide exciting bird-watching. Arnold's Marsh, viewable from the East Bank, attracts waders and a few ducks. The grazing marsh and pools of Salthouse to the east are favoured by many species and should not be ignored.

ACCESS: The reserve is open throughout the year daily, except Mondays (bank holidays excluded). Permits must be obtained from the visitor centre (free to NWT members), open from 10am to 5pm. From November to March, the centre is closed, and permits can be obtained from the warden at Watcher's Cottage. There is one public hide just to the east of the visitor centre, and the East Bank is a public footpath allowing views across the reserve. The reserve is situated just to the east of Cley village.

DISABLED ACCESS: Wheelchair-friendly boardwalks are currently being installed and new hides are being built. For an update on access, contact the visitor centre. Tel: 01263 740008.

2

Blakeney Point and Harbour

Blakeney Point was purchased by the National Trust in 1912. It lies at the end of a shingle ridge that runs from Weybourne, protecting the coastal marshes from the sea. The point is of most interest for its migrant birds and tern colonies.

BIRDS
A boat can be taken from Morston Quay to the point, but to do it justice it is necessary to walk the 3 miles from Cley along the shingle. For every two steps forward it feels that you are taking one back, so it is a hard slog! However, in August and September the bird-watching can be outstanding. During easterly winds, impressive falls are possible. Drift migrants from early August regularly include Wrynecks and the more numerous Pied Flycatchers, Redstarts and Willow Warblers. During September there is a good chance of seeing Red-breasted Flycatcher and Barred Warbler. Falls of Goldcrests and thrushes occur in late autumn.

Spring falls do occur, but not on the scale of those in

The colourful Bluethroat is an annual visitor to Blakeney Point.

autumn. Stunning spring plumage Bluethroats are possible in easterly winds, as are the occasional Icterine Warbler, Red-backed Shrike or Wryneck. The presence of migrants at either season is dependent on the weather; an easterly

An inquisitive Common Seal.

or north-easterly wind is best, but do not ignore south-easterlies, especially in spring. Migrants may occur anywhere where there is cover. Sites that are worth covering thoroughly include Halfway House, The Hood and Long Hills.

The tern colony consists of around 3000 pairs of Sandwich Terns, with 150 pairs of Common Terns, lesser numbers of Little Terns and a few pairs of Arctic Terns on the southern limit of their breeding range. The colonies can be viewed from

well-placed hides. If you take a boat out to the point in summer, it is unusual not to see Common and Grey Seals. Special seal trips are run from Blakeney Quay.

In winter, Blakeney Harbour attracts the typical estuarine species, in particular Wigeon and Brent Geese, plus waders such as Bar-tailed Godwit, Dunlin and Curlew.

 ACCESS: The point can be reached by walking along the shingle from Cley coastguards' car park, itself reached by taking the left turn just east of the village. Alternatively, boats can be taken in summer from Morston Quay, west of Blakeney.

3

Holkham and Wells

These two adjoining sites provide excellent bird-watching in autumn. The belt of pines was planted from 1850 onwards to act as a shelter, and runs from

the Wells Beach Road to the west of Holkham. At Holkham, there is a large coastal marsh.

 BIRDS
Wells Harbour and the sea off Holkham can be productive in winter for divers, grebes and seaduck. However, of the most interest are the belt of pines for migrants and rarities in autumn, and the marsh in winter for wintering geese.

The marsh is a reclaimed saltmarsh that was farmed before becoming a National Nature Reserve. The marshes now support breeding Redshank, Snipe, Lapwing, Avocet, Shoveler, Gadwall and Marsh Harrier, to name a few. In winter, thousands of Pink-footed and Brent Geese, and small numbers of White-fronted Geese graze the meadows. In the past few years, Wigeon have increased dramatically, with recent peaks of over 9000. Unfortunately, viewing is somewhat restricted, being confined to the A149 or from the pines.

In spring, the pines attract migrants, though in

Holkham Bay

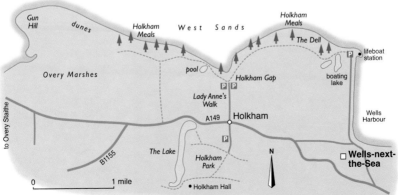

autumn the numbers and variety are greater. From August, chats, warblers and flycatchers start to appear. Winds with an easterly influence are needed for good numbers and for scarce drift migrants. Those that appear regularly in such conditions include Icterine and Barred Warblers, Red-backed Shrikes and Wrynecks. September is the month in which to search for Yellow-browed Warblers, which are found within the pines annually. By October, the variety will have decreased, but there is more chance of a vagrant such as Pallas's Warbler or Olive-backed Pipit. Influxes of Goldcrests, Firecrests and thrushes occur at this time.

OTHER ANIMALS
The dunes at Holkham support Natterjack Toads, one of our rarest amphibians. Butterflies include the Dark Green Fritillary and Grayling. In early spring, look out for the Brimstone and Orange Tip.

FLOWERS
Of interest in the pinewoods are the rare Creeping Lady's-tresses, a

small orchid with cream flowers which can be located in August.

ACCESS: There are two main access points. Take the road north from Wells alongside the harbour. Park at the end and proceed along the path.

At Holkham, the main access is via Lady Anne's Drive opposite Holkham Park. The marshes can also be viewed from the A149, but do not park on the road.

4

Titchwell
RSPB Reserve

Until the 17th century, when the land was drained and converted to farmland, Titchwell consisted entirely of saltmarsh. In 1953, however, the sea breached the sea wall and the land reverted to the saltmarsh it once was. Montagu's Harriers subsequently nested in the early 1970s, highlighting the site as a potential reserve. In 1973, the RSPB purchased 420 acres and built a wall preventing flooding

Natterjack Toad.

from the sea, thereby creating a brackish marsh.

There are a number of hides, excellent paths and a visitor centre.

BIRDS
A lagoon with much exposed mud attracts a good variety of passage waders and wintering wildfowl. Avocets breed on the muddy islands, arriving back in March. The autumn passage of waders is excellent, with similar species to those recorded at Cley. The neighbouring reedbed has breeding Marsh Harriers, Bearded Tits, Water Rails and Reed and Sedge Warblers. Much work is being done to attract the Bittern back as a regular breeding bird, as single birds are already sometimes present. In winter, the reedbed is used by roosting Hen Harriers.

The saltmarsh is of most interest in winter, when a regular flock of Twite can be located. The beach attracts waders, complementing those on the brackish marsh. Twittering flocks of Snow Buntings and, in some years, Shorelarks inhabit the edge of the dunes. Thornham Point, easily reached from the main part of the reserve by walking west along the beach, is one of the more reliable sites in Norfolk for Shorelarks. A few grebes, divers, seaduck and sometimes auks can be seen offshore.

The trees around the centre attract a few migrants and woodland birds.

ACCESS: The reserve lies just off the A149 between Titchwell and Thornham.

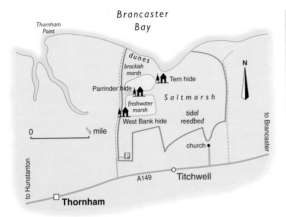

Brancaster Bay

Thornham Point

dunes

brackish marsh

Parrinder hide

Tern hide

freshwater marsh

West Bank hide

Saltmarsh

tidal reedbed

church

0   ½ mile

to Hunstanton

P

A149   Titchwell

Thornham

to Brancaster

N

owned by the Norfolk Wildlife Trust; and a small plot of land east of the Firs administered by the Norfolk Ornithologists' Association, where there is a bird observatory.

There are hides and a visitor centre, which is situated at the Firs. Board-walks alleviate erosion of the dunes by visitors, and well-marked paths allow the wooded areas to be explored.

Titchwell RSPB Reserve.

 DISABLED ACCESS: There is wheelchair access to most of the hides along good paths.

5

Holme

Holme's habitats include wader scrapes, Marram- and scrub-covered dunes, pines, grazing marsh and saltmarsh. Holme is separated politically into two blocks: Holme Dunes,

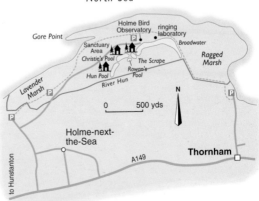

North Sea

Gore Point

Holme Bird Observatory   ringing laboratory

Broadwater

Sanctuary Area

Christie's Pool

The Scrape

Ragged Marsh

Hun Pool

Rowan's Pool

River Hun

Lavender Marsh

P

P

P

0   500 yds

N

Holme-next-the-Sea

A149   Thornham

to Hunstanton

BIRDS

Spring and autumn are the best times to visit, when there is a variety of migrants. Scarce drift migrants are regular, and each year a number of first-class rarities are recorded. Early spring sees the arrival of Chiffchaffs, Wheatears and Firecrests. By May, the commoner summer migrants may be joined by annually appearing drift migrants such as Bluethroat, Red-backed Shrike and Icterine Warbler. On some days, large numbers of birds may be migrating.

northerly or easterly winds often being productive. Wryneck, Red-backed Shrike, Red-breasted Flycatcher, and Barred, Icterine and Yellow-browed Warblers are all seen in most years. By late autumn, Goldcrests can be abundant and large movements of thrushes, finches and Skylarks occur. Waders, ducks and geese will be on the move offshore.

In winter, divers, grebes and seaduck such as Long-tailed Ducks, scoters, Eiders and Mergansers are regular. Brent Geese and Wigeon

Wryneck.

There is a lull in summer, when breeding birds include Shelducks and Avocets, and Yellow Wagtails, Snipe and Redshank all rear families on the grazing marsh. Offshore, Sandwich, Common and Little Terns pass, coming and going from breeding colonies near by. By mid-July, a few waders will be appearing and, by early August, the first Pied Flycatchers and Redstarts of the autumn are making an appearance. The numbers of warblers, chats and flycatchers are dependent on the weather,

graze the marshes, while raptors may include Short-eared Owls, resident Barn Owls, Merlin and Hen Harrier.

 OTHER ANIMALS

During summer, Common Lizards bask in the dunes, these also supporting the Natterjack Toads that were introduced in the 1980s. Hares favour the grasslands, while other mammals to look out for include Noctule and Pipistrelle Bats in summer.

ACCESS: Turn off the A149 towards the sea at the Hunstanton end of Holme village. Take the second turning on the right along a gravel track to the reserve. Park either at the western end of the reserve (on the left past the bungalows) or continue to the reserve's car park. A permit is required for non-members to visit both reserves, which are open from 10am to 5pm daily.

_____ **6** _____

Snettisham
RSPB Reserve

ONE OF Britain's greatest wildlife spectacles can be enjoyed at Snettisham. On each high tide from autumn through to spring, tens of thousands of waders are pushed off the vast expanse of mud on the Wash to roost on the RSPB reserve's gravel pits.

 BIRDS

Knot average over 80,000 birds each winter but have peaked at over 120,000. Also prominent are Dunlins, Redshanks and Oystercatchers. As the tide rises, clouds of waders take to the air, twisting and turning in unison. Once the mud is covered, they settle on the pits to roost. When these huge flocks rise together, there are few more impressive sites. To witness this spectacle it is imperative you plan your visit well. Spring tides are best, and while neap tides produce few birds they do provide the spectacle of wheeling flocks as the birds are pushed closer to the shore.

The Wash at low tide.

during the week in autumn and winter.

DISABLED ACCESS: Wheelchair access is possible to the first hide. However, contact the warden at the visitor centre for permission to drive to this point.

The Wash is the most important area of estuarine mudflat in Britain, annually supporting approximately 300,000 birds in winter. Many waders use the site as a refuelling point *en route* to and from their northern breeding grounds. In winter, wildfowl are also prominent. Thousands of Pink-footed Geese roost out on the mud, passing over Snettisham at dusk and then again at dawn. Brent Geese, Shelduck, Wigeon and Pintail are just a few of the species that occur in significant numbers.

The pits at Snettisham often attract seaduck such as Scaup, Long-tailed Duck and Red-breasted Merganser. On occasions, divers and the rarer grebes turn up and, from late October, Little Auks are a possibility if there are large numbers of them in the North Sea. Common Terns, Ringed Plovers and Oystercatchers nest on and around the pits in summer.

A number of hides overlook the pits, the furthest hide being one of the best for viewing roosting waders. Occasionally, Twite and Snow Bunting may be encountered along the foreshore, and hunting raptors such as Hen Harrier, Merlin and Short-eared Owl are regular.

See also Hunstanton and Heacham, listed under Additional Sites.

ACCESS: The reserve is open at all times. From the A149 at Snettisham, take a minor road to the caravan park and large car park. From here, walk along the shore past the holiday chalets to the reserve. There is a visitor centre open from 10am to 4pm at weekends throughout the year, and

BIRDS THROUGH THE SEASONS

ALL YEAR: Little Grebe, Bittern (Cley), Grey Heron, feral Greylag and Canada Geese, Egyptian Goose (Cley and Holkham), Gadwall, Shoveler, Tufted Duck, Sparrowhawk, Water Rail, Lapwing, Snipe, Redshank, Ringed Plover, Oystercatcher, Black-headed Gull, Barn Owl, Little Owl, Tawny Owl, Kingfisher, Lesser Spotted, Great Spotted and Green Woodpeckers, Stonechat,

Map: to Hunstanton, B1454, N, The Wash, Snettisham Scalp, BEACH ROAD, Snettisham, caravan site, Wolferton Creek, A149, Dersingham, B1440, 0   1 mile, B1439, to King's Lynn

Goldcrest, Bearded Tit (Cley, Titchwell), Marsh Tit, Willow Tit, Corn Bunting, Reed Bunting and Crossbill (Holkham).

SPRING: Spoonbill (annual), Shelduck, Garganey (Cley), Shoveler, Tufted Duck, Eider, Common Scoter, Red-breasted Merganser, Marsh Harrier, Hobby, Avocet, Little Ringed Plover, Kentish Plover (Cley), Dotterel, Golden Plover, Grey Plover, Sanderling, Little Stint, Temminck's Stint, Curlew Sandpiper, Dunlin, Knot, Ruff, Black-tailed and Bar-tailed Godwits, Whimbrel, Curlew, Spotted Redshank, Greenshank, Green, Wood and Common Sandpipers, Turnstone, Sandwich, Common, Arctic, Little and Black Terns, Yellow Wagtail, Tree Pipit, Bluethroat (possible in May), Redstart, Whinchat, Stonechat, Wheatear, Ring Ouzel, Chiffchaff, Willow Warbler, Wood Warbler (scarce passage migrant), Grasshopper Warbler, Savi's Warbler (very rare), Sedge Warbler, Reed Warbler, Lesser Whitethroat, Whitethroat, Blackcap, Firecrest, Pied Flycatcher (scarce), Spotted Flycatcher.

SUMMER: Breeding birds include tern colonies at Blakeney. In reedbeds; Marsh Harrier, Bittern and Bearded Tits. Little Gulls often at Cley. Most of the above-mentioned warblers breed. A few waders summer and Avocets breed.

AUTUMN: Same species as in spring but in higher numbers. Waders in particular are much more abundant. Redstarts and Pied Flycatchers are much more numerous. Additional species after easterlies may include Wryneck, Black Redstart, Icterine, Barred and Yellow-browed Warblers, Red-breasted Flycatcher and Red-backed Shrike. Offshore: auks, divers, grebes, skuas, terns, gulls and waders may be moving. During rough weather, there is a chance of shearwaters and petrels. Little Auks in late autumn. Falls of Goldcrests in late autumn. Thrush movements from mid-October.

WINTER: Offshore: Red-throated Diver, Great Northern and Black-throated Divers (scarce), Great Crested, Red-necked and Slavonian Grebes, Long-tailed Duck, Velvet and Common Scoters, Red-breasted Merganser, Eider, Scaup, and a few Guillemots and Razorbills. Pink-footed, Brent and a few White-fronted Geese, Shelduck, Wigeon, Teal, Shoveler, Gadwall, Pochard, Tufted Duck, Goldeneye, Hen Harrier, Merlin, Peregrine, Oystercatcher, Grey Plover, Golden Plover, Knot, Dunlin, Bar-tailed and Black-tailed Godwits, Sanderling, Curlew, Redshank, Spotted Redshank (very few), Turnstone, Short-eared Owl, Shorelark, Rock Pipit, Stonechat, Twite, and Lapland and Snow Buntings.

 ACCESS:
See site guide.

 DISABLED ACCESS:
See site guide.

OTHER ATTRACTIONS

THE WILD north Norfolk coast receives over one million visitors a year. The long sandy beaches are popular with walkers, though the sea can be decidedly chilly for bathing. There are quaint villages such as Blakeney, characterised by flint cottages. Trips to see the seals leave Blakeney and Morston during summer, and the harbours are popular with sailors.

The royal Sandringham estate is a popular attraction, and the house is open to the public when members of the royal family are not in residence. Penthorpe Waterfowl Park near Fakenham has over 100 species of wildfowl, and makes a good day out for a family.

Cley Reserve in one of the best sites for Garganey in spring.

CAMBRIDGE-SHIRE

Nene Washes
RSPB Reserve

This reserve is a mosaic of wet meadows, ditches and marsh lying between the River Nene and Morton's Leam. In winter, Hen Harriers and Merlins are joined by Bewick's Swans and a good variety of dabbling ducks. Passage waders include Ruff and Whimbrel. The typical wet-meadow breeding species are graced by the rare Black-tailed Godwit and Garganey. There are no facilities but the drove can be walked. The reserve is situated 5 miles east of Peterborough; take the B1040 Whittlesey–Thorney road. Just before the bridge over the River Nene, there is a grassy lay-by on the right; you can walk from here.

ESSEX

Fingeringhoe Wick

This Essex Wildlife Trust Reserve is centred around disused gravel pits, which attract a variety of wildfowl, waders and passage migrants. The foreshore along the River Colne provides feeding for large numbers of wintering estuarine wildfowl and waders. There are hides, a visitor centre and facilities for the disabled. The reserve is open daily, except Mondays, from 9am to 4.30pm. From Colchester, take the B1025 to Abberton. Turn off to Fingeringhoe and then on to a road signposted to South Green. The reserve is well signposted from here.

Stour Estuary
RSPB Reserve

Situated on the border of Essex and Suffolk border, this reserve incorporates the shallow Stour Estuary and Stour Wood, and comprises oak and Sweet Chestnut coppice. The estuary is best in winter, and is favoured by Wigeon, Pintail and Brent Geese, while there is a good variety of estuarine waders – Black-tailed Godwits and Dunlin in particular. The woodland has breeding Nightingales and all three species of woodpecker. Dormice, White Admiral butterflies and the wild Service tree are some of the other interesting inhabitants of the wood. There are three hides, but it can be wet underfoot. The reserve lies west of Harwich, and is reached off the B1352 Manningtree–Ramsey road, 1 mile east of Wrabness village.

Walton-on-the-Naze

The Naze can be good in autumn for migrants, especially after easterly winds. Park in the cliff-top car park north of the town and proceed north, checking the bushes.

NORFOLK

Berney Marshes and Breydon Water
RSPB Reserves

Breydon water is a vast expanse of tidal mudflats, surrounded by dykes and grazing marsh. The area can seem quite daunting to cover, but the bird-watching can be excellent. Wildfowl and waders, along with wintering raptors, are the main attractions. Berney Marshes are best visited by train from Great Yarmouth. Disembark at Berney Arms Halt, and return on a 4-mile walk along the Weavers Way. There is limited parking at the Asda superstore in Yarmouth.

Hunstanton and Heacham

These two neighbouring resorts, on the eastern side of the Wash, are excellent for divers, grebes and seaduck in winter. Hunstanton, famous for its coloured cliffs, can also be a good sea-watching site. Purple Sandpipers can be seen below the cliffs in winter and Fulmars nest in them. View from the promenade at the top of the cliffs, and from the beach at Heacham.

Scolt Head Island

Situated on the north Norfolk coast, this island of sand dunes bordered by saltmarsh is a National Nature Reserve. It is of most interest for its large tern colonies. In winter, the saltings support estuarine wildfowl and waders, with large numbers of Brent Geese. Access is by boat from Brancaster Staithe. The tern colonies should be avoided during the breeding season.

Surlingham Church Marsh

RSPB Reserve

This is a small broadland reserve on the south bank of the River Yare. Breeding birds include Little Ringed Plover, Common Tern and various warblers. Marsh Harriers and, in winter Hen Harriers visit regularly. Two hides overlook the marsh and pools. Take the A146 Norwich–Lowestoft road, and then take the minor roads to Surlingham. Park at the church and enter the reserve from here.

SUFFOLK

Alde Estuary

Reached along footpaths from Aldeburgh, the estuary regularly attracts over 700 wintering Avocets, along with Pintail and Wigeon and the commoner estuarine waders.

Boyton Marshes

RSPB Reserve

Grazing marsh and salt-marsh attract estuarine birds. Marsh Harriers occasionally hunt over the reserve, which overlooks Havergate Island. Footpaths cross the marshes, which are reached from along the river at Boyton.

Landguard Point

Bordered by Felixstowe Docks, Landguard is certainly not picturesque. However, the bird-watching in spring and autumn can be excellent, with a wide range of migrants recorded annually, including rarities. The area is managed as a nature reserve by the Suffolk Wildlife Trust, and there is a bird observatory, established in 1983. Take the A14 to the south of Felixstowe almost to the port, turn down Manor Terrace, parking in the car park at the end.

North Warren

RSPB Reserve

North Warren, between Thorpeness and Aldeburgh, has coastal grazing marshes, woodland and heath. A wide variety of birds range from wintering Bewick's Swans, White-fronted Geese and various ducks to breeding wildfowl, waders, Woodlarks, Kingfishers and Yellow Wagtails. In spring, Garganey and Ruff are regular, as are a number of passage migrants in autumn.

Both Purple and Green Hairstreak butterflies occur, and Adders frequent the heaths. Public footpaths cross the reserve, and can be reached from either Aldeburgh or Thorpeness. The adjoining coast road allows views across the marshes.

Wicken Fen

The fen lays claim to being the oldest nature reserve in Britain, and is managed by the National Trust. In winter, Hen Harriers sometimes roost, and Short-eared Owls and Merlins are regular. A good variety of summer migrants breed, including Grasshopper Warbler. However, the fen is best known for its abundance of plants and insects. From the A10 north of Cambridge, take the A1123 towards Wicken. The reserve is signposted as you enter the village.

Wolves Wood

RSPB Reserve

Wolves Wood is a small mixed deciduous woodland, attractive to Nightingales and a variety of woodland birds. Hawfinches occasionally breed, and both Lesser Spotted and Great Spotted Woodpeckers are residents. Interesting plants include Herb Paris, Yellow Archangel and Violet Helleborine. White-letter and Purple Hairstreaks are two of over 20 species of butterfly regularly recorded. The wood is accessed off the A1071, 2 miles east of Hadleigh.

NORTHERN ENGLAND

67 – 79

For the purpose of this guide, the North covers the area south of the Scottish border as far as a line running between the Wash in the east and the Dee Estuary in the west. Within this region there are some outstanding areas of natural beauty, including the upland areas of the Pennines, the North York Moors and the Lake District, and the Northumberland coast.

The Northern region's coastline is perhaps of most interest to bird-watchers. The east coast, especially Spurn Head and Flamborough Head, offers some of the best migrant hot spots in Britain, although both coasts have a reputation for excellent sea-watching opportunities.

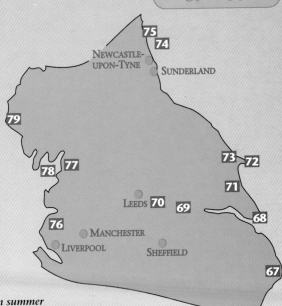

A visit to the Farne Islands in summer will guarantee close encounters with Arctic Terns!

Northumberland is home to one of our most popular seabird cities, the Farne Islands, renowned for their birds since the days of St Cuthbert. On the west coast, Morecambe Bay is second only to the Wash in its importance for passage and wintering wildfowl and waders, while neighbouring Leighton Moss is the British stronghold of the Bittern.

Many of the northern rivers support trout and salmon, prey for the Otter that can regularly be seen on the lowland reserve of Leighton Moss. Red and Roe Deer are found across much of the region, and in places the Red Squirrel and a few Pine Marten survive. The Northern region forms the southern and northern boundaries for some summer migrant birds, and for many plant and insect species.

GIBRALTAR POINT Local Nature Reserve extends from the Wash for 3 miles along the Lincolnshire coast to Skegness. Saltmarsh, sand dunes, scrub and freshwater marsh are the main habitats found on the reserve.

BIRDS

Visible migration can be witnessed during spring and autumn, when a variety of chats, warblers and flycatchers pass through. Movements of thrushes, buntings and finches can be impressive in late autumn. To observe birds on the move, an early morning visit to the Mill Hill observation platform is recommended. As at all migration watchpoints, sightings depend on weather conditions. Poor visibility and easterly or south-easterly winds can produce falls, which may include scarce drift migrants such as Bluethroat, Wryneck or, more likely, Pied Flycatcher and Ring Ouzel.

Mill Hill, the highest point on the dunes.

In autumn, Red-backed Shrike, Red-breasted Flycatcher, and Icterine and Barred Warblers can appear in the right conditions.

A good range of birds can be found in winter, including raptors, Snow Buntings and Twite. At high tide, large numbers of waders are pushed from their feeding grounds in the Wash up on to the spit to roost, while offshore you should look for divers, grebes and seaduck.

Little Terns breed close by, and they often fish over the lagoon. By mid-July, the Fenland Lagoon is attracting waders such as Wood Sandpiper, Ruff and Spotted Redshank.

FLOWERS

Both the saltmarsh and dune grasslands support a specialised flora. The Sea Buckthorn, a common shrub at Gibraltar Point, is restricted to the east coast. It provides cover for migrants, and its orange berries are a food source for thrushes in autumn and winter. Sea Lavender adds colour to the saltmarsh from late July to September, and Pyramidal Orchids can be found on the freshwater marsh. Name-plates assist visitors not familiar with the more common plants.

An information centre, field station and bird observatory serve the visitor. From the visitor centre, a walk south will take you to the Wash viewpoint. A brick-built hut with picture windows provides a dry and draught-free haven; on a clear day you can see the white cliffs of Hunstanton on the north Norfolk coast, 13 miles south across the Wash.

A path runs from the front of the visitor centre across an area of saltmarsh lying between the east and west sand dunes. These dunes run roughly parallel from north to south, and are the main topographical feature of the reserve. Turn right at the end of this track to reach the bird observatory and spit. Alternatively, follow the path north for the lagoons, marsh, hides and Mill Hill.

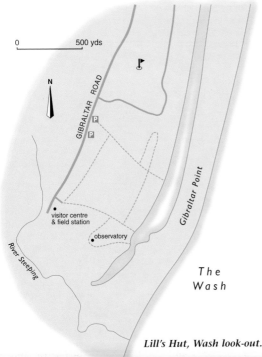

Lill's Hut, Wash look-out.

large numbers of Dunlin and Knot in the Wash.
AUTUMN: As for spring, scarce drift migrants may include Red-backed Shrike, Red-breasted Flycatcher, Bluethroat and Barred and Icterine Warblers. Skuas, gulls, wildfowl and waders occur in the Wash. Late autumn can produce large thrush movements.
WINTER: Hen Harrier and Short-eared Owl are regular. Twite and Snow Buntings occur on the saltmarsh, and divers, grebes and seaduck offshore. Waders roost on the spit at high tide; those using the Wash include Knot, Dunlin, Oystercatcher, Curlew, Bar-tailed Godwit, Grey Plover and Redshank.

ACCESS: The reserve is well signposted from the centre of Skegness. Take the coast road, which runs alongside the golf course, to the pay and display car park at the end. The visitor centre is open daily between May and October, and at weekends for the rest of the year.

There is a bird observatory and a field station with accommodation for up to 28 people. Further information from Gibraltar Point Field Station, Skegness, Lincolnshire PE24 4SU.

DISABLED ACCESS: Wheelchair access is possible in the vicinity of the visitor centre.

OTHER ATTRACTIONS

THE SEASIDE resort of Skegness is close by. The Skegness Seal Sanctuary, along the promenade, is an ideal attraction for children.

BIRDS THROUGH THE SEASONS

SPRING: Migrants will include warblers, chats and flycatchers, plus the chance of a Bluethroat. Waders include Greenshank and Whimbrel. Poor visibility with an easterly or south-easterly wind may produce falls.
SUMMER: Little Terns breed. Returning waders by the end of July may include Curlew Sandpiper, Wood Sandpiper, Black-tailed Godwit, Ruff and Spotted Redshank on the mere, and

THE SPURN Peninsula, a shingle and sand spit covered in Marram Grass and Sea Buckthorn, is one of the top migration watch-points in Europe. At its narrowest, at the Neck, it is just a few yards across, before gradually widening to the head. A road runs along the 3½-mile spit to the head, where there is a pilots' launch, and coastguard's and lifeboat station. The spit is owned by the Yorkshire Wildlife Trust, and a bird observatory has operated here since 1946, the first to be established on mainland Britain.

The current spit is probably the fifth to have existed since records began. A 250-year cycle of breaching followed by regrowth means that Spurn may now be on borrowed time. Sea defences have been erected to try to ensure that the head does not become cut off, yet during storms the road can become flooded and covered with sand.

During February 1996 storms broke through the Neck, washing away the road. At the time of writing there are no plans to rebuild. To enable access a moveable roadway has been introduced.

BIRDS

Spring and autumn are the optimum times to visit. In early spring, large numbers of our wintering birds may be on the move to mainland Europe. Thousands of Starlings, Chaffinches, Rooks, Jackdaws and Lapwings can pass on some days. Later in spring, hirundines and Swifts, and various chats, flycatchers and warblers arrive.

Offshore between March and May, divers, grebes, gulls, terns and waders will be on the move, and will be visible from the Neck in favourable conditions.

Spurn is at its best in autumn. The Neck is the best spot in both seasons to view visible migration, and is probably the best site in Britain for this. Early mornings are usually most productive, though birds can be on the move all day. As the birds become funnelled along the Neck, they pass low overhead and along the shore. Hirundines, wagtails, finches, pipits and Skylarks are some of the species that can pass by. August and September are prime months for Redstarts,

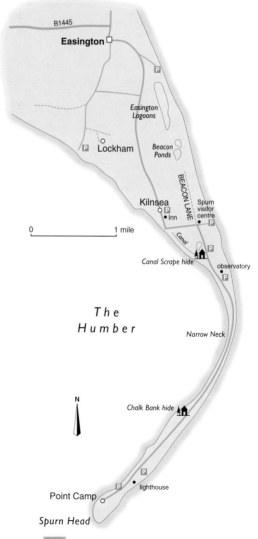

B1445

Easington

Easington Lagoons

Lockham

Beacon Ponds

BEACON LANE

Kilnsea
Inn

Spurn visitor centre

0   1 mile

Canal

Canal Scrape hide

observatory

The Humber

Narrow Neck

N

Chalk Bank hide

Point Camp

lighthouse

Spurn Head

Spurn Head; will it soon be an island?

Pied Flycatchers, Whinchats, Wheatears and warblers. The head and bushes along the spit can be alive with birds, especially after easterly winds, and such falls often contain drift migrants such as Barred and Icterine Warblers, Red-backed Shrike and Wryneck. During October and November, spectacular arrivals of thrushes, Starlings and finches may occur. Goldcrests, a few Firecrests, Long-eared Owls and Woodcocks are all recorded at this time.

Sea-watching can be excellent in autumn. There are hides for sea-watching located behind the observatory and a concrete shelter that gives some protection on the Neck.

Winter can be bleak and birdless, but occasionally hard-weather movements of Skylarks, finches, buntings and Starlings can be impressive. A variety of wildfowl and waders feed out on the Humber. At Chalk Bank there is a hide that looks out on to a wader roost, which is best visited up to two hours before high tide, when it consists mainly of Oystercatchers and the common estuarine species.

Just before the entrance gate to the spit, a hide looks over a scrape attractive to passage waders such as Little Stint and Greenshank. Travel a little further north to the caravan park, and a lane bordered by hedges running to the north. This is Beacon Lane and is a good site for searching out migrants. Beacon Ponds and Easington Lagoon to the north can be productive for wildfowl and waders.

OTHER ANIMALS
In summer, Harbour Porpoises are occasionally seen offshore, and Grey and Common Seals are often observed on sandbanks.

FLOWERS
Spurn has an interesting flora, including Pyramidal Orchid, Yellow Wort and Common Centaury. Sea Buckthorn covers the peninsula, its orange berries a welcome food source for birds in autumn and winter.

BIRDS THROUGH THE SEASONS
ALL YEAR: Ringed Plover, Wren, Tree Sparrow, Greenfinch, Linnet, Yellowhammer, Reed Bunting and Corn Bunting. SPRING: Migrants may include Sparrowhawk, Merlin, Hobby, Wood Pigeon, Turtle Dove, Cuckoo, Swift, Wryneck, Skylark, Sand Martin, Swallow, House Martin, Tree and Meadow Pipits, Yellow, Grey and Pied Wagtails, Robin, Nightingale, Bluethroat (after easterly winds in May), Black Redstart, Redstart, Whinchat, Stonechat, Wheatear, Ring Ouzel, Grasshopper, Sedge and Reed Warblers, Lesser Whitethroat, Whitethroat, Garden Warbler, Blackcap, Chiffchaff, Willow Warbler, Goldcrest, Firecrest, Spotted Flycatcher, Pied Flycatcher, Chaffinch, Greenfinch, Goldfinch, Siskin, Linnet, Redpoll, Bullfinch,

Yellowhammer and Reed Bunting. Passing seabirds can include Arctic, Common, Sandwich, Little and Black Terns, and gulls and skuas. Waders on the Humber are as for winter, and passage waders include Whimbrel, Greenshank and Common Sandpiper.
SUMMER: Breeding birds include Sedge Warbler and Whitethroat. A few waders occur on the Humber.
AUTUMN: As listed for spring, with the addition of Ruff, Little Stint, Curlew Sandpiper, Wood Sandpiper and Jack Snipe. Offshore, sea-watching in north-westerly to north-easterly

Spectacular arrivals of Fieldfares may occur during late autumn.

winds may produce Leach's and British Storm-petrels, skuas, auks and, regularly, Sooty Shearwater. Little Auks from October. Passerines include Blackbird, Robin, Fieldfare and Redwing, sometimes in large numbers plus Goldcrest, Firecrest and Pied Flycatcher. The following are annual: Icterine, Barred and Yellow-browed Warblers, Red-breasted Flycatcher, Red-backed and Great Grey Shrike and, annually, vagrants from the east.
WINTER: In the Humber and offshore: Red-throated Diver, Great Crested Grebe, Brent Goose, Wigeon, Teal, Mallard, Pintail, Tufted Duck, Goldeneye, Eider, Common Scoter, Red-breasted Merganser,

Guillemot, Razorbill, Kittiwake, Bar-tailed Godwit, Curlew, Oystercatcher, Dunlin, Knot, Grey Plover, Redshank and Turnstone. Inland: Golden Plover.

ACCESS: Leave Hull on the A1033, and at Patrington take the B1445 to Easington. From Easington take the minor road to Spurn Head, where, just before the entrance on the right, there is a car park and hide by the Canal Scrape. For the head, either drive to the old lighthouse where there is parking, or park by the observatory and visitor centre inside the main gate. There is a charge for cars.

For Easington Lagoons and Beacon Ponds, park in the cliff-top car park just to the south of Easington, reached by taking the turning on the left south of the village. Walk south from here. Alternatively, continue to Kilnsea, pass the Crown and Anchor pub and continue to the Blue Bell. Park here and proceed north along Beacon Lane. The Spurn Point Visitor Centre is located at the Blue Bell, and is worth a look if it is open.

DISABLED ACCESS: The Canal Scrape Hide is accessible to a wheelchair. Otherwise, wheelchairs are restricted to the roads.

OTHER ATTRACTIONS

H ULL IS a good shopping centre and has many museums and galleries. It is Britain's third-largest port. There are a number of pleasant pubs in the Spurn area, and there is plentiful B&B accommodation in Easington.

BLACKTOFT SANDS lies at the head of the River Humber where the Ouse and Trent rivers meet. A large tidal reedbed, lagoons and rough grazing marsh annually attract approximately 180 species.

BIRDS
The reserve has year-round appeal, but is particularly good for waders

Marsh Harriers pass through on passage and breed. Bearded Tits fluctuate widely in their numbers, but are at their most abundant in autumn, when the young of the year swell the population. Bearded Tits undergo what are known as irruptive movements. In autumn, a flock will suddenly rise from the reedbed, calling

Blacktoft Sands RSPB Reserve.

in autumn. It is necessary to visit at high tide for the best variety and highest numbers of birds. At low tide, the scrapes can be almost empty as birds move out on to the Humber to feed. Some of the typical species present from mid-July include Spotted Redshanks, Little Stints, Ruffs and Wood Sandpipers. Rare waders turn up annually and have included Red-necked Stint and Hudsonian Godwit.

During the winter, wildfowl numbers can be high. Dabbling ducks are most numerous, inhabiting the lagoons and grazing marsh. Pink-footed Geese sometimes overfly the reserve. Hen Harriers roost in the reedbed, while Merlins and the occasional Peregrine hunt over the reserve and surrounding fields.

excitedly before heading off elsewhere to winter.

OTHER ANIMALS
Water Voles and Water Shrews frequent the waterways. Hares and Roe Deer are easier to see, and during summer evenings look out for the small Pipistrelle and larger Noctule Bat. Insects include some of the rare reed-loving Wainscot moths, and around 20 species of butterfly and 10 species of dragonfly.

Reedbed at Blacktoft Sands visitor centre.

BIRDS THROUGH THE SEASONS

ALL YEAR: Little Grebe, Cormorant, Grey Heron, Shelduck, Gadwall, Teal, Shoveler, Pochard, Tufted Duck, Sparrowhawk, Kestrel, Water Rail, Moorhen, Coot, Lapwing, Dunlin, Redshank, Barn Owl, Bearded Tit, Reed Bunting and Corn Bunting.
SPRING: Occasional Garganey, Marsh Harrier, Hobby, Oystercatcher, Ringed Plover, Knot, Sanderling, Curlew Sandpiper, Ruff, Little Stint, Black-tailed and Bar-tailed Godwit, Whimbrel, Curlew, Spotted Redshank, Greenshank, Green, Wood and Common Sandpipers, Little Gull, Common and Black Tern, Yellow Wagtail, Whinchat and Wheatear.
SUMMER: Marsh Harrier, Avocet, Little Ringed Plover, Ruff, Turtle Dove, Cuckoo, Swift, Sand Martin, Swallow, House Martin, Grasshopper and Sedge and Reed Warblers.
AUTUMN: As for spring, plus a good chance of a rare wader. Also Grey Wagtail and Goldcrest.
WINTER: Occasional visits by Bittern, Bewick's and Whooper Swans and overflying Pink-footed Geese. Regulars include Wigeon, Pintail, Goldeneye, Hen Harrier, Merlin, Peregrine, Short-eared Owl, Golden Plover, Grey Plover, Snipe, Water and Rock Pipit, Stonechat, and thrushes.

ACCESS: From Goole, take the A161 east to Swinefleet. Turn left here for Reedness, continuing along this road to Ousefleet. The reserve is on the left 1½ miles beyond the village, and is open daily from 9am. There are six hides and a visitor reception.

DISABLED ACCESS: Most of the hides are accessible to wheelchair users.

OTHER ATTRACTIONS

YORK IS not to be missed, home of York Minster, Britain's largest cathedral, and the National Railway Museum.

FAIRBURN INGS stretches west from below the village of Fairburn. The lakes were formed through mining subsidence, and adjoining them are patches of deciduous woodland, pools and flashes among grazing marsh.

🦆 BIRDS

A good range of species can be seen throughout the year, but Fairburn is best in winter for its wintering wildfowl. A regular herd of Whooper Swans is joined by Mallard, Teal, Tufted Ducks and Pochard, with small numbers of Shoveler, Pintail, Gadwall and Goldeneye. Goosanders are regular and, in cold weather, may be joined by Smew and perhaps one of the rarer grebes or divers.

A good variety of migrants is recorded on passage, including Black Terns and Little Gulls, and waders such as Green Sandpiper and Greenshank. Passerines include wagtails, chats and warblers. On dull, damp days during summer, large concentrations of Swifts can appear. In late summer, Yellow Wagtails and Swallows roost.

BIRDS THROUGH THE SEASONS

ALL YEAR: Great Crested and Little Grebes, Mute Swan, Mallard, Gadwall, Tufted Duck, Sparrowhawk, Red-legged and Grey Partridge, Moorhen, Coot, Lapwing, Redshank, Snipe, Little Owl, Kingfisher, Reed Bunting and Corn Bunting. SPRING: Passage birds may include Garganey, Osprey, Common, Arctic and Black

In late summer Swallows roost in the reserve.

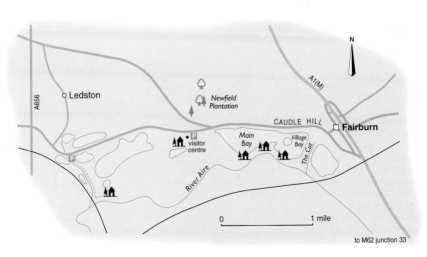

Male Teal.

Terns, Little Gull, Yellow Wagtail, Redstart, Whinchat and Wheatear. Passage waders may include Common, Green and Wood Sandpiper, Greenshank and Spotted Redshank.
SUMMER: Breeding birds include Little Ringed Plover and Common Tern. Garganey are sometimes present. Swifts and hirundines can be abundant on the reserve.
AUTUMN: As for spring. Yellow Wagtails and Swallows roost. Passage waders are more numerous than in spring, and might include Little Stint, Curlew Sandpiper and Ruff.
WINTER: Rarer grebes, divers and sawbills are occasional. Regulars include Whooper Swan, Goosander, Wigeon, Teal, Pintail, Goldeneye, Golden Plover, Redwing, Fieldfare, Redpoll and Siskin. A large mixed gull roost may include Mediterranean Gull and occasional Glaucous or Iceland Gull.

ACCESS: Fairburn lies beside the A1, a few miles north of the M62 junction. Leave the A1 at Fairburn and drive into the village. *See* map for further directions. There are three main parking areas. The first two allow access to the lakes, where there are three public hides, the third to a hide overlooking the flashes. The information centre is open at weekends and on bank holidays from 10am to 5pm.

DISABLED ACCESS: The lakes can be viewed from lay-bys. At the second car-parking area by the information centre there is a boardwalk and hide overlooking a pool, accessible to wheelchairs.

OTHER ATTRACTIONS

THE SPA town of Harrogate is near by. Harewood House, between Harrogate and Leeds, is one of the country's most impressive stately homes, its grounds housing a bird garden with over 100 species. Haworth, to the west of Leeds, is where the Brontës lived. The parsonage is now a museum furnished as it was when they lived there.

HORNSEA MERE is the largest natural lake in Yorkshire. Because it lies less than a mile from the coast, it attracts large numbers of wintering wildfowl and a variety of passage migrants.

The lake is very shallow and is rich in nutrients, leading to an abundance of insect and plant life. This rich food source ensures a breeding population of several species of waterfowl.

There are two main areas from which to view the mere: either the boating point on the eastern side, or from a public footpath along the southern shore. The latter allows a limited amount of walking and reasonable views of most of the mere.

BIRDS

During late summer, Little Gulls arrive to feed over the mere. This gathering can number up to 200, with August being the peak month. Spring and autumn see a good scattering of migrant passerines. Large numbers of hirundines, Swifts and terns can gather over the mere, with Black Tern being regular. The limited amount of mud exposed in autumn attracts passage waders.

Ducks are abundant in winter. The mere is important as a wintering site for Goldeneye and Gadwall. Goosanders are frequent visitors, whereas Red-throated Diver, seaduck and the rarer grebes occur occasionally, generally in hard weather.

BIRDS THROUGH THE SEASONS

ALL YEAR: Great Crested Grebe, Little Grebe, Mute Swan, feral Greylag and Canada Geese, Gadwall, Teal, Mallard, Shoveler, Pochard, Tufted Duck, Ruddy Duck, Sparrowhawk,

The mere is an important wintering site for Gadwall.

Great Spotted Woodpecker and Kingfisher.
SPRING: Occasional Garganey, Marsh Harrier, Osprey, Green, Wood and Common Sandpipers, Greenshank, Dunlin, Curlew Sandpiper, Little Stint, Little Gull, Common, Arctic and Black Terns, Rock Pipit, Yellow Wagtail, Whinchat, Wheatear and warblers.
SUMMER: Hirundines and Swifts feed over the mere, and the former roost in the reedbed. Sedge and Reed Warblers breed. Little Gulls and returning waders appear.

Great Crested Grebes breed at Hornsea Mere.
(Left) Golden Plover.

AUTUMN: As for spring. Little Gulls peak in August. Hobby may be attracted by roosting hirundines. Passerine migrants in addition to those seen in spring may include Redstart, Pied Flycatcher and Goldcrest.
WINTER: Occasional divers, rarer grebes and seaduck.

Regulars include Wigeon, Gadwall, Teal, Pintail, Shoveler, Pochard, Tufted Duck, Goldeneye, Goosander, Ruddy Duck, Golden Plover, Lapwing, Dunlin and Snipe. Gulls roost and may include a Glaucous or Iceland Gull. Bearded Tits occasionally appear, plus Redpoll, Siskin and Corn Bunting.

Access: There are two access points. If entering Hornsea from the south on the B1242 to view the south side, take Hull Road on the left opposite a garage. After half a mile, park in Mere View Avenue on the left and cross the road to the path.

The second site, the boating area, is reached by carrying on past the garage. After approximately 160 yards there is a narrow entrance gate to the mere. Follow the track to the end. Beware of a tame Whooper Swan here that can be a little intimidating.

DISABLED ACCESS: Wheelchair users can view the mere from the boating area car park.

OTHER ATTRACTIONS

HORNSEA HAS a well-known pottery factory among its many other attractions.

FLAMBOROUGH HEAD projects 6 miles into the North Sea, making it one of the top sites on the east coast for migrants, rarities and sea-watching. Much of the headland is arable farmland with hedgerows, and there is a golf course and woodlands.

BIRDS

Spring passage is largely overshadowed by autumn. However, sea-watching can be excellent, with divers moving north from February to mid-April, and the first Sandwich Terns arriving in late March. A good variety of chats, pipits, wagtails, flycatchers and warblers appear in spring, and there are occasional falls that may include a rarity. As for other east coast sites, weather is important, easterly winds being best.

During June and July, particularly in the evenings, Guillemots and Puffins can

on the move. Flamborough has a reputation for rare seabirds, such as Great and Cory's Shearwater and, rarer still, the occasional Little Shearwater and Soft-plumaged Petrel. Sea-watching can be productive during the winter months, too, involving a range of seabirds, ducks and divers, and a good possibility of Little Auks from late October.

In August, passerine migrants start to appear again in numbers. Falls have on occasions been spectacular, involving thousands of birds. On easterly winds the hedgerows can be alive with tacking warblers and Redstarts. Pied Flycatchers may sally to and fro from hedgerows, though more prominent are Wheatears and Whinchats. In late autumn, large arrivals of thrushes, finches and Goldcrests can occur. Each autumn, rarities are discovered. In September and October, Yellow-browed Warblers usually appear, often with a Red-breasted Flycatcher or Barred Warbler.

While anywhere on the headland is potentially good for migrants, the sites listed below are well-known hot spots.

North Sea

Thornwick Bay

North Landing

to Bempton

Danes Dyke

B1229

Flamborough

tower

lighthouse

Flamborough Head

New Fall Hedgerow

Old Fall

B1255

South Landing

0   1 mile

Redstarts can be abundant during easterly winds in autumn.

be watched offshore flying in to their breeding colonies. Various seabirds breed on the cliffs, though the really big concentrations are further back along the headland at Bempton. By July, a more interesting assortment of terns, and possibly skuas and shearwaters, will be passing, though this depends on the weather. Strong north-westerly to easterly winds associated with poor visibility are best. From August to October, Manx and Sooty Shearwaters, petrels, skuas, auks, terns and gulls will be

SITE GUIDE

Lighthouse

To sea-watch, walk from the car park down to the cliff top below the fog-horn station, a noisy spot at times. Early mornings and evenings can be productive,

Yellow-browed Warblers often favour South Landing in autumn.

although it is always best to check the weather first as described previously.

2
New Fall Hedgerow

This hedge runs from north to south along the southern side of the headland. A circular walk can be taken from the car park at the head south along the headland, and then inland along the hedge, passing the Old Fall Plantation, which is strictly private but can be viewed from the path. The path comes out on the main road to the car park. The hedge can be full of birds, as can the plantation. Scan the fields for partridges and migrants such as Wheatears.

3
South Landing

South Landing can be reached from the head by walking along the southern side, past New Fall Hedgerow. Alternatively, after entering the village of Flamborough, and after a left-hand bend, turn right on to the B1259 signposted to South Landing.

This is a popular spot with bird-watchers in autumn, as the mass of cover attracts and holds migrants. Thrushes can pile into the trees here in late autumn in huge numbers, the thin 'sueep' call of Redwings and the deep 'chak-chak' call of Fieldfares filling the air as flocks arrive off the sea and move through the trees. Listen out for the calls of Yellow-browed Warbler and Firecrest. This is one of the

best spots for rarities. From the car park, take the concrete path down the valley to the boulder beach, and cross the ravine for a circular walk. Alternatively, you can walk to the head and back.

4
Dane's Dyke

Dane's Dyke is an old line of defence, now covered in trees, which runs across the entire headland from north to south, and which is positioned to the west of Flamborough. Much of the northern end is private, but the southern section is easily accessed by turning right off the B1255 at a dip in the road west of Flamborough. Park in the car park and follow the paths. Owing to the amount of cover, this site also tends to retain migrants and is best worked after a fall.

5

North Landing

The North Landing ravine is reached from Flamborough village. Although it is private, it is overlooked by the cliff-top path.

BIRDS THROUGH THE SEASONS

ALL YEAR: Cormorant, Shag, Gannet, Fulmar, Kittiwake, Guillemot, Razorbill, Sparrowhawk, Rock Dove. SPRING: Offshore: Red-throated Diver, less regularly Black-throated and Great Northern Divers,

arriving on land may include Cuckoo, Swift, hirundines, Tree Pipit, Yellow Wagtail, Black Redstart, Redstart, Whinchat, Stonechat, Wheatear, Ring Ouzel, Sedge, Reed, Willow and Garden Warblers, Blackcap, Lesser Whitethroat, Whitethroat, Goldcrest, Firecrest and Spotted and Pied Flycatcher. On easterly winds, scarce drift migrants such as Bluethroat and Wryneck are possible. SUMMER: Breeding seabirds on the cliffs and, offshore, Puffins and Guillemots flying by in the evening. Manx Shearwaters pass from July.

larger numbers, and the chance of Icterine, Barred and Yellow-browed Warblers, Red-breasted Flycatcher, Richard's and Tawny Pipits, Red-backed Shrike and vagrants. From October, in the right weather, mass arrivals of thrushes (particularly Redwings and Fieldfares), Goldcrests, and finches. WINTER: Offshore: divers, grebes, Brent Goose, Wigeon, Teal, Scaup, Eider, Long-tailed Duck, scoters, Red-breasted Merganser, Goldeneye, chance of Iceland and Glaucous Gull.

ACCESS: Flamborough Head is north of Bridlington, but *see* site guide for specific directions. Boat trips are run during the summer months from North Landing to view the cliff-nesting seabirds. In autumn, pelagic trips are run by the RSPB, departing from Bridlington. These give the opportunity of seeing shearwaters and skuas at close quarters. Details from the RSPB North of England Office, 4 Benton Terrace, Sandyford Road, Newcastle Upon Tyne NE2 1QU, or from the Bempton RSPB Reserve (Site 73).

DISABLED ACCESS: For wheelchair users, this is restricted to a limited area at South Landing and at Danes Dyke. Sea-watching is possible from the lighthouse area. There are some steep inclines at these sites.

Little Auks are seen annually offshore in late autumn.

grebes, Red-breasted Merganser, Eider, scoters, various ducks and waders, Pomarine, Arctic and Great Skuas, Little Gull, the commoner gulls, Sandwich, Common, Arctic, Little and Black Terns, Guillemot, Razorbill, Black Guillemot and Puffin. Migrants

AUTUMN: As for spring, plus the chance offshore of Sooty Shearwater and, much more rarely, Cory's and Great Shearwaters, Mediterranean and Manx Shearwaters, Leach's and British Storm-petrel, Long-tailed Skua and Sabine's Gull. Passerine migrants in

OTHER ATTRACTIONS

*S*EE UNDER Bempton (Site 73).

ON THE north side of Flamborough Head, 4 miles from the head itself, stretch the 430-foot high chalk cliffs of Bempton RSPB Reserve. Bempton has the largest concentration of breeding seabirds on the English mainland. To enjoy this spectacle, a visit between late April and early July is necessary.

Puffins. Shags breed along the base of the cliffs. Gannets first colonised the cliffs in the 1920s and now exceed 1000 pairs. Outside the breeding season, Bempton can be good for migrants. Anywhere with cover should be checked for birds, and one of the best spots to search is along Hoddy Cows Lane, reached by walking north for about half a mile along the cliff top.

OTHER ANIMALS
Offshore, seals are regularly seen and Harbour Porpoises occasionally pass in summer.

FLOWERS
On the narrow strip of rough ground between the cultivated fields and the cliff top, over 200 species of flowering plant have been recorded, including Greater Knapweed and Pyramidal Orchid.

BIRDS THROUGH THE SEASONS
SPRING AND SUMMER: Breeding seabirds include Fulmar, Gannet, Shag, Herring Gull, Kittiwake, Guillemot, Razorbill and Puffin. Migrants in spring. Rock doves breed on the cliffs. AUTUMN: Migrants can be searched for in the limited cover.

ACCESS:
Bempton Cliffs are on the north side of Flamborough Head. From the B1229 at Bempton, turn down Cliff Lane to the reserve.

The visitor centre is open from 10am to 5pm from April to September.

DISABLED ACCESS:
There is wheelchair access to two viewpoints on the cliff top.

OTHER ATTRACTIONS

FILEY, to the north, has some excellent beaches, and is quieter than Bridlington to the south. The fish and chips found in this part of Yorkshire are to be recommended.

Bempton Cliffs.

From the car park, paths lead off in both directions along the cliff top. Viewing areas with safety barriers are placed strategically along the cliff.

BIRDS
Tens of thousands of Kittiwakes crowd on to the ledges, alongside the next most numerous species, the Guillemot. There are lesser numbers of Razorbills and

THE FARNE Islands lie from 1½ to 4½ miles off the Northumberland coast, and are owned by the National Trust. Fifteen species of seabird breed, and as the majority allow very close views the Farnes are a popular destination for photographers.

The Farne Islands are rich in history. Their most notable inhabitant was St Cuthbert, who lived on Inner Farne from AD676 to 684, and then returned to die on the island in AD687.

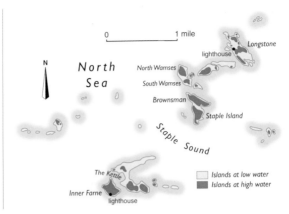

North Sea

0 — 1 mile

N

Longstone
lighthouse
North Wamses
South Wamses
Brownsman
Staple Island
Staple Sound
The Kettle
Inner Farne
lighthouse

☐ Islands at low water
■ Islands at high water

Guillemots on Staple Island.

He protected the birds, ensuring special care for the Eider ducks. Various other monks followed in Cuthbert's footsteps and, in 1255, a Benedictine monastery was established on Inner Farne, which remained until 1536. The present chapel on Inner Farne was built in 1370, but has since been restored. Various lighthouses have existed on the islands, along with their keepers, none more famous than the Darling family. Grace Darling became a national heroine after the rescue she undertook with her father in 1838 of the stricken crew of the *Forfarshire*.

🦆 **BIRDS**
Daily boat trips are run from Seahouses, allowing landings on Staple Island and Inner Farne. The best time to visit is from May through to early July. On Staple Island hordes of Guillemots crowd the cliffs,

Shags on the Farne Islands.

BIRDS THROUGH THE SEASONS

SPRING AND SUMMER: Breeding birds include Fulmar, Cormorant, Shag, Eider, Oystercatcher, Ringed Plover, Black-headed, Lesser Black-backed and Herring Gulls, Kittiwake, Sandwich, Roseate, Common and Arctic Terns, Guillemot, Razorbill, Puffin and Rock Pipit. Migrants occur in spring.

AUTUMN: Migrants and impressive falls can occur.

ACCESS: Boats run from the harbour at Seahouses from April to September, weather permitting. Landing is allowed on Staple Island and Inner Farne, where a National Trust landing fee is payable. Boats generally depart from 10am onwards. Ensure you book with a boat that will give a reasonable amount of time on each island, as not all boats allow you to land. If faced with a choice of which island to visit, then Inner Farne offers the most in terms of variety and interest of both birds and history.

OTHER ATTRACTIONS

EVEN FOR those with no interest in birds, the spectacle of the breeding colonies, the islands' fascinating history and the seals all add up to an excellent day out. There is plentiful accommodation and campsites in and around Seahouses, and some excellent fish and chip shops. Just to the north is impressive Bamburgh Castle, housing collections of weapons and tapestries.

along with a few Razorbills, Shags and large numbers of Kittiwakes. Close encounters with Puffins can be enjoyed by the landing stage.

Inner Farne has a large colony of Arctic Terns. On landing, visitors have to run the gauntlet past these nesting terns, which rise to the air and mob human invaders. For this reason, a hat is recommended. Smaller numbers of Common and Sandwich Terns and a few pairs of Roseate Terns also nest. The latter species has become very rare and you have to be lucky to enjoy a sighting. In recent years a vagrant Lesser-crested Tern,

affectionately named Elsie, has taken up residence with the Sandwich Terns, and has successfully reared hybrid young. Eiders are a common nesting bird on Inner Farne, and on the cliffs a variety of other seabirds can be seen.

In spring and autumn falls of migrants occur, and over 250 species have been recorded. Numbers and variety greatly increase in autumn, although few bird-watchers visit outside the breeding season.

OTHER ANIMALS
The islands have a population of Grey Seals, which can be viewed during boat trips to and from Staple Island.

LINDISFARNE NATIONAL Nature Reserve encompasses a massive area of intertidal mudflats, sand dunes, grassland, scrub and rocky shoreline. Rising above this is the picturesque Lindisfarne Castle on Holy Island, swamped by holidaymakers in summer. However, the area is large enough to get away from the crowds and enjoy the solitude of this beautiful coastline.

BIRDS

The reserve is best for birds from September to May. Passage migrants abound and, in winter, tens of thousands of estuarine wildfowl and waders swarm over the mudflats.

Lindisfarne is the most important site on the British mainland for wintering light-bellied Brent Geese, which originate in Svalbard. They winter both here and in Denmark, and numbers depend on the severity of the weather in Denmark. Wigeon can reach 20,000, making this the most important coastal site for this species. Other birds occurring in nationally and internationally important numbers include Greylag Geese, Whooper Swan, Red-breasted Merganser and a variety of waders. An incoming tide allows the best viewing, as feeding birds are pushed close to the shore and rise in restless flocks. Raptors hunt the meadows, dunes and saltmarsh in winter, while Twites and Snow Buntings are a feature of the shore. At sea, divers, the rarer grebes and rafts of seaduck can all be enjoyed.

In spring and autumn, the coastline welcomes a variety of migrants, from geese and waders to warblers and thrushes. Rarities are regular, with the chance of a Bluethroat after easterly winds in May, or perhaps a Barred Warbler in similar conditions in autumn.

OTHER ANIMALS

Grey Seals can be seen on the sandbanks.

FLOWERS

The dune slacks support an interesting flora, highlights including Grass of Parnassus, Bog Pimpernel, Creeping Willow, Early and Northern Marsh Orchids and Marsh Helleborine.

Owing to the vast size of the reserve, the following site guide highlights some of the more productive areas. To do Lindisfarne justice, a few days are needed for a full exploration and just about anywhere will provide exciting bird-watching in winter.

SITE GUIDE

Budle Bay

The bay is a good site for viewing wildfowl and waders. There are lay-bys overlooking the bay on the B1342. Budle Point is reached by taking a minor road from Bamburgh to the golf course (do not park in golf club car park). The point is productive for seaducks, such as Long-tailed Duck, scoters, Scaup, Red-breasted Mergansers, Eider and Red-throated Divers, and Slavonian and Red-necked Grebes. Great Northern and Black-throated Divers are less regular. Greylag Geese are sometimes present in the bay.

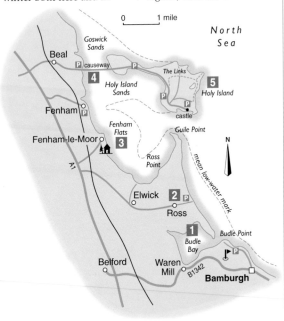

2
Ross Links

Take the minor road out beyond Ross and walk across the links to the dunes. This can be a good site for Greylag and sometimes Pink-footed Geese. Raptors hunt over the area and Snow Buntings are regular among the dunes. Offshore, here and along to Guile Point, a variety of divers, grebes and seaduck congregate.

3
Fenham Flats

At the end of the Fenham le Moor road a small hide overlooks Fenham Flats, which, on a rising tide, is excellent for estuarine wildfowl and waders.

4
Holy Island Causeway

This is the best spot for observing the large numbers of wildfowl and waders out on the mudflats. A rising tide is best as, at low tide, birds can be very distant. The dunes on the approach to Holy Island can be searched for migrants in spring and autumn. The area known as the Snook often holds migrants, and is reached along a track from the car park in the dunes.

Lindisfarne Castle on Holy Island.

5
Holy Island

Before crossing to Holy Island, consult the tide tables displayed as the causeway is impassable for two hours either side of high tide. Anywhere with cover may hold migrants; in easterly winds drift migrants may include Bluethroat and Wryneck. Large falls can occur in autumn. A hide overlooks the lough, which attracts waders and ducks. Offshore, seaduck, divers and grebes are present in winter. Terns feed around the mouth of the bay in summer, when Arctic Skuas are often present. Sea-watching in autumn can be good, with shearwaters, petrels, skuas, auks, terns and gulls all passing in favourable conditions. Holy Island can become very crowded in summer and at weekends.

BIRDS THROUGH THE SEASONS
ALL YEAR: Fulmar, Shag, Shelduck, Eider, Oystercatcher, Ringed Plover and Rock Pipit.
SPRING: Passage migrants include Black-tailed Godwit, Spotted Redshank, Greenshank, Wood Sandpiper, Little Gull, and a variety of warblers, chats and flycatchers. Easterly winds may produce drift migrants; Bluethroat are just about annual.
SUMMER: Common and Arctic Terns breed. Offshore, seabirds from the Farnes to

the south may be seen, also Gannets and a chance of Manx Shearwater. Wheatears on the golf course.

AUTUMN: Arriving winter birds and passage migrants as for spring, plus Curlew Sandpiper, Little Stint and Arctic Skua. Offshore, seabirds passing may include terns, gulls, skuas, shearwaters and petrels, with the chance of Little Auks in late autumn. Rarities are recorded annually.

WINTER: Red-throated and scarcer Black-throated and Great Northern Divers, Slavonian and Red-necked Grebes, Whooper Swan, Pink-footed, Greylag and light-bellied Brent Geese, Wigeon, Teal, Pintail, Scaup, Long-tailed Duck, Common and Velvet Scoter, Goldeneye, Red-breasted Merganser, Merlin, Peregrine, occasional Hen Harrier, Lapwing, Golden Plover, Grey Plover, Knot, Sanderling, Purple Sandpiper (scarce), Dunlin, Bar-tailed Godwit, Curlew, Redshank, occasional Spotted Redshank, Short-eared Owl, Twite, Lapland and Snow Buntings, and occasional Shorelarks.

ACCESS: Lindisfarne is south of Berwick-upon-Tweed, and is easily reached off the A1. There is unrestricted access; *see* the above site guide for more detail. Hides are at Fenham le Moor and overlooking the lough on Holy Island.

DISABLED ACCESS: Wheelchair users are restricted to the roads.

Good views of Budle Bay are possible from lay-bys, and the causeway across to Holy Island allows viewing from a vehicle. Disabled access is planned for the hide overlooking the lough on Holy Island.

OTHER ATTRACTIONS

NORTHUMBERLAND HAS a host of attractions. Holy Island is popular for Lindisfarne Castle, which dates back to 1550. Monks settled on the island in the 7th century, and made it a place of scholarship. The holy relics of St Cuthbert were buried in the priory here and as a result pilgrims from throughout Europe came to pay homage.

MARTIN MERE was once a huge lake, but, after drainage, winter flooding of the grazed marshland began to attract large numbers of birds. In 1969 the Wildfowl and Wetlands Trust, realising the importance of the area, purchased Martin Mere and started to develop the area for birds.

Martin Mere has many attractions aside from its birds, and as such is an ideal location for a family day out. The wildfowl collection includes flamingos, and is laid out so that the various sections have representative wildfowl from different regions of the world. Attractions for children include the wetland adventure, a tearoom (called the Pinkfoot Pantry), and a gift shop and bookshop. Winter is the best time to visit, and on most winter evenings the swans can be watched under floodlights.

BIRDS

Each winter, large numbers of wildfowl are attracted to the site, which also has an extensive captive collection of waterfowl. The land is very flat with flashes in the fields, these are dissected by drainage ditches.

Thousands of Pink-footed Geese are one of the main attractions, harbouring among them small parties of other species. Over 20,000 have been counted on the reserve. A series of hides overlooks their preferred grazing areas, and allows a variety of other species to be seen. Whooper and Bewick's Swans can be watched just a few yards away from the hides. Dabbling ducks are here in their thousands in winter, with often up to 3000 Pintail, and as many as 20,000 Wigeon. Teal and Mallard are the two other abundant species. Over 100 Ruff regularly winter among the thousands of Golden Plover and Lapwings that favour the wet fields.

In spring and autumn there is a light passage of waders, while Ruff and Black-tailed Godwit summer and have bred. Garganey also appear, and a few Marsh Harriers pass through. Barn Owls breed

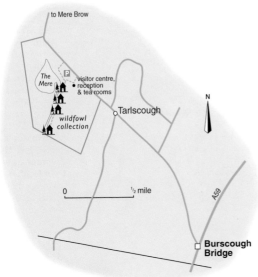

Up to 3000 Pintail spend the winter at Martin Mere.

locally and regularly hunt over the fields towards dusk.

BIRDS THROUGH THE SEASONS

ALL YEAR: Grey Partridge, Barn Owl, Little Owl, Collared Dove, Corn Bunting and Tree Sparrow. SPRING: Garganey, Black-tailed Godwit, Green, Wood and Common Sandpipers, Ruff, Spotted Redshank, Dunlin, Redshank, Lapwing, Snipe, Whimbrel, Curlew, Marsh Harrier and Yellow Wagtail. SUMMER: Breeding birds include Shelduck, Mallard, Gadwall, Shoveler and Pochard. Other species sometimes summer, along with the occasional injured Pink-footed Goose and swan. Breeding waders include Little Ringed Plover, Redshank, Snipe and Lapwing. Breeding and/or summering waders include Ruff and Black-tailed Godwit.

AUTUMN: Passage migrants as for spring, plus Greenshank and Little Stint. Pink-footed Geese start to return in mid-September.
WINTER: Whooper and Bewick's Swans, Pink-footed Geese, Shelduck, Wigeon, Mallard, Teal, Gadwall, Pintail, Pochard, Tufted Duck, Goldeneye, Ruddy Duck, Hen Harrier, Merlin, Peregrine, Short-eared Owl, Golden Plover, Lapwing, Ruff, Snipe, Redshank and Corn Bunting.

ACCESS: Martin Mere is well signposted. On the A59 at Burscough Bridge, take the minor road off to the left just after the hump-back bridge over the railway line. The reserve is along this lane on the left. Open daily from 9.30am except Christmas Eve and Christmas Day. Admission charge for non-members. Families can request a special all-inclusive low-price ticket

DISABLED ACCESS: This is excellent and nowhere is inaccessible. There is free wheelchair loan, a special parking area and reduced rates for helpers.

OTHER ATTRACTIONS

MARTIN MERE is an ideal place for a family day out, even for non-bird-watchers. Liverpool lies a few minutes away and has various museums, an impressive planetarium and a large shopping centre. At the Liverpool Docks are the Seaforth Nature Reserve and Crosby Marina, two excellent bird sites (*see under* Additional Sites).

LEIGHTON MOSS RSPB Reserve lies in a wooded valley that was once an inlet of Morecambe Bay. After reclamation from the sea, the valley was flooded with fresh water in 1917 from several streams that drain the surrounding hills. The reserve's large reedbed is bordered by woodland and scrub, and within the reeds are open stretches of water and the old drainage dykes.

Six hides can be visited along excellent paths, and the picturesque location of the reserve adds to the variety of birds on offer. Spring is best for the reedbed specialities, although a visit in autumn or winter can be just as rewarding.

There is a visitor centre, shop and tearoom.

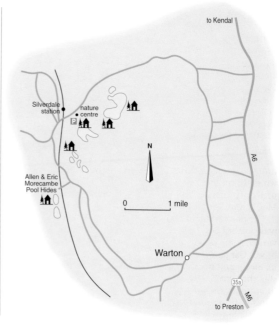

The reedbeds at Leighton Moss are home to Britain's main population of breeding Bitterns.

BIRDS

The reedbeds are one of the last British strongholds of the Bittern. Bitterns boom from late January to mid-June, and in 1995 there were four booming males. Bearded Tits, Water Rails and Marsh Harriers all breed among the reeds. During autumn, the reeds are used by roosting wagtails, hirundines and Starlings, which in turn attract predators such as Hobby, Merlin and Peregrine.

The open water attracts a wide variety of wildfowl in winter, some of which breed. Garganey are annual in spring and occasionally stay through the summer. In autumn, the brackish pools in front of the Allen and Eric Morecambe hides attract a few passage waders. August is a good month for Spotted Crakes, and these have bred on the reserve in the past.

OTHER ANIMALS

Otters are regularly seen on the reserve, one of the best spots for them being the Lower Hide. Roe and Red Deer inhabit the reedbeds and surrounding woodlands, and may sometimes be seen from Grisedale Hide grazing at the water's edge. Scarce butterflies such as Pearl-bordered, Small Pearl-bordered and High Brown Fritillaries are found along the woodland edge.

BIRDS THROUGH THE SEASONS

ALL YEAR: Grey Heron, Bittern, Mallard, Teal, Gadwall, Pochard, Tufted Duck, Shoveler, Water Rail, Peregrine, Sparrowhawk, Buzzard, Barn Owl, Green, Great Spotted and Lesser Spotted Woodpeckers, Kingfisher, Bearded Tit, Marsh Tit, Redpoll and Reed Bunting.

SPRING: Garganey, Marsh Harrier, Osprey, Black Tern, Little Gull, Hobby and a few passage waders.

SUMMER: Breeding birds include Marsh Harrier, Black-headed Gull, Reed, Sedge and Grasshopper Warblers, Whitethroat, Lesser Whitethroat, Blackcap, Chiffchaff, Willow Warbler and resident woodland birds.

AUTUMN: As for spring, plus Greenshank, Ruff, Green, Common and Wood Sandpipers, Little Stint, Spotted Redshank, and roosts of wagtails, hirundines and Starlings.

WINTER: Pintail, Wigeon, Goldeneye, Hen Harrier, Merlin and Snipe.

Channel through reedbeds.

ACCESS:

Take the A6 north from Morecambe through Carnforth, and turn off to Yealand Redmayne and Silverdale. The reserve is close to Silverdale station. The Allen and Eric Morecambe hides are reached from the Carnforth–Silverdale road near the railway line just to the south of the reserve.

DISABLED ACCESS:

There is wheelchair access to four hides, and there is an invalid lift to reach the tearoom and display area. A wheelchair is available on loan.

OTHER ATTRACTIONS

LEIGHTON HALL, home of the Gillow family, is close by. It was built around 1800 and contains a collection of Gillow furniture. The largest collection of birds of prey in northern England is housed here and there are regular flying displays. Open between May and the end of September on Tuesdays, Fridays and Sundays.

MORECAMBE BAY is one of the largest estuarine areas in Britain. Five rivers drain into the bay through intertidal mudflats, mussel beds and saltmarsh. A rich invertebrate life and safe roosting areas for birds mean that Morecambe Bay is second only to the Wash for the diversity of wildfowl and waders it attracts. Numbers wintering and passing through on passage are huge, with an average 200,000 birds present in winter.

 BIRDS

Over 4000 Eider, more than 3000 Pintail and 3000 Shelduck are just some of the numbers of wildfowl that occur. Waders are represented by over 50,000 Oystercatcher and tens of thousands of Knot and Dunlin, and a number of other species of wader occur in internationally and nationally important numbers. Terns breed in summer, along with the only breeding population of Eider on the west coast of Britain.

On arrival, the thought of finding birds can seem quite daunting due to the size of the bay, but many concentrate in particular areas. At low tide the sea can be so far out as to be almost out of sight, but once the tide turns it can come in quickly. It is best to watch on an incoming tide, when birds will be pushed close inshore and on to roosts. Midsummer is the least interesting time; otherwise, wildfowl and waders are present throughout in large numbers. Effort is best concentrated at the following sites.

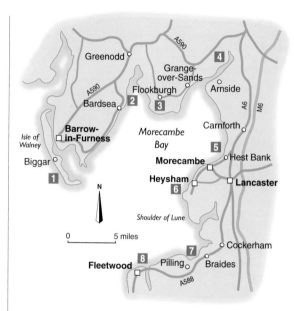

SITE GUIDE

1

Walney Island

Walney Island is at the westernmost point of the bay. The south of the island is of most interest for birds. There is a bird observatory and the South Walney Nature Reserve, run by the Cumbria Wildlife Trust. Large numbers of waders feed and roost, along with a good variety of wildfowl in winter. Offshore, seaduck are joined by grebes and Red-throated Divers. Seabird passage can be excellent in autumn in westerly or south-westerly gales, when Leach's Storm-petrels are regularly seen. In spring and autumn, a good variety of migrants pass through, rarely in large numbers, although falls do occur. Walney Island is well known for its breeding Eiders and large gull colony.

Three species of tern also nest. Three well-placed hides on the nature reserve allow sea-watching in relative comfort in wet and windy conditions, and offer views of many of the other birds that use the area.

ACCESS: Walney is reached by crossing the bridge from Barrow-in-Furness, and driving south past the village of Biggar to the South End caravan site. Take the track past South End Farm to the reserve.

DISABLED ACCESS: Sea-watching and the viewing of waders and wildfowl on the move are possible from a vehicle in places.

2
Leven Estuary

Chapel Island in the lower estuary is the site of a large wader roost, and there are often wildfowl to be seen. The upper estuary, north of the railway line, attracts Teal, Wigeon, Pintail, Shelduck and waders.

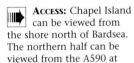 **ACCESS:** Chapel Island can be viewed from the shore north of Bardsea. The northern half can be viewed from the A590 at Greenodd.

3
Flookburgh Marshes

This area of intertidal mud and saltmarsh lies between Humphrey Head and the Leven, and is best visited on an incoming tide. There are wader roosts and wildfowl. Hen Harrier, Merlin and Peregrine hunt over the area.

ACCESS: Flookburgh lies west of Grange-over-Sands. Access is either from the village or by walking out to Humphrey Head.

4
Kent Estuary

This estuary attracts the typical estuarine wildfowl and waders, and alongside

its upper reaches Greylag Geese can be found in winter. The mudflats off Grange-over-Sands attract large flocks of Pintail and Wigeon.

 ACCESS: Viewing is easy from Grange-over-Sands and Arnside promenades.

5
Hest Bank
RSPB Reserve

Knot, Dunlin and Redshank are some of the waders that favour these saltings. On spring tides, this area can have masses of roosting waders. The state of the tide is the main factor dictating how many birds will be seen.

Knot winter in large numbers.

 ACCESS: From Morecambe, take the A5105 towards Carnforth. Turn off to Hest Bank, cross the level crossing and park in the car park by the shore.

 DISABLED ACCESS: Viewing is possible from a vehicle.

6
Heysham

Heysham is the most reliable site in Britain for Leach's Storm-petrels in autumn, both after and during south-westerly to westerly gales. September and October are the months to try for this species in the right conditions. Other seabirds that appear regularly include Little Gulls, a few skuas and terns. The power station outflow often tempts terns and gulls to linger. In winter, divers, grebes and seaduck are regular. Purple Sandpipers frequent the harbour. At the rear of the power station is

an area of scrub with an observation tower and a ringing station. Passerine migrants are frequent, with some falls producing the occasional rarity.

ACCESS: From the A589 south through Heysham, turn right at the traffic lights for Heysham Harbour. Turn left along Moneyclose Lane at the next set of lights. The right-hand turning then takes you to the observation tower and ringing station. Continue straight on for the outflows, pass through the caravan park to the sea wall and follow it round to the hide. For the North Harbour Wall, turn right at the second set of lights for the heliport.

DISABLED ACCESS: Sea-watching from a vehicle is possible along the harbour wall.

7

Pilling and Cockerham Moss

From February to April, the fields at Cockerham Moss to Pilling attract a few thousand Pink-footed Geese, these roosting on Pilling Sands. Peregrine hunt over the area, often putting to flight the Golden Plovers and Lapwings that use the fields.

 ACCESS: Access is off the A588. There are a number of access points to the shore, and minor roads border Cockerham Moss.

8

Fleetwood

Situated at the southern end of the bay, Fleetwood can be a good sea-watching point in north-westerly gales in autumn. Leach's Storm-petrel, terns and skuas can be pushed close to the promenade in such conditions. Wintering seaduck are regular, and a good variety of waders is usually on offer.

 ACCESS: Viewing from the promenade and Rossall Point at the western end is best.

BIRDS THROUGH THE SEASONS
ALL YEAR: Eider, Peregrine, Sparrowhawk, Oystercatcher, Ringed Plover and Dunlin.
SPRING: Passage waders include the wintering species, plus Greenshank, Whimbrel, Spotted Redshank, and Green, Common and Wood Sandpipers. Passerine migrants at Heysham and Walney Island.
SUMMER: Breeding birds include Eider, Lesser Black-backed, Great Black-backed and Herring Gulls,

Bar-tailed Godwit.

Sandwich, Common, Arctic (very few) and Little Terns and Yellow Wagtail. Waders start to build in number from July.
AUTUMN: As for spring, plus Little Stint, Curlew Sandpiper, Ruff, Little Gull and Black Tern. Offshore in right conditions: Leach's and British Storm-petrel, skuas, possible Grey Phalarope, Sabine's Gull and Sooty Shearwater.
WINTER: Red-throated Diver, a few Great Northern and Black-throated Divers, Red-necked, Slavonian and Great Crested Grebes, Brent Geese, Pink-footed Geese, Cormorant, Shelduck, Wigeon, Teal, Pintail, Pochard, Tufted Duck, Scaup, Long-tailed Duck, Goldeneye, Red-breasted Merganser, Merlin, Peregrine, Hen Harrier, Oystercatcher, Ringed Plover, Golden Plover, Grey Plover, Lapwing, Knot, Sanderling, Dunlin, Black-tailed Godwit, Bar-tailed Godwit, Curlew, Redshank, Turnstone, Purple Sandpiper, Greenshank, Short-eared Owl, Rock Pipit, Twite and occasional Snow Buntings.

 ACCESS: *See* site guide above.

DISABLED ACCESS: *See* site guide above.

OTHER ATTRACTIONS

THE LAKE DISTRICT and its many attractions lie close by. Both Morecambe and Blackpool to the south are popular seaside resorts. The Blackpool illuminations are worth a look after dark in winter.

AUTUMN: As for spring, plus chance of petrels and shearwaters.

WINTER: Offshore: chance of divers and seaduck.

ACCESS: The reserve is west of the A595 and south of Whitehaven. Park in the car park at the beach at St Bees, and walk north along the cliffs.

DISABLED ACCESS: Disabled visitors in vehicles can use the private road from Sandwith to the lighthouse.

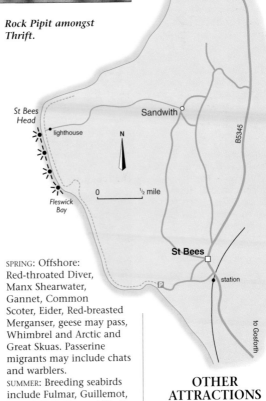

THE SANDSTONE cliffs at St Bees Head, Cumbria's westernmost point, rise to 300 feet and are of interest for their breeding seabirds.

Rock Pipit amongst Thrift.

BIRDS
Guillemots are most numerous, and there are a few Puffins and Black Guillemots, the latter species breeding nowhere else in England.

Peregrines, Ravens and Rock Pipits are also inhabitants of the cliffs. Offshore, seaduck can often be seen in winter. During autumn, sea-watching can be productive. There is little cover for passerine migrants, the best spot being Fleswick Bay, which has Gorse and Bramble cover.

There is a cliff-top path with four viewing areas. The best period to visit for seabirds is from April to early July.

BIRDS THROUGH THE SEASONS
ALL YEAR: Fulmar, Cormorant, Kittiwake, Peregrine, Rock Pipit, Stonechat and Raven.

SPRING: Offshore: Red-throated Diver, Manx Shearwater, Gannet, Common Scoter, Eider, Red-breasted Merganser, geese may pass, Whimbrel and Arctic and Great Skuas. Passerine migrants may include chats and warblers.

SUMMER: Breeding seabirds include Fulmar, Guillemot, Razorbill, Puffin and Black Guillemots (both scarce), Kittiwake, Herring Gull, Rock Pipit and Raven.

OTHER ATTRACTIONS

THE LAKE District, with its scenery and family attractions, is just to the east.

CHESHIRE

Frodsham Marsh and the Weaver Bend

Bordering the Mersey Estuary, Frodsham Marsh comprises a number of embanked lagoons, areas of rough ground and fields. The Weaver Bend is a meander of the River Weaver which has mud banks, and above the bend is a lagoon particularly attractive to birds. Passage waders are one of the main attractions. In autumn, Little Stints, Curlew Sandpipers and Ruff are just three species that occur in good numbers. These migrants are often joined by roosting waders from the Mersey. In winter, large numbers of duck use the lagoons, and raptors hunt over the area. This site regularly turns up rarities, and has been particularly good for American waders. Pass through Frodsham heading south, go past the main shopping area and then turn right down Marsh Lane, which leads over the motorway. Take the right-hand fork to the Weaver Bend.

Gayton Sands
RSPB Reserve

This reserve covers part of the Dee Estuary. Intertidal mudflats, saltmarsh and a reedbed are the main habitats. The reserve is best visited from autumn to spring on a rising tide. Large flocks of wintering estuarine waders and wildfowl are the main interest, particularly Pintails, along with hunting Peregrine, Merlin, Hen Harrier and Short-eared Owl. Finch flocks feed along the tide line and, in some years, these may include Bramblings. Noctule Bats can sometimes be seen in summer. From the A540 Chester–West Kirby road, turn off to Neston and Parkgate. Viewing is possible from the footpath adjacent to the Old Baths car park near the Boathouse Restaurant in Parkgate.

Hilbre Island

This island has long been famous as a major roost for waders which use the Dee Estuary on passage and in winter. The island has a regular wintering flock of

Dunlin at a winter roost.

Purple Sandpipers. During autumn, if north-westerly gales persist, then Leach's Storm-petrels are likely to appear along with skuas and gulls. Migrants appear in spring and autumn, though variety and numbers are often higher in spring. Hilbre can only be reached on foot at low tide, and you must set out at least 3½ hours before high tide. To avoid difficult conditions, set out from the end of Dee Lane at West Kirby, aiming for the left-hand end of Little Eye. You will not be able to leave until 2 hours after high water.

New Brighton

On the tip of the north Wirral, on the Mersey and next to Wallasey, is New Brighton. North-westerly gales in autumn produce Leach's Storm-petrels, along with skuas, gulls and terns. Viewing is from the promenade.

CLEVELAND

South Gare

This promontory, on the south shore of the Tees Estuary, is particularly good for passerine migrants and for sea-watching in autumn, which can be outstanding in north-easterly to north-westerly winds. Little Terns breed in summer, and by August large numbers of terns will have gathered in the estuary. Drive west from Redcar seafront to a boating lake and then turn right along Majuba Road. Turn right at the roundabout and cross over the railway line on to the access road. Ignore the private road signs (motorists are welcome), and either continue to the end or stop *en route* to explore, ensuring your vehicle does not impede other traffic.

Long-tailed Skua is a possibility off South Gare during autumn gales.

CUMBRIA

Campfield Marsh
RSPB Reserve

Campfield Marsh borders the southern shore of the Solway, and its saltmarsh and grazing land attract large numbers of estuarine wildfowl and waders. Scaup, divers and grebes may be seen, and the saltmarsh has the largest wader roost on the Solway. Raptors present in winter include Peregrine, Merlin and Barn Owl. Pink-footed Geese are regular visitors in late winter. Roe Deer and Adders are present, and on the mire, plants such as Mire Sundew and Bog Rosemary occur. The wader roosts can be seen easily from roadside lay-bys along the minor road that runs from Bowness-on-Solway to Cardurnock.

Geltsdale
RSPB Reserve

Geltsdale is situated in the northern Pennines. The heather-cloaked fells and rushing streams are home to Red Grouse, Raven, Short-eared Owl, Merlin, Peregrine, Dipper and Twite, which are joined by Curlew, Golden Plover, Wheatear, Ring Ouzel, Tree Pipit, and, in the woodlands, Redstart, Pied Flycatcher and Wood Warbler. The reserve lies to the south of Brampton between the A69 and the B6413. Access is from either the B6413, 3 miles south of Brampton at the railway viaduct (suitable for wheelchairs), or from the west side off the A69.

Haweswater
RSPB Reserve

The Haweswater RSPB Reserve has in recent years been home to the only nesting pair of Golden Eagles in England. They have nested near the head of the valley, and from April to August an observation post is wardened by the RSPB, providing they are present. The surrounding fells support Ring Ouzel, Wheatear, Raven, Peregrine and Golden Plover. The woodlands have breeding Buzzard, Pied Flycatcher, Redstart, Wood Warbler and woodpeckers. Common Sandpiper and Red-breasted Merganser are two species found on Haweswater.

Some of the more interesting plants include Globe Flower, Bird's-eye Primrose and Lesser Twayblade, while Roe and Red Deer and Red Squirrel are present.

There is a car park at the southern end of the reservoir. A path leads from here to the eagle observation point.

Hodbarrow
RSPB Reserve

Hodbarrow is on the north side of the Duddon Estuary, approached along Mansgate Road from Millom. The lagoon is used by a variety of wildfowl throughout the year. Seaduck, divers and grebes occur in winter, and in autumn the area supports a moulting flock of Red-breasted Mergansers. Passage and wintering waders inhabit the lagoon and estuary, while the surrounding scrub acts as a refuge for passerine migrants. Sandwich and a few pairs of Little and Common Terns nest along the sea bank. There is a colony of Natterjack Toads.

LANCASHIRE

Marshside
RSPB Reserve

Marshside is close to Southport on the south side of the Ribble. The wet grazing marsh attracts thousands of wildfowl in winter, including Pink-footed Geese, Bewick's Swans, Pintail, Teal and Wigeon. Waders include Black-tailed Godwit, Ruff and Golden Plover. Various raptors hunt over the marshes. In summer, Redshank, Snipe and Lapwing breed, and it is hoped Ruff and Black-tailed Godwit will be persuaded to nest. The reserve is reached via Marine Drive at the northern end of Southport. There is a car park next to the sand-winning plant. Views can be obtained from the roads or from the sea

wall that runs along the south-eastern boundary of the reserve.

Pendle Hill

North of Burnley is Pendle Hill, best approached from the village of Barley. The summit of the hill is well known for its attraction to trips of Dotterel in the first two weeks of May. Ring Ouzel, Whinchat, Twite and Red Grouse are some of the other species found here.

Seaforth Nature Reserve and Crosby Marina

Seaforth Nature Reserve lies within Liverpool Docks and comprises fresh- and saltwater pools. The reserve is managed by the Lancashire Wildlife Trust and is owned by the Mersey Docks and Harbour Company. It is outstanding for gulls and terns, and, along with neighbouring Crosby Marina, is the best site in the country for Little Gulls in spring. Passage peaks in mid-April when hundreds may be present. Rare gulls are regular, notably Mediterranean and Ring-billed, and Ross's Gulls have occurred more than once. In autumn, waders pass through and sea-watching can be excellent. In winter, wildfowl occur in moderate numbers. There are two hides. Access is through the main Freeport entrance, off the roundabout at the end of the A5036 where it meets the A565.

NORTH YORKSHIRE

Filey Brigg

Just north of Flamborough is Filey Brigg, a small finger of land protruding into the North Sea. The same birds at the same seasons as at Flamborough can be expected, though in fewer numbers. From the A165, turn on to the A1039 to Filey, and then take Church Cliff Drive to North Cliff Country Park.

Filey Dams

This reserve on the west side of Filey has a wader scrape and pools overlooked by two hides. Passage waders occur and, in winter, there are a few wildfowl. From the southern roundabout on the A165, take the A1039 to Filey, and after a short distance turn left into Wharfedale Road. After a phone box, turn left to the reserve car park.

Swaledale

Swaledale, in the Yorkshire Dales, has many roads that can be used to view the beautiful scenery and to find birds. Typical species in spring and summer are Red and Black Grouse, Golden Plover, Curlew, Short-eared Owl, Wheatear and Ring Ouzel. Along the streams, look for Common Sandpiper, Dipper and Grey Wagtail, and in the woodlands look for Redstart.

SCOTLAND

SCOTLAND OFFERS a remarkable diversity of habitats, from fertile low-lying islands to bleak mountain tops. The Scottish Highlands harbour some of Britain's last great wilderness areas, where sparsely populated moorlands, mountains, forests, lakes and a rugged coastline support their own special bird communities. The Scottish 'specialities', such as Capercaillie, Crested Tit, Ptarmigan and Scottish Crossbill, are found nowhere else in Britain.

The Highland scenery is diverse, encompassing the beauty of the Spey Valley – home to Wild Cat, Pine Marten and Red Squirrel – and the contrasting, almost featureless expanse of the Flow Country. The Flows and the uplands of north-west Sutherland are as close as you will get to real wilderness in Britain, and remain the domain of the Golden Eagle.

The Highlands offer a range of climates, from the Arctic-like conditions of Cairn Gorm, to the wet and mild climate of the west coast. Land use varies from forestry and hill sheep farming, to traditional keepered estates where grouse moors and forests attract sportsmen from around the world. Fish farms are prominent on the larger lochs and coastal bays, but the most important industry for much of the region is tourism.

The lowlands are often ignored by birders travelling north, yet take a closer look and you will realise the region has much to offer. Cliffs, such as those at St Abb's, become seabird cities during summer.

Few experiences, however, can match the sight and sound of thousands of geese on a crisp winter's day. The Solway on the west coast, and Loch Leven on Tayside, are two of the British Isles' premier sites for such an experience.

The Shetland Archipelago is the northernmost outpost of the British Isles. Its moorlands and cliffs host breeding waders and sea-birds. In spring and autumn migrants bring with them a host of rarities. To the south, Orkney in contrast to Shetland is green and fertile, and has among its islands out-standing sites for birds.

Scattered along Scotland's west coast are islands with landscapes that vary from low-lying areas to rugged mountains with peat bogs and high cliffs. Some of the best-known to birders are the Hebrides, the breeding stronghold of the Corncrake. Finally, mention must be made of St Kilda, Britain's remotest and most difficult-to-reach archipelago. St Kilda in summer provides arguably the greatest spectacle of them all: breathtaking scenery and hundreds of thousands of seabirds make a visit here unforgettable.

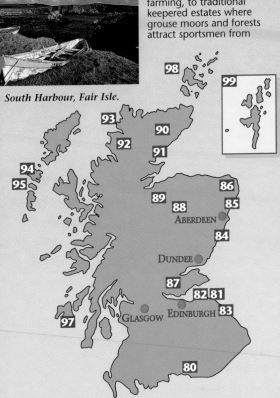

South Harbour, Fair Isle.

98

99

93

90

92

91

94

95

86

89

88

85

ABERDEEN

84

DUNDEE

87

82 81

GLASGOW EDINBURGH 83

97

80

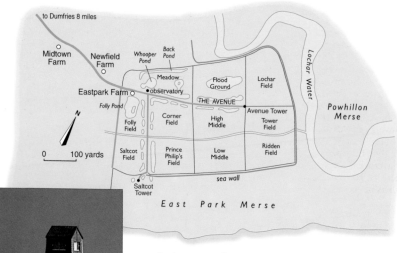

to Dumfries 8 miles

Midtown Farm
Newfield Farm
Whooper Pond
Back Pond
Meadow
Eastpark Farm
observatory
Flood Ground
Lochar Field
Lochar Water
Folly Pond
THE AVENUE
Powhillon Merse
Avenue Tower
Folly Field
Corner Field
High Middle
Tower Field
N
0   100 yards
Saltcot Field
Prince Philip's Field
Low Middle
Ridden Field
Saltcot Tower
sea wall
East Park Merse
Solway Firth

Sir Peter Scott once wrote, 'Large flocks of geese are the last great wildlife spectacles left in Britain'. Caerlaverock provides such a spectacle. Between October and March the entire Spitzbergen population of Barnacle Geese – currently numbering some 14,000 birds – winter here, along with a few thousand Pink-footed Geese.

The Wildfowl & Wetlands Trust (WWT) reserve at Caerlaverock covers 1400 acres along the northern edge of the Solway coast. A National Nature Reserve also runs for 6 miles along the shore, and includes mudflats, saltmarsh and meadows.

Observation tower.

Barnacles are thought to have wintered on the Solway for hundreds of years, the population numbering at least 10,000 at the turn of the last century. In the 1930s Peter Scott estimated the population to be around 5000, and this decline continued until just 400 remained in the winter of 1948/9. A series of poor breeding seasons, use of the foreshore as a practice ground for bombers during World War II and an increase in wildfowling were thought to be the causes. Action was needed, and by 1954 the Barnacle Goose received protection in Britain. The following year saw protection granted in Spitzbergen, and Norway further introduced a shooting ban in 1971.

The reserve is run as a farm with cattle grazing during the summer. This ensures a close sward which provides good grazing for the geese.

BIRDS

The WWT provides excellent facilities for winter bird-watching. A heated observatory overlooking Whooper Pond allows close views of a variety of wildfowl. Whooper Swans entertain as they feed and squabble only feet away. Wigeon are a common sight, while the occasional wader

Numbers of Barnacle Geese peak in November.

such as Oystercatcher or Curlew may drop in. From the observatory tower, look south and you will see a lone wind-shaped Sycamore, a tree that appeared in many of Scott's paintings of Barnacle Geese. Two more observation towers and 20 small hides overlook a patchwork of fields all named individually by Scott.

For the bird-watcher, Caerlaverock is primarily a winter site. For the largest numbers of geese, late

Rainbow over Caerlaverock.

October through to mid-November is best.

 OTHER ANIMALS
For the naturalist, this reserve has much to offer during summer. A colony of the localised Natterjack Toad thrives here on the north-western limit of its European range. Roe Deer are seen all year round, being especially common in winter. Otter are resident yet rarely seen.

 FLOWERS
The *merse* (the local name for a saltmarsh) holds a variety of interesting plants, including Northern Marsh Orchid, Common Spotted Orchid and

Twayblade. During the summer, walks can be taken out on to the meadows.

BIRDS THROUGH THE SEASONS
ALL YEAR: Shelduck, Teal, Shoveler, Sparrowhawk, Peregrine, Buzzard, Snipe, Redshank, Barn Owl.
SPRING: Sanderling, Whimbrel and the occasional Osprey.
SUMMER: Little bird interest; a few resident breeders include Barn Owl.
AUTUMN: Green Sandpiper, Curlew Sandpiper, Little Stint, Whimbrel, Ruff, Spotted Redshank and Black-tailed Godwit.
WINTER: The Barnacle Geese peak in mid-November when up to 14,000 may be present. Pink-footed Geese reach a peak in late winter with up to 5000. Greylag Geese are seen in small flocks. Whooper Swans (up to 350), Bewick's Swans in small numbers. Dabbling duck include Pintail, Wigeon, Teal, Gadwall and Shoveler. Hen Harrier, Merlin, Peregrine and Sparrowhawk are all seen regularly. Thousands of Golden Plover and Lapwing feed on the fields. Dunlin, Oystercatcher and Curlew roost in large numbers on the *merse*.

ACCESS: The Trust reserve at Eastpark Farm is signposted from the A75. Access is via the minor road off the B725. The reserve lies 8 miles south-east of Dumfries.

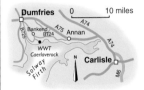

 Open daily from 10am to 5pm except Christmas Day. Admission for WWT members is free. Charge for non-members.
Special events and activities are run. Contact The Wildfowl & Wetlands Trust, Eastpark Farm, Caerlaverock, Dumfries and Galloway, Scotland DG1 4RS. Tel: 01387 770200 for further information and group bookings.

DISABLED ACCESS:
Wheelchair access is good. The ground floors of Avenue Tower, the observatory and the Folly Pond hide are all accessible. Authority to drive to the Avenue Tower may be granted on request.

OTHER ATTRACTIONS

CAERLAVEROCK CASTLE: A romantic-looking castle dating back to the 13th century. Close to the WWT reserve.

DUMFRIES: Known as the Queen of the South, Dumfries is the largest town in south-west Scotland and has much of historical interest.

FROM LAND, it appears as a shimmering white mass; closer inspection reveals the island to be covered in thousands of pairs of Gannets. This is the Bass Rock, a volcanic plug over 325 feet high within sight of North Berwick at the mouth of the Firth of Forth.

The Gannets were harvested up to 1885, but are now left in peace. To land on the Bass in summer and walk amongst the

BIRDS THROUGH THE SEASONS

SUMMER: The Gannets are best viewed on the rock from late May to late July. Puffin, Shag, Guillemot, Razorbill, Herring Gull and Kittiwake breed in small numbers. Similar species breed on Craigleath, although there are no Gannets.

 ACCESS: Boats trips are run throughout the

summer from North Berwick, subject to weather. Landing on Bass Rock is restricted to the latter end of the breeding season to avoid undue disturbance. There is no guarantee of landing on either island; this is at the discretion of the boatman. For further information, contact the boatman, Fred Marr, on Tel: 01620 893863, or the tourist information office on Tel: 01620 892197.

DISABLED ACCESS: Landing is not possible. Contact the above for possibility of boat trips.

OTHER ATTRACTIONS

HAILES CASTLE: Ruins in an attractive setting. Close to Haddington.

PRESTON MILL: This 17th-century water-powered mill, owned by the National Trust for Scotland, is one of the most attractive in the country. Preston lies just off the A1, south of North Berwick.

Gannets on the Rock.

colony is truly memorable. Quite unperturbed by human presence, the Gannets make this a photographer's paradise. A few other species of seabird breed in very small numbers.

The nearby island of Craigleath has a thriving colony of Puffins, as well as Razorbills and Guillemots. Landing is permitted on this island, which is another very good place for photography.

Bass Rock.

EAST OF Edinburgh on the Firth of Forth are Aberlady Bay and the adjacent Gosford and Gullane Bays, offering some of the best bird-watching in Scotland. Extensive mudflats are used by large numbers of waders and wildfowl during the winter and on passage. Sand dunes, grassland, scrub and mixed woodland all attract a variety of migrant and breeding species.

Aberlady Bay is a Local Nature Reserve, and much of the protected 1430 acres lies below the high-water mark. Pink-footed Geese and, often, Whooper Swans roost on the reserve. Offshore a variety of divers, grebes and wildfowl winter.

Gosford Bay is known for its wintering population of Red-necked Grebes. From mid- to late August they arrive offshore, annually reaching double figures; Ferny Ness on the west side

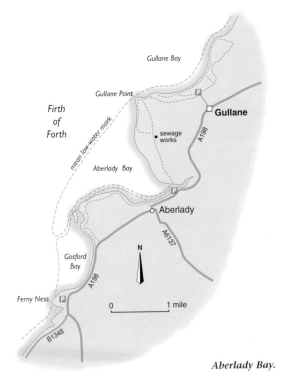

Aberlady Bay.

of Gosford Bay is one of the best places from which to observe them. Numbers tend to drop a little in mid-winter, perhaps due to dispersal up and down the coast. Slavonian Grebes winter between here and Gullane Bay; up to 160 have been counted. Gullane Bay attracts Red-throated Divers, which arrive in September and remain until April. Common and Velvet Scoters have been accompanied by at least one Surf Scoter during recent winters. Gosford Bay is often the more attractive location for this North American species.

From Aberlady Bay, walks can be taken either round Gullane Point into Gullane Bay, or round the coast into Gosford Bay. On the latter route there is a hide at the mid-way point.

Whilst winter provides excellent bird-watching, Aberlady Bay provides much interest throughout the year, especially during passage periods for migrants and waders.

Aberlady Bay is the most important site in Britain for wintering Red-necked Grebes.

BIRDS THROUGH THE SEASONS

SPRING: Red-necked Grebes may be present into May in Gosford Bay or Gullane Bay. Passage waders and passerine migrants come through.

SUMMER: A few waders in summer, including Grey Plover, Bar-tailed Godwit, Knot and Sanderling. Breeding birds include Little Grebe, Shelduck, Eider, Ringed Plover, Lapwing, Redshank, Snipe, Sedge Warbler and Lesser Whitethroat. Sandwich Terns are often numerous in late summer.

AUTUMN: Red-necked Grebes arrive in Gosford Bay in August. Red-throated Divers from September in Gullane Bay. Common Scoter, Velvet Scoter and other species of wintering wildfowl appear during September and October. From late July through to October, passage waders may include Greenshank, Spotted Redshank, Wood Sandpiper and Little Stint. Skuas, various gulls (including Little Gull) and Black Tern are seen during August and September. Passerine migrants can be searched for.

WINTER: Red-necked Grebe, Slavonian Grebe, Great Crested Grebe and Red-throated Diver all on the sea. Pink-footed Geese roost on the mudflats and reach peak numbers in late October to early November. Whooper Swan roost, while other species include Common Scoter, Velvet Scoter, Surf Scoter (almost annual), Eider, Wigeon, Teal, Red-breasted Merganser, Shelduck, Goldeneye, Long-tailed Duck, Short-eared Owl, Long-eared Owl, Peregrine, Merlin, Twite, Brambling, Snow Bunting, Lapland Bunting and the occasional Shorelark.

Access: For Aberlady Bay take the A198 North Berwick–Musselburgh road, which passes the bay just east of Aberlady village. Park in the reserve car park. A track leads across the footbridge round to Gullane Point. Alternatively, walk back along the road and then round the headland to Gosford Bay.

Gullane Bay can also be reached by turning off the A198 in Gullane along Sandy Loan and parking in the car park.

Gosford Bay can be viewed from a number of points along the A198. For Ferny Ness, which is best for the grebes, park in the car park by the bay.

DISABLED ACCESS: All three bays can be accessed. Viewing is possible from a vehicle at a number of points along the A198.

OTHER ATTRACTIONS

EDINBURGH: This attractive city has many sights and lies only a few miles away.

MUIRFIELD GOLF COURSE: Championship golf course at North Berwick.

See also entries under Bass Rock (Site 81).

NATIONALLY IMPORTANT numbers of breeding seabirds and a rich botanic and geological interest ensured that St Abb's Head was declared a National Nature Reserve in 1983.

The reserve is owned by the National Trust for Scotland and is jointly managed by the Scottish Wildlife Trust. Sea cliffs rising to 330 feet, a man-made freshwater loch, grassland areas and a few trees all feature in the 200 acres of the reserve. St Abb's Head owes its name to the daughter of King Edilfred of Northumbria. Whilst escaping from King Mercia in the 7th century, Aebbe (otherwise known as Abb) was shipwrecked here, later becoming leader of a local monastic settlement.

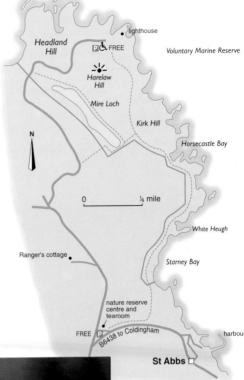

Guillemots cram together on tiny ledges at St Abb's.

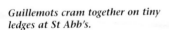

BIRDS

St Abb's offers the opportunity to watch thousands of Guillemots and Kittiwakes perched on their tiny cliff ledges. The indented coastline aids viewing, and the most densely populated cliffs are on Headland Hill. As at all big seabird colonies, the sound of thousands of calling birds adds to the experience.

During spring and autumn, migrants should be searched for, especially in the vicinity of the loch, which regularly turns up a rarity. East or south-easterly winds are best when accompanied by rain or drizzle. Sea-watching is best from the lighthouse and can be productive in autumn when a variety of skuas, Manx Shearwater and, less regularly, Sooty Shearwater fly past.

FLOWERS

Over 250 species of flowering plant occur on the reserve, including the rare Scots Lovage, found on

St Abb's.

White Heugh. Primrose and Early Purple Orchid add colour in spring as the seabirds return to breed. Below the cliffs, submarine kelp forests are washed by strong tides that keep the sea free from pollution. Such conditions allow marine animals and plants to thrive, making this a popular site for divers.

BIRDS THROUGH THE SEASONS

ALL YEAR: Fulmar, Gannet and Shag.
SPRING: Seabirds return to nest. Migrants in April and May include warblers, chats

and flycatchers. Bluethroat and Red-backed Shrike are almost annual.
SUMMER: Mid-May to July is best for breeding seabirds that include Guillemot, Razorbill, a few Puffin, Shag, Fulmar, Kittiwake and Herring Gull. Wheatear and Rock Pipit breed.
AUTUMN: Sea-watching for

Manx Shearwater, Sooty Shearwater, skuas, Common Scoter and Red-throated Diver. Passerine migrants can be abundant. An impressive list of rarities has been recorded and the following are almost annual in autumn: Yellow-browed Warbler, Common Rosefinch, Red-breasted Flycatcher, Wryneck, Red-backed Shrike and Firecrest.
WINTER: The loch can hold a variety of wildfowl, including Tufted Duck, Goldeneye and Wigeon. Offshore, look for Red-throated Diver, Common Scoter and Eider. Purple

Sandpiper can be found on the rocks.

ACCESS:

A circular walk starts at the nature reserve information centre and tearoom. The path leads east and then north along the cliffs. The road or footpaths can then be used to return.

Car parking is free at the Northfield Farm reserve centre, reached by turning off the A1 to Coldingham, then taking the B6438 to St Abb's. Alternatively, the Head can be reached directly by road; there is a small car park by the lighthouse.

For information on guided walks and bookings for group and school visits, contact the ranger at: Ranger's Cottage, Northfield, St Abb's, Eyemouth, Berwickshire TD14 5QF. Tel: 01890 771443.

DISABLED ACCESS:

There is limited access for wheelchair users at the Head. Further information from the ranger, details as above.

OTHER ATTRACTIONS

DUNS: An interesting market town. Within the castle can be found the Jim Clark memorial room, a commemoration to the World Champion racing driver.

MANDERSTON HOUSE: An Edwardian interior, some of the finest stuccoed ceilings completed this century and a grand stable block add to the grandeur of this house. There are gardens and various walks. To the south-west of St Abb's on the A6105 near Duns.

THIS LINE of cliffs, to the south of Stonehaven and overlooking the North Sea, is crammed with seabirds in summer. The tens of thousands of birds make Fowlsheugh one of the more densely populated seabird cities in Britain.

The Old Red Sandstone cliffs rise from 100 to 200 feet in height, the crumbly rock providing nesting seabirds with innumerable ledges. Indentations along the coastline make life easier for the bird-watcher as seabirds can be observed at close quarters.

The cliff-top path leads to several viewpoints. One of the best is the first major indentation reached from the car park. Here, Fulmars

BIRDS THROUGH THE SEASONS
SUMMER: Kittiwake, Razorbill and Guillemot breed in large numbers. There are smaller breeding populations of Shag, Fulmar, Herring Gull and Puffin. Eiders occur offshore and Rock Pipit along the cliff top.

 ACCESS: There is a small cliff-top car park at Crawton, reached from the A92 Inverbervie–Stonehaven road. Three miles south of Stonehaven take the minor road to the car park. Proceed north along the cliff top. Extreme care should be taken when close to the cliff edge.

 Visit Fowlsheugh between April and mid-July as there is little bird interest outside of the breeding season.

DISABLED ACCESS: None.

OTHER ATTRACTIONS

DRUM CASTLE: A 13th-century tower house complete with antiquities. Gardens and nature trails. East of Banchory off the A93.

HOUSE OF DUN: A Palladian house owned by the National Trust for Scotland. Overlooks the Montrose Basin just west of Montrose.

Fowlsheugh is one of the more densely populated seabird 'cities' in Britain. (Right) Razorbill and Guillemot.

glide past on stiffly held wings, often chancing a sideways glance as they rush by. A few Puffins can also be seen close to this spot. Shags breed in caves and on ledges at the cliff base.

THE SPECTACULAR sand dunes and coastal moorland of the Sands of Forvie border the Ythan, a long, narrow estuary with extensive mussel beds towards its mouth. There are areas of inter-tidal mud, sandflats and saltmarsh, all feeding grounds for a wide variety of birds. The area is noted for the wildfowl and waders that winter and pass through in large numbers during spring and autumn.

BIRDS

Situated 12 miles north of Aberdeen, this National Nature Reserve supports Britain's largest concentration of breeding Eider, one of our most attractive and long-lived ducks. During early spring, the males' amusing 'oo-hooo' courtship call can be heard as they attempt to woo females. Once mated and with the female incubating, the males then gather in large flocks in the estuary mouth, spending the summer loafing on sandbanks. During June, females caring for large crèches can be seen further up the estuary in the vicinity of the mussel beds that provide an important food source for this species. With careful scanning of the Eider flocks at any time of year, a King Eider may be seen. At least one male of this Arctic species has been present in the Ythan for the last few years, and during the summer it can often be located towards the mouth of the estuary among the hundreds of male Eiders.

The dunes support four species of breeding tern. On the rising tide, terns can be watched feeding on sand-eels and fish fry close to the estuary mouth. The terns attract both Great and Arctic Skuas in small numbers during late summer.

During spring and autumn, skeins of Pink-footed Geese pass through. A few thousand stay for the winter and are joined by waders and wildfowl, such as Golden Plover, Redshank, Curlew, Teal, Wigeon and, often, Whooper Swans, while in excess of 1000 Eider remain.

Snow Buntings are a common winter visitor to the beaches and dunes.

Sands of Forvie.

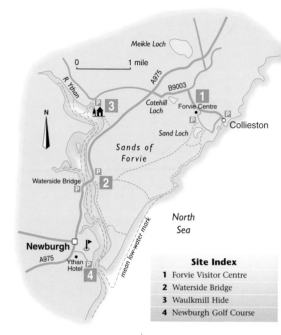

Site Index

1 Forvie Visitor Centre
2 Waterside Bridge
3 Waulkmill Hide
4 Newburgh Golf Course

SITE GUIDE

1

Forvie Visitor Centre

A circular walk can be taken from the visitor centre out on to the moorland that is covered in a rich blanket of Heather, Crowberry and lichens. Boardwalks protect the most vulnerable areas of this fragile environment which support breeding Eider and Curlew. During the winter the moor can be a good location for Short-eared Owls. Sand Loch, close to the visitor centre, often attracts a few duck, and Otter are occasionally seen here.

ACCESS: From the A975 north of the estuary, take the B9003 to Collieston. The visitor centre is on the right just before the village. Access is possible at all times. The reserve manager can be contacted at the Forvie Centre, Collieston, Ellon, Aberdeenshire.

DISABLED ACCESS: None.

2

Waterside Bridge

The bridge allows good views of the estuary. Looking upstream can be particularly productive for wildfowl and waders at low tide. The road north of the bridge follows the estuary for a little way, enabling further viewing from lay-bys.

A walk can be taken from the bridge towards the sea along the north shore of the estuary into the dunes.

ACCESS: Park by the bridge to view the estuary, or walk along the north shore to the dunes. Viewing is possible from lay-bys to the north of the bridge.

DISABLED ACCESS: Much can be seen from the roadside, both from the bridge and from lay-bys to the north. There is no disabled access on to the reserve.

3

Waulkmill Hide

This hide provides good views over the inner estuary. At low tide large areas of mud are exposed, providing a feeding ground for wildfowl and waders.

ACCESS: On the A975, 3 miles north of Newburgh, take the left-hand turn signed to Ellan. After 1½ miles and just before a right-hand bend, take the track off to the left to reach the hide.

DISABLED ACCESS: A vehicle can be driven right up to this hide which allows wheelchair access.

4

Newburgh Golf Course

The outer estuary can be viewed from here. Large numbers of Eiders loaf on

Eider with young.

the sandbanks, and this is also the best place to look for the King Eider. The tern breeding colonies, notably of Sandwich Terns, can be viewed from here by looking across the estuary to the dunes.

ACCESS: Travelling north on the A975 as you enter Newburgh, take the right-hand turn by the Ythan Hotel signed to the golf course. Drive through

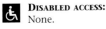

the car park and along the track to the edge of the estuary.

♿ DISABLED ACCESS: None, other than limited viewing from a vehicle.

BIRDS THROUGH THE SEASONS

ALL YEAR: Eider.

SPRING: Shelduck, Teal, Wigeon, Mallard and Goosander on the estuary. Migrant geese include Pink-footed and Greylag, with smaller numbers of Brent, Barnacle and White-fronted Geese. Terns return, with Sandwich being first in early April. Passage waders include Greenshank, Green Sandpiper, Curlew Sandpiper, Ruff, Ringed Plover, Knot, Whimbrel, Bar-tailed Godwit, Golden Plover, Lapwing and Redshank.

SUMMER: Eider will have young out on the estuary. Sandwich, Common, Arctic and Little Tern nesting in the dunes. Great and Arctic

Skua in late summer in the estuary mouth and offshore. Oystercatcher, Curlew and Ringed Plover all breed. Stonechat may be found in areas of bramble and gorse.

AUTUMN: Passage waders, in particular Golden Plover. Migrating geese, most notably Pink-footed. Wild-fowl, both passing through and arriving for the winter, include scoter, Long-tailed Duck and Goldeneye.

WINTER: Over-wintering

Ythan Estuary.

geese, mainly Pink-footed and Greylags. Whooper Swans often winter. Wigeon, Mallard, Teal, Goldeneye, Red-breasted Merganser, Long-tailed Duck, Common and Velvet Scoter, Red-throated Diver, Short-eared Owl, Merlin, Peregrine and Snow Bunting can all be seen. There are a variety of wintering waders on the estuary and surrounding fields, with notable numbers of Redshank and Golden Plover.

OTHER ATTRACTIONS

CRUDEN BAY: A popular tourist resort with golf courses, sandy beaches and a number of historical sites. Just south of Peterhead.

FYVIE CASTLE: Situated in a wooded park on the River Ythan, this castle dates back to the 13th century. Reached off the A947 due north of Inverurie.

PETERHEAD: Once a whaling port, the town has a variety of attractions.

A male King Eider has been present on the estuary for many years.

THIS LOCH is the largest dune slack pool in Britain, and is internationally important as a staging post and wintering ground for thousands of ducks, geese and swans.

The loch's attraction is due both to its position just a few hundred yards from the North Sea and to the scarcity of large expanses of water in the region.

BIRDS
Whooper Swan, Pink-footed and Greylag Geese, and Teal are particularly abundant during winter, when the reserve can support upwards of 30,000 birds. The Pink-footed Geese start to arrive during September and peak by November. During early October, Barnacle Geese stop off on their journey from Spitzbergen to the Solway on Scotland's west coast, and in recent years some have remained to winter.

Birds inhabit the surrounding fields, marshes, dunes and scrub throughout the year. During spring and autumn, waders pass through on passage, while in summer Marsh Harriers are often present. A variety of wildfowl and terns breed.

Winter bird-watching can be enjoyed from a number of hides, some of which overlook the loch while others have views on to

The rare Temminck's Stint is an annual passage migrant.

wader scrapes. The reserve centre has a viewing gallery overlooking the marsh and pools.

OTHER ANIMALS
Roe deer are conspicuous, but the resident Otters and Badgers are rarely seen.

FLOWERS
The dunes are home to some interesting plants, including Scots Lovage, Grass of Parnassus, and both Field and Autumn Gentian.

BIRDS THROUGH THE SEASONS
SPRING: Most of the wintering wildfowl have departed by the end of April. Passage waders include Wood Sandpiper and, regularly, Temminck's Stint.

(map)
to St Combs
B9033
North Sea
Loch of Strathbeg
P Savoch
Starnafin
to Fraserburgh
Crimond
access by permit only
A952
N
0   1 mile
to St Fergus & Aberdeen

SUMMER: Breeding birds include Shelduck, Shoveler (a few pairs), Teal, Tufted Duck, Eider, Water Rail and Sedge Warbler. Garganey are often recorded, while Marsh Harrier and Black-tailed Godwit summer. Sandwich and Common Tern breed. Large numbers of Mute Swan visit the loch to moult.

AUTUMN: During August, passage waders include Ruff, Greenshank, Black-tailed Godwit, Green Sandpiper, Spotted Redshank, Dunlin, Curlew Sandpiper and Little Stint. Pink-footed Geese start to arrive in September, while Barnacle Geese stop off in October. By the end of September, wildfowl numbers are beginning to build up.

WINTER: Pink-footed, Greylag and Barnacle Geese, Whooper Swan, Mute Swan, Mallard, Teal, Wigeon, Pochard, Tufted Duck, Goldeneye, Red-breasted Merganser, Goosander, Smew, Sparrowhawk and Coot.

Access: Reached from the A952 Peterhead–Fraserburgh road. There are three separate locations that can be reached by car from the village of Crimond. To reach the visitor centre, follow the signs from the A952. Detailed directions to the hides can be obtained from here.

DISABLED ACCESS: Wheelchair access to Savoch hide only. The viewing gallery is accessible by just a few steps. Very limited views of parts of the loch from a vehicle.

OTHER ATTRACTIONS

DEER ABBEY: A 13th-century Cistercian abbey. There is a country park and visitor centre near by at Old Deer. Due west of Peterhead on the A950.

FRASERBURGH: Fraserburgh has a few places of interest and a couple of attractive golf courses.

See also entries under Sands of Forvie and the Ythan Estuary (Site 85).

Whooper Swans are one of the main winter attractions.

THE SIGHT and sound of skeins of wild geese is the main attraction to be enjoyed at Vane Farm, an RSPB reserve since 1967. Shore, marsh, grassland, woodland and heather moorland comprise the reserve's 571 acres in the south-east corner of the loch.

in Britain for this species. They start to appear in late September, reaching a peak in early November. Many then disperse to leave a reduced winter population that remains until May. Up to 5000 Greylag Geese also winter, with a few remaining to breed during the summer months. The

other obvious winter visitor is the Whooper Swan.

The loch is a wetland of international importance, and is designated a Ramsar Site as over 20,000 wildfowl are regularly present in winter.

The RSPB visitor facilities at Vane Farm include a heated observation room that is ideal for viewing the geese. Arable farmland and grassland managed by the RSPB attract the geese away from the surrounding private farmland. Small pools and scrapes have been created, providing wildfowl and passage waders with feeding and resting sites. To experience the vastness of the loch, a circular walk can be taken from the reserve centre up Vane Hill behind it. The loch stretches out below, with St Serf's Island on the right and Castle Island on the left, the latter being where Mary Queen of Scots was once held prisoner.

Tufted Ducks are one of five duck species that nest on St Serf's Island.

BIRDS

Loch Leven is of major importance not only for wintering wildfowl (in particular Pink-footed Geese), but also for its large numbers of breeding wildfowl. Several islands provide nesting sites for duck, in particular St Serf's Island, which supports up to 1000 pairs. These include large numbers of Mallard, a few pairs of Shoveler and Wigeon, and up to 60 pairs of Gadwall. A large colony of Black-headed Gulls are attractive to a few hundred pairs of Tufted Duck that nest here.

In winter, up to 20,000 Pink-footed Geese arrive from their breeding grounds in Iceland and Greenland. Loch Leven is one of the main arrival sites

to Perth

Milnathort

A911

A922

7

Kinross

6

to Scotlandwell

Castle Island

Loch Leven

M90

St Serf's Island

B996

N

B9097

P

Vane Farm

to Kinglassie

B9097

5

0   1 mile

to Edinburgh

The approach to the top of the hill passes through birch woodland. A hide provides views of the more common woodland birds. In summer, Spotted Flycatcher, Tree Pipit and Willow Warbler breed. Green and Great Spotted Woodpeckers occur throughout the year.

BIRDS THROUGH THE SEASONS

ALL YEAR: Great Crested Grebe, Cormorant, Grey Heron, Mute Swan, Greylag Goose, Wigeon, Teal, Mallard, Shoveler, Pochard, Tufted Duck, Ruddy Duck, Sparrowhawk, Oystercatcher, Curlew, Redshank, Snipe, Green and Great Spotted Woodpecker.

SPRING: Many wintering species are still present into April and some geese into early May. Passage waders may be seen on the scrapes and loch shore.

SUMMER: Nesting wildfowl out on the loch include Wigeon, Gadwall, Mallard, Shoveler, Tufted Duck, and a few Greylag Geese. Breeding waders include Common Sandpiper, Redshank, Curlew, Snipe, Lapwing, Oystercatcher and Ringed Plover. In the woodland there are Spotted Flycatcher, Willow Warbler, and Tree Pipit. Wheatear are found on Vane Hill.

AUTUMN: Passage waders include Greenshank, Green Sandpiper, Wood Sandpiper and Black-tailed Godwit. The geese start to arrive in late September.

WINTER: By late October/early November the Pink-footed Geese have peaked in number, and dispersal is under way before the population stabilises. Greylag Goose, Whooper Swan, and often

Loch Leven viewed from the top of Vane Hill.

small numbers of Bewick's Swan, Goldeneye, Goosander, Smew and Long-tailed Duck are seen out on the loch. Gadwall, Shoveler, Mallard, Wigeon, Tufted Duck and Pochard are numerous.

ACCESS: Although there are a couple of other access points around the loch, Vane Farm is by far the best site from which to observe birds and for an excellent view of the whole lake. A hide overlooking some pools and the shore is reached by a walkway under the road from the car park. A further woodland hide is situated on the nature trail on Vane Hill.

The reserve is reached from Junction 5 of the M90. Take the B9097 towards Glenrothes for 2 miles; the reserve centre is on the right. The nature trail giving access to the viewpoint on Vane Hill is open at all times.

The nature centre with observation room is open daily from April to Christmas from 10am to 5pm, and from January to March from 10am to 4pm. Closed between Christmas and the New Year. For group visits, contact the warden in advance at Vane Farm Nature Centre, Kinross, Tayside KY13 7LX. Tel: 01577 862355.

DISABLED ACCESS: A ramp allows access to the observation room.

OTHER ATTRACTIONS

CULROSS: On the Firth of Forth just east of Kincardine is this small town, with a 13th-century abbey and a superb example of a 16th-century palace.

DEWAR'S DISTILLERY: Visitors are welcome to tour this distillery in Perth.

PERTH: This town, lying to the north, contains a mix of 18th- and 19th-century buildings, and has a long and chequered history.

SPEYSIDE ENCOMPASSES some of Scotland's most beautiful scenery. Pine-fringed lochs, tumbling streams and heather moorland flank the River Spey. Overlooking the area is the imposing Cairngorm Plateau, rising to over 3000 feet and supporting an Arctic–Alpine flora and a select band of bird species adapted to the harsh environment.

The whole area is subject to tens of thousands of visitors every year, who come to enjoy the beauty of the landscape, to walk, fish, shoot and just relax. During winter, too, the main tourist resort of Aviemore is alive with skiers who use a restricted area on Cairn Gorm. Due to the popularity of the region, there is a tourist infrastructure providing plentiful accommodation and facilities for the visiting bird watcher.

 BIRDS
Most of the Scottish speciality birds can be seen year-round, with the exception of Osprey and Dotterel which are present

Dotterel can be found on the top of the Cairngorm Plateau in summer.

Capercaillie displaying.

only in summer. Within the native Scots Pine forest of Abernethy, an RSPB reserve, can be found Crested Tit, Capercaillie and Scottish Crossbill, three specialists found only in this habitat. Loch Garten, within Abernethy, is home to the famous nesting Ospreys, these having witnessed over 1.5 million visitors since the start of Operation Osprey in 1959.

During the latter half of the last century, Ospreys in Scotland came under increasing pressure from egg collectors and hunters until they finally ceased to breed in 1916. They returned to breed successfully in 1954, and their increase to almost 100 breeding pairs today is one of the great

conservation success stories of the last 50 years.

Another species persecuted was the Capercaillie, a huge turkey-like bird dependent on native pine forest for its survival. Eventually made extinct in the late 18th century, they were reintroduced in 1837. Today, these birds roam the pine forests unmolested, but as they are very shy, they are best searched for at dawn.

Capercaillies have a remarkable courtship ritual. In April, males lek in clearings in the forest, gathering within the lekking arena before dawn. Fanning their tails, they strut up and down uttering a series of clicking noises. This behaviour is acted out to attract females which gather in trees to decide which male to mate with. Successful males can be surrounded by females.

The Caledonian pine forests, on which the Capercaillie is so dependent, have stood for hundreds of years. Only pockets of the original forest remain as many areas were deforested and replanted for commercial purposes, but

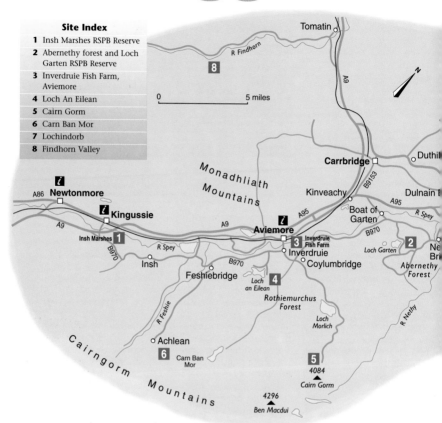

much work is now being done to return sites to their former appearance. The old forests have a rich, shrubby ground layer of Bilberry, Heather and Juniper, providing food and shelter for a range of wildlife, and also contain flowering plants such as Twinflower and wintergreens.

The Scottish Crossbill is confined to these forests, being endemic to Scotland with a population of 1500 birds. The birds are best looked for at the tops of pines, where they feed on pine-cone seeds. Britain's rarest tit, the Crested Tit, is native to these forests. With a distinctive crest

and trilling call, these can also be difficult to see. With patience, however, all the forest birds can be tracked down.

The lochs not only support fishing Ospreys but also the rare Slavonian Grebe that breeds in a few discrete locations. Another rare breeder is the Golden-eye, this nesting in tree holes. To encourage more pairs to breed, the RSPB has erected over 500 nestboxes which the birds readily use.

The rivers and streams in the area are home to Dippers and Grey Wagtails, while the surrounding moorlands have good populations of Red Grouse and a small number of

Black Grouse. Hen Harrier and Merlin both breed.

Bordering the Spey Valley is Cairngorm. A very specialised bird community exists on the plateau, numbering only a very few species. Dotterel are summer visitors that arrive to nest on the montane plateau. Ptarmigans, hardy members of the grouse family, live up on the mountain tops all year, experiencing the hardest weather Scotland can muster. Other specialities include Snow Bunting and Golden Eagle. The latter hunt the Mountain Hare which, during the winter months, can be hard to spot in its seasonal white coat.

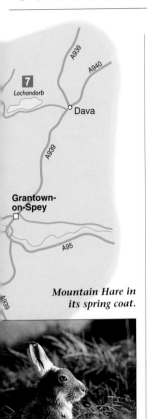

Mountain Hare in its spring coat.

OTHER ANIMALS

Speyside is a good location in which to see the Red Squirrel. Much more elusive are the Pine Marten and Wild Cat, both of which are resident but rarely seen. Besides Red Deer, Roe Deer are plentiful, especially in the forest mires. Important populations of insects include the Scotch Argus butterfly, on the wing in July and August. The rare Northern Damselfly breeds in the forest mires and lochans of Abernethy, while over 400 species of beetle have been recorded from this one site.

SITE GUIDE

1

Insh Marshes
RSPB Reserve

Adjacent to the town of Kingussie, the RSPB manages 2100 acres of marsh, woodland and moorland in the flood plain of the River Spey. The marshland birds can be tricky to see here and are often quite distant. Two hides and a couple of trails lead out from a small information centre. Breeding birds include Greylag Goose, Shoveler, Wigeon, Teal, Tufted Duck, Goldeneye, Curlew, Redshank, Snipe and Grasshopper Warbler. Ospreys are a regular feature in summer as they fish over the reserve. Spotted Crakes have been heard to call in some years and are best listened for after dark. The woodland supports breeding Tree Pipit and Redstart in summer.

During winter there is often a large herd of Whooper Swans and Hen Harriers. Greylag and Pink-footed Geese use the marshes in spring and autumn.

 ACCESS: The reserve information centre and car park are reached off the B970 Kingussie–Insh village road approximately 1½ miles from Kingussie. Views across the marshes can be obtained from several points along the B970.

There are two trails and two hides. The reserve is open daily from 9am.

 DISABLED ACCESS: None on the reserve. A limited area can be viewed from the B970.

2

Abernethy Forest and Loch Garten
RSPB Reserve

Loch Garten, famed for the nesting Ospreys that have returned annually since 1959, is within the 30,760-acre Abernethy Forest Reserve. Capercaillie, Scottish Crossbill and Crested Tit are all resident breeders. The lochs support breeding Goldeneye.

Insh Marshes.

Abernethy Forest is the largest tract of native pinewood in Britain. The reserve also incorporates the Nethy River, farmland, moorland and mountain plateaux.

The Ospreys usually return during the first week of April, laying their eggs at the end of the month. Closed-circuit TV relays pictures live to the visitor centre, thereby offering a fascinating view of life in the nest. From the Osprey hide it is sometimes possible to see Capercaillie; in some years they have even lekked within sight of the hide. The path from the car park to the hide should provide views of Crested Tit and, if you are lucky, Scottish Crossbill too.

There are a number of tracks into the forest that will allow you to search for these species; one of the best is at Forest Lodge. Here, two tracks lead through the pinewoods, the area close to the car park being especially good for Scottish Crossbill. Try also the tracks leading to Loch Mallachie; a pleasant circular walk can be taken to the loch and back. Early mornings along the tracks and on the surrounding forest roads may produce a Capercaillie if you are lucky.

Around 60 species of bird nest on the reserve, including Redstart, Goldcrest, Siskin, Spotted Flycatcher and Coal Tit. Woodcock can be seen roding in the spring. Black Grouse and Long-eared Owl are much more elusive. Loch Garten has breeding Goldeneye, while, during the winter, groups of Goosander, large numbers of Greylag Geese and a variety of gulls come here to roost.

ACCESS: Close to the village of Boat of Garten, Loch Garten is signposted from the B970 and, during the summer months when the Ospreys are present, is usually signposted from Aviemore. See map for various access points. The tracks should be kept to at all times when walking in the reserve.

Binoculars and telescopes are available at the Osprey observation hide to view the birds, as is the closed-circuit TV. There are a number of volunteers on hand to answer questions, and there is a shop. Group visits should be arranged with the warden by writing to RSPB, Abernethy Forest, Grianan, Nethybridge, Highlands PH25 3EF.

The Osprey observation hide does not open immediately the birds return in spring, as a settling down period is allowed. If planning an early spring visit, it may be wise to check with the Aviemore tourist office first.

DISABLED ACCESS: This is good, with wheelchair access along the track to Loch Mallachie if with a strong pusher. A firm track leads to the Osprey observation centre, where there are disabled viewing facilities. Cars with disabled occupants can be driven to the centre.

3

Inverdruie Fish Farm, Aviemore

This fish farm, within walking distance of Aviemore, is famous for its fishing Ospreys. Birds visit daily in summer. There is a hide that overlooks a well-stocked pool, left uncovered for the birds. The most productive time to visit is early morning or evening. The Ospreys can be viewed over the farm from the tourist information centre car park in Aviemore by looking beyond the railway line.

ACCESS: If travelling south through Aviemore, take the turning on the left to Coylumbridge after the tourist information centre. The fish farm is on the left, just past the bridge over the River Spey.

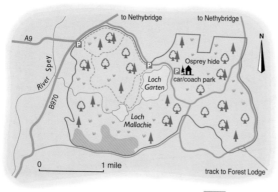

DISABLED ACCESS:
This is possible at the fish farm, but wheelchair users would need assistance throughout.

4

Loch An Eilean

Scenically superb, Loch An Eilean is one of the region's most attractive lochs. The ruined castle in the middle of the loch is an old Comyn stronghold, and was once used by nesting Ospreys. The loch often has Red-throated Diver and Goldeneye during the summer. The surrounding pine forest supports Redstart and Crested Tit, and can be a good site for Scottish Crossbill. Several of the large pines are more than 250 years old. A nature trail leads around the loch shore. Loch An Eilean does suffer from hordes of tourists during the summer months, so an early morning or evening visit may be preferable.

ACCESS: Head south on the B970 from Inverdruie. After 1 mile there is an unclassified road on the left signed to the loch. A nature trail leads from the car park.

DISABLED ACCESS: There is access to the loch shore.

5

Cairngorm

Ptarmigan, Dotterel and Snow Bunting are the specialist species found on Cairngorm. Britain's highest mountain plateau extends for 160 square miles and is home to four out of the five highest summits in Britain. The highest peak is Ben Macdui, rising to 4300 feet. Covered in snow for much of the year, the plateau endures a subarctic climate, reflected in its flora and fauna.

Cairngorm enjoys the highest annual snowfall of anywhere in Britain, and the area has become popular with skiers. A complete tourist infrastructure has developed, putting immense pressure on this fragile environment. The ski-lifts, however, do enable easy access to the high tops for the bird watcher. Between May and August, Dotterel, Snow Bunting and Ptarmigan can be found on the tops. Indeed, the latter two species are present all year round, although in times of heavy snow cover they may be best looked for at lower altitudes.

Ptarmigan inhabit the boulder fields. They have a distinctive croaking call to listen out for. Often remarkably tame, this species is best spotted by

The Cairngorms viewed from Cairn Gorm.

walking slowly, and scanning ahead regularly.

Dotterel are also tame and again can be difficult to locate. This species is a very rare breeding bird in Britain, and you should be aware that it is a criminal offence to disturb a Dotterel at or near its nest.

Snow Buntings vary annually in their abundance but are the easiest of the three species to locate. During the winter they are often found around the Ptarmigan Restaurant just below the Cairn Gorm summit and around the car parks at the bottom of the chair-lifts. You may be lucky enough to see a Golden Eagle – a few pairs breed in the more remote areas.

 ACCESS: From Aviemore take the Coylumbridge road and continue past Loch Morlich up to the car parks below the ski-lifts. Once on the tops, it is more productive to walk on past the Cairn Gorm summit along the ridge towards Ben Macdui. The boulder field leading away from this ridge is a good site for Ptarmigan.

Ptarmigan moulting from winter to summer plumage.

The further you walk from the chair-lifts, the better the chances of finding birds. The weather on Cairn Gorm can change in an instant, so you should ensure you are fully prepared for walking in the mountains. A compass and a good map are essential as it is easy to get lost once away from the chair-lifts.

 DISABLED ACCESS: None.

6

Carn Ban Mor

Much less disturbed than the Cairn Gorm summit area, this site is particularly good for the high-top specialities, especially Dotterel and Ptarmigan. There is also a better chance of seeing Golden Eagle and the occasional Peregrine here. A path climbs 2297 feet to the tops.

 ACCESS: Approached from the B970 from Inverdruie or Kingussie. At Feshiebridge, take the road to Lagganlia. Follow this road for 5 miles to its end at Achlean. Take the track from here to the summit.

 DISABLED ACCESS: None.

7

Lochindorb

Grouse moor surrounds this large freshwater loch. The moorland, which is easily explored from the roads, has a good population of Red Grouse because this is a managed estate. Short-eared Owl and Hen Harrier breed, as do small numbers of Twite. There are often Red-throated Divers on the loch. The shoreline may produce a few waders, such as locally breeding Dunlin, Golden Plover, Common Sandpiper, Lapwing, Curlew and Redshank. Raven and Golden Eagle occur.

 ACCESS: The area is easily worked from a vehicle. Take the B9007 north from the A938 between Carrbridge and Dulnain Bridge. The next road on the right along this minor road takes you down to the loch.

 DISABLED ACCESS: As above, the area can be worked from a vehicle.

8

Findhorn Valley

Steep-sided mountain ridges in the upper reaches of this valley are particularly attractive to soaring Golden Eagles. The picturesque River Findhorn is home to Dipper, Grey Wagtail, Common Sandpiper and Oystercatcher, as well as the occasional Goosander.

The raptors are the principal attraction. Merlin, Buzzard, Kestrel and Sparrowhawk can all be located. For the Golden Eagles, constant scanning of the skies and along the mountain ridges on clear, dry days should, with perseverance, produce results.

A road follows the river up the valley for some 9

River Findhorn in the Findhorn Valley.

miles to the start of a track. Cars must be parked here, but the track has a number of paths leading off it which can be walked – except in the stalking and grouse-shooting seasons from mid-August to February.

A population of feral goats inhabits the valley. Red Deer are farmed and so are numerous, especially during the winter. During summer they tend to move up to the mountain tops. The only turning to the right a little way along the valley takes you up on to some moorland that is excellent for Red Grouse and Mountain Hares.

ACCESS: Turn off the A9 15 miles south of Inverness at Tomatin and take the minor road on the north side of the bridge up the valley. Just past the right-hand turn that leads up on to moorland is a wooden bridge. This is a good place at which to stop and look for Dipper. Where the road eventually ends, park and walk.

DISABLED ACCESS: Much can be seen from a vehicle as the road follows the river closely. The right-hand turn up on to the moor is easily worked from a vehicle.

BIRDS THROUGH THE SEASONS

ALL YEAR: Goldeneye, Sparrowhawk, Goshawk, Kestrel, Buzzard, Peregrine, Hen Harrier, Golden Eagle, Long-eared Owl, Red Grouse, Black Grouse, Ptarmigan, Capercaillie, Woodcock, Great Spotted Woodpecker, Grey Wagtail, Dipper, Crested Tit, Coal Tit, Raven, Scottish Crossbill, Crossbill and Snow Bunting.
SPRING: Pink-footed and Greylag Geese pass through on passage. The Ospreys usually return in the first week of April. Dotterel arrive back on the tops in early May.
SUMMER: Breeding birds other than the specialities already mentioned include: Slavonian Grebe, Red-breasted Merganser, Goosander, Short-eared Owl,

Merlin, Golden Plover, Common Sandpiper, Dunlin, Curlew, Redshank, Lapwing, Redstart, Tree Pipit, Wood Warbler, Pied Flycatcher, Spotted Flycatcher, Ring Ouzel, Wheatear, Whinchat, Siskin and Redpoll. A handful of Red-throated Divers are often present on the various lochs.
AUTUMN: Pink-footed Geese pass through.
WINTER: Whooper Swan, Greylag Goose, Goosander, Redwing, Fieldfare and Brambling.

OTHER ATTRACTIONS

AVIEMORE CENTRE: This complex has a cinema, ice rink, shopping centre and swimming pool. In Aviemore.

THE HIGHLAND FOLK MUSEUM: An insight into Highland life through history is offered in this Kingussie museum.

HIGHLAND WILDLIFE PARK: A range of native species can be seen here. Includes a drive-through section. North-east of Kingussie on the A86.

LANDMARK VISITOR CENTRE: Situated at Carrbridge, the centre has an interesting exhibition of the story of man in the Highlands. There is also a sculpture display, nature trails and a restaurant.

RUTHVEN BARRACKS: Illuminated at night, this stronghold dates back to the 13th century and has a fascinating history. It stands on a hill opposite Kingussie and overlooks the Insh Marshes reserve.

LOCH RUTHVEN is the most important breeding site for Slavonian Grebes in Britain. During summer they can be watched from the RSPB reserve at the eastern end of the loch. A hide overlooks Bottle Sedge beds in a sheltered bay where some of the birds nest.

Slavonian Grebes were first recorded nesting in the Highlands in 1908. Today, the British breeding population numbers around 60 pairs, a quarter of which nest on Loch Ruthven. Red-breasted Merganser, Teal, Tufted Duck and Wigeon also breed here.

The loch is surrounded by birch woodland, heather moorland and rocky crags. The woodland supports a few Siskin and Redpoll. Black Grouse are seen occasionally. The best sites for this species are the fields on the north-eastern side of the loch, which can be viewed from the hide by looking to the extreme right across the loch.

BIRDS THROUGH THE SEASONS

SPRING AND SUMMER: The Slavonian Grebes gather in early spring on the loch. Between May and July is probably the optimum time for a visit. Other breeding birds include Red-breasted Merganser, Mallard, Teal, Wigeon, Tufted Duck, Coot, Raven, Kestrel, Buzzard, Black Grouse, Siskin and Redpoll. Peregrine, Hen Harrier and Osprey are seen regularly.

 ACCESS: From the A9, turn west on to the B851 6 miles from Inverness. Fork right at East

Loch Ruthven.

Croachy on to a minor road where there is a car park by the loch shore. A trail from here leads to the hide.

♿ **DISABLED ACCESS:** None.

OTHER ATTRACTIONS

DRUMNADROCHIT: On the west bank of Loch Ness, this village offers a range of activities from pony trekking to angling and climbing. Also home to the Loch Ness monster exhibition.

FOYERS: On the east side of Loch Ness, this was the site of the first hydro-electric power scheme in Britain. After heavy rain, the falls here are spectacular.

LOCH NESS: Narrow, deep 20-mile long loch famous for its monster.

URQUHART CASTLE: On the west side of Loch Ness; dates to the Norman period.

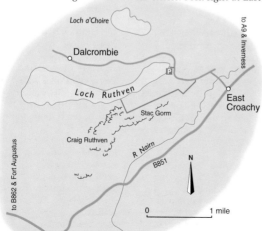

THIS 17,570-acre reserve is the RSPB's second-biggest land holding. The Flow Country, of which the Forsinaird reserve is part, is of major importance for breeding birds that include Red-throated and Black-throated Divers, Greenshank and Golden Plover.

Just 35 miles from John O' Groats, this reserve represents a vast area of peatlands that form the largest stretch of blanket bog in Britain.

Blanket bog develops in wet, cool climates where sphagnum-dominated vegetation can grow. The sphagnum mosses are the powerhouse of the bog, enabling the surface to be kept moist even in the driest conditions. The mosaic of pool systems are essential for supporting a variety of insects, the food source for many of the birds that breed here.

Few roads intrude into the Flow Country. Bird-watching is difficult as breeding-bird density is low and the land area is vast and featureless. The Flows are of interest for birds only during the breeding season. Those species present are typically northern species breeding on the southern limit of their range.

The RSPB has converted the railway station at Forsinaird into the Flow Country Visitor Centre. This gives an insight into the ecology of blanket bogs, the birds and wildlife of the Flows, and their vulnerability to human interference. Guided walks are given, usually twice a week between April and the end of July. A self-guided trail leads down to the Dubh Lochan cluster. Many of the breeding waders feed in the fields viewable from the road-side north of the visitor centre, in March/April and again in June. The breeding birds are very sensitive to disturbance. Due to the scarcity of many species, you are unlikely to see many of the birds listed. Forsinaird allows the visitor

to experience the habitat more than the birds.

 OTHER ANIMALS
Various dragonflies here include the Azure Hawker.

 FLOWERS
Within the bogs an interesting flora includes Dwarf Birch, three species of sundew, Bog Bean and Deer Grass.

BIRDS THROUGH THE SEASONS
SUMMER: Breeding birds include: Red-throated Diver, Black-throated Diver, Wigeon, Common Scoter, Hen Harrier, Golden Eagle, Merlin, Peregrine, Golden Plover, Curlew, Dunlin, Greenshank, Short-eared Owl, Dipper, Twite, Wheatear, Raven and Ptarmigan.

 ACCESS: Forsinaird is midway along the A897 that runs between the A836 on the north coast and the A9 on the east coast. This is a spectacular road with views across the peatlands. Alternatively, Forsinaird is on the Inverness–Thurso railway. British Rail enquiries, Tel: 01463 242124. Some walks coincide with a return journey from the south.

RSPB visitor centre at Forsinaird.

The visitor centre is open from 1 April to 31 October, 9am to 6pm.

There are usually two, 3-hr walks a week, plus the occasional early morning walk to listen for singing waders. For further details contact the warden, Norrie Russell on Tel: 01641 571225.

The B871 that forks off the A897 at Kinbrace south of Forsinaird is worth exploring if time permits.

DISABLED ACCESS:
Roadside viewing is all that is currently possible at this site.

OTHER ATTRACTIONS

DOUNREAY EXHIBITION: Dounreay, on the north coast, is dominated by the nuclear reactor. An exhibition details the story of nuclear energy.

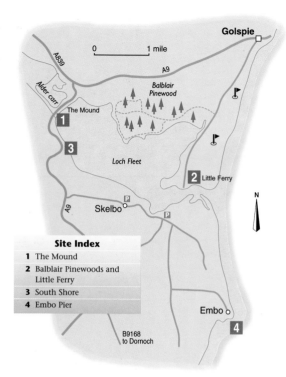

Balblair
Pinewood

The Mound

1

3

Loch Fleet

2 Little Ferry

Skelbo

Site Index

1 The Mound
2 Balblair Pinewoods and Little Ferry
3 South Shore
4 Embo Pier

Embo

4

B9168
to Dornoch

Golspie

0   1 mile

A9

A839

Alder carr

A9

N

2866 acres of the loch and surrounding habitats as a reserve. Pinewoods, sand dunes, heath and Alder carr surround the loch.

At low tide extensive areas of mud are exposed, yet Loch Fleet does not support a particularly large wader population, although a good variety can sometimes be seen on passage.

BIRDS

Regular wintering species include Curlew, Golden Plover, Knot, Wigeon, Mallard and Teal. The surrounding fields are attractive to a small herd of Whooper Swans and Greylag Geese. Balblair Pinewood supports Scottish Crossbill and Redstart in summer. Ospreys are regular and Peregrines rarer.

The coast between Embo and Golspie is of most interest. Autumn and late spring see the largest numbers of seaduck. During the winter, Eider are numerous, with smaller numbers of Red-breasted

THIS TIDAL basin and coast-line to the south of Golspie is best visited from winter to late spring. Wildfowl occur in impressive

numbers both in the loch and offshore, where they are joined by divers and grebes. The Scottish Wildlife Trust manages

Loch Fleet.

Merganser, Common Scoter, Long-tailed Duck and Goldeneye. All three species of diver, both Red-necked and Slavonian Grebe and Velvet Scoter may be on the sea. In some years a King Eider and the odd Surf Scoter winter. During April and May up to 2000 Long-tailed Ducks gather before their departure north to breed.

 OTHER ANIMALS
Common Seals regularly loaf on sand banks.

 FLOWERS
The pinewoods support a rich ground flora that includes One-flowered Wintergreen, Twinflower and Creeping Lady's Tresses.

SITE GUIDE

The Mound

A car park by the A9 at the head of the loch allows views into an area of Alder carr which has resulted from an abortive attempt to drain the loch. Passage waders may include Greenshank on the Mound Pool.

Balblair Pinewood and Little Ferry

From Golspie take the minor road south to Little Ferry. There are car parks from which exploration of the woods can take place. For views of the seaduck, park at Little Ferry and walk east to the loch mouth.

South Shore

A minor road running from the A9 along the south shore of the loch provides various viewing points.

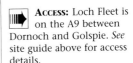

Embo Pier

Reached by going through the caravan site at Embo to its far south-east corner. This is an excellent site for seaduck, and favoured by King Eider when present. If there are few birds, it is worth walking back along the shore towards the loch mouth.

BIRDS THROUGH THE SEASONS
ALL YEAR: Eider, Buzzard, Sparrowhawk, Goldcrest, Coal Tit, Siskin and Scottish Crossbill.
SPRING: Long-tailed Ducks peak in April and May. Many other species of wildfowl that have wintered are present into May. Passage waders include Greenshank.
SUMMER: Breeding birds include Fulmar, Shelduck, Arctic Tern and Redstart. Osprey visit.
AUTUMN: Passage waders include Greenshank, Dunlin, Bar-tailed Godwit, Knot and Golden Plover. Seaduck start to increase in numbers. During north-westerly or northerly winds and in poor visibility skuas and the occasional shearwater are possible.
WINTER: Offshore and in the estuary mouth, Long-tailed Duck, Goldeneye, Red-breasted Merganser,

Long-tailed Duck.

Common and Velvet Scoter, Slavonian and occasional Red-necked Grebe, and all three species of diver occur. Dabbling duck in and around the estuary include Mallard, Wigeon and Teal. Greylag Goose and Whooper Swan occur in the fields. Peregrine and Hen Harrier are occasionally seen. Short-eared Owl are regular. Twite and Snow Bunting may be found in the dunes.

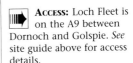 **ACCESS:** Loch Fleet is on the A9 between Dornoch and Golspie. *See* site guide above for access details.

DISABLED ACCESS: Viewing from a vehicle is possible along the minor roads around the loch. Wheelchair users may need assistance if further exploration is desired.

OTHER ATTRACTIONS

DORNOCH: This town has a golf course and much of historical interest.

DUNROBIN CASTLE: Just north of Golspie, this is a fine castle with a mix of French and Scottish architecture.

SCENICALLY BREATHTAKING Inverpolly lies in a region of the British Isles that is as close to wilderness as you are likely to find. Rugged peaks tower over a landscape of rocky hummocks that are interspersed with peat bogs and lochs. This is the domain of the Golden Eagle, Black-throated Diver and Greenshank.

The Inverpolly reserve covers 26,825 acres and is

A mountain stream at Inverpolly.

the second-largest National Nature Reserve in Britain. The Knockan Cliff, famous for its geology, is owned by Scottish Natural Heritage. Most of the rest of the reserve is owned by three different estates. Three peaks dominate, the highest being Cul Mor at 2786 feet.

The reserve can be covered well by the few roads that penetrate this vast area. If walking away from the paths, care is needed as within minutes you can be out of sight of roads and walk all day without encountering another person.

BIRDS
Ptarmigan may be found on the higher ground, whilst frequent scanning with binoculars should eventually provide views of Golden Eagle. The Knockan Cliff nature trail off the A835 provides a good vantage point from which to look for eagles, and is worth a visit purely for its views across the reserve. During spring and summer the lochs below the cliff often have Red-throated Divers on them

and, occasionally, Black-throated Divers. Greenshank nest alongside Golden Plover and Ring Ouzel on the moorland. Scattered patches of birch forest support breeding Woodcock, Wood Warbler and Spotted Flycatcher. The reserve also includes some inaccessible offshore islands that have a few breeding seabirds and are used by wintering Barnacle Geese.

Male Ptarmigan in spring plumage.

OTHER ANIMALS
Around 500 Red Deer roam the reserve, so a few are likely to be encountered during a visit. Wild Cat and Pine Marten are rarely seen. The lochs and rivers contain Eels, Char, Salmon and Trout, all prey for the elusive Otter.

FLOWERS
During July, the boggy moorland is carpeted with the yellow flowers of the Bog Asphodel. Over 360 species of plant have been recorded within the reserve.

SITE GUIDE

Knockan Cliff

Midway between Drumrunie and Elphin on the A835. The nature trail affords one of the most spectacular views to be had anywhere in the Scottish Highlands. Golden Eagle can be looked for and the lochs checked for divers. A reserve centre with local information and displays is open from May to September between 10am and 6pm.

Drumrunie to Lochinver

The reserve can be viewed from this route along roads bordering its edge. Turn west off the A835 at Drumrunie and then, after approximately 7 miles, turn right to Lochinver. You eventually reach the River Kirkaig. This route is one of the best for seeing Red Deer. A good cross-section of birds should be seen by stopping regularly at the various habitats encountered.

River Kirkaig

A walk up the River Kirkaig leads to a series of impressive waterfalls and beyond. The path leads from a car park near Inverkirkaig on the minor road south of Lochinver. From the car park the falls are an easy climb that takes approximately an hour. Upstream from the falls, where the river widens, is an excellent place to watch Dippers. Beyond the falls are bogs and moor stretching away to the dominating peak of Suilven, this rising to 2398 feet.

BIRDS THROUGH THE SEASONS

ALL YEAR: Golden Eagle, Raven, Red Grouse, Ptarmigan and Dipper.

SPRING AND SUMMER: Additional breeding birds to the above include: Red-throated Diver, Black-throated Diver, Red-breasted Merganser, Goosander, Wigeon, Greylag Goose, Buzzard, Merlin, Peregrine, Golden Plover, Greenshank, Woodcock, Ring Ouzel, Wheatear, Stonechat, Wood Warbler, Treecreeper, Long-tailed Tit, Spotted Fly-catcher, Twite and Grey Wagtail. Breeding seabirds on the coast and islands include: Fulmar, Shag, Eider and Black Guillemot.

WINTER: Barnacle Goose on the offshore islands. Snow Buntings often along the roadside.

ACCESS: Inverpolly is reached by taking the A835 north from Ullapool. See site guide for specific information on access.

The best time for a visit is between April and the end of June for the breeding birds.

DISABLED ACCESS: None away from the road. However, much can be seen from a vehicle.

OTHER ATTRACTIONS

This area is remote. The scenery is dramatic, with fishing, walking and climbing being the main activities. The nearest town is Ullapool to the south, which has a plentiful supply of accommodation. Otherwise, accommodation is few and far between, although there are a number of well-placed campsites.

A loch in Inverpolly.

BORDERED ON three sides by high sea cliffs, this 900-acre island is a few hundred yards from the west Sutherland coast. Formerly an RSPB reserve, Handa is now managed by the Scottish Wildlife Trust.

BIRDS
Seabirds breed in large numbers, in particular Guillemot, Razorbill, Kittiwake and Great Skua. The cliff-nesting seabirds are best viewed in the north-west of the island on the Great Stack.

Arctic Skua.

The interior of the island has rough pasture, moorland and a few lochans on which Red-throated Divers occasionally breed. The moorland has a breeding population of both Arctic and Great Skuas. A path leads through the Great Skua colony, allowing close views. The birds are quite tolerant of human visitors.

During spring and autumn, the sandy bays in the south attract a few waders, such as Greenshank, Sanderling and Whimbrel. A small stand of trees around the bothy attracts passerine migrants. During winter a small flock of Barnacle Geese uses the island to graze on. Divers, including Great Northern, can be seen on the sea, sometimes lingering into late spring.

FLOWERS
There are a few plants of interest, including Royal Fern and Scots Lovage. In the damper areas, Bog Asphodel, Pale Butterwort, Heath-Spotted Orchid and Northern Marsh Orchid grow.

The island is of interest for its breeding seabirds, so a visit between mid-April and July is recommended.

BIRDS THROUGH THE SEASONS
SPRING: Passage waders may include Greenshank, Whimbrel, Sanderling, Dunlin and Turnstone. Pomarine Skuas in May. Wintering Great Northern Diver often linger into May. The auks start to come ashore in April, laying eggs in early May. However, cold weather can delay the birds settling down to breed.
SUMMER: Breeding birds include Red-throated Diver, Eider, Shelduck, Oyster-catcher, Ringed Plover, Guillemot, Razorbill, Puffin, Fulmar, Kittiwake, Shag,

A Kittiwake with young.

Great Skua, Arctic Skua, Rock Dove, Snipe, Wheatear and Stonechat. Black Guillemot and Black-throated Diver can be seen offshore and in the sound in summer.
AUTUMN: A few passage waders. Offshore Manx and a few Sooty Shearwaters may be seen.
WINTER: A few Barnacle Geese use the island. Wintering Great Northern Divers in the sound and offshore.

ACCESS: Boats for Handa leave from Tarbet and run daily except Sundays from 1 April to September. The first boat departs at 10am and then according to demand until 2pm. Tel: Scourie 01971 502056 or 502340. If travelling north on the A894, take the first turning on the left after Scourie to Tarbet. The boats depart from the jetty next to the car park.

DISABLED ACCESS: None.

OTHER ATTRACTIONS

See Inverpolly (Site 92).

A BREEDING stronghold for the Corncrake, this reserve reverberates to their monotonous rasping call during the day and night in spring and summer. Balranald is also important for supporting one of the highest breeding densities of waders found anywhere in Europe.

Balranald incorporates a rocky headland, sand dunes, marshland, rough pasture and machair. The latter is a habitat unique to north-west Scotland, created as wind-blown sand has mixed with the underlying peat. During summer, the reserve is awash with colour. Ragged

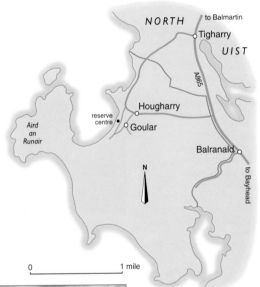

RSPB visitor centre.

Robin is abundant in the meadows close to the reserve centre, while the uncultivated machair is covered in clover, Corn Marigolds and vetches.

The Corncrake benefits from the traditional agricultural methods employed by the local crofters who farm on the reserve. Modern farming practices and especially early silage-making has, in recent years, caused alarming declines in this bird's population. In 1995, however, for the first time in 100 years, the Corncrake population increased in the Scottish Islands. This is the result of a campaign by the RSPB to implement Corncrake-friendly management regimes on crofts and reserves.

The Corncrakes arrive back at Balranald at the end of April from their wintering quarters in south-east Africa. May is the best month in which to see this elusive bird, for as soon as the vegetation starts to grow, they become impossible to spot although infuriatingly easy to hear. Although Corncrakes can be heard calling throughout the day, they are most vociferous between midnight and 3am.

One of the most abundant birds breeding on the machair is the Corn Bunting, its tinkling rattle-like song making it easy to locate. Twite breed and can often be seen along the

Corn Bunting, a common breeding bird at Balranald.

roadside. Some of the freshwater lochs are also best viewed from the road. These lochs support nesting Shoveler, Little Grebe and Tufted Duck. Otters breed on the reserve and are frequently seen on the lochs. During winter a variety of raptors and wildfowl visit.

The rocky headland of Aird an Runair is an excellent sea-watching point. Manx Shearwater are commonly seen from spring to autumn. Sooty Shearwater, skuas – including Pomarine and Long-tailed – and Leach's Storm-petrel are all regularly recorded, especially in strong westerly winds.

A circular route can be taken around the reserve, starting at the reserve centre and car park. The area around the reserve centre is one of the best sites in Britain to see and hear Corncrakes.

BIRDS THROUGH THE SEASONS
SPRING: Corncrakes arrive at the end of April. Red-throated Diver breed near by and can often be seen in flight between their breeding lochs and the sea. Scan the sea for lingering Great Northern Diver. Sea-watching in spring during northerly and north-westerly winds may produce a passage of skuas, especially Long-tailed and Pomarine. The second and third weeks of May are generally best.
SUMMER: Breeding birds on the reserve include Mallard, Teal, Shoveler, Gadwall, Wigeon, Tufted Duck, Lapwing, Redshank, Oystercatcher, Ringed Plover, Dunlin, Corn Bunting and Twite. Sooty

Ragged Robin grows abundantly in the meadows.

and Manx Shearwaters may be seen offshore.
AUTUMN: Sea-watching may produce Leach's and British Storm-petrel, Grey Phalarope, and a variety of auks, skuas and gulls in strong westerly winds.
WINTER: The following inhabit the freshwater lochs: Whooper Swan, Greylag Goose, Wigeon, Pochard, Tufted Duck, and Goldeneye. Offshore, Great Northern Diver, Slavonian Grebe and a few Red-throated Divers are regular. Wintering waders include Grey Plover, Bar-tailed Godwit, Purple Sandpiper, and large numbers of Ringed Plover and Sanderling. Snow Bunting are often on the machair.

 ACCESS: By sea: Caledonian MacBrayne runs daily ferries from Uig (Skye) and Tarbet (Harris) to Lochmaddy on North Uist. Tel: 01475 650000.

By air: British Airways Express flies daily, Monday to Saturday to Benbecula.

Tel: 0181 8974000. Further information from the North Uist Tourist Office, Pier Road, Lochmaddy, Tel: 01876 500321.

Balranald RSPB reserve is reached by turning off the A865 3 miles north of Bayhead to Hougharry. The reserve centre and car park are at Goular Cottage.

DISABLED ACCESS:
The road and some of the tracks in the area are ideal for bird-watching. Wheelchair users may not be able to gain access to some of the more sandy areas of the reserve.

OTHER ATTRACTIONS

BARPA LANGASS: 5000-year-old chambered cairn. On the slope of Ben Langass off the A867.

CLACHAN SANDS: A large sandy beach not far from Clachan on the B893 road.

DUN AN STICAR: At Newton Ferry. The last inhabited *dùn* in North Uist, occupied until 1602.

POBULL FHINN: A standing stone circle at Langass, close to Barpa Langass.

TAIGH CHEARSABHAGH: Museum and arts centre in Lochmaddy.

TEMPULL NA TRIONAID: Ruined remains of an ecclesiastical site dating from 1203. Close to A865 road at Carnish.

VALLAY STRAND: Beautiful views across a large sandy strand to where Erskine Beveridge's mansion still stands.

BIRDS THROUGH THE SEASONS

SUMMER: Breeding birds include: Common Tern, Arctic Tern, Little Tern, possibly Sandwich Tern, Black Guillemot, Fulmar, Shag, Cormorant, Eider, Ringed Plover, Dunlin, Wheatear and Twite. Manx Shearwater and British Storm-petrel feed in the surrounding waters.

WINTER: Barnacle Geese use the island on passage and during winter.

THE MONACHS are a low-lying chain of five islands 6 miles off the west coast of North Uist and largely inaccessible. Grazed by sheep and Rabbits, they were once occupied and farmed. The machair that covers the islands is regarded as the best example left in Britain.

During summer the islands are important for breeding seabirds and waders, and during the winter they provide a refuge for passage and wintering Barnacle Geese.

Due to the flat landscape and lack of ground predators, cliff-nesting birds such as Fulmar nest on the ground along with the occasional pair of Buzzards. Breeding terns are represented by Little, Arctic and Common. Black Guillemots breed and are numerous, especially off the rocks of Sillay.

During late autumn, the Monachs become a pupping ground for hundreds of Grey Seals. During summer and autumn the sea can be a mass of bobbing heads; the seals' mournful cries send a shiver down the spine when heard in the dead of night.

As long ago as 1263, the islands yielded a living for a few people. There was once

Grey Seal.

a nunnery from where the nuns would regularly row to North Uist to collect peat for fuel. There have been up to 100 residents at any one time, and at one point over 1000 cattle were grazed. In 1864 the lighthouse on Sillay was built, this being finally extinguished in 1942 during World War II; it was then that the last inhabitants left.

 ACCESS: It is only possible to visit the Monach Islands during the summer months on organised boat charters that operate in the Western Isles. There are no regular boat services. Most charters that sail to the St Kilda archipelago stop off here as there is a sheltered anchorage. It may be possible to go out to the islands with lobster fishermen from the Uists who sometimes stay for short periods.

DISABLED ACCESS: None.

The Arctic Tern is one of the four species of tern that regularly breed here.

FEW BIRD-WATCHERS have ever made it out to St Kilda, Britain's remotest archipelago 50 miles out in the Atlantic. It is easy to run out of superlatives when attempting to describe the scenery, the numbers of birds and often the journey to St Kilda. The island has the highest sea cliffs in Britain, as well as some of the most majestic

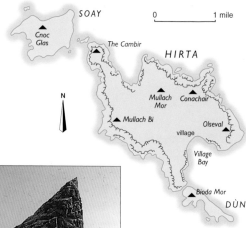

(Above) Stac An Amin.   *(Below) Gannets.*

sea stacks to be found anywhere in the world. Sprawled across a natural amphitheatre is the old village; like a lost world this is a monument to a community that may have existed for 4000 years but which finally died when the last St Kildans were evacuated in 1930.

Spectacular scenery and an amazing history are good enough reasons to brave the Atlantic Ocean, but when you add the spectacle of the seabird colonies, then a visit to St Kilda becomes an experience that will never be forgotten. The sea stacks tower out of the ocean and are covered in tens of thousands of Gannets. To sail under these stacks and to watch the Gannets being mobbed by Great Skuas at such close quarters is truly spectacular. Early sailors journeying from the Western Isles to St Kilda in fog would follow the long lines of Gannets flying back from their fishing grounds rather than trust their compasses.

If approached by boat from the north-east, the great stacks and the island of Boreray first come into view as a black mass rising sheer from the ocean. After drifting close to the stacks packed with Gannets you sail under Conachair, the highest sea cliff in the British Isles at 1398 feet. Finally, you round the corner and enter Village Bay. The old village street stretches along the bottom of the hillside and everywhere are dotted *cleits*, round, stone buildings that were used to dry and store the Gannets and auks that were caught for food. Village Bay is the only safe

numbers of seabirds. The surface of the island is riddled with Puffin burrows. Within the St Kilda group it is estimated that an amazing quarter of a million pairs of Puffins breed. There are over 60,000 pairs of Gannets centred on Stac an Amin, Stac Lee and Boreray. Of the other species of breeding seabird, one of the rarest is the Leach's Storm-petrel, which can be encountered out at sea when *en route* to St Kilda. This species can be found on Hirta, as can British Storm-petrel and Manx Shearwater; all three

species come ashore to their nest sites at night. Hirta is also home to a growing Great Skua colony. These first bred in 1963 and now number 200 pairs.

A bird unique to the islands is the St Kilda Wren, a subspecies that is around a third larger and has a greyer plumage than its mainland relative. It nests in the walls of the village and on the cliffs and stacks. Reduced to just 15 pairs by 1894, a bill known as the Wild Birds Protection (St Kilda) Act was introduced to Parliament and passed in 1904. This gave the Wren an opportunity to regain its numbers to a present population of around 125 pairs.

 OTHER ANIMALS
Also unique is the St Kilda Field Mouse, a form of the wood mouse found only on Hirta and Dùn. It favours the village area, stone walls and cliffs. Almost twice the size of a House Mouse, it may have been introduced by the Vikings. Much easier to see are the Soay sheep, a

The Old Village, Hirta.

The museum on Hirta.

anchorage, but in south-easterly winds the swell in the bay makes even this too uncomfortable. The archipelago was designated a World Heritage Site in 1987.

St Kilda was bequeathed to the National Trust for Scotland by the Marquis of Bute in 1956.

BIRDS
Dùn, an island separated by the tiniest of gaps on one side of Village Bay, is home to huge

primitive breed resembling the Moufflon and thought to be another Viking introduction. Once confined to Soay, 107 were introduced to Hirta after the 1930 evacuation. The sheep are easily seen around the village area.

During summer, cetaceans are regular. Large pods of Killer Whales have been spotted, while Minke Whale, Pilot Whale, Harbour Porpoise and dolphins are all frequently seen.

 FLOWERS
The islands are one of the windiest places in the British Isles and so are drenched in salt spray, yet 141 species of plant have been identified, including Primrose, Honeysuckle, Wild Angelica, Bog Asphodel, Mountain Everlasting and Bog Orchid.

BIRDS THROUGH THE SEASONS
SUMMER: Breeding birds include Eider, Fulmar, Gannet, Guillemot, Black Guillemot, Razorbill, Puffin, Great Black-backed Gull, Lesser Black-backed Gull, Herring Gull, Kittiwake, Leach's Storm-petrel (largest colony in east Atlantic), British Storm-petrel, Shag, Great Skua, Manx Shearwater, Hooded Crow, Oystercatcher, Meadow Pipit, Rock Pipit, Snipe, Starling, Wheatear, St Kilda Wren and Raven. Peregrines are often present and sometimes breed.

 ACCESS: Only accessible during the summer. The Army has a missile-tracking station in Village Bay served by a helicopter. There is no airstrip and no civilian helicopter service, leaving a sea crossing as the only option. Due to the uncertainty of the Atlantic weather there are no guarantees that St Kilda can be reached. A number of charters advertise in various national magazines, trips to St Kilda usually lasting a week. If taking this option, be sure the company has the main aim of reaching the islands, as many do not even though they mention St Kilda.

The islands take around 8 hours to reach from the Uists. Most charters, however, tend to leave from Oban, the journey taking up to 48 hours. If on a charter, you sleep on the boat as it lies moored in Village Bay. The Army has an officers' mess called the Puff Inn. Visitors are often invited ashore by the commanding officer to drink in this extraordinary pub.

A small number of people are allowed to camp on the island. Permission needs to be gained from the National Trust for Scotland. The Trust organises work parties that stay for two-week periods. In between assisting with various conservation tasks, there is plenty of spare time to explore the islands. Details from The Secretary, St Kilda Club, National Trust for Scotland, 5 Charlotte Square, Edinburgh EH2 4DU.

🕐 Late May to early July is the best time to visit for the seabirds, and provides the best opportunity of good weather for the journey to the islands.

♿ **DISABLED ACCESS:** None.

Soay Sheep.

ISLAY (pronounced 'eye-la') is famed for its malt whiskies and wintering geese. The latter arrive in their thousands during October, providing one of the most dramatic bird-watching experiences in Britain.

BIRDS
On arrival, Barnacle Geese concentrate on the Loch Gruinart RSPB Reserve, where numbers can peak at 20,000 birds before dispersal. Greenland White-fronted Geese rarely exceed 1000 on the reserve and then only when there is autumn stubble. Their numbers vary annually depending on breeding success in Greenland and, after arrival, they form small groups that become scattered throughout the island. Gruinart remains one of the best sites to see the geese during the rest of the winter. A car acts as a good mobile hide, enabling close views of the geese from the roadside.

Islay's mild winter climate allows grass to grow throughout the year, thereby

Barnacle Geese.

providing a continual food source. During the summer, cattle and sheep graze the pasture on the 3950-acre Loch Gruinart reserve, ensuring conditions are perfect for the returning geese in autumn.

The goose and the whisky distillery have not always lived in harmony. The island was pushed under the media spotlight in 1985 when a firm of distillers applied to drain and cut an area of peat at Duich Moss, which happened to be an important roosting site for Greenland White-fronts. The peat is used by distillers in the malting stage of whisky production; smoke from the peat fire helps to give a malt whisky its own distinctive flavour. Conflict between conservationists and islanders was eventually settled so that today both live in relative harmony.

Islay has more to offer than geese and whisky. Birds that can be seen throughout the year include Golden Eagle, Black Guillemot and Chough. The latter species has a breeding population of around 75 pairs.

OTHER ANIMALS
The islands are well suited to the Brown Hare, particularly abundant here.

Roe Deer are often seen from the road that dissects the Gruinart flats. Red Deer are far more numerous than the Roe and, during April and May, small groups of them can be seen grazing on the goose fields on the RSPB reserve. There are a few introduced Fallow Deer around Kidalton. At Portnahaven Harbour both Grey and Common Seals are often present, seen basking on the rocks. Islay is a stronghold for the Otter, which can be encountered throughout the year.

SITE GUIDE

1

Loch Gruinart
RSPB Reserve

The B8017 and the unclassified road leading to Ardnave Loch give excellent views of the reserve, which is to the south and west of Loch

Gruinart. The RSPB has a visitor centre at Aoradh Farm, open from 10am to 5pm seven days a week. There are informative displays and a closed-circuit TV gives live close-up pictures from the reserve. A small hide can be reached by walking a short way up the Ardnave road opposite the farm. There is a car park opposite the hide.

The Gruinart area is important for its wintering geese. Barnacle and Greenland White-fronts congregate in late October. A variety of wintering and passage waders use the mudflats in the loch and can be searched for from the minor road running along its east side. The reserve is also important for breeding waders and ducks. Over 300 pairs of Lapwing and 60 pairs of Redshank nest. Several pairs of Shoveler, Teal and Mallard breed, while Garganey, Pintail, Wigeon and Gadwall are often present and probably attempt to breed. Up to 11 pairs of Hen Harrier have bred on the reserve, and recently, due to management work, Corncrake have increased.

Machir Bay.

2

Ardnave Loch

Take the minor road running along the west side of Loch Gruinart. The fields on the right and the dunes close by often have feeding Chough. Loch Ardnave attracts a variety of wildfowl and, along the shoreline, waders in winter. Breeding waders include Redshank, Lapwing, Curlew and Oystercatcher. Look out for Otter around the loch and along the Loch Gruinart shoreline close by.

3

Machir Bay

This area of sand dune, cliff and grazing land is one of the best sites for seeing Chough. Before reaching the church at Kilchoman, take the lane down to the sea and walk through the dunes. The fields bordering the small car park often have waders and gulls feeding on them in winter.

4

Bridgend

The mudflats at the head of Loch Indaal at Bridgend is a good wader site, best viewed from various points along the A847 and A846. Barnacle Geese roost in Bridgend Bay. The woodlands in Bridgend were planted from 1820 onwards, and from late January through February can be covered in a carpet of Snowdrops. During the summer, Wood Warbler and Spotted Flycatcher breed.

5

Port Askaig

This is one of the best sites for close views of Black Guillemots.

6

Bunnahab-hainn

Reached by taking a minor road off the A846. Park at the distillery and walk north along the coast. Look for Otter, especially in the vicinity of the river mouth just north of the distillery. Between October and April, divers should be looked for on the Sound of Islay. Eider and Red-breasted Merganser are present all year.

7

Bowmore Pier

Park in Bowmore adjacent to the pier and walk to the end to view Loch Indaal. During winter a variety of duck are present. Scaup can number over 1000, and Long-tailed Duck and Slavonian Grebe occur in small numbers. Great Northern Diver, Red-throated Diver and the scarcer Black-throated Diver are all possible.

8

Bowmore Rubbish Tip

From Bowmore leave the town south on the A846 and take the first right after the church (opposite Seafield), then first left. Follow this road for approximately 2 miles; the rubbish tip is on the left. Both Glaucous and Iceland Gull can occur during winter.

9

Port Ellen Harbour

Divers, grebes and seaduck occur in the mouth of the harbour in winter. This is a reliable site for Black Guillemot.

10

The Oa

Take the minor road out on to The Oa and park in the small car park a short distance along the track to Upper Killeyan, signposted 'American Monument'. Peregrine, Raven, Chough and Golden Eagle should all be searched for. Wild goats inhabit these dramatic cliffs. During summer, cliff-breeding birds include Fulmar, Shag, Razorbill, Guillemot and Black Guillemot. Special care should be taken here during wet and blustery weather as the grass-covered cliff edge can be very slippery.

11

Rubha Na Faing

This peninsula is the most westerly point on Islay and can produce seabirds during passage periods. Sooty Shearwaters, often in the company of Manx Shearwaters, are regular. The first Sooty Shearwaters occur in early August, with the main passage peaking in the first half of September. Sooty Shearwaters breed on sub-Antarctic islands; non-breeding birds undergo a remarkable journey, circum-navigating the Atlantic Ocean clockwise, thus almost all pass southwards through Islay. Gannet, divers, and both Leach's and British Storm-petrel can be seen. A dramatic auk passage occurs between August and October, with thousands per hour passing at times. For the auks and petrels, onshore winds (from north-west round to south-west) are best.

12

Jura

Separated from Islay by the Sound of Islay is Jura, just a 10-minute ferry ride away.

In contrast to the rolling landscape of Islay, Jura is mountainous and rugged, with much of the island remote and uninhabited. Three peaks dominate the landscape and are known as the Paps, the highest reaching 2572 feet.

Golden Eagle breed but are easier to see on Islay. Other breeders include Red-throated Diver, Golden Plover, Whinchat and the most southerly breeding Arctic Skuas in Britain. In winter the bays support Black Guillemot, grebes and Great Northern Diver.

The name Jura comes from the Norse meaning Deer Island, and with very good reason as over 5000 Red Deer roam the hills. Otters are also numerous, one of the best sites for them being the area of shore north of Craighouse. On the road north you may notice a standing stone at the roadside at Tarbert; this dates back to the Bronze Age. At the north end of the island is Barnhill, where George Orwell stayed during the summers of 1946 to 1949 while writing his futuristic novel, *1984*.

BIRDS THROUGH THE SEASONS

ALL YEAR: Red-throated Diver, Red-breasted Merganser, Eider, Common Scoter, Teal, Tufted Duck, Golden Eagle, Buzzard, Merlin, Peregrine, Hen Harrier, Short-eared Owl, Barn Owl, Black Guillemot, Stonechat, Twite, Chough and Raven. No more than 30–40 Black Grouse and approximately 50 pairs of Red Grouse on the whole island.

WINTER: From late October to early April there is the spectacle of thousands of

The Paps of Jura.

geese. Barnacle and Greenland White-fronts are joined by a handful of Pink-footed Geese, and 20–40 Greylag Geese winter. The occasional Snow Goose and Canada Goose of one of the smaller North American races have been recorded. These are likely to be genuine vagrants originating from North America and arriving with the geese from Greenland.

Other winter visitors include Great Northern Diver, Black-throated Diver (scarce), Slavonian Grebe, Scaup, Goldeneye and Wigeon. Small numbers of Whooper Swans arrive in autumn but are usually absent between mid-December and February. A few Purple Sandpiper winter. Glaucous and Iceland Gulls are annual in small numbers.

SPRING: A few geese linger into May. Corncrake breed in a few locations, and are best listened for in late spring to early summer in the Gruinart area and in the vicinity of Machir Bay. Passage waders include Whimbrel.

SUMMER: Breeding birds include Fulmar, Shag, Kittiwake, Black Guillemot, Guillemot, Razorbill, Hen Harrier and Corncrake. Wood Warbler, Tree Pipit

(scarce) and Whinchat are all summer visitors.

AUTUMN: Sea-watching can produce Sooty and Manx Shearwater, and Leach's and British Storm-petrel. Pink-footed and Brent Geese pass *en route* south, as do flocks of Whooper Swans. A variety of passage waders are seen. Redwing and Fieldfare can occur in large numbers.

Greenland White-fronted Geese.

 ACCESS: Islay can be reached by air or sea. Caledonian MacBrayne operates a car and passenger ferry from Kennacraig to Port Ellen and Port Askaig. The voyage takes 2 hours and can be good for birds. During the winter there are two sailings a day from Monday to Saturday, with one sailing on Sundays. From mid-April to late October there are three sailings a day and two on Sunday. Reservations can be made by calling Tel: 01475 650000; general enquiries on Tel: 01475 650100, or write to Caledonian MacBrayne, The Ferry Terminal, Gourock PA19 1QP.

Loganair makes two flights a day from Glasgow airport on weekdays and one on Saturdays. Contact Loganair at Glasgow airport on Tel: 0141 8891311.

The Islay field centre shares a building with a

youth hostel where accommodation can be sought and information found on Islay's natural history. Further details from the Islay Natural History Trust, Port Charlotte, Isle of Islay, Strathclyde PA48 7TX.

Information is also available from the Islay Tourist Office, The Square, Bowmore, Isle of Islay, Strathclyde Tel: 01496 810254.

DISABLED ACCESS: Islay is tailor-made for bird-watching from a vehicle. The network of roads that criss-crosses the island provides excellent opportunities. All the island's specialities can be seen from a vehicle, and indeed this is often the best way to bird-watch.

OTHER ATTRACTIONS

Apart from the numerous opportunities to sample the island's famous malt whiskies, there is much to discover as Islay has a fascinating history. Standing stones dating back to the Bronze Age are dotted around the island. At Bowmore, the round church of Kilarrow dates back to 1769. It was built, legend has it, so that there would be no corners in which the devil could hide.

The Rhinns in the south-west of the island have some fine sandy beaches and dramatic cliff scenery. The castle at Finlaggan Loch was once the base for the Lords of the Isles, where the Clan Donald chiefs resided. They ruled much of the Atlantic seaboard during the 14th and 15th centuries.

CENTRAL

Inversnaid
RSPB Reserve

An RSPB reserve of 924 acres on the eastern shore of Loch Lomond. Deciduous woodland covers a steep hillside that leads to a ridge with moorland beyond. Wood Warbler, Pied Flycatcher, Redstart, Tree Pipit and Buzzard breed, as do the Dipper, Grey Wagtail and Common Sandpiper that inhabit the loch shore and tumbling streams. Wildfowl frequent the loch and, during passage periods, waders may be encountered. The reserve is important for its diverse community of bryophytes and lichens.

Inversnaid is reached by taking the B829 westwards from Aberfoyle, then turning on to an unclassified road that takes you to the Inversnaid Hotel. From the car park here, take the West Highland Way northwards; the trail through the woodland starts shortly past the boathouse.

DUMFRIES AND GALLOWAY

Loch Ken
RSPB Reserve

Situated north-west of Castle Douglas, the loch has wintering Greenland White-fronted Geese, Whooper Swan and Hen Harrier. Barn Owls hunt over the area throughout the year. Goosander and Kingfisher inhabit the River Dee. In summer the deciduous woodlands support breeding Redstart, Pied Flycatcher, Tree Pipit and Wood Warbler. There are a number of paths in the area. The RSPB owns various plots of land.

Access to the reserve can be made at the entrance to the Mains of Duchrae Farm on the C50 minor road which leaves the northbound B795 immediately west of Glenlochar Bridge. The road affords views of the loch, and is a good route to follow when looking for wintering geese.

Loch Ryan

The loch is of most interest during winter for wildfowl and the rarer grebes, including Slavonian and Black-necked. Scaup can occur in large numbers in winter, during which time Iceland and Glaucous Gulls are often present.

The loch can be viewed from the A77 that leads to Stranraer and from the A718 that follows the west shore.

Mull of Galloway
RSPB Reserve

A rocky peninsula 22 miles south of Stranraer. This reserve's granite cliffs are of interest in spring and summer for their nesting Guillemots, Razorbills, Kittiwakes, Black Guillemots, Shags, Cormorants and Fulmars. Extreme care should be taken as the cliffs are dangerous. The birds are best viewed from the lighthouse, accessible at all times. The reserve is reached by taking the A715 or A716 to Drunmore, then the B7041 to the lighthouse.

Nesting Shags can be watched at the Mull of Galloway.

Wood of Cree
RSPB Reserve

A reserve covering 660 acres of broad-leaved woodland. Redstart, Pied Flycatcher, Wood Warbler, Tree Pipit and Woodcock breed. Buzzard, Sparrowhawk and Great Spotted Woodpecker can be seen throughout the year. Along the streams there are Dipper, Grey Wagtail and Common Sandpiper, the latter during summer.

The reserve is 4 miles north-west of Newton Stewart. From Minnigaff, take the minor road north that runs parallel with the A714. There is a roadside car park; accessible at all times.

FIFE

Eden Estuary

An important site for passage and wintering wildfowl and waders. The estuary lies to the north of St Andrews. Scaup, Common and Velvet Scoter, Eider and Long-tailed Duck in particular are found in large numbers in St Andrews Bay. The following access points are best. To reach Out Head: follow the coast road north out of St Andrews signed to West Sands. Follow the road to the car park at the end and walk out to the peninsula. For Coble Shore: take the A91 St Andrews–Cupar road and turn off it on to a track 3½ miles east of Guardbridge. Good views of the inner estuary can be had from a lay-by immediately past the bridge east of Guardbridge on the A91.

Fife Ness

Situated on the eastern tip of the Fife Peninsula, this site is best in spring and autumn for migrants, when there is an easterly influence in the wind. At other times the area can be very quiet. Fife Ness Muir is probably the most productive site, an area of scrub and trees reached by parking at Balcomie Golf Course and walking through the gate to the right of the road and then turning left to the sea. Fife Ness Muir is on the right and is reached from the cottage on the shore. Denburn Wood, bordering

Juvenile Raven.

the churchyard in Crail, has hosted a variety of rare birds in recent years and is always worth a look.

Isle of May

This small island, lying at the entrance to the Firth of Forth, has large numbers of breeding seabirds but is best known for its migrants and for some impressive rarities. A bird observatory was established in 1934, and self-catering accommodation is available on a weekly basis. Contact the bookings secretary: Mike Martin, 36 Main Street, Ratho, West Lothian EH28 8RB. Tel: 0131 333 1547. Day-trips can be arranged from Anstruther.

Largo Bay

This deep tidal bay east of Leven on the south Fife coast is a wintering site for a variety of duck, divers and grebes. Red-throated and Black-throated Diver, Slavonian and Red-necked Grebe, Scaup, Long-tailed Duck, Eider, Common and Velvet Scoter, Goldeneye and Red-breasted Merganser can all be seen in varying numbers. Largo Bay is an annual site for wintering Surf Scoter.

There are a number of sites from which the bay can be viewed. Two of the best are from Ruddon's Point, accessed by leaving the A917 near Kilconqhar Loch and driving through the caravan park. Alternatively, try the free car park at the east end of Lower Largo.

GRAMPIAN

Banff Harbour

A good site for wintering seaduck and Iceland and Glaucous Gulls. Banff is on Grampian's north coast, 25 miles west of Fraserburgh.

Findhorn Bay

An almost land-locked tidal basin on the Moray Firth that attracts a variety of passage waders and large numbers of seaduck, especially Long-tailed Ducks in winter. Take the B9011 from Forres via Kinloss. After 2 miles, the road follows the bay.

Glen Muick and Lochnagar

This area lies south-east of Braemar in the eastern Grampians, and supports a similar range of species to that of Speyside. The high tops have Ptarmigan, Dotterel and Golden Eagle. Black Grouse, Red Grouse, Peregrine, Merlin, Hen Harrier, Golden Plover, Dunlin and Common Sandpiper can all be found.

The area is reached by leaving the B976 westwards from Ballater; after half a mile turn left on to a minor road at Bridge of Glen Muick. The car park is 8 miles further on, where there is a visitor centre.

Glen Tanar

Lying between Banchory and Ballater in the eastern Grampians, this area of Caledonian pine forest supports Capercaillie and Scottish Crossbill. There are Ptarmigan on the mountain tops. From Aboyne on the A93 between Banchory and Braemar, cross the River Dee and travel west on the B976. After 1½ miles take the minor road left to Braeloine where there is a car park and visitor centre. Any of the trails from Glen Tanar House can be productive for birds.

Spey Bay

Between Buckie and Lossiemouth on the north coast of Grampian are a number of access points from which to view the bay. Of most interest in winter for its large numbers of seaduck and Red-throated Divers.

THE HEBRIDES AND OUTLYING ISLANDS

Coll
RSPB Reserve

The reserve at the western end of this Hebridean island has an increasing population of Corncrakes. The machair supports breeding waders, while winter attractions include Barnacle and Greenland White-fronted Geese. Coll is reached by ferry from Oban. The RSPB reserve is at the end of the B8070 from Arinagour.

Mull

Close to Coll is this mountainous island, interesting for its raptors, including Golden Eagle, Hen Harrier, Merlin and Peregrine, and for passage and wintering birds. Reached by ferry from Oban and Lochaline.

Rhum

This large, mountainous island has the biggest Manx Shearwater colony in the world, the birds nesting high on the mountains. Golden Eagle breed, but the island is best known as the centre of the White-tailed Sea Eagle reintroduction programme. Rhum is a National Nature Reserve and can be reached by ferry from Mallaig.

Tiree

This low-lying island with machair and low moorland lies west of Mull. Excellent for Corncrake in summer, the island also supports high breeding densities of waders. The island has a wintering

Golden Eagle.

Rhum has the largest Manx Shearwater colony in the world.

population of Greenland White-fronted and Barnacle Geese, divers and wildfowl. Reached by ferry from Oban. There is no public transport on the island.

HIGHLANDS

Beinn Eighe

A remote National Nature Reserve to the south-west of Ullapool and bordering Loch Maree. Pinewoods, heather moorland, bogs and the loch support a variety of typical Highland species. The loch has both Black-throated and Red-throated Diver, and Tree Pipit and Redstart breed in the woods. Golden Eagle, Merlin, Peregrine and Raven should be looked for. The A832 runs along the south shore of the loch, providing a number of viewing points. Two nature trails lead off from a car park, 3 miles north-west of Kinlochewe.

Clo Mor

In Scotland's far north-west corner, 4 miles east of Cape Wrath, moorland-topped cliffs rise to almost 985 feet. Breeding seabirds on the cliffs are joined by Peregrine, Golden Eagle and Rock Dove. Red Grouse, Ptarmigan and Greenshank occur inland.

A pedestrian ferry operates across the Kyle of Durness at Keoldale just off the A838, 1 mile south-west of Durness (Tel: 01971 81377). A connecting minibus operates on the far side to Cape Wrath several times daily during summer (Tel: 01971 81287). Request to be dropped off at the Kearvaig track and walk to Kearvaig. From here, follow the Clo Mor cliffs east for 3 miles before turning back inland to the track and meeting the minibus at Inshore by prior arrangement. Access is sometimes restricted in this area due to military activity.

Culbin Sands
RSPB Reserve

Best in winter for waders and wildfowl, especially Common and Velvet Scoter. This reserve borders the south side of the Moray Firth. The shore is backed by Britain's largest sand dune system, this covered in forest. There is access at all times from Kingsteps (1 mile east of Nairn) along a minor road past the golf course.

Peregrines are found throughout the Highlands.

A number of Scottish harbours attract Iceland Gulls in winter.

Dunnet Head

The most northerly headland on mainland Britain, just east of Thurso. The sea cliffs support breeding Puffins, Guillemot, Black Guillemot, Razorbill, Kittiwake and Fulmar. Raven, Twite and Rock Dove also breed locally. Dunnet Bay has divers, seaduck and Iceland and Glaucous Gulls in winter. From the village of Dunnet, take the road out to the lighthouse.

Fairy Glen
RSPB Reserve

A woodland reserve of just 6 acres in a steep-sided valley, with Great Spotted Woodpecker, Buzzard and Treecreeper. Along the stream are Grey Wagtail and Dipper. Accessible at all times. The reserve is reached from the car park on the northern edge of Rosemarkie, off the A832, and is 15 miles north of Inverness.

Glen Affric

West of Loch Ness is Glen Affric Forest Reserve, managed by the Forestry Commission and a good site for Scottish Crossbill and Crested Tit. Black Grouse and Capercaillie are resident but difficult to see. The loch has Red-throated Diver, Goosander and Red-breasted Merganser during summer, with Dipper and Grey Wagtail along the streams. It is reached by turning off the A831 at Cannich on to an unclassified road, then proceeding past Fasnakyle. There are a number of car parks along here from which the area can be explored.

Glenborrodale
RSPB Reserve

A beautiful reserve in the western Highlands by Loch Sunart. There is a circular trail through bogs, heath and woodland. Breeding birds include Wood Warbler, Tree Pipit, Redstart and Raven. Merlin and Golden Eagle are sometimes seen. The reserve is on the B8007 half a mile west of Glenborrodale village.

Noss Head

A headland 3 miles north of Wick that is good for passerine migrants in spring and autumn. Sea-watching can produce a variety of shearwaters and skuas.

Udale Bay
RSPB Reserve

A 1922-acre reserve on the Cromarty Firth. Mudflats, saltmarsh and grazing marsh attract a variety of wildfowl and waders in autumn and winter. Accessible at all times, with wheelchair access to a hide that overlooks the mudflats. The reserve is reached along the B9163 just to the west of Jemimaville.

LOTHIAN

John Muir Country Park

This 1730-acre country park, to the west of Dunbar, incorporates the estuary of the River Tyne. The area is good for wintering and passage wildfowl and waders. Migrants during spring and autumn can be searched for, and during the summer months there is often something of interest. The park is reached by turning off the A1 on to the A1087 1 mile west of Dunbar. After half a mile take the minor road on the left to Linkfield car park. A second car park, the South Shore car park in Dunbar, can be reached by carrying on along the A1087 through West Barns and then turning left. Both car parks are linked by a footpath.

Musselburgh

Musselburgh, east of Edinburgh, is best in winter for its wildfowl, divers and grebes offshore, and for a variety of waders. Over the years an impressive array of rarities has been found. Birds offshore can be watched from the A199 Leith–Musselburgh road. The sea and the Esk river mouth can be viewed from an embankment reached by turning north off the main road just before the racecourse, then right to the River Esk. Follow the river downstream to Goosegreen Crescent and park.

STRATHCLYDE

Barons Haugh
RSPB Reserve

The *haugh* (marsh), woodland and meadows attract a variety of

wintering and breeding birds to this 264-acre reserve. Close to Motherwell in the Clyde Valley, the marsh hosts an array of wintering wildfowl that include Whooper Swans. Little Grebe, Grasshopper Warbler, Kingfisher, Common Sandpiper and Whinchat breed. There are four hides, two of which are suitable for wheelchairs. The reserve is reached by turning down Adele Street, opposite Motherwell Civic Centre.

Lochwinnoch
RSPB Reserve

Lochwinnoch, 18 miles south-west of Glasgow, is composed of open loch, marsh, willow scrub and some mature woodland. Breeding birds include Great Crested Grebe, Shoveler, Tufted Duck and Grasshopper Warbler. Wildfowl over-winter on the loch. The reserve is open from 9am to sunset. There is a visitor centre with observation tower, open from 10am to 5pm. The reserve is half a mile east of Lochwinnoch on the A760 Largs–Paisley road.

TAYSIDE

Loch of Kinnordy
RSPB Reserve

This reserve, situated 18 miles from Dundee, is best known for its breeding Black-necked Grebes. Marsh

Harrier and Osprey are regular during the summer. In winter there is a large roost of Pink-footed Geese. Open daily from 9am to sunset, except for Saturdays in September, October and November. The reserve is 1 mile west of Kirriemuir on the B951.

Loch of the Lowes

This Scottish Wildlife Trust reserve is a regular breeding site for Ospreys. A variety of wildfowl both breed and winter here. There is a visitor centre and hide accessible to wheelchair users. To reach the reserve, turn off the A923 on to a minor road 1½ miles east from Dunkeld.

Montrose Basin

Forming the estuary of the River Esk, the Montrose Basin regularly supports over 20,000 waterfowl. Internationally important numbers of Pink-footed Geese roost in October and November. Notable numbers of waders and sea duck occur. During the summer there is a large breeding population of Eider. Passage waders may include Wood Sandpiper and Spotted Redshank. Post-breeding flocks of terns use the basin in late summer. There is access at the Mains of Dun off the A935, and from the A92 which runs through Montrose.

A FIRST impression of Orkney is likely to be of a gentle, fertile landscape. Yet amongst the 70 or so islands are some of Britain's most dramatic sea cliffs, none more so than the cliffs that adjoin the huge sea stack, the Old Man of Hoy. The Island of Hoy has a rugged moorland contrasting markedly with the green, low-lying islands of the rest of Orkney.

Although Orkney lies closer to the Arctic Circle than to London, its climate is mild, courtesy of the Gulf Stream. With such a climate and fertile soil, rich pasture land supports the rearing of beef cattle, one of the island's mainstays. During spring and early summer, before the grass is cut for silage, the green patchwork of fields is rich with flowers. Some fields turn completely yellow with buttercups, while orchids are a common sight along roadside verges.

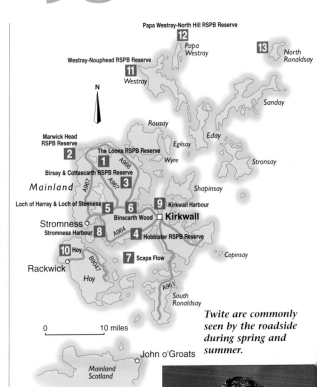

Papa Westray–North Hill RSPB Reserve — **12**
Papa Westray
13 North Ronaldsay
Westray–Nouphead RSPB Reserve — **11**
Westray
Sanday
Rousay
Marwick Head RSPB Reserve — **2**
Eday
Egilsay
Wyre
Stronsay
1 The Loons RSPB Reserve
Birsay & Cottascarth RSPB Reserve — **3**
Mainland
Shapinsay
Loch of Harray & Loch of Stenness
5 **6** **9** Kirkwall Harbour
Binscarth Wood □ **Kirkwall**
Stromness
Stromness Harbour **8**
4 Hobbister RSPB Reserve
10 Hoy
Copinsay
Rackwick
7 Scapa Flow
Hoy
South Ronaldsay
0   10 miles
John o'Groats
Mainland Scotland

Twite are commonly seen by the roadside during spring and summer.

BIRDS
Birds are abundant. In spring and summer breeding Curlews, Oyster-catchers and Redshank call from fence posts pro-claiming their territory. The moors have breeding Red-throated Diver, Short-eared Owl and Hen Harrier. Seabirds are numerous, too, with densely populated cliffs on Westray, Mainland and Hoy. In recent years, the islands of North Ronaldsay and Stronsay have become known for their attraction to vagrant birds. The winter months are not dull on Orkney either. Large concentrations of seaduck congregate in Scapa Flow and other sheltered inlets, while thousands of waders arrive in the islands for the winter.

OTHER ANIMALS
Most of the mammals have been introduced. These include Brown Rat, Rabbit, Brown Hare and Hedgehog. During the first half of this century, two cargo boats, the *Busy Bee* and *Cormorant*, docked in Kirkwall every summer. The crews gave out Hedgehogs to the boys playing on the pier, and by the 1950s Hedgehogs were well established. The Orkney Vole, a subspecies of the continental Common Vole, was probably introduced during the Stone Age. Voles are essential prey for breeding Short-eared Owl and Hen Harrier.

Otter are widespread but much more elusive than those on Shetland. Mountain Hares are restricted to Hoy and are perhaps a remnant from the last Ice Age. Grey and Common Seals are common around the coastline. There is always the prospect of a chance encounter with dolphins, Harbour Porpoises and whales, although you are most likely to see Minke Whale, Killer Whale and Pilot Whale.

Harbour Porpoises are often in Scapa Flow, while dolphins are occasional, including White-sided Dolphin and the rarer Risso's Dolphin. Late summer provides the best opportunity for a sighting.

 FLOWERS The Scottish Primrose survives at a few localities in Orkney, favouring maritime heaths. Flowering in May and July, this rarity is best found on Westray, the North Hill of Papa Westray and at Yesnaby on mainland Orkney.

MAINLAND ORKNEY

THE MAINLAND can be divided into east and west by running a line through the capital Kirkwall. The most interesting half for birds is the western side. Heather moorland, wetlands and cliffs support a variety of breeding birds, the wetlands being perhaps Orkney's most threatened habitat. Small bogs dotted across the rural landscape are an essential breeding ground for waders such as Snipe.

■ **THE MOORLANDS** These have been the stronghold for Britain's breeding Hen Harrier population, and a good example is the Birsay Moors RSPB Reserve. Orkney's harriers are polygamous, with one male having a number of mates due to the rich food supply available. During spring you may encounter a male skydancing, a display of dives, twists and turns. The Short-eared Owl also has a strong breeding population and is dependent on the Orkney Vole as a source of food. Less conspicuous is

the Merlin, often seen dashing low against a hillside. Important populations of Golden Plover, Dunlin and Curlew rely on this moorland to breed. Small moorland lochans provide nesting sites for Red-throated Divers, which can often be seen flying to and fro between the sea.

■ **THE WETLANDS** Ten species of duck use the few wetlands to breed. The Pintail has its British breeding stronghold of a few pairs on Orkney. Red-breasted Merganser, Wigeon and Shoveler all rear families in relative secrecy.

■ **THE CLIFFS** Marwick Head RSPB reserve, the best example of a sea cliff on mainland Orkney, is densely populated with Guillemots and Kittiwakes. Close to the eastern end of Mainland is Copinsay, a small island with large numbers of cliff-nesting seabirds.

During the winter months, thousands of wildfowl and waders arrive, including large numbers of Purple Sandpiper which inhabit the rocky coastline. Most prominent are thousands of Curlew roosting and feeding in the fields. Long-tailed Duck, Velvet Scoter,

Great Northern Diver and Slavonian Grebe join residents such as Black Guillemot, Eider and Red-breasted Merganser to winter in the bays and inlets, especially in Scapa Flow.

SITE GUIDE

1

The Loons
RSPB Reserve

The Loons is a marsh covering 180 acres, and is worth a visit at any time of year. A roadside hide allows views of breeding wildfowl that include Red-breasted Merganser, Shoveler, Teal, Wigeon, Tufted Duck and Pintail. The pool in front of the hide often tempts many of the aforementioned species out from the vegetation. Arctic Terns breed and often fish over the pool, occasionally perching on a post. Snipe, Redshank and Curlew are easily seen during the breeding season. Kittiwakes from nearby Marwick Head arrive in flocks to bathe and

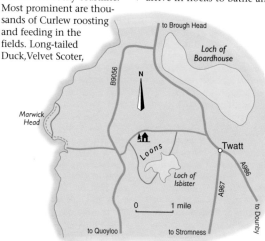

A Kittiwake panting on a hot summer's day. Their distinctive cries fill the air at Marwick Head and at the Noup on Westray.

collect nesting material. In winter, a flock of Greenland White-fronted Geese inhabit the marsh. The elusive Otter can occasionally be seen.

ACCESS: There is no access on to the reserve due to the nature of the habitat and susceptibility to disturbance. However, good views of many of the birds are possible from the roadside hide on the western side. Just north of Twatt on the A986, take a left turn on to a minor road. The hide is approximately 1½ miles along on the left.

DISABLED ACCESS: No disabled access to the hide, although the marsh can be viewed from a lay-by.

2

Marwick Head
RSPB Reserve

The most accessible seabird colony in Orkney, where red sandstone cliffs rise to 328 feet and extend for over a mile. Thousands of seabirds breed, including Kittiwake, Guillemot, Razorbill and Fulmar, as well as a few rather elusive Puffins. Rock Dove and Raven breed, and Twite are worth looking for in the vicinity. Marwick Bay has breeding Eider.

ACCESS: The cliffs can be reached by parking at the car park at Marwick Bay. From the B9056 take the minor road signed Marwick Bay and walk north to the cliffs. Great care should be taken when near the edge of these cliffs as they are crumbly with dangerous overhangs.

Marwick Head is best visited between May and July. There is little bird interest at other times.

DISABLED ACCESS: None.

Marwick Head.

3

Birsay and Cottascarth
RSPB Reserve

This large reserve of heather moorland, blanket bog and small lochans is especially important for breeding Hen Harrier. A few pairs of Short-eared Owl and Merlin also breed, while the lochans hold breeding Red-throated Diver. Kestrels nest on the ground on this reserve, no doubt a reflection of the lack of ground predators. Other breeding birds include small colonies of Great and Arctic Skua, and eight species of wader that include Golden Plover, Dunlin and large numbers of Curlew. Red-breasted Merganser, Teal and Wigeon breed, whilst passerines include Twite, Wheatear, Stonechat and large numbers of Meadow Pipit and Skylark.

Short-eared Owl and Hen Harrier are regularly seen from the hide at Cottascarth during spring and summer.

ACCESS: The reserve can be viewed from the B9057 and from the minor road running alongside the Burn of Hillside.

A hide at Cottascarth is excellent for Short-eared Owl and Hen Harrier. From Finstown, turn left off the A966 after 3 miles just past a garage on the right, then take the first turning on right signed Cottascarth. Drive to the farm at the end and park in the RSPB car park. From here, walk to the hide which is sited at the bottom of the hillside.

A hide at Burgar Hill is very good for viewing some of the typical moorland

breeders, especially Red-throated Diver. It is reached by taking a track off the A966 to the left half a mile after the B9057 junction. The wind generators by the car park are a good reference.

🕐 The best time to visit is between May and July.

♿ **DISABLED ACCESS:** As mentioned above, much of the moors can be viewed from the road. There is wheelchair access to the hide at Burgar Hill.

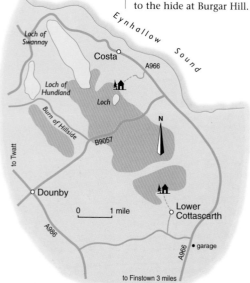

4

Hobbister
RSPB Reserve

Like Birsay and Cottascarth, this is a moorland reserve with similar breeding species. Interest is maintained outside of the breeding season as Waulkmill Bay is good for seaduck and passage waders. Red-throated Diver can be seen on the nearby Loch of Kirbister.

ACCESS: Turn down the road signed Waulkmill Bay 1½ miles east of Orphir on the A964, or alternatively park in the car park half a mile further along the A964 on the right.

DISABLED ACCESS: Very limited for wheelchair users. However, Waulkmill Bay can be viewed from a vehicle.

Loch of Harray is home to thousands of wintering wildfowl.

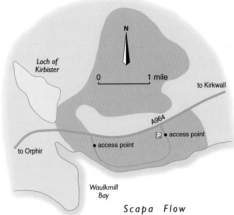

Loch of Kirbister

0   1 mile

to Kirkwall

A964

P • access point

• access point

to Orphir

Waulkmill Bay

Scapa Flow

5

Loch of Harray & Loch of Stenness

The two largest lochs in Orkney. Loch of Harray is a freshwater loch and is one of Britain's most important wintering sites for ducks. Pochard and Tufted Duck winter in large numbers, while over 200 Scaup may be present. The Loch of Stenness is tidal and attracts large numbers of Long-tailed Duck, Goldeneye and Slavonian Grebe. Greylag Geese and Whooper Swans can be found in the fields around the lochs during winter.

ACCESS: Best reached from the A966, 4 miles east of Stromness. There are numerous viewpoints from the surrounding roads and tracks, one of the best being

from the car park at the Ring of Brodgar.

 DISABLED ACCESS: The surrounding roads are ideal for watching from a vehicle.

Binscarth Wood

A mix of Sycamore and conifer dominate the largest stand of trees on Orkney. Long-eared Owls roost during winter. Passage periods can produce passerine migrants.

 ACCESS: On the A965 1 mile west of the centre of Finstown, right down to Binscarth farm. Drive past the farm until the road becomes a track. At the sharp left turn park and enter the woodland.

 DISABLED ACCESS: None.

Scapa Flow

Famed for its wartime history, Scapa Flow holds thousands of wintering seaduck. Long-tailed Ducks can number in excess of 1000 birds, with smaller numbers of Velvet Scoter present. Over 100 Great Northern Divers are joined by Slavonian Grebe, Black-throated Diver, Eider, Red-breasted Merganser and Black Guillemot.

 ACCESS: This large area can be viewed from numerous points on

southern Mainland, Burray, South Ronaldsay and Hoy. On the mainland, one of the best vantage points is from the Churchill Barriers. These barriers were erected in World War II after a German U-boat slipped through the sea defence and sank HMS *Royal Oak*. The barriers are crossed by a road.

Waulkmill Bay on the Hobbister RSPB reserve is another productive site (*see* above).

 DISABLED ACCESS: Numerous roads allow viewing from a vehicle.

Stromness Harbour

During winter the harbour has a few wildfowl. However, it is best for gulls, with Glaucous and Iceland Gull being regular.

 ACCESS: View from road and harbour area in Stromness.

 DISABLED ACCESS: View from road.

Kirkwall Harbour

Like Stromness, the harbour is best for gulls, including Glaucous and Iceland Gull in winter. Wintering wildfowl include Goldeneye and Long-tailed Duck.

 ACCESS: Various points from roads.

 DISABLED ACCESS: Roadside viewing.

BIRDS THROUGH THE SEASONS
ALL YEAR: Black Guillemot, Eider, Red-breasted Merganser, Curlew, Oystercatcher, Dunlin, Redshank, Snipe, Red Grouse, Buzzard, Peregrine, Kestrel, Rock Dove, Raven and Hooded Crow.
SPRING: Many of the breeding and wintering birds are present. Passage waders include Greenshank, Whimbrel, Curlew Sandpiper, Black-tailed Godwit and Spotted Redshank. Rarities such as Bluethroat, Icterine Warbler, Red-backed Shrike, Wryneck and Common Rosefinch are regular. South-east winds are best for the more unusual visitors.
SUMMER: In addition to those species present all year, the following also breed: Red-throated Diver, Fulmar, Pintail, Wigeon, Gadwall, Shoveler, Hen Harrier, Merlin, Short-eared Owl, Corncrake (now very rare), Golden Plover, Guillemot, Razorbill, Puffin, Arctic Tern, Kittiwake, Common Gull, Arctic Skua, Great Skua, Rock Dove, Meadow Pipit, Stonechat, Wheatear, Ring Ouzel and Twite.
AUTUMN: As listed under spring.
WINTER: Great Northern Diver, Black-throated Diver, Velvet Scoter, Long-tailed Duck, Goldeneye, Tufted Duck, Pochard, Slavonian Grebe, Whooper Swan, Greenland White-fronted Goose, Greylag Goose, Barnacle Goose, Pink-footed Goose (occasionally, more often on passage), Iceland Gull and Glaucous Gull.

ACCESS: To reach Orkney by sea: P&O Ferries operates a roll-on/roll-off service from Scrabster to Stromness, from Aberdeen to Stromness and from Lerwick in Shetland to Stromness. Booking enquiries can be made, Tel: 01856 850655. John O' Groats Ferries has a passenger-only service which runs during the summer from John O' Groats to Burwick, the southern tip of South Ronaldsay, Tel: 01955 81353. There are bus connections between Burwick and Kirkwall for all ferry sailings.

By air: British Airways flies from Glasgow, Edinburgh, Aberdeen and Inverness, with connections from Heathrow, Birmingham and Manchester.

For further information contact the Orkney Tourist Board at 6 Broad Street, Kirkwall, Orkney KW15 1NX, Tel: 01856 872856, Fax: 01856 875056.

HOY

RUGGED Hoy, with its dramatic cliffs, seems quite out of place compared with the green, low-lying islands of the rest of Orkney. The twin peaks of Cuilags and Ward Hill rise to nearly 1640 feet and dominate the landscape.

BIRDS

A feeling of remoteness can be enjoyed on walks across the moorland. Amidst the spectacular coastal scenery the bird-watching can be impressive. Around 1500 pairs of Great Skua nest. Stray too close to a nest and they make their presence known by flying straight towards the intruder, pulling out of a certain collision course right at the last moment, but often dealing a blow with their feet or bill. Over 200 pairs of Arctic Skuas also breed. The moorland that makes up much of the RSPB's 10,000-acre reserve supports Red Grouse, Dunlin, Golden Plover, Curlew and Snipe. The latter species often gives away its presence during the breeding season by uttering a curious call that sounds like a squeaky bicycle pump.

Small numbers of Short-eared Owl and Hen Harrier nest, their low breeding density is attributable to the absence of the Orkney Vole. One mammal that is abundant is the Mountain Hare. Around half the Orkney breeding population of Red-throated Divers are on Hoy, while Wheatear, Twite, Willow Warbler and a few pairs of Teal add interest. The cliffs support over 40,000 pairs of Fulmar, along with the usual auks. A

(Left) *Great Skua on the attack! Over 1500 pairs nest on Hoy.*
Ward Hill and the Cuilags dominate the Hoy landscape.

scan of Rackwick Bay on a summer's evening may reveal a few Manx Shearwaters waiting to come ashore under the cover of darkness.

Hoy is worth visiting for its scenery alone. St John's Head, a 984-foot high sea cliff, is one of the most dramatic in Britain, while Britain's most famous sea stack, the Old Man of Hoy, scene of a number of epic televised climbs, reaches 492 feet. Hoy means 'High Island', and is taken from the Old Norse *haey*.

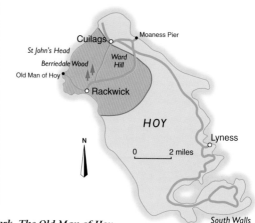

Orkney's most famous landmark, The Old Man of Hoy.

FLOWERS

The upland environment of Hoy is very suitable for Arctic–Alpine plants, Yellow Mountain Saxifrage, Purple Saxifrage, Wild Azalea and Least Willow being just a few of the species likely to be encountered. In Rackwick Valley at Berriedale, Orkney's only native and Britain's most northerly natural woodland survives. Rowan, Aspen, Downy Birch and Hazel trees all provide shelter for migrants and a few breeding birds such as Goldcrest and Willow Warbler.

BIRDS THROUGH THE SEASONS:

ALL YEAR: Black Guillemot, Red Grouse, Rock Dove, Buzzard, Peregrine, Raven. SPRING: Migrants and the occasional rarity are found. SUMMER: Breeding birds include Red-throated Diver, Manx Shearwater, Teal, Golden Plover, Dunlin, Snipe, Curlew, Hen Harrier, Merlin, Short-eared Owl, Great Skua, Arctic Skua, Arctic Tern, Great Black-backed Gull, Kittiwake, Fulmar, Puffin, Shag, Guillemot, Razorbill, Wheatear, Twite, Stonechat, Goldcrest, Willow Warbler. AUTUMN: As per spring. WINTER: Sea duck in Scapa Flow. A flock of Barnacle Geese winter in the South Walls area.

ACCESS: A roll-on/roll-off car ferry operated by the Orkney Islands Shipping Company departs from Houton on Orkney Mainland to Lyness on Hoy. Advance booking is advisable. Tel: 01856 811397.

A passenger-only ferry run by Hoy Sailings departs from Stromness daily, arriving at Moaness Pier in North Hoy. Tel: 01856 850624 or 01856 850678.

The North Hoy RSPB reserve, which includes the entire north-west of Hoy, can be explored along a path that leads to Rackwick through a glen between Ward Hill and the Cuilags. To view the Old Man of Hoy, a path leads from the activity centre at Rackwick (near the phone box) up along the cliff. The walk takes around 45 minutes.

The best time to visit is between May and July for breeding birds.

DISABLED ACCESS: None. A limited amount of bird-watching can be achieved from a vehicle, although much walking is required to find the majority of the birds on Hoy.

WESTRAY: NOUP HEAD RSPB RESERVE

A S IT is one of the most densely populated seabird cliffs in Britain, a visit to Noup Head is a must for the sheer spectacle of the birds in their thousands. Around 50,000 Guillemots and 20,000 pairs of Kittiwake dominate the 1½ miles of cliff on the RSPB reserve. Razorbill, Fulmar, Black Guillemot, Shag and a few Puffin can be seen. A few pairs of Raven nest on the cliffs. Although mainly of interest during the summer months, the lighthouse area is worth exploring during spring and autumn for migrants. A variety of rarities have been recorded.

Inland from the reserve, the maritime heath supports breeding Arctic Tern and Arctic Skua.

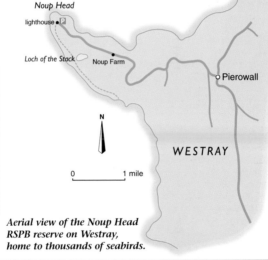

Aerial view of the Noup Head RSPB reserve on Westray, home to thousands of seabirds.

ACCESS: By sea: The Orkney Islands Shipping Company operates a twice-daily roll-on/roll-off ferry service to Rapness on Westray. Tel: 01856 872044.

By air: British Airways Express operates a twice-daily (excluding Sunday) eight-seater Islander aircraft to the airstrip at Skaill. Tel: 01856 872494.

The Noup on the west coast of the island can be reached from Pierowall along a minor road leading to Noup Farm. Take the track past the farm and park at the lighthouse.

DISABLED ACCESS: None.

PAPA WESTRAY: NORTH HILL RSPB RESERVE

REFERRED TO as Papay by Orcadians, Papa Westray is just over 4 miles long by 1 mile wide. The cliffs on the North Hill reserve are said to have been the last refuge of the Great Auk, made extinct in 1813. Papay also boasts being in the *Guinness Book of Records* for having the world's shortest scheduled air service, a trip of just 100 seconds from Westray.

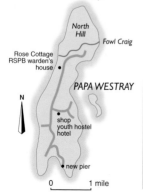

The Curlew's bubbling song and characteristic display flight is a feature of the summer.

BIRDS
The North Hill RSPB reserve's maritime heath is one of the best examples of this habitat remaining in Britain, and is important for its Arctic Tern colony. This remarkable migrant flies all the way to the Antarctic and then back again every year, covering some 24,000 miles during its round trip. Breeding alongside the terns are Arctic Skuas, which rely on robbing the terns and other nesting seabirds of their food, most notably sand eels.

The heath hosts breeding waders, including Lapwing, Snipe and Curlew, whilst a few Eider are likely to be encountered. It is worth searching for the rare Scottish Primrose which flowers in May and July.

Fowl Craig, the tallest section of cliff, is where many of the nesting auks, Kittiwakes and Fulmar are found. A visit between mid-May and July is recommended. Mull Head, the most northerly point on Papay, can be a good sea-watching point in late summer and early autumn.

BIRDS THROUGH THE SEASONS
SUMMER: Eider, Curlew, Snipe, Arctic Tern, Arctic Skua, Black Guillemot, Guillemot, Kittiwake, Fulmar, Shag, Puffin.
AUTUMN: Migrants. Sea-watching often produces Long-tailed Skua, Pomarine Skua, Leach's Storm-petrel and Sooty Shearwater.

ACCESS: By sea: Orkney Islands Shipping Company runs a twice-weekly ferry service. Tel: 01856 872044. A shuttle service from Westray runs daily during summer.

By air: British Airways Express operates flights from Kirkwall six days a week. Tel: 01856 872494.

To reach North Hill, take the only main road north until it ends. The RSPB warden should be contacted in advance of a planned visit to arrange for an escorted tour round the perimeter path to view the nesting colonies. The warden resides at Rose Cottage, Papa Westray, Orkney KW17 2BU, Tel: 0185 74240.

NORTH RONALDSAY

FEW ISLANDS exhibit more of an attraction to rare birds than North Ronaldsay. Being the most north-easterly island in the Orkney group, the island is well placed to receive drift migrants and vagrants from the east. Yellow-browed Bunting, Siberian Thrush and Pallas's Grasshopper Warbler are just three examples of the vagrants that have appeared in recent years.

BIRDS
North Ronaldsay's 5 square miles are rich in breeding birds. Small but important wetlands support breeding Pintail, Shoveler and various waders. The rocky coastline is home to a healthy population of Black Guillemot, and lots of sheep! The sheep graze on seaweed and are retained along the shore by a 6-foot high wall built over 100 years ago. Known as the 'Sheep Dyke', the wall is maintained by a 'sheep court' of 12 islanders.

In 1987 a bird observatory was established in the south-west of the island. Since then, the true potential of the island has been realised, with dramatic falls of migrants in both spring and autumn. South-easterly winds prove to be the most rewarding for migrants, which include pipits, warblers, chats, flycatchers and thrushes. During autumn the arrival of thousands of thrushes, especially Redwings, can be spectacular. Late September onwards is good for geese and wild swans, which make their stopping off on their way to more southerly wintering grounds.

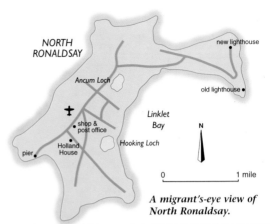

A migrant's-eye view of North Ronaldsay.

The walled garden at Holland House can be alive with migrants. Its stunted Sycamores and shrubs are often home to some of the outstanding rarities that can occur.

North Ronaldsay is ideally situated for sea-watching. Many seabirds moving between the Atlantic and North Sea pass, including Leach's Storm-petrel, Sooty Shearwater and the occasional Sabine's Gull. The best point from which to watch is the old beacon in the north-east corner of the island.

BIRDS THROUGH THE SEASONS
SPRING: Migrants often include Bluethroat, Common Rosefinch and Red-backed Shrike. The number and diversity of birds is dependent on the weather, and anything is possible.
SUMMER: Fulmar, Cormorant, Black-headed Gull, Arctic Tern, Black Guillemot, Shelduck, Teal, Gadwall, Pintail, Eider, Oystercatcher, Curlew, Lapwing, Ringed Plover, Snipe, Redshank, Rock Dove, Rock Pipit, Twite.
AUTUMN: Passage waders and wildfowl, Long-tailed Skua, Sooty Shearwater, Sabine's Gull and Leach's Storm-petrel. Migrants and vagrants: recent sightings have included Yellow Warbler, Pine Bunting and Spanish Sparrow.

ACCESS: By sea: Orkney Islands Shipping Company runs a weekly service, weather permitting. Tel: 01856 872044.

By air: by far the best way to visit; British Airways Express has a regular service. Tel: 01856 872494.

There is a comfortable bird observatory on North Ronaldsay offering dormitory and twin-room accommodation. For details, contact The Warden, North Ronaldsay Bird Observatory, Orkney, KW17 2BE, Tel: 01857 633267.

DISABLED ACCESS: A lot of bird-watching can be done from the roads on the island, which are free from traffic.

ORKNEY'S OTHER ATTRACTIONS

Orkney has a long, well-documented history. With over 1000 historical sites dotted around the islands, there is much to see. A variety of sports can also be enjoyed, including golf, fishing, sailing and diving. Orkney is a relaxing, peaceful place offering a chance to get away from it all.

Listed below are some of the main attractions.

MAINLAND

EARL'S PALACE, KIRKWALL: Fine example of French Renaissance architecture.

HIGHLAND PARK MALT WHISKY DISTILLERY: Founded in 1798. The visitor centre includes an audio-visual display on Orkney.

ITALIAN CHAPEL, HOLM: Built by Italian POWs during the construction of the Churchill Barriers in World War II.

MAES HOWE, STENNESS: Raided by the Vikings in the 12th century, this is the finest example of a chambered tomb in Western Europe, and was built before 2700 BC.

THE RING OF BRODGAR: Arguably the best example of a stone circle in Britain, this is one of Orkney's most impressive sites. During the summer, a visit at sunset is recommended.

SKARA BRAE, SANDWICK: The best-preserved neolithic village in Europe, probably built around 3000 BC.

ST MAGNUS CATHEDRAL, KIRKWALL: Built 1137.

OTHER ISLANDS

DWARFIE STANE, HOY: The only example in Britain of a rock-cut tomb (3000 BC).

KNAP OF HOWAR, PAPA WESTRAY: The earliest standing dwelling house in north-west Europe (pre-3500 BC).

LYNESS NAVAL BASE INTERPRETATION CENTRE, HOY: Wartime Naval base.

ADDITIONAL SITES

Copinsay
RSPB Reserve

Dedicated to the memory of James Fisher, author and broadcaster, this small island lies only 2 miles off east Mainland and is important for its cliff-nesting seabirds. It is possible to take a boat and land, or alternatively be taken under the cliffs. Contact S. Foubister, Tel: 01856 741252.

Rousay and Egilsay

Rousay has breeding Short-eared Owl, Merlin, Hen Harrier, Golden Plover and a few Common Sandpiper on its moorland. Egilsay has many lochs supporting a variety of breeding duck and waders. Winter visitors include large numbers of Purple Sandpiper and numerous wildfowl offshore. Accessible by ferry from Tingwall.

Sanday

Situated in the east between North Ronaldsay and Stronsay, it is not surprising that this island can be excellent in spring and autumn for migrants. Lady Parish in the north-east of the island is the best area. Access is as for Stronsay.

Stronsay

Stronsay has small breeding communities of Arctic Tern, Great Skua and Arctic Skua. It is good in winter for wildfowl, Whooper Swan, Greylag Geese, Greenland White-fronted Geese and waders. This island has become better known in recent years for rarities due to increased coverage. As on North Ronaldsay, autumn can provide much excitement. British Airways Express flies daily (except Sunday). A ferry leaves from Kirkwall daily except Sundays in winter.

ROUGHLY 100 islands stretch in a chain for some 70 miles between the Atlantic Ocean and North Sea. These are the Shetland Isles. Closer to the Arctic Circle than to London, the archipelago enjoys the 'simmer dim', endless twilight during summer nights that can allow bird-watching at midnight during June!

You are never more than 3 miles from the sea on Shetland, and the islands are peppered with deep inlets known as *voes*. There are few trees, and those that do exist have been planted mainly around habitation. For the most part, the islands are covered in heather and dotted with lochans.

The coming of the Vikings to Shetland shaped the island's culture and gave it the character it bears today. The other main event in history to have such an impact was the North Sea oil boom of the 1970s. This has brought many benefits to the islands, not least the vast improvement in roads, and ferry and air transport

that assists the visiting bird watcher in covering the main islands with the minimum of fuss.

The main centre of population is the capital Lerwick, situated on South Mainland. Its natural harbour hosts visiting vessels from around the globe. Supertankers ply in and out of Shetland's waters, visiting Europe's largest oil terminal, hidden away in Sullom Voe in the north of the mainland.

🦆 BIRDS

The sea is rich in marine life, and is the provider for the thousands of seabirds that breed. The bird-watching spectacle is enriched with a sprinkling of species on their southern breeding limit, such as Red-necked Phalarope.

Snowy Owls once bred and individuals still occur.

During spring and autumn, searching for migrants is made all the more exciting by Shetland's reputation for turning up outstanding rarities. One island, Fair Isle, is justly famous amongst bird watchers for providing such excitement. Weather is the decisive factor as to variety and numbers, and south-easterly winds are best. If an easterly airflow originates from deep inside Siberia, then the chances are that something really exciting might be found. Such vagrants as White's Thrush, Thick-billed Warbler and Great Knot have all put in

Fair Isle is famous for attracting some of Britain's most sought-after vagrants, such as this Red-flanked Bluetail.

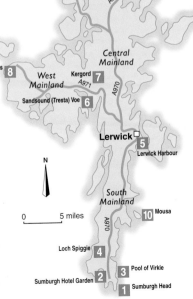

an appearance in recent years. American vagrants make landfall, too, with recent records of Ovenbird, Yellow Warbler and Western Sandpiper.

Largely neglected in winter, the islands are home to a variety of exciting birds, although the weather can be bleak and day length is short. Sea duck, grebes and divers abound in the voes. Lerwick Harbour annually hosts both Glaucous and Iceland Gull, while winter gems may include a White-billed Diver, Gyr Falcon or Ivory Gull.

Whenever you visit, Shetland has much to offer. For the best weather, an excellent variety of breeding birds, such as Red-necked Phalaropes, and the spectacle of large seabird colonies, not to mention the chance of a rarity or two, then the first two weeks in June is the optimum time. For autumn rarities, the last two weeks of September and first two weeks of October are hard to beat.

OTHER ANIMALS
There are few better places in Britain in which to observe Otters. They are adapted to life on the seashore. Mammals that have been introduced include Hare, Rabbit, Stoat, Hedgehog, and Field and House Mouse. Both Grey and Common Seals are frequently seen around the coast. During summer Shetland waters also host a variety of cetaceans.

During spring and autumn, migrants often take refuge along the stone walls leading up to Sumburgh Head.

MAINLAND SHETLAND

THE SOUTHERN limb of the mainland is of most interest. The Sumburgh area can be outstanding for migrants, and is where most spring and autumn rarities are found. The tidal Pool of Virkie, by the airport, hosts the widest variety of waders in Shetland. Near by, the Sumburgh Hotel garden, with its stunted bushes and limited cover, is remarkable for the number of rare birds it shelters each year. During the summer months, Sumburgh Head is an excellent place to watch Puffins. Autumn sea-watching from here regularly turns up Sooty Shearwaters.

Close by is Loch Spiggie, an RSPB reserve. Large numbers of wildfowl linger in autumn, including Whooper Swans. In spring, Long-tailed Ducks gather.

Tresta Voe in the west of the mainland is good for grebes and divers, and is the most reliable site in Shetland for King Eider, a colourful Arctic visitor and an individual of which has been present in the voe for the last few years. One of the largest inlets, Sullom Voe, is also good for seaduck, divers and grebes, as well as being one of the better areas in which to find Otter.

Jutting out on the western side of the mainland is Sandness. Its many lochs hold a variety of wintering wildfowl, whilst sea-watching can also be rewarding.

SITE GUIDE

1

Sumburgh Head

High cliffs surround the lighthouse on the head, an excellent site in which to enjoy the antics of Puffins. The eastern side has a steep thrift-covered slope, home to hundreds of Puffins. Puffins can be seen at any time of day, although activity increases in early

evening. Kittiwakes, Fulmar and Guillemot can also be watched. The area can be good for migrants, and in autumn it is a good vantage point from which to sea-watch.

ACCESS: The road past the airport leads naturally round to the lighthouse. Park in the car park at the bottom of the hill and walk to the lighthouse.

DISABLED ACCESS: Limited viewing is possible. There is some parking by the lighthouse entrance. High stone walls may impede viewing for wheelchair users.

2

Sumburgh Hotel Garden

This site is always worth checking for migrants, although like all other migrant hot spots it is dependent on weather. Red-backed Shrike, Common Rosefinch, Yellow-browed Warbler and Bluethroat are all regular.

ACCESS: The hotel is opposite Sumburgh airport. Park in the hotel car park and enter the garden.

DISABLED ACCESS: There is a gate that opens on to a large ramp. The garden is surrounded by a concrete pathway.

The Loch Spiggie RSPB Reserve is an important refuge for passage wildfowl in both spring and autumn.

3

Pool of Virkie

This tidal pool, just north of Sumburgh airport, attracts a variety of passage waders. In winter, duck use the pool. The bushes and gardens are attractive to migrants. The privacy of residents should be respected.

ACCESS: Easily viewed from a minor road off the A970 signposted to Eastshore.

DISABLED ACCESS: Viewed easily from a vehicle from the road mentioned above.

4

Loch Spiggie
RSPB Reserve

A reserve of 284 acres. Whooper Swans use the loch as a staging post in autumn, as do Greylag Geese. Various species of wildfowl winter, while in spring Long-tailed

Duck congregate and can often be seen displaying. Skuas use the loch to bathe in during summer, and Arctic and Common Terns, Snipe, Redshank and Lapwing all breed here. Rarities have included Black Duck and Lesser Scaup.

ACCESS: From the A970 take the B9122 at Boddam. Turn left on to a minor road just before Scousburgh. The loch can be viewed from various points along this road.

DISABLED ACCESS: Excellent viewing from a vehicle as above.

5

Lerwick Harbour

The harbour is of most interest during the winter when good numbers of Iceland and Glaucous Gulls may be seen. Little Auks are regular. Black Guillemot are present all year.

ACCESS: The harbour is on the east side of the town.

 DISABLED ACCESS: Much of the harbour is visible from a vehicle.

6

Sandsound (Tresta) Voe

Tresta Voe is one of the most productive inlets in Shetland. A drake King Eider has been present in the area since 1987. A few Great Northern Diver and Long-tailed Duck are present all through the year. In winter, they increase in number and are joined by Slavonian Grebe, Red-throated Diver, Red-breasted Merganser and Eider. Tresta village can be good in spring and autumn for migrants; the Sycamores around the post office in particular are worth checking.

 ACCESS: The voe is viewable from the A971, and from one or two points along minor roads.

 DISABLED ACCESS: Viewable from a vehicle as mentioned above.

7

Kergord

Conifers and broad-leaved trees make up the longest-established woodland in Shetland. Breeding species include Goldcrest and Rook. Migrants should be searched for. Stay out of the gardens of Kergord House.

 ACCESS: (OS ref: HU: 395542). Take the B9075 along the Weisdale valley. The plantations are on either side of the road and cannot be missed.

 DISABLED ACCESS: None.

8

Sandness

Many lochans support a variety of wintering wildfowl at Sandness, the western-most point of the mainland. Sea-watching may produce Pomarine and Long-tailed Skua in spring. The best place for sea-watching is the headland of Watsness when there are strong north-westerly or westerly winds.

 ACCESS: The area is reached along the A971. The lochans can be explored from the roads in the Sandness area. To reach Watsness for sea-watching, take the offshoot of the A971 to Walls and then the minor road to Dale. Before reaching Dale, take the road off to the left after Skarpigarth and walk to the headland.

 DISABLED ACCESS: Many of the lochans can be viewed from the road, as above.

9

Sullom Voe

Famed for its oil terminal, this large inlet is good in winter for Great Northern Diver, Slavonian Grebe, Long-tailed Duck and Eider. Look out for Otter. The

Houb of Scatsa, just past the airfield north of the B9076, can be productive for waders.

 ACCESS: The voe can be viewed from the B9076, and from one or two unclassified roads on the north shore.

 DISABLED ACCESS: Viewing from roads as above.

10

Mousa

Lying just half a mile off the east mainland coast opposite Sandwick is Mousa, probably the best place in Shetland to see British Storm-petrels. A night trip is required to see this tiny seabird which comes ashore to nest in stone walls and amongst boulders. The birds can be heard singing from their burrows at night, though it is usually necessary to place your ear close to the entrance to hear them.

 ACCESS: Overnight trips are organised during the summer months to see the British Storm-petrels. Details from the tourist office in Lerwick.

BIRDS THROUGH THE SEASONS
ALL YEAR: Fulmar, Shag, Eider, King Eider, Black Guillemot, Rock Dove, Raven and Twite.
SPRING: Passage and wintering birds still lingering include: Long-tailed Duck, Pomarine Skua, Long-tailed Skua, Pink-footed Goose, Greylag Goose. Passage waders

include Knot, Bar-tailed Godwit and Sanderling, Greenshank, Ruff, Spotted Redshank. South-easterly winds are likely to produce a variety of migrants that can include warblers, chats, buntings, thrushes and flycatchers, along with scarce migrants such as Bluethroat, Common Rosefinch and Red-backed Shrike. Spring rarities have included Pallas's Sandgrouse and White-throated Needle-tailed Swift.

SUMMER: Breeding birds include British Storm-petrel, Red-throated Diver, Red-breasted Merganser, Merlin, Whimbrel, Curlew, Dunlin, Snipe, Wheatear. One of the main summer attractions are the large seabird colonies: Great Skua, Arctic Skua, Common Tern, Arctic Tern, Shag, Guillemot, Razorbill, Puffin, Gannet, Kittiwake and Fulmar.

AUTUMN: Whooper Swan, Pink-footed Goose and Greylag Goose pass through in late September. Passage waders include Little Stint. As in spring, south-easterly winds are best for variety and numbers of passerine migrants. Ring Ouzel, Wryneck, Yellow-browed, Barred and Icterine Warblers, Common Rosefinch, Red-breasted Flycatcher, Richard's Pipit and Little Bunting are all regular. Impressive numbers of thrushes can appear, in particular Redwing and Fieldfare. Every autumn, Shetland turns up an outstanding rarity or two; almost anything is possible. Sea-watching in autumn can produce Sooty Shearwater, Leach's and British Storm-petrel, and skuas.

WINTER: Great Northern Diver are conspicuous around the coast and in the voes, with small numbers of Red-throated Diver. Long-tailed Duck, Slavonian Grebe and occasional Little Auks also populate coastal waters. On the lochs Whooper Swan, Greylag Geese, Tufted Duck, Teal, Goldeneye and a few Wigeon can be seen. There are often Iceland and Glaucous Gull in the harbours and Purple Sandpiper on the rocky foreshore.

ACCESS: To reach Shetland by sea: P&O Scottish Ferries operates a passenger and vehicle service five times a week between Aberdeen and Lerwick. There is also a service between Aberdeen, Stromness (Orkney) and Lerwick, enabling Orkney to be visited in the same trip. Brochure and booking enquiries from PO Box 5, Jamieson's Quay, Aberdeen AB9 8DL. Tel: 01224 572615.

By air: British Airways operates four flights per day to Sumburgh Airport (South Mainland) from Aberdeen during the week and a reduced service at weekends. There are connections from most major UK airports. For further information on schedules, fares and bookings, Tel: 0181 897 4000; Shetland Tel: 01950 460345; Central reservations Tel: 01345 222111. Business Air runs flights from Edinburgh, Glasgow, East Midlands and Manchester. Tel: Freephone 0500 340146 or Tel: 01382 566345.

Further information on travel, accommodation and places to visit can be obtained from the Shetland Tourist Office, Market Cross, Lerwick, Shetland ZE1 OLU, Tel: 01595 693434.

NOSS

THE NAME Noss comes from the Norse for nose. The 590-foot high cliff, the Noup of Noss, is a superb spectacle from both sea and land. Packed with seabirds, the cliffs provide a home for thousands of Guillemots, Razorbills, Kittiwakes and Gannets, all creating a memorable cacophony of sound.

Bridled Guillemots make up almost a quarter of the Guillemot population of Noss.

Managed by Scottish Natural Heritage and owned by the Garth Estate, the island was declared a National Nature Reserve in 1955. A 4000-year-old Bronze Age burnt mound at Helia Cluve is the first sign of human habitation. The last permanent resident left the island in 1939.

Visitors today are ferried across on an inflatable from Bressay. However, one of the best ways to experience the seabird colonies is by taking a boat trip along the base of the cliffs.

Away from the cliffs, the moorland supports a colony of Great Skuas and much smaller numbers of the daintier Arctic Skua.

BIRDS THROUGH THE SEASONS

SUMMER: The island is of interest for its breeding

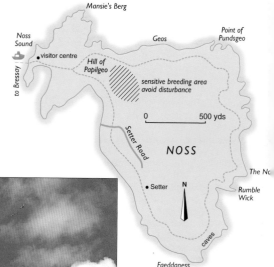

The map shows: Mansie's Berg, Noss Sound, to Bressay, visitor centre, Hill of Papilgeo, Geos, Point of Pundsgeo, sensitive breeding area avoid disturbance, 0 — 500 yds, Setter Road, NOSS, N, Setter, The No, Rumble Wick, caves, Faeddaness

The Noup of Noss, breeding site of thousands of seabirds, is most impressive when viewed from the sea.

seabirds, these including Great Skua, Arctic Skua, Arctic Tern, Gannet, Fulmar, Guillemot, Razorbill, Puffin, Black Guillemot, Shag, Herring Gull and Great Black-backed Gull.

ACCESS: Noss is open to the public from mid-May to September except Mondays and Thursdays, and is reached by crossing Bressay. A regular roll-on/roll-off ferry service runs from Lerwick to Bressay. It is 3 miles across Bressay to the car park and ferry point for Noss. Scottish Natural Heritage operates an inflatable boat across to the island. During bad weather, a red flag is flown if the island has to be closed. Check with the tourist office in the centre of Lerwick if in doubt.

To view the island from the sea, various boat trips depart from Lerwick during the summer; further details from the Lerwick tourist office.

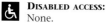 **DISABLED ACCESS:** None.

FETLAR

A GREEN, fertile island, Fetlar became headline news in 1967 for hosting the first pair of breeding Snowy Owls in Britain. The Secretary of State for Scotland granted a sanctuary order that enabled the RSPB to establish a reserve that now covers 1700 acres.

Five young Snowy Owls successfully fledged that first year, and breeding continued until 1975. Since then, individuals have often been present here and on neighbouring Unst.

A variety of waders breed, some in nationally important numbers. These include Red-necked Phalarope which, like the

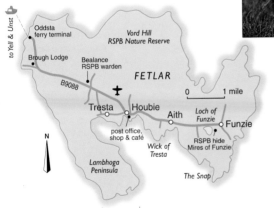

Red-necked Phalaropes breeding on Fetlar are right on the southern limit of their range.

(Right) Fetlar is the British breeding stronghold for Whimbrel.

the other breeding waders such as Golden Plover, Dunlin, Curlew and Snipe.

On the Lambhoga Peninsula, a few pairs of Manx Shearwater and British Storm-petrel breed, although both these breeding populations have declined in recent years.

During spring and autumn the island is worth a visit for migrants as some impressive rarities have been found.

BIRDS THROUGH THE SEASONS

SPRING: Migrants and breeding waders arrive. Red-necked Phalaropes start to arrive in late May.

SUMMER: Breeding birds include: Red-throated Diver, Eider, Great Skua, Arctic Skua, Arctic Tern, Common Tern, Fulmar, Kittiwake, Shag, Puffin, Black Guillemot, Manx Shearwater, British Storm-petrel, Red-necked Phalarope, Whimbrel, Golden Plover, Ringed Plover, Lapwing, Oystercatcher, Dunlin, Curlew, Wheatear, Twite and Raven.

AUTUMN: Migrants and rarities.

WINTER: A few wildfowl winter on Papil Water. Divers and duck can be found around the coast.

Snowy Owl, is a species right on the southern limit of its range. Over 90 per cent (31 pairs in 1995) of the British breeding population nest on the island. These hyperactive birds can be seen feeding off flies that cling to the rocks around the shore of the Loch of Funzie. A hide overlooks the nearby mire where they breed. The first phalaropes arrive in late May, and are only on the Loch of Funzie on warm sunny days when there are flies to be preyed upon. Otherwise, time spent in

the hide should be productive. Phalaropes have their sexual roles reversed, the females being the more colourful and the males staying behind to incubate and rear their young.

The RSPB reserve protects areas of serpentine moorland, a tundra-like habitat. Found only here and on neighbouring Unst, it is attractive to Whimbrel, which breed in high density. Their evocative call, a trill, echoes across the island. Pairs of Whimbrel are often encountered along the roadside, as are many of

ACCESS: A daily roll-on/roll-off ferry service operates from Gutcher on Yell and from Belmont on Unst across to Oddsta on Fetlar. Crossing time is approximately 25 minutes. Booking is advisable. For times and bookings, Tel: Burravoe 01957 722259.

To reach Fetlar by public transport, take the bus from Viking bus station in Lerwick at 8am daily except Sunday or from the dockside by the P&O ferry terminal at 8.10am. This bus takes you to the Yell ferry. On Yell, another bus takes you to Gutcher to catch the ferry to Fetlar. There is no public transport on Fetlar.

The RSPB reserve is closed during the breeding season, although escorted visits by the warden can be arranged, especially if there is a Snowy Owl present. The warden can be contacted at the Bealance, Tel: 01957 733246. All of Fetlar's birds can be seen outside the reserve from the roadside. The area around the airstrip is good for waders, and Red-necked Phalaropes can be watched from the roadside at the Loch of Funzie, or from a hide reached from the loch.

DISABLED ACCESS:
As mentioned above, excellent bird-watching can be experienced from the roads.

UNST–HERMANESS NATIONAL NATURE RESERVE

ONE OF the largest seabird colonies in Britain, cliffs rising to 650 feet and views of Muckle Flugga, Britain's most northerly point, make Hermaness one of Shetland's main attractions. The reserve was declared a National Nature Reserve in 1955.

BIRDS
Walk to the top of Hermaness Hill during the breeding season and you will be greeted by 'bonxies', a Shetland name for the Great Skua. Any intruder is dive-bombed, so to avoid being hit hold up a stick or your arm. Around 60 per cent of the world population of the Great Skua nests on Shetland. Skuas are the pirates of the bird world, preying on neighbouring breeding seabirds and forcing them to drop their catch.

The Great Skua has not always thrived. A population decline to just three pairs in 1831 prompted protective action against egg collectors and taxidermists by the landowners, the Edmonston family. Today, there are over 800 pairs on the reserve.

Golden Plover can be seen close to the path, often giving themselves away by uttering a sad-sounding plaintive whistle. The lochans support breeding Red-throated Divers.

Tens of thousands of seabirds breed along the cliffs and can be viewed by taking a circular route. Turn left off the main path from the car park along the Burn of Winnaswarra. Once at the cliff top, a left turn takes you to Gannet

Hermaness is one of the best sites in Shetland to get really close to Puffins.

colonies and to the cliffs, most famous inhabitant, a Black-browed Albatross affectionately known as 'Albert'. Since 1972, Albert has returned to the point of Saito and sat on a nest amongst the Gannets, no doubt waiting in forlorn hope for a mate! Since the late 1980s Albert has been less reliable, disappearing for long periods. Early spring is often the best time to visit in the hope of finding him home.

Retrace your steps from the point of Saito and continue north along the cliff path for views of Guillemots and Razorbills. Close encounters with Puffins can be enjoyed along the cliff top. Eventually, Muckle Flugga lighthouse comes into view. The path turns back up to the top of Hermaness Hill through more breeding Great Skuas, before leading back downhill to the car park. This route will take three to four hours if walked at a leisurely pace.

 FLOWERS
Hermaness has some interesting plants. Field Gentian, a purple flower, can be found in late summer on the grassland. Thrift graces the cliff tops, as do the deep pinks of Red Campion. The most interesting flora is found in those areas inaccessible to sheep, which are grazed throughout the year.

BIRDS THROUGH THE SEASONS
SUMMER: Hermaness is of most interest for its breeding birds. A visit between May and July is best. Gannet, Great Skua, Arctic Skua, Razorbill, Guillemot, Puffin, Fulmar, Kittiwake, Black-browed Albatross (often from March and on through summer), Dunlin, Golden Plover, Snipe, Raven, Rock Pipit, Wheatear and Twite (around car park).

 Access: Unst is reached by roll-on/roll-off ferry from Yell. From the ferry terminal at Belmont in the south of Unst, drive north and follow signs for Burrafirth. The road narrows and leads round to a car park at the bottom of the reserve.

There is a visitor centre in the shore station below the car park, where the summer warden is based. There are no access restrictions on the reserve, but you should ensure that you keep to the marked paths to minimise disturbance to nesting birds. The weather can be very changeable and the paths wet, so decent footwear and warm clothing are advisable. Take care when close to the cliff edge, especially when looking for Albert!

DISABLED ACCESS: None.

FAIR ISLE

FAIR ISLE has long been a mecca for bird-watchers. It attracts rare birds from all directions, and first records for Britain turn up with amazing regularity. The isle is also famed for its falls of common migrants.

Owned by the National Trust for Scotland, the island has a rugged beauty. It measures some 3 miles long by 1½ miles wide, and is perched 24 miles off the south-west tip of mainland Shetland. Cliffs rise to 650 feet, while inland, heather-clad hills give way

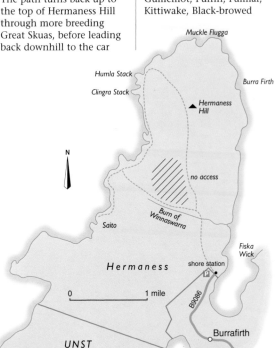

Muckle Flugga

Humla Stack

Clingra Stack

Burra Firth

Hermaness Hill

N

no access

Burn of Winnaswarra

Saito

Fiska Wick

Hermaness

shore station

P

0   1 mile

B9086

Burrafirth

UNST

to a patchwork of green fields, rough pasture, and a few crops, bogs and ditches. The isle is also world-famous for its distinctive knitwear.

The Fair Isle Bird Observatory provides a range of comfortable accommodation, and is where most visitors stay. It was started by the late Dr George Waterston in 1948, and has facilitated the study of migration and monitoring of the island's breeding seabirds.

weather and in particular on having the right winds. South-easterly to easterly winds are best, but any wind with a hint of easterly can produce rarities. Autumn in particular can produce totally birdless periods if the wind is westerly for prolonged periods. However, when the weather is right and birds arrive in numbers, often with a sprinkling of rarities, there is arguably no more exciting place. A vagrant,

perhaps a first for Britain, can be watched with just a handful of fellow birders.

April and May are good for the common and scarce spring migrants which include Wryneck, Red-backed Shrike and Bluethroat. Sandhill Crane, Lesser Kestrel, Bimaculated Lark and Song Sparrow have occurred in spring.

The peak time for a visit is from the second week in September through to the second week of October. During this period, if the winds have an easterly bias, both Yellow-breasted Bunting and Lanceolated Warbler, which are both Fair Isle specialities, have a good chance of being found. Lanceolated Warbler can be particularly confiding, often running around on the ground like a mouse. Regular rarities on

Fair Isle displays a rugged beauty and the promise of outstanding bird-watching.

 BIRDS

Over 350 species have been recorded, a figure that illustrates Fair Isle's importance. During June and July, the 18 species of breeding seabird are of most interest. Puffins frequent the cliff tops, with Razorbills, Guillemots, Gannets, Kittiwakes and Fulmars on the cliff ledges. Great Skua and Arctic Skua are joined by Common and Arctic Terns inland.

Spring and autumn are the two periods that provide the magic for the many bird-watchers who are hooked on this mystic isle. The occurrence of migrants, as on mainland Shetland, is dependent on

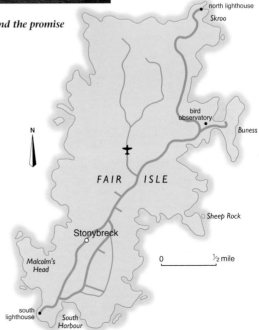

This Heligoland trap at the Plantation is one of several on the island used to trap migrants for ringing.
(Left) White-beaked Dolphins are regularly seen in the summer on the sea journey to Fair Isle.

the island include Barred Warbler, Olive-backed Pipit, Greenish and Arctic Warbler, and Little Bunting. Huge falls of thrushes may occur, especially Redwings – often in their thousands. Whooper Swans and skeins of Pink-footed, Greylag and Barnacle Geese are an annual feature over the isle during late autumn.

OTHER ANIMALS

Fair Isle can be a good locality for observing cetaceans during the summer. The sea crossing from Sumburgh Head is often productive. White-beaked Dolphin, Harbour Porpoise and Minke Whale are seen regularly during calm conditions between late May and September. Risso's Dolphin, Killer and Pilot Whale are rarely seen but possible.

BIRDS THROUGH THE SEASONS

ALL YEAR: Fulmar, Shag, Eider, Black Guillemot, Rock Dove, Rock Pipit, Fair Isle race of Wren, Twite, Raven.
SPRING: Migrants start arriving in March, mainly thrushes. May through to early June produces the best variety. As long as the winds are right, Red-backed Shrike, Golden Oriole, Common Rosefinch, Wryneck, Bluethroat, Icterine Warbler, Marsh Warbler, Ortolan Bunting and Lapland Bunting may all put in an appearance. Regularly recorded rarities during spring have included Thrush Nightingale, Subalpine Warbler and Red-throated Pipit.
SUMMER: During the summer there is always the chance of a very rare bird turning up. Breeding seabirds include British Storm-petrel, Puffin, Gannet, Fulmar, Kittiwake, Shag, Razorbill, Guillemot, Black Guillemot, Arctic Tern, Common Tern, Great Skua and Arctic Skua. Wheatear, Twite, Rock Pipit and Rock Dove are resident breeders.

AUTUMN: Late August can be very good for migrants, September and early October being the prime time. Annual visitors include Wryneck, Bluethroat, Barred, Icterine and Yellow-browed Warblers, Red-backed Shrike, Lapland Bunting and Red-breasted Flycatcher. Rarities that have occurred on a number of occasions include Greenish Warbler, Booted Warbler, Pallas's Warbler, Arctic Warbler, Dusky Warbler, Olive-backed Pipit, Red-throated Pipit, Great Snipe and Spotted Crake. Yellow-breasted Bunting and Lanceolated Warbler are a good bet during the latter half of September if the winds are easterly. The majority of Britain's Pechora Pipit records have come from here. Pallas's Grasshopper Warbler, Paddyfield Warbler, Blyth's Reed Warbler, Red-flanked Bluetail and White's Thrush can all be prayed for! American vagrants have included Tennessee Warbler, Savannah Sparrow and Bobolink. Impressive falls of thrushes often occur. Skeins of migrant geese and swans are annual in autumn.

ACCESS:

Fair Isle Bird Observatory provides comfortable accommodation on a full-board basis. A variety of accommodation is available from dormitory to single room. Open from late April to the end of October, it is advisable to book up for the peak period (mid-September to early October) well in advance. Bookings and further information from the Fair Isle Bird Observatory, Bookings Secretary, Fair Isle, Shetland ZE2 9JU. For booking enquiries, Tel: 01595 760258.

To reach Fair Isle from mainland Shetland:

By air: Loganair flies twice daily on Monday, Wednesday and Friday and once on Saturday from Tingwall airport just north of Lerwick. Tel: 01595 840246. Central reservations Tel: 01345 222111.

By sea: The mailboat *Good Shepherd* sails on Saturdays and alternate Thursdays to Grutness one week and Lerwick the next. The crossing takes approximately 2½ hours. Tel: 01595 760222.

Flights and sea crossings are subject to the weather.

SHETLAND'S OTHER ATTRACTIONS

The Vikings have left their mark on Shetland unlike anywhere else in the British Isles. The majority of place names are Norse. Every year the mid-winter festival of Up Helly Aa attracts over 1000 torch-carrying islanders and a squad of Vikings. A Longship is ceremoniously burnt in Lerwick as part of the festival.

The islands are rich in archaeological sites, which include Jarlshof and the Broch of Mousa. If you are keen on walking, then the islands have 900 miles of coastline to be discovered. Diving is good as there are a variety of wrecks, plentiful marine life and clear water. Over 350 lochs are available to the Trout angler, and Sea Trout can be caught along the shore. Riding and pony-trekking are available, and golf can be played at mid-night on midsummer's day at Britain's most northerly course on Whalsay!

ADDITIONAL SITES

Bressay

This island faces Lerwick and can be good for migrants. Try the crofts in the west during passage periods. There is a regular ferry service from Lerwick.

Foula

Lying 14 miles west of Mainland, Foula has some of the most spectacular sea cliffs found in Britain, these rising to a height of 1210 feet. It is important for its huge seabird colonies, some 12 species breeding here. Britain's largest breeding colony of Great Skua is joined by large numbers of Fulmar, Puffin, Guillemot, British Storm-petrel and small numbers of Leach's Storm-petrel. Flights operate into Foula throughout the year. The mail boat takes passengers twice weekly from Walls on West Mainland, weather permitting.

Out Skerries

This group of small islands forms the most easterly point in Shetland, and as such has attracted an impressive number of rare birds over the years. A passenger ferry runs from Vidlin in East Mainland on Monday, Friday, Saturday and Sunday, and from Lerwick on Tuesday and Thursday. The crossing takes approximately 1½ hours and is good for cetaceans, especially Harbour Porpoise. Loganair flies weekly in summer.

The largest Great Skua colony in the British Isles is found on Foula.

Whalsay

Whalsay, lying off East Mainland's coast, is particularly good for migrants. Crofts around the Skaw area in the north-east can be particularly rewarding. The seaward side of Ibister and Brough in the west are also worth checking in spring and autumn. Recent rarities include Ruppell's Warbler and Lesser Grey Shrike. There are daily flights by Loganair from Tingwall (except Sundays). A car ferry runs from Laxo (Mainland).

Yell

Any excursion to Unst or Fetlar requires a journey across Yell. Heather moorland and numerous bogs support breeding Red-throated Diver and Merlin. The RSPB reserve at Lumbister on the western side of the island supports the typical breeding species.

IRELAND

*Kebble NNR,
Rathlin Island.*

IRELAND SUPPORTS some outstanding sites for birds, despite the fact that two-thirds of the breeding species found in the rest of Britain are absent. Notable among these are the Tawny Owl, all three species of woodpecker, Nuthatch, Willow Tit and Marsh Tit. This deficit of woodland birds is more than compensated for by the varied experiences available to the bird-watcher, whether watching vast flocks of wildfowl and waders in winter on the loughs and estuaries, or an American vagrant on a coastal headland in autumn.

There are impressive seabird colonies both in the north and south. Perched on the western edge of the European landmass, Ireland is well placed to witness large-scale movements of seabirds in the eastern Atlantic. In the south and west, headlands and the island of Cape Clear provide some of the most exciting sea-watching to be enjoyed anywhere in Europe. This western position means Ireland is the first landfall for many American vagrants. The headlands and coast of the west and south-west are sparsely covered by bird-watchers in autumn, allowing visitors the opportunity to make exciting finds.

A mild climate means good feeding for many species in winter. During cold spells in Europe, Ireland enjoys mass influxes of birds from Britain and the Continent. At these times wildfowl, waders, larks, finches and thrushes flood across the Irish Sea in search of ice-free feeding grounds.

Annual winter visitors such as Great Northern Divers are joined by Greenland White-fronted and Barnacle Geese from Greenland, and by light-bellied Brent Geese from Canada. Thousands of waders flock to the estuaries and coastline, whereas the lakes and turloughs are attractive to wildfowl.

Some mammals common on the British mainland are also absent from Ireland – for instance, the Mole, Harvest Mouse and Weasel. However, there are some interesting endemic forms, such as the Irish Hare, a variety of the Mountain Hare. Red Squirrels inhabit the woodlands, Otters are widespread, and in a few sites the rare Pine Marten can be found. Around the coasts there are both Common and Grey Seals.

There are some outstanding sites for flora. The Burren, a limestone pavement in Co Clare, attracts botanists from far and wide, and is one of Ireland's most impressive landscapes. The bogs support a specialised plant life, as do the cliffs, hills and mountains of Northern Ireland.

LYING 3 miles off the north Antrim coast is this L-shaped island of 3500 acres, of most interest for its seabird colonies.

Much of the western end of the island is part of the Kebble National Nature Reserve, owned by the Environment Service. The RSPB owns 2½ miles of the northern cliffs and also leases the West Lighthouse platform from the

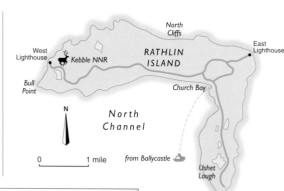

Cliffs and stacks on Kebble NNR, Rathlin Island.

Commissioners for Irish Lights. The platform is a dramatic viewpoint from which to scan the cliffs.

BIRDS

At the western end, high basalt cliffs and stacks are packed with Guillemots, Razorbills, Fulmars and Kittiwakes. Lesser numbers of Puffins nest in burrows on the steep grassy slopes. Black Guillemots breed amongst the boulders at the base of the chalk cliffs west of Church Bay, and can be seen just offshore. There is a small colony of Manx Shearwater, a species commonly seen on the boat

crossing from Ballycastle during summer. Buzzard, Raven and Peregrine have a healthy breeding population on Rathlin, but the Chough appears to have departed as a regular breeder. The moorland, rough pasture, scattered pools and marsh support breeding Tufted Duck, Snipe, Lapwing, Sedge Warbler, Skylark and Wheatear.

The best time to observe seabirds on Rathlin is between late May and early July. There are a number of walks, two of the best being the roadway out to West Lighthouse and the path down to Rue Point, where

Manx Shearwater often congregate offshore before coming in to their nesting burrows during the late evening.

OTHER ANIMALS

Mammals include a few introduced Irish Hares, rabbits, and both Grey and Common Seals around the shore.

FLOWERS

During summer the island has a fine display of orchids. Early Purple Orchid

The rare Pyramidal Bugle is only an inch or so tall and can be found by the entrance to the Kebble Reserve.

are common in spring, while in early summer the moorlands are carpeted with Heath Spotted Orchid. Other orchid species which occur in the rough pastures and marshes include Common Spotted Orchid, both varieties of Butterfly Orchid, Northern Marsh Orchid and Fragrant Orchid. In May you can find the rare Limestone or Pyramidal Bugle by the gateway into the Kebble reserve.

**BIRDS THROUGH
THE SEASONS**
SUMMER: Breeding birds include Little Grebe, Manx Shearwater, Shag, Shelduck, Mallard, Tufted Duck, Eider, Buzzard, Peregrine, Kestrel, Coot, Oystercatcher, Ringed Plover, Lapwing, Snipe, Redshank, Common Gull, Black-headed Gull, Herring Gull, Lesser Black-backed Gull, Great Black-backed Gull, Kittiwake, Razorbill, Guillemot, Black Guillemot, Puffin, Rock Dove, Skylark, Raven, Hooded Crow, Wheatear, Stonechat, Whinchat, Sedge Warbler, Meadow Pipit, Rock Pipit, Linnet, Reed Bunting and, sporadically, Twite. Non-breeding birds likely to be encountered include Gannet and, occasionally, skuas and Sooty Shearwater offshore. Chough are often seen.

ACCESS: Boats leave the quay at Ballycastle at around 10am on most days during summer. Advance booking is advisable with Rathlin Ferries, Tel: 012657 63907 or 63915, or with Rathlin Ferry Company, Tel: 012657 63917 or 63934. The crossing takes approximately 40 minutes.

A bus meets the boat on Rathlin and can take passengers to the West Light. It is advisable to contact Liam McFaul, the RSPB warden, before you intend to visit as the platform is only open under his supervision. The warden can be contacted at South Cleggan, Rathlin Island, Co Antrim. Tel: 012657 63935. The RSPB organises round-island boat trips during the summer; details from the warden.
Visitors may stay at the guest-house, Tel: 012657 63917, and there is also dormitory-style accommodation on the island at the activity centre by the harbour, Tel: 012657 63971.

 DISABLED ACCESS: None.

OTHER ATTRACTIONS

BRUCE'S CAVE, on Rathlin, the famous sea cave where Robert the Bruce was said to have watched the spider, is only visible by taking a boat trip. The activity centre on the island provides opportunities for scuba diving. The island's history can be explored at the Boat House Visitor's centre.
The following places of interest lie along the north Antrim Coast.

BUSHMILLS DISTILLERY: The oldest working whiskey distillery in the world is located at Bushmills.

CARRICK-A-REDE ROPE BRIDGE: This bridge is not for the faint-hearted as it spans a chasm above the sea to reach a small island used

by fishermen. Only open between May and September, and reached from a National Trust car park at Larrybane near Ballintoy. Close views of seabirds can be had on the cliffs.

DUNLUCE CASTLE: The romantic remains of an old castle near Portrush.

Giant's Causeway.

GIANT'S CAUSEWAY: This World Heritage Site, in the care of the National Trust, is an amazing formation of thousands of six-sided basalt columns, reached off the main coast road some 3 miles north-east of Bushmills. Peregrines, Ravens and Buzzards all breed in this part of the Antrim coast, and Eider duck may be seen offshore.

PORTRUSH: A seaside holiday resort with family attractions that include Waterworld, an indoor holiday centre and a number of excellent golf courses.

STRANGFORD LOUGH, 13 miles from Belfast, is of international importance for its wintering wildfowl and waders. The lough is over 18 miles long and is connected to the sea by the Strangford Narrows, which, with a minimum width of just 550 yards, has strong, turbulent currents. The estuarine habitats within the lough are some of the best studied in the British Isles and support a remarkable diversity of species.

There are over 120 islands in the lough, mainly along the west side. Most are drowned, rounded hills called drumlins, formed by glacial deposits during the last Ice Age.

BIRDS

The inter-tidal mudflats comprising 40 per cent of the lough are the attraction for the majority of the birds. Most prominent are the light-bellied Brent Geese that start to arrive from Arctic Canada by September, reaching a peak population of several thousand in October and early November. The northern end of the lough is an important staging post for the geese, providing rich feeding on the extensive areas of Eel-grass that grow here. Once this food source diminishes, many of the geese disperse to other sites within Ireland, most notably Wexford and the Dublin area. One or two Black Brant are recorded in most years, a race of Brent Goose that breeds in Alaska and western Arctic Canada, and winters on the Pacific coast of North America.

A few Whooper Swans winter here, favouring fields between Newtownards and Comber. Various other species of wildfowl occur in small numbers, including Red-breasted Merganser, Goldeneye, Gadwall and Shelduck. A few Slavonian Grebes and three diver species favour the deeper southern waters of the lough.

The common species of wader are represented in autumn and winter by large numbers of Golden Plover, Lapwing, Redshank, Knot, Oystercatcher, Dunlin, Curlew and Bar-tailed Godwit, and small numbers of Black-tailed Godwit and Greenshank. Passage waders include Spotted Redshank and Ruff, which may be looked for at favourable sites such as Castle Espie and Quoile Pondage. Sandwich and Common Terns nest on the inaccessible islands.

Although there is bird interest throughout the year, autumn and winter are best, particularly September and October for large numbers of birds. To ensure reasonable views of many of the birds, a visit within two hours of high tide is recommended.

OTHER ANIMALS

Common Seals and a few Grey Seals are the obvious marine animals, but if you dive below the water surface you enter Strangford Lough's most densely

Strangford Lough.

populated habitat. With each tide, 12,000 million cubic feet of water streams through the narrows, bringing with it microscopic life that supports millions of filter-feeding animals. Soft corals and anemones in the narrows are replaced further up the loch by brittle stars and mussels. This rich, marine environment has led to the proposal that Strangford Lough should become a Marine Nature Reserve.

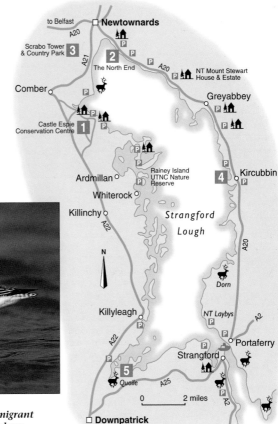

The Greenshank is a passage migrant and winters in very small numbers.

SITE GUIDE

1

Castle Espie
Wildfowl & Wetlands Trust Centre

Situated at the northern end by the Comber Estuary, this small reserve has a variety of habitats that overlook the shore. The centre has a varied wildfowl collection, and the lagoons within the reserve attract waders. The shore of the lough can be viewed from the comfort of a hide inside the WWT reserve or by taking the lane on the Comber side.

ACCESS: On the north-west shore, 13 miles from Belfast. From Comber, travel south on the A22 and, after 550 yards, turn left on to the minor road signed to Mahee Island and Castle Espie. The centre is open daily from 10.30am to 5pm Monday to Saturday, and from 11.30am to 5pm on Sunday (admission charge for non-members). There is a visitor centre, restaurant and art gallery.

DISABLED ACCESS: This is good, with access to the hides and along all the main paths.

2

The North End

Apart from Castle Espie, mentioned above, the A20 running along the east shore has a number of lay-bys, these allowing the lough to be viewed very easily by car. The area between Newtownards and Greyabbey is best for Brent Geese, and for a variety of ducks and waders.

Scrabo Tower

A pair of Peregrines have bred on the cliffs here for many years. During the breeding season, the warden of the country park normally sets aside a small area for viewing the birds. Access is from the A21; the country park is well signposted.

Kircubbin

This site lies half-way along the east shore, and can be good for wintering Black Guillemots, Slavonian Grebes and divers, including Black-throated Diver. Park near the Kircubbin Yacht Club and walk north along the shore.

5

Quoile Pondage

This freshwater lagoon, now a National Nature Reserve, was formed in 1957 by the building of a barrage across the River Quoile. A good diversity of species can be seen here. Passage waders include Spotted Redshank, Greenshank, and occasional Green and Wood Sandpiper. Garganey are sometimes seen while, in summer, terns fish over the open water. The best place for watching

is Castle Island, where there is a comfortable hide.

 ACCESS: Castle Island is reached by turning right off the A25 approximately 2½ miles west of Strangford. Much of the lagoon can be seen from the hide and the road that leads to a sailing club.

DISABLED ACCESS: The hide allows disabled access, and much can be seen from the road.

BIRDS THROUGH THE SEASONS
ALL YEAR: Great Crested Grebe, Little Grebe, Cormorant, Grey Heron, Mute Swan, feral Greylag, Canada and Barnacle Geese, Shelduck, Mallard, Gadwall, Shoveler, Tufted Duck, Pochard, Eider, Red-breasted Merganser, Coot, Moorhen, Ringed Plover, Lapwing, Snipe, Curlew, Redshank, Black Guillemot.
SPRING: A few passage waders occur, notably Whimbrel and Common Sandpiper. Occasional Garganey.
SUMMER: Breeding terns include Arctic, Common and Sandwich Tern. Roseate Tern used to breed; now the odd individual sometimes lingers. Breeding Peregrines.

Strangford Lough (north end) at low tide.

AUTUMN: Wildfowl and waders start to arrive for the winter. Passage waders include Whimbrel, Common Sandpiper, Spotted Redshank, Ruff, Greenshank, and occasional Wood and Green Sandpiper.
WINTER: Slavonian Grebe, Great Northern Diver, Red-throated Diver, Black-throated Diver, Whooper Swan, light-bellied Brent Goose, Wigeon, Teal, Pintail, Scaup, Goldeneye, Golden Plover, Grey Plover, Curlew, Oystercatcher, Knot, Dunlin, Purple Sandpiper, Black-tailed Godwit, Bar-tailed Godwit, Snipe, Jack Snipe and Greenshank.

OTHER ATTRACTIONS

BELFAST: This is the capital of Northern Ireland, and is a city with a multitude of attractions.

MOUNT STEWART HOUSE: This National Trust property is the family home of the Marquess of Londonderry. There are themed gardens and an 18th-century house containing family treasures.

LOUGH NEAGH is the largest freshwater lake in the British Isles, and is one of the most important sites for wintering wildfowl in Europe, regularly supporting between 60,000 and 80,000 birds. Due to its vast size, there are a number of sites favoured by birds, one of the best of which is Oxford Island, with excellent facilities for the visitor.

 BIRDS

Oxford Island National Nature Reserve is not an island but a peninsula on the lough's south shore. The site covers 290 acres and is managed by Craigavon Borough Council. The sheltered bays on either side are overlooked by five hides. Both bays support large concentrations of diving duck in winter;

most numerous are Pochard, Tufted Duck and Goldeneye, with smaller numbers of Teal, Mallard, Scaup and Great Crested Grebe.

Willow and Alder scrub, small patches of reeds and open fields attract a variety of species. Both Bewick's and Whooper Swans use the fields close by. During summer, Grasshopper Warbler, Sedge Warbler,

Lough Neagh.

Willow Warbler and Reed Bunting breed. Over 150 pairs of Great Crested Grebe nest, together with a few wildfowl. The small islands viewable from Oxford Island attract breeding Common Tern and Black-headed Gull.

The best time to visit for large numbers of wildfowl is winter. During weekends this site can become quite crowded.

OTHER ANIMALS

The Kinnegoe Meadows support a variety of butterflies and flowers. A network of footpaths leads through the varied habitats. Wood White butterfly is one of the more interesting species to be found. Badger, Mink and Otter use the reserve but are rarely seen. Lough Neagh is Europe's largest inland fishery, with 700 tons of Eels being caught annually, a harvest that has continued for centuries.

BIRDS THROUGH THE SEASONS

ALL YEAR: Little Grebe, Great Crested Grebe, Sparrowhawk, Tufted Duck, Pochard, Mallard, Water Rail, Kingfisher, Treecreeper and Reed Bunting.
SPRING: Passage waders may include Oystercatcher, Ringed Plover, Ruff, Black-tailed Godwit, Common Sandpiper and Whimbrel. Arrival of summer visitors.
SUMMER: Breeding birds include Gadwall, Ruddy Duck, Black-headed Gull, Common Tern, Willow Warbler, Sedge Warbler, Grasshopper Warbler, Blackcap and Cuckoo.
WINTER: Large rafts of diving duck, mainly Tufted Duck, Pochard and Goldeneye. Smaller numbers of Teal, Mallard and Scaup. Occasional Smew and Goosander. Whooper and Bewick's Swan and Golden Plover on surrounding fields.

Access: The reserve lies 20 miles west of Belfast, and is clearly signposted from junction 10 of the M1.

There are five hides and various paths. The Discovery Centre has displays on the history and wildlife of the lough. Facilities include a restaurant, information desk, a play area for children, and a gift and craft shop.

For more information, contact the Lough Neagh Discovery Centre, Oxford Island, Craigavon, Co Armagh BT66 6NJ. Tel: 01762 322205.

DISABLED ACCESS:

Most of the paths are surfaced, and two of the hides are accessible to wheelchairs.

OTHER ATTRACTIONS

LOUGH NEAGH is a popular centre for watersports, and there are a number of activity points around the shore where equipment can be hired. Several historical sites are worth visiting near by; details are available from the Discovery Centre.

Lough Neagh Discovery Centre.

THE BELFAST Harbour Estate, on the south shore of Belfast Lough, has an excellent area for birds throughout the year within its industrial surroundings.

During winter the inner lough attracts a few seaduck, such as Common Scoter and Scaup. Nearer the mouth of the lough, larger numbers of Eider and

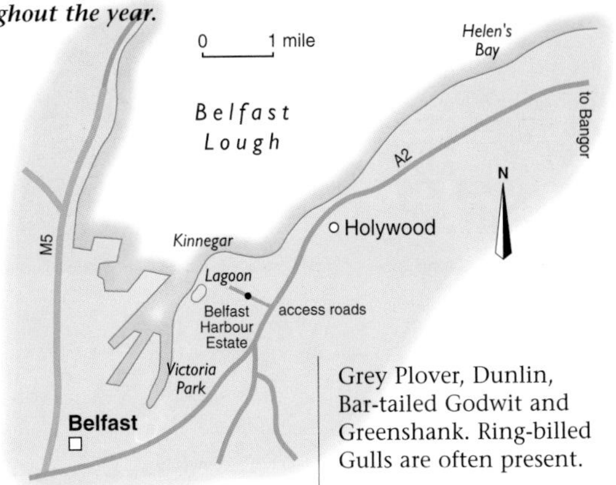

SUMMER: Breeding birds include a few species of wildfowl and waders.

AUTUMN: Passage waders include Spotted Redshank, Greenshank, Little Stint, Curlew Sandpiper, Ruff, Grey Plover, Black-tailed Godwit, Common Sandpiper and Little Stint. Vagrant North American waders and gulls are found regularly.

WINTER: On the lough: divers and grebes, Scaup, Long-tailed Duck, Common Scoter, Goldeneye and Brent Goose. Waders include Golden Plover,

The lagoon attracts birds throughout the year.

Belfast Harbour is Ireland's largest port, and so invariably there is much pressure on the land for development. In 1990 an agreement was reached between various conservation bodies and the Belfast Harbour Commissioners to safeguard 200 acres of inter-tidal mudflats and lagoons. As a result, two of the three lagoons have been filled in, but the third is now safe from future development. It is attractive to a range of breeding and wintering species; during spring and autumn a variety of migrants occur.

🦆 BIRDS
The lagoon is an important wader roost, and various species of wildfowl and gulls winter there. During spring and autumn a variety of migrants use the lagoon. Garganey are annual each spring, while waders such as Little Stint, Curlew Sandpiper, Ruff and Spotted Redshank are seen in autumn. During both seasons there is always a chance of a rarity.

a few Long-tailed Ducks can be found. Peregrines hunt over the area throughout the year.

BIRDS THROUGH THE SEASONS
ALL YEAR: Great Crested Grebe, Cormorant, Mute Swan, Shelduck, Mallard, Moorhen, Coot, Peregrine, Kestrel, Sparrowhawk, Oystercatcher, Lapwing, Snipe, Redshank, Black-headed Gull, Herring Gull, and Stonechat.

SPRING: Passage waders such as Whimbrel and Common Sandpiper. Garganey are annual.

Grey Plover, Dunlin, Bar-tailed Godwit and Greenshank. Ring-billed Gulls are often present.

▶ ACCESS:
To enter Belfast Harbour Estate to view the pool and lough, take the A2 from Belfast towards Holywood. The estate is signposted at the second set of traffic lights. The outer lough can be viewed from a number of access points.

♿ DISABLED ACCESS:
The pool is viewable from a vehicle.

OTHER ATTRACTIONS

THE CENTRE of Belfast and its various attractions are a few minutes' drive away.

Map labels: Belfast Lough · Helen's Bay · to Bangor · A2 · Holywood · Kinnegar · Lagoon · Belfast Harbour Estate · access roads · Victoria Park · Belfast · M5 · N · 0   1 mile

THIS PICTURESQUE estuary, close to Coleraine on the North Antrim coast, attracts a range of species, especially waders. A National Trust hide provides a good view over the estuary, and is the best site for viewing during an incoming tide.

BIRDS THROUGH THE SEASONS

SPRING: Lingering winter visitors and passage waders pass through, notably Whimbrels – often in numbers exceeding 100.

SUMMER: A few waders may be present.

WINTER: Great Northern Diver, Red-throated Diver and Great Crested Grebe on the sea and estuary mouth. Within the estuary: Eider, Mallard, Teal, Wigeon, Goldeneye, Oystercatcher, Ringed Plover, Golden Plover, Lapwing, Dunlin, Sanderling, Curlew and Greenshank. Snow Buntings in the dunes.

ACCESS: Travelling west on the A2 from Coleraine, turn right at Articlave and, after approximately 1 mile, turn left at a T-junction. Cross a bridge and then turn right. Park before the railway line, and proceed on foot to the estuary and hide. Castlerock is reached by continuing on the A2 past Articlave to the coast.

Bann Estuary.

BIRDS
A few Snow Buntings occasionally winter in the sand dunes on the seaward side. Castlerock Strand, a popular sandy beach bordering the dunes, has a pier which can make a good vantage point for sea-watching during onshore winds in autumn. Sanderlings occur on the beach in autumn.

Several rarities have been recorded in recent years, including Forster's Tern and Semi-palmated Sandpiper. The optimum time to visit is during autumn.

FLOWERS
There is a fine orchid flora that includes Common Spotted, Northern Marsh, Pyramidal and Bee Orchids.

(Map) North Channel · Ramore Head · Portrush · Portstewart · Castlerock · A2 · Bann Estuary · A2 · Articlave · A2 · Coleraine · 0 — 1 mile · N

AUTUMN: Winter wildfowl and divers arrive. Waders include Oystercatcher, Ringed Plover, Golden Plover, Lapwing, Knot, Dunlin, Sanderling, Curlew Sandpiper, Little Stint, Curlew, Spotted Redshank, Redshank, Greenshank and occasional rarities. Offshore skuas, terns, gulls (notably Sabine's Gulls) and shearwaters are possible in strong onshore winds.

DISABLED ACCESS:
Although there is wheelchair access to the hide, this is not particularly practical and assistance may be required, particularly in wet weather.

OTHER ATTRACTIONS

SEE ENTRIES under Rathlin Island (Site 100).

LOUGH FOYLE is a large, shallow estuary stretching for nearly 20 miles and separating Co Londonderry from Co Donegal. Extensive inter-tidal mudflats on the southern and eastern shores are backed by farmland.

The best time to visit is in winter, with late October/early November being optimum for the highest numbers of birds.

BIRDS
The Londonderry side of the lough is of most interest for birds as 3400 acres of the south-east shore is a nature reserve. This is an important winter refuge for wildfowl, especially Whooper Swan, light-bellied Brent Goose and Wigeon.

many of them of Icelandic origin, arriving on the lough in October before dispersing to other sites within Ireland.

Divers and grebes occur away from the shallow feeding areas used by wildfowl. Great Northern Diver, Red-throated Diver and Slavonian Grebe are often present in very small numbers, along with larger numbers of Great Crested Grebe.

A few Greenshank winter, but most obvious are Curlew, Dunlin, Golden Plover, Lapwing, Oystercatcher and Bar-tailed Godwit. In bad weather during autumn, seabirds occasionally find their way into the lough.

SITE GUIDE

1

Magilligan Point

The point is one of the best places to see skuas and terns using the narrows in summer and autumn. Divers and grebes favour the deep water off the point. Along the sandy shore there are often Sanderling in winter. Magilligan Point is part of one of the largest sand-dune systems in the British Isles.

Creeping Thyme and Pyramidal Orchids grow here in summer, and a variety of common butterflies can be seen.

ACCESS: The point is approximately 10 miles north of Limavady. Take the B202 off the A2 to the point.

Whooper Swans.

Average winter wildfowl counts exceed 25,000 birds, of which over 15,000 are waders. Over 1000 Whooper Swans spend the winter feeding on the surrounding farmland, along with much smaller numbers of Bewick's Swans. Both Brent Goose and Wigeon populations vary annually. In some winters Wigeon numbers can exceed 20,000 birds,

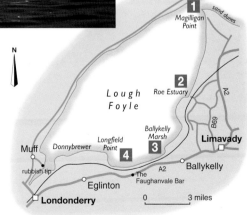

DISABLED ACCESS:
None, but the strand along the Lough Foyle side of the point can be viewed from a car.

Roe Estuary.

2

Roe Estuary

The Roe Estuary lies in the imposing shadow of Binevenagh, supposedly where the last Irish Wolf roamed. This site is best visited at high tide, when waders and wildfowl are pushed towards the shore and roost on the saltmarsh. Slavonian Grebes favour this area of the lough. Sometimes large numbers of Whooper Swans, and smaller numbers of Bewick's Swans, Greenland White-fronted Geese and Greylag Geese graze on the Myroe Levels behind the embankment. These fields also attract finches in winter, and a few Snow Buntings can often be located in the vicinity. Peregrines and other raptors often hunt over the estuary and low-lying fields behind the sea wall. Part of the area is a National Nature Reserve.

ACCESS: From the car park, walk along the river embankment and over the railway line. The Myroe Levels are behind the sea wall.

The car park is reached by taking the B69 north out of Limavady. After 1½ miles take a left turn to Limavady Junction Railway Station. After a further 1½ miles you reach a T-junction; turn right here and drive down to the estuary.

DISABLED ACCESS:
None.

Lough Foyle viewed from Ballykelly.

3

Ballykelly Marsh

Ballykelly Marsh is an expanse of saltmarsh that is a wader roost at high tide.

Access: Turn off the A2 down Station Road by the Bridgehouse restaurant in Ballykelly.

DISABLED ACCESS:
None.

4

Longfield Point

The Longfield Levels behind the point are low-lying pastures and arable fields. They are attractive to Whooper and Bewick's Swans, often in large numbers, and to a few geese in winter. Occasional Merlins, and more regularly Peregrines patrol the area. The point overlooks an expanse of mud, inhabited by wildfowl and waders.

Access: If travelling west along the A2, turn right following the signs for Donnybrewer. Drive over the railway line and follow the track. From here, the levels up to Longfield Point can be explored.

♿ **DISABLED ACCESS:**
The levels along the many tracks can be watched from a car, as can the lough from Longfield Point.

BIRDS THROUGH
THE SEASONS

SPRING: Lingering winter visitors, including Whooper and Bewick's Swans, depart in March and early April. A few Whimbrel pass through.
SUMMER: Terns and skuas may be seen off Magilligan Point.
AUTUMN: Passage waders include Curlew Sandpiper, Little Stint, Spotted Redshank and Ruff. In bad weather, sea-watching can be very rewarding at Magilligan Point.
WINTER: Red-throated Diver, Great Northern Diver, Great Crested Grebe, Slavonian Grebe, Whooper Swan, Bewick's Swan, light-bellied Brent Goose, Greylag Goose, Greenland White-fronted

Grazing marsh behind Longfield Point. (Right) male Wigeon.

Goose, Wigeon, Teal, Mallard, Pintail, Peregrine, Merlin, Sparrowhawk, Kestrel, Oystercatcher, Golden Plover, Lapwing, Dunlin, Sanderling, Knot, Curlew, Redshank, Snow Bunting and Twite.

➡ **ACCESS:** *See* site guide above for detailed access arrangements.

♿ **DISABLED ACCESS:**
This is very limited, other than sites where viewing is possible from a car. *See* site guide above.

OTHER
ATTRACTIONS

DOWNHILL HOUSE: The ruins of this magnificent former bishop's palace lie in a landscaped park overlooking Lough Foyle. Mussenden Temple, a circular neoclassical building on the cliff top, was once the bishop's library. There are breathtaking views of the north coast of Ireland.

ROE VALLEY COUNTRY PARK: A picturesque woodland area with riverside walks which can provide good opportunities to see the Irish races of Coal Tit and Dipper. The park is signposted from Dungiven.

See also entries under Rathlin Island (Site 100).

This shallow lough is situated on the River Bann about 2 miles north of Lough Neagh, and is attractive to passage waders and wildfowl.

Surrounded by flood meadows, Church Island, with its unusual 18th-century spire, along with Scab and Ceney islands, was once surrounded by flooded meadows. The lough has now shrunk owing to the erection in the 1930s of flood gates where the River Bann leaves Lough Neagh.

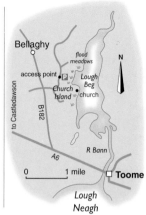

View of Church Island.

When the meadows do flood during winter rains, they provide a rich feeding ground for wildfowl.

Lough Beg is worth visiting at any time of year. However, it is at its best in autumn for passage waders, and during the winter months for wildfowl.

BIRDS
Waders use the route between Lough Neagh and the Bann Estuary as a flyway. Most just fly straight through, but those that linger include flocks of Icelandic Black-tailed Godwits which use the lough as a staging-post in spring. In autumn, a variety of passage waders may be found around the shoreline.

A long list of rarities have been observed at this site, most notably American waders such as Greater and Lesser Yellowlegs and White-rumped Sandpiper. During winter, Golden Plover and Lapwing are numerous, with small populations of Curlew, Redshank and Dunlin. Wildfowl numbers can be high, with good numbers of Whooper Swans and fewer Bewick's Swan. Wigeon, Teal, Mallard and Pochard are prominent and increase in times of hard weather.

FLOWERS
Some interesting plants grow, including Flowering Rush and the rare Irish Ladies Tresses. These plants are protected within a nature reserve that encompasses the meadows around Church Island.

BIRDS THROUGH THE SEASONS
ALL YEAR: Great Crested Grebe, Grey Heron, Mute Swan, Teal, Mallard, Shoveler, Tufted Duck, Pochard, Kestrel, Sparrowhawk, Moorhen, Coot, Lapwing, Snipe, Curlew, Redshank, Black-headed Gull, Kingfisher and Reed Bunting.

SPRING: Passage waders include Black-tailed Godwit and Whimbrel. Garganey are near annual.

SUMMER: Breeding birds include Great Crested Grebe, Mallard, Teal, Shoveler, Tufted Duck, Red-breasted Merganser, Shelduck, Lapwing, Snipe, Curlew and Redshank.

AUTUMN: Passage waders include Black-tailed Godwit, Ruff, Curlew Sandpiper, Little Stint, Greenshank, Common Sandpiper, Green Sandpiper and Wood Sandpiper. Rarities in recent years have included a variety of American waders.

WINTER: Whooper Swan, Bewick's Swan, Wigeon, Pintail, Peregrine, Hen Harrier, Merlin, Short-eared Owl, Golden Plover, Grey Plover and Greenshank.

ACCESS:
The best access is along the western shore. About 1 mile from Toome, take the Bellaghy road (B182), turning down Ballydermott Road. The church spire can be seen some distance away and can be used as a point of reference. Park opposite Church Island and proceed across the meadows to the lough.

DISABLED ACCESS:
None.

OTHER ATTRACTIONS

*S*EE ENTRIES for Lough Neagh (Site 102).

THE NORTH Bull, on the outskirts of Dublin City, offers some of the best winter bird-watching within the republic. A causeway cuts through saltmarsh and mudflats to the sand dunes of North Bull, where there is an interpretive centre.

BIRDS

The causeway was built in 1964 to carry traffic across to the island, and offers the best vantage point for observing the thousands of wildfowl and

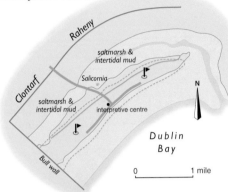

Raheny
saltmarsh & intertidal mud
Salicornia
Clontarf
saltmarsh & intertidal mud
interpretive centre
N
Dublin Bay
Bull wall
0   1 mile

waders that feed on the inter-tidal mud. Arrive three hours before high tide and watch large numbers of waders as they fly in from Dublin Bay and are pushed close to the causeway by the incoming tide. One of the attractions of the Bull is the tameness of the birds. Tamest of all are the few hundred light-bellied Brent Geese. They tolerate approach to within a few yards. The geese are winter visitors from the Canadian Arctic, and on arrival feed out on the saltmarsh. Later in the winter they favour areas of grass such as the golf courses.

The Bull island has grown considerably since the Bull wall was constructed in 1825 to improve the approach into Dublin Harbour. The island has two golf courses among its dunes, and on the seaward side there is a wide sandy beach that attracts a few waders. During the summer months the island can be very crowded, especially at weekends, and so is best avoided. Bird interest is maintained by a few breeding Little Terns, and there are always a few waders on the mud.

OTHER ANIMALS

The golf courses are attractive to Irish Hares.

FLOWERS

An interesting flora includes Pyramidal Orchid, Marsh Helleborine, Autumn Ladies Tresses Orchid, Cat's-ear and Yellow Rattle.

(Top) Interpretive centre.

Light-bellied Brent Geese feed within a few yards of the causeway.

Rainbow over the saltmarsh and mudflats of the North Bull.

BIRDS THROUGH THE SEASONS

ALL YEAR: Cormorant, Shelduck, Mallard, Oystercatcher, Dunlin, Ringed Plover, Kestrel, Curlew and Reed Bunting.

SPRING: A few lingering winter visitors. Whimbrel pass through. A few migrants often occur on the island.

SUMMER: Little Terns attempt to breed.

AUTUMN: Curlew Sandpiper, Spotted Redshank, Ruff and Little Stint are annual. Rare waders often occur.

WINTER: Off the Bull wall and shore in Dublin Bay look for Red-throated and Great Northern Divers, Red-breasted Merganser, scoters, grebes and seabirds. On the inter-tidal mud there are Grey Heron, light-bellied Brent Goose, Wigeon, Teal, Pintail, Shoveler, Dunlin, Black-tailed Godwit, Bar-tailed Godwit, Redshank, Knot, Grey Plover, Golden Plover, Oystercatcher, Lapwing and Curlew, with Sanderling on the beach and Purple Sandpiper on the Bull wall. Raptors include Merlin, Peregrine and Short-eared Owl. A few Snow Buntings often winter on the Bull wall or along the beach.

ACCESS: North Bull is just a few minutes' drive from Dublin City centre, and is reached by taking the coast road north from the docks towards Raheny and Howth. You can drive along the Bull wall to the beach at the end. The causeway is the best access point; park and view on either side.

DISABLED ACCESS: This is excellent. Viewing is easy on the causeway from a vehicle or from the pavements on either side. You can drive on to the beach behind the dunes.

OTHER ATTRACTIONS

LYING AT the mouth of the River Liffey, Dublin has a host of attractions, from guided tours of the Guinness factory to a lively night out in one of the city's many pubs.

THIS RESERVE, on the north side of Wexford Harbour, is famous for its winter concentrations of geese. The Slob covers 2500 acres of low-lying farmland reclaimed from the sea in 1847. The reserve of 510 acres is run by the Irish Wildbird Conservancy. Greenland White-fronted Geese started using the Slob in the 1920s. You may notice some of the geese have neckbands; they are trapped using a canon net populations of Brent Geese and often a few Pink-footed Geese. Among these there is often a Snow Goose or one of the small sub-species of Canada Goose, both of which are likely to have originated from across the Atlantic.

A herd of Bewick's Swan feeds on the Slob, along with a variety of other wildfowl. Lapwing, Curlew and Golden Plover are numerous. In front of the Tower Hide, a small pool is attractive to passage waders and to the occasional rarity. Rarities recorded on the reserve have included Western Sandpiper, Cattle Egret, Lesser White-fronted Goose, Black Duck and Paddyfield Warbler.

Wexford Harbour is a wide sea inlet that holds good numbers of sea and estuarine ducks in winter. It also has small numbers of Slavonian and Black-necked Grebes, and occasional Red-necked Grebe. The stretch of

North Slob Wildfowl Reserve.

on the North Slob as part of an on-going study.

The best time for a visit is between October and April. During spring and autumn there may be passage waders present.

BIRDS
Greenland White-fronted Geese can reach 10,000 birds, with smaller

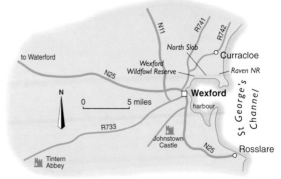

Up to 10,000 Greenland White-fronted Geese winter on the Slobs.

coast from Curracloe sand dunes to Raven Point, close to North Slob, often has Common Scoter offshore and is worth visiting to check for Surf Scoter.

BIRDS THROUGH THE SEASONS

ALL YEAR: Great Crested Grebe, Mute Swan, Mallard, Kestrel and Sparrowhawk
SPRING: Passage waders. Winter visitors departing.
SUMMER: A few Black-tailed Godwits may be present in summer.
AUTUMN: Passage waders, with the chance of a rarity. Winter visitors arrive.
WINTER: Bewick's Swan and sometimes a few Whooper Swan. Greenland White-fronted, light-bellied Brent and often a few Pink-footed Geese, possibility of Snow Goose and small race of Canada Goose, Wigeon, Pintail, Shelduck, Mallard, Teal, Gadwall, Shoveler, Tufted Duck, Pochard, Goldeneye, Red-breasted Merganser, Lapwing, Golden Plover, Curlew, Black-tailed Godwit, Redshank, Dunlin, Hen Harrier, Merlin and Peregrine.

ACCESS: From Wexford, travel north on the road to Gorey. A further 1½ miles after the bridge is a right-hand turn signposted to the reserve.

There is no admission charge.

Visitor facilities include a comfortable viewing hide, a visitor centre with audio-visual display, and a small collection of wildfowl. Guided tours by the warden are available on request. Contact Chris Wilson on Tel: 053 23129.

The reserve is open from 9am to 6pm daily between 16 April and 30 September, and from 10am to 5pm daily between 1 October and 15 April.

DISABLED ACCESS: This is difficult, but arrangements can be made by contacting the warden (details above).

OTHER ATTRACTIONS

WEXFORD TOWN is well worth exploring as it contains much of considerable historic interest.

THE LARGEST of the two Saltee islands, Great Saltee is approximately 1 mile long by half a mile wide. Steep cliffs along the south and west of the island are inhabited by breeding seabirds, while the northern shoreline has a boulder-strewn beach at the base of low boulder-clay cliffs. A few trees survive around the farmhouse, and stone walls border overgrown fields.

From spring through to autumn, there is much to see. The best time for a visit would be mid- to late May for the chance of a few migrants and the opportunity to see all the breeding seabirds.

 BIRDS
While the seabird colonies are a big attraction in summer, Great Saltee is one of the most productive migration watch-points in Ireland. The country's first bird observatory was established here in 1950, but was later closed in 1963. During spring there can be some dramatic falls, and occasional rarities are recorded at both passage periods. Common migrants can include large numbers of Willow Warblers, Chiffchaffs, Wheatears and Swallows. During autumn, rarities are found regularly amongst the commoner migrants.

The seabird colonies are viewed easily. Most impressive is the growing Gannet colony; the birds first bred in 1929, and now number over 1000 pairs. Guillemots and Razorbills are easily watched from the cliff top and a few hundred pairs of Puffins nest in burrows half-way along the south side. The most

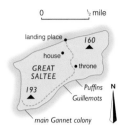

difficult seabird to see on the island is the Manx Shearwater as it only comes ashore to its nesting burrow at night. During the day, however, this species and British Storm-petrel can often be seen on the boat crossing during summer.

The island's owners, the Neale family, have declared it a bird sanctuary and have erected a throne in the middle of the island.

 FLOWERS
There is an interesting maritime flora; in spring and early summer the ground is carpeted in Bluebells.

BIRDS THROUGH THE SEASONS
ALL YEAR: Cormorant, Shag, Peregrine, Oystercatcher, Raven, Chough and Rock Pipit.
SPRING: Seabirds arrive and will be on the cliffs by mid-

Great Saltee Island.

May. Migrants include Cuckoo, Redstart, Whinchat, Wheatear, Swallow, Willow Warbler and Chiffchaff. Possible rarities might include a Hoopoe or Golden Oriole.
SUMMER: Breeding seabirds include Manx Shearwater, Fulmar, Shag, Gannet, Guillemot, Razorbill, Puffin, Herring Gull, Lesser Black-backed Gull, Great Black-backed Gull and Kittiwake. British Storm-petrels are regularly seen on the boat crossing. Other breeders include Shelduck, Mallard, Oystercatcher, Ringed Plover, Snipe, Raven, Chough and Peregrine.
AUTUMN: Various migrants including warblers, chats and flycatchers. Rarities occur. During southerly and south-westerly winds, skuas and shearwaters can occur offshore.

 ACCESS: Great Saltee is reached from Kilmore Quay. Day-trips are possible during the summer months; enquiries for boats to the island should be made at the quay.

Permission is required from the owners if an overnight stay is desired.

 DISABLED ACCESS: None.

KNOWN AS a back-barrier seepage lagoon, Lady's Island Lake is separated from the sea by a shingle bank that is breached each spring to release the water that accumulates through seepage, rainfall and from feeder streams (*see also* following site and map).

BIRDS

The lagoon is of most importance for its breeding terns, especially Sandwich and Roseate Terns. The Roseate Terns number around 70 pairs, and nest on a small island off Lady's Island. The latter is a place of pilgrimage from which the lake gets its name, and is linked to the mainland by a causeway.

As well as the large numbers of Sandwich Terns, there are a few Common and Arctic Terns. In winter, a few wildfowl occur and a few species nest at Ring Marsh, a small lagoon to the east of the lake. During autumn, the lake is worth checking for waders and, although not so attractive to rarities as nearby Tacumshin, a number of American waders have been found here.

FLOWERS

The lake has some interesting plants around its shores. The gravel barrier has growing on it the only stand of Cottonweed in the whole of Ireland. Burnet Rose is common in the south-eastern corner, where there is also a well-developed community of annual herbs.

BIRDS THROUGH THE SEASONS

ALL YEAR: Mute Swan, Mallard, Great Crested Grebe, Little Grebe, Tufted Duck, Coot and Moorhen.
SPRING: A few passage waders. Terns arrive.
SUMMER: Breeding birds include Shoveler, Herring Gull, Lesser Black-backed Gull, Black-headed Gull, Roseate Tern, Sandwich Tern, Arctic Tern, Common Tern, Sedge Warbler and Reed Warbler.
AUTUMN: Passage waders may include Curlew Sandpiper and Little Stint. There is always the chance of an American wader.
WINTER: Occasionally a few Bewick's and Whooper Swans. Wigeon, Teal, Gadwall, Shoveler, Pochard, Tufted Duck, Goldeneye, Red-breasted Merganser, Coot, Oystercatcher, Golden Plover, Lapwing, Curlew, Redshank and Greenshank. Generally, wildfowl and wader numbers are low, most birds concentrating at nearby Tacumshin.

 ACCESS: The east side provides the easiest access. The path that runs around the shore is the best way to explore the area if time allows. Lady's Island is the best place to see the Roseate Terns, either off the causeway or looking across to the island on which they breed. Good views can also be had by watching the birds passing to and from the sea at the shingle bank barrier.

Lady's Island Lake is one of the most important breeding sites for Roseate Terns in Ireland.

To reach the lake, take the road leading south from the N25 Wexford–Rosslare road at Tagoat; the lake is signposted. Ring Marsh in the south-east corner is reached by taking the road to Carnsore Point. After the Lobster Pot, which incidentally is an excellent bar and restaurant for a meal, drive to the point where road becomes track. The lake can now be seen, and there is a track on the right leading to the marsh.

DISABLED ACCESS:

A track in the south-eastern corner allows viewing from a vehicle, as does the causeway that runs across to Lady's Island.

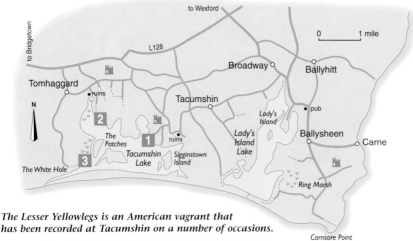

*The Lesser Yellowlegs is an American vagrant that
has been recorded at Tacumshin on a number of occasions.*

Carnsore Point

TACUMSHIN IS legendary for
its attraction to American
waders. Buff-breasted
Sandpipers are almost
annual, with a record nine
birds seen in September
1980. Nearly all the
American waders on the
British and Irish list have
been recorded here over the

years. September and
October are best, and are
the months when
Tacumshin is most
intensively watched.

Like Lady's Island Lake,
this is a brackish lagoon cut
off from the sea by dunes.
The lagoon had a tidal
outlet until 1972. Since that

time, a one-way pipeline
has drained the lagoon,
resulting in high water
levels in winter and a
drying out of much of the
lagoon in summer. There
are a number of islands on
the lake, and extensive reed
swamps, areas of sedge and
marsh, and vast sandflats.
In the south-west corner
there is a small marsh
separated from Tacumshin
by a sluice and dyke. This is
known as the White Hole
and often attracts Bewick's
Swans and Brent Geese.

BIRDS
Autumn is the peak
time to visit, both for the
chance of a rarity and for
the diversity of wildfowl and
waders that occur. The
waders should be studied
carefully, with each Dunlin
flock checked thoroughly
for a vagrant. During winter,
Tacumshin supports large
numbers of wildfowl,
especially Wigeon. Hen
Harrier and Merlin patrol
the area regularly, often
provoking panic amongst

the ducks. One of the attractions of a winter visit is the impressive numbers of birds, and with not another bird-watcher in sight.

Rarities turn up throughout the year, but autumn is the best time. There are both interesting breeding birds in summer and impressive numbers of wintering wildfowl, these giving Tacumshin year-round appeal.

BIRDS THROUGH THE SEASONS
ALL YEAR: Mute Swan, Shelduck, Mallard, Moorhen, Water Rail, Oystercatcher, Ringed Plover and Redshank.
SPRING: A few terns and Little Gulls pass through. Garganey are sometimes seen. A few passage waders.
SUMMER: Breeding birds (see All year).
AUTUMN: Passage waders include Ruff, Curlew Sandpiper, Little Stint, Spotted Redshank, Black-tailed Godwit and American vagrants. Passerines include a variety

Tacumshin.

of migrants, notably large numbers of hirundines.
WINTER: Bewick's Swan, Whooper Swan, light-bellied Brent Goose, Wigeon, Teal, Gadwall, Shoveler, Pintail, Tufted Duck, Pochard, Hen Harrier, Merlin, Golden Plover, Grey Plover, Lapwing, Bar-tailed Godwit, Black-tailed Godwit and Dunlin.

Access: Tacumshin lies about 1 mile west of Lady's Island Lake, and is reached along country lanes. Due to its size, there are a number of access points; the following are recommended (see map).

1 The north-east shore can be reached at two points. If driving from Lady's Island Lake, pass through Tacumshin, go straight over a crossroads and then turn left at the ruins of an old castle. Follow this road and then fork either left or right to reach the shore.

2 To explore the north-west corner, turn right at a sign marked 'cul-de-sac' approximately half a mile from Tomhaggard travelling towards Tacumshin. This road leads down to the shore, where there is a large reed bed.

3 The White Hole and south-western corner are reached by turning left half a mile west of Tomhaggard. Follow this road to a small parking area. The White Hole can be covered from here and, by walking east, you will reach the lagoon.

DISABLED ACCESS: At access points 1 and 3, viewing is possible from a car, especially in winter when water-levels are high and birds may be seen closer to the tracks. At point 3, a couple of the tracks can be followed by car for a short way. Nowhere is suitable for wheelchair access.

BALLYMACODA IS a large area of inter-tidal mud in the estuary of the Womanagh River, and is bordered along its southern flank by Knockadoon Head.

BIRDS

The mudflats and surrounding fields attract thousands of waders in winter. Golden Plover can exceed 10,000, up to 1000 Black-tailed Godwit winter, and in spring Grey Plover congregate before migrating north. The headland attracts migrants in spring and autumn.

Many of the surrounding marshy fields provide a feeding ground for wildfowl, and light-bellied Brent Geese winter here in small numbers along with a few duck. Raptors include Short-eared Owl during most winters, while Hen Harrier, Merlin and Peregrine are regular visitors.

Knockadoon Head is under-watched in autumn when it is at its best. The hedgerows on the head attract Goldcrests, Chiffchaffs, finches and chats. Rarities have included Pied Wheatear and Woodchat Shrike. Chough are a year-round feature.

The estuary is best in winter and on a rising tide.

BIRDS THROUGH THE SEASONS

ALL YEAR: Kestrel, Sparrowhawk, Peregrine, Shelduck, Mallard and Chough.

SPRING: Wintering waders. Grey Plover gather. A few migrants on the headland.

SUMMER: A few waders on the mudflats and breeding residents.

AUTUMN: The rarer passage waders may include Ruff, Curlew Sandpiper, Green Sandpiper, Wood Sandpiper and Little Stint. On Knockadoon Head, Goldcrests and Chiffchaffs can be numerous, together with chats, flycatchers, warblers and rarities.

WINTER: Light-bellied Brent Goose, Wigeon, Teal, Mallard, Shelduck, Oystercatcher, Curlew, Black-tailed Godwit, Bar-tailed Godwit, Redshank, Dunlin and large flocks of Golden Plover and Lapwing. Merlin, Peregrine, Hen Harrier and often Short-eared Owl.

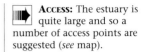 **ACCESS:** The estuary is quite large and so a number of access points are suggested (*see* map).

1 Park at Crompaun Bridge on the road between Ballymacoda and Youghal. Walk south along the river to the point where the estuary widens.

2 If time is limited or if a short walk is required, park at Clonpriest graveyard and take the track to the shore 100 yards further on. The graveyard is situated east of Crompaun Bridge.

3 In the north-east of the estuary is Pillmore Strand, reached by turning right off the Ballymacoda–Youghal road about 1 mile to the north of Clonpriest.

4 The south side can be reached by taking one of a number of roads off to the left after leaving Ballymacoda in an easterly direction.

5 Knockadoon Head lies east of Ballymacoda, and birds may be seen anywhere here. The caravan park has been the site for some interesting birds in recent years.

DISABLED ACCESS: None.

OTHER ATTRACTIONS

LISMORE VILLAGE, situated on the N72 directly north of Ballymacoda, has a fascinating history. Lismore Castle stands on a sheer cliff overhanging the River Blackwater, and was once owned by Sir Walter Ralegh.

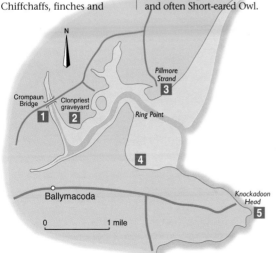

FOR MANY bird-watchers the name Ballycotton is synonymous with rare birds, especially the North American waders for which this site is famous.

Ballycotton contains a mixture of habitats. Intertidal mud borders an often dry lagoon known as Ballycotton Lake. A few hundred yards north are the muddy Shanagarry Pools, particularly good for waders. The town itself has many hedgerows and gardens that attract a wide variety of passerine migrants, especially in autumn.

Ballycotton is worth a visit at any time, although weekends in high summer are best avoided as there are crowds. Spring and autumn are best, and autumn in particular for waders and migrants.

village of Ballycotton should be checked for migrants. During winter there are fewer waders but there is often a good variety of wildfowl. Merlins hunt the area in this season, and they are sometimes joined by Hen Harrier and Short-eared Owl.

BIRDS THROUGH THE SEASONS

ALL YEAR: Mute Swan, Shelduck, Mallard, Gadwall, Teal, Oystercatcher, Ringed Plover, Curlew, Redshank, Dunlin, Reed Bunting and Chough.
SPRING: Passage waders include Whimbrel, Black-tailed Godwit, Bar-tailed Godwit, Common Sandpiper and Sanderling. Summer migrants include hirundines, Wheatear, Cuckoo and Sedge Warbler.

reedbeds. There are often a few summering waders such as Bar-tailed Godwit and Dunlin.
AUTUMN: Waders include Black-tailed Godwit, Bar-tailed Godwit, Redshank, Greenshank, Curlew, Dunlin, Grey Plover, Sanderling, Spotted Redshank, Ruff, Little Stint, Curlew Sandpiper and, irregularly, Green and Wood Sandpiper. American waders are annual, with Pectoral, White-rumped and Baird's Sandpipers being most frequently recorded. Passerines along the beach and in the town may include Pied Flycatcher, Redstart and Whinchat. Wheatears are common.
WINTER: A few waders. Wildfowl often include a few Bewick's and Whooper

American waders are annual at Ballycotton in autumn.

BIRDS

In autumn, flocks of godwits are joined by Curlew Sandpiper, Little Stint, Spotted Redshank and often an American species. The gardens in the fishing

SUMMER: Breeding birds include a few wildfowl. Large numbers of Sedge Warblers, and a few Reed Warblers nest in the

Swans. Regular are Wigeon, Teal, Gadwall, Mallard, Shoveler, Tufted Duck, Pochard and Red-breasted Merganser. American

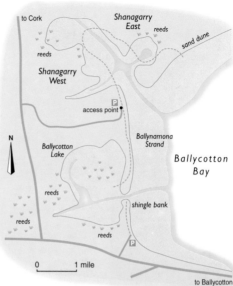

Shanagarry Pools.
(Below) Ballycotton Harbour.

Wigeon and Green-winged Teal have been recorded on a number of occasions. Both Iceland and Glaucous Gull are almost annual in the bay.

ACCESS: The mudflats, Ballycotton Lake and Shanagarry Pools are all reached by turning left to Ballynamona Strand, about half a mile from Shanagarry on the Ballycotton road. Park at the end and walk north for the pools and south for the mudflats and lake. For Ballycotton town, turn left at the end of the main road.

DISABLED ACCESS: The Shanagarry Pools can be viewed from a vehicle by driving north along the strand.

OTHER ATTRACTIONS

BALLYCOTTON: This is a popular resort in the summer. The village has a number of pleasant pubs and an attractive harbour.

BLARNEY CASTLE: To the north of Cork. This is the home of the Blarney Stone; kiss it, and you are granted the gift of the gab!

CORK CITY: Cork has a number of attractions, not least its beautiful French gothic cathedral.

Old Head of Kinsale.

THE OLD Head of Kinsale, a long, thin headland on the south coast, is second only to Cape Clear in autumn for watching passing Cory's and Great Shearwaters, along with a host of other seabirds.

BIRDS

Sea-watching is best in strong south-westerly winds in autumn, although even on days of light winds there are often auks, skuas, Gannets and Manx Shearwaters flying past.

During summer, the headland is alive with breeding seabirds. The steep cliffs on the western side have several thousand pairs of Kittiwakes and Guillemots breeding on their ledges. Chough are conspicuous, either flying along the cliff tops or feeding on the short turf.

There is little cover on the headland and so passerine migrants are best searched for further inland. One of the most productive sites is the area from the Kinsale Head car park back towards the Speckled Door pub.

OTHER ANIMALS

In summer and autumn the seas around the head can be excellent for seeing dolphins and porpoises, along with the occasional Basking Shark and even turtles.

BIRDS THROUGH THE SEASONS

ALL YEAR: Peregrine, Raven, Chough and Rock Dove.
SPRING: There are often seabirds passing offshore, with the possibility of Pomarine Skuas in May and a few passerine migrants.
SUMMER: Breeding seabirds include Shag, Fulmar, Kittiwake, Guillemot, Razorbill and Black Guillemot. Offshore, Gannets and Manx Shearwaters are passing regularly. There are Sooty Shearwater and Great Skua in late summer, with the chance of Cory's Shearwater.

AUTUMN: Passage seabirds include Manx Shearwater, Gannet, Great Skua, Arctic Skua, terns, Guillemot, Razorbill, Kittiwake and Fulmar. During south-westerlies, expect Great Shearwater, Cory's Shearwater, Sooty Shearwater and British Storm-petrel, and there is always the chance of the unexpected; Little Shearwater and Black-browed Albatross are just two of the rarities that have passed by.

ACCESS:
At the time of writing, a golf course is being constructed which is due to be completed on the end of the headland in the spring of 1997. Access for bird-watchers is permitted by the owners, and an assurance has been given that this will continue once the course has been completed. You may be asked to sign an indemnity with regard to potential accidents. Extreme care should be taken if walking along the cliff top.

The headland is reached by leaving the town of Kinsale in a westerly direction. Cross the bridge and follow signs for the Old Head of Kinsale. Park by the old tower and proceed through the gates. The seabird colonies are on the western side.

DISABLED ACCESS:
None.

OTHER ATTRACTIONS

THE TOWN of Kinsale was home to James II in 1689 before his defeat at the Battle of the Boyne.

THESE TWO estuaries midway along the Cork coast lead out into a sandy bay. In its north-west corner, a causeway separates the Inchydoney Estuary from a series of freshwater pools.

BIRDS

Waders are the principal attraction, with Clonakilty being used by up to 800 Icelandic Black-tailed Godwits during autumn and winter. Most of the waders prefer the Clonakilty Estuary, while passage waders such as Little Stint and Curlew Sandpiper are more likely to be found on the lagoons. Wildfowl winter mostly on the Inchydoney, while out in Clonakilty Bay Red-throated and Great Northern Divers are regular.

BIRDS THROUGH THE SEASONS

ALL YEAR: Shelduck, Mallard, Oystercatcher, Ringed Plover, Sparrowhawk, Kestrel and Kingfisher.
SPRING: There are a few passage waders and lingering winter visitors. The pools have attracted rarities such as Black-winged Stilt and Little Egret.
SUMMER: Waders including Black-tailed Godwits start to return in July.
AUTUMN: Passage waders include Curlew Sandpiper, Little Stint, Ruff, Spotted Redshank, Wood Sandpiper and Greenshank, with the possibility of an American wader. There are terns and skuas in the bay.
WINTER: There are Mallard, Wigeon, Teal, Golden Plover,

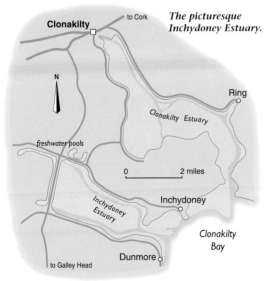

The picturesque Inchydoney Estuary.

Grey Plover, Bar-tailed Godwit, Black-tailed Godwit, Lapwing, Knot, Dunlin and a few spotted Redshank on the Inchydoney. Greenshank, Short-eared Owl, Hen Harrier, Peregrine and a large gull roost are found in Clonakilty Bay.

ACCESS: Both estuaries and the pools are bordered by roads, making viewing easy. Both estuaries are reached from Clonakilty town. Dunmore is a good point from which to view the bay.

DISABLED ACCESS: This is excellent, as all bird-watching is done from the roads.

Galley Head.

THIS PICTURESQUE headland, not far from Clonakilty, can harbour some exciting migrants in autumn and, in south-westerlies, is an excellent sea-watching site.

BIRDS
Permission is required to enter the tip of the head at the lighthouse, but migrants are best searched for in the trees and in the bays leading up to the head. The gardens and hedgerows should be checked thoroughly in autumn. Outstanding vagrants that have occurred include Philadelphia Vireo and American Redstart.

Both Red and Long Strand on either side of the head are attractive to divers. Kilkerran Lake, on the west side, has a few wildfowl and is always worth checking in autumn.

OTHER ANIMALS
During the summer months cetaceans, especially porpoises can occur close inshore. Although best visited in autumn, a spring visit might also be productive.

BIRDS THROUGH THE SEASONS
ALL YEAR: Shag, Rock Dove, Stonechat and Chough.
SPRING: Seabirds passing may include Pomarine Skua, Manx Shearwater and terns. Look for passerine migrants.
SUMMER: Fulmar and Wheatear breed on the head. Kilkerran Lake has Little Grebe and Mallard. Offshore are Manx Shearwater, Gannet, British Storm-petrel and terns.
AUTUMN: Firecrest and Yellow-browed Warbler are almost annual. Warblers, flycatchers and chats occur, plus the chance of a vagrant.

Offshore in strong south-westerlies, Great Shearwater, Sooty Shearwater, Manx Shearwater, Great Skua, Arctic Skua, Gannet and British Storm-petrel occur.

ACCESS: From Clonakilty, drive across the causeway at the head of the Inchydoney Estuary. On reaching the crossroads at the end, drive straight on to Galley Head.

DISABLED ACCESS: None.

to Cork

Clonakilty

N

Inchydoney

Clonakilty Bay

Long Strand

Kilkerran Lake

Sand's Cove

Atlantic Ocean

Red Strand

Dirk Bay

Galley Head • lighthouse

0 — 3 miles

Cape Clear.

per hour. Cape Clear provides one of the best opportunities in Britain and Ireland to see Great Shearwaters. They nest in the southern oceans, migrating north along the American seaboard before swinging across into the eastern Atlantic in late summer. In July and August they are seen off Cape Clear, often in their hundreds and in some years in their thousands. Their rarer cousin, Cory's Shearwater, is annual but occurs in smaller numbers between June and October. Sooty Shearwaters are much more numerous and occasionally occur in spring. Among other passing seabirds, British Storm-petrels are common, along with auks, Kittiwakes and skuas.

CAPE CLEAR, with the exception of the Fastnet Rock just offshore, is the most southerly point in Ireland. The island has long been a migration watch-point, drawing bird-watchers in September and October due to its attraction to rare birds. A bird observatory was established in 1959, and it was not long before large numbers of seabirds were recorded passing the island in summer and autumn. Today, Cape Clear is internationally renowned for its seabird passage.

It is worth a visit at any time between April and November, with July to September being best for seabirds, and September and October best for rarities and migrants.

BIRDS

Huge numbers of Manx Shearwaters pass in July and August – on some days over 20,000 birds pass

The annual occurrence of rare birds from both east and west attracts bird-watchers in autumn. Over the years, American species have included Black and White Warbler, Yellow-bellied Sapsucker and White-throated Sparrow, while from the east have

*This young Chough was reared in a nest situated in a
deserted building on Cape Clear island.*
(Right) *Cape Clear.*

come Lesser Grey Shrike,
Fan-tailed Warbler and
Siberian Thrush. Each
autumn, a sprinkling of
rarities are found. Red-
breasted Flycatcher and
Yellow-browed Warbler are
annual. Spring and summer,
however, should not be
ignored for passerines.

BIRDS THROUGH
THE SEASONS

ALL YEAR: Gannet, Peregrine,
Sparrowhawk, Kestrel, Rock
Dove, Stonechat, Meadow
Pipit, Raven and Chough.
SPRING: Pomarine Skuas in
May. Passerine migrants
include chats, warblers,
Turtle Dove and Cuckoo.
SUMMER: Breeding birds
include Guillemot, Black
Guillemot, a few Puffins,

Great Black-backed Gull,
Lesser Black-backed Gull,
Herring Gull, Wheatear,
Chough and Peregrine.
Passage seabirds include
Manx Shearwater, Sooty
Shearwater, Great
Shearwater (in late July
and August), Cory's
Shearwater, Gannet, Fulmar
and British Storm-petrel.
AUTUMN: Passage seabirds as
for summer, plus Great
Skua, Arctic Skua, Pomarine
Skua, Kittiwake, auks and
terns. Red-breasted
Flycatcher and Yellow-
browed Warbler are annual
visitors, and chats, warblers,
flycatchers and always a few
rarities may be seen.
WINTER: Red-throated Diver,
Great Northern Diver and
thrushes.

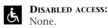

ACCESS: Head for
Baltimore from Cork
via the N71 and then the
R595. If there is time, good
birding can be had from
the car at Rosscarbery Bay,
which is along the route.
Ferries leave Baltimore
daily; information on times
from the Cape Clear Co-
operative, Tel: 028 39102.
   To stay at the bird
observatory, contact
Sean Farrell, 81 Ferndale
Avenue, Dublin 11.
Tel: (01) 834 3620.

DISABLED ACCESS:
None.

AKERAGH LOUGH in northern Kerry has, over many years, attracted a variety of North American wildfowl and waders. The lough can dry out in summer, but in winter it often floods on to the surrounding marshes, creating attractive conditions for wintering wildfowl. The site is at its best in autumn when North American waders are annual. If there is little suitable wader habitat in the vicinity of the lough, then waders use the beach to feed on.

A visit in autumn, winter or spring should provide some interesting birds.

 BIRDS
Past records have included a flock of 13 American Wigeon in October 1968, and 11 Pectoral Sandpipers in September 1971. Although numbers of rarities may have decreased a little in recent times, Akeragh remains one of the outstanding sites for rare birds in Ireland. Passage waders such as Little Stint and Green Sandpiper are

(Above) The shoreline in the vicinity of Black Rock often hosts waders.

The Pectoral Sandpiper is just one of several American visitors to have made landfall in autumn on the lough.

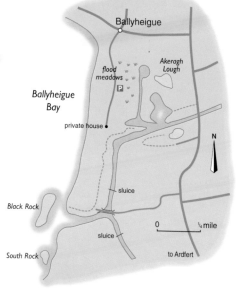

regular in autumn. Although numbers of birds may not be high, the quality is usually good.

The shoreline in the vicinity of Black Rock should always be checked for birds, as the waders will often be on the beach if the lough is proving unattractive.

🌸 FLOWERS

During summer there is little bird interest, but the site is still worth visiting for the flower meadows bordering the lough. Yellow Iris,

SPRING: A few passage waders.
SUMMER: *See* All year.
AUTUMN: Passage waders include Golden Plover, Lapwing, Ruff, Sanderling, Greenshank, Dunlin, Curlew Sandpiper, Little Stint, Black-tailed Godwit, Bar-tailed Godwit, Redshank, Green Sandpiper, Wood Sandpiper and American waders.
WINTER: Bewick's Swan, Whooper Swan, Wigeon, Teal, Shoveler, Red-breasted Merganser, Golden Plover, Lapwing, Dunlin,

past the caravans and park near the farmhouse on the right. The lough is directly inland across the field – note that this can be very wet. The farmhouse that lies at the end of the track is strictly private.

To reach Black Rock, walk through the dunes and along the beach in a southerly direction.

The lough and Black Rock can also be reached by driving from Ballyheigue towards Ardfert. After crossing the river and half a

Akeragh Lough provides excellent conditions for wildfowl.

Ragged Robin and Broad-leaved Marsh Orchid add to the blaze of colour.

BIRDS THROUGH THE SEASONS

ALL YEAR: Mute Swan, Mallard, Oystercatcher, Ringed Plover, Chough and Peregrine.

Sanderling, Bar-tailed Godwit, Greenshank and Redshank.

▶ ACCESS:

From the centre of Ballyheigue, drive down the track that runs parallel with the sea

mile beyond the Ranch House guest-house, turn right. From here, the lough, is to the north and Black Rock offshore.

DISABLED ACCESS:
None.

THIS LARGE estuary at the head of Dingle Bay has a magnificent mountain backdrop. Sand spits, saltmarsh, inter-tidal mudflats and surrounding fields are the main habitats.

Due to the size of the area, there are a number of access points (*see* Access below). A walk out to Inch Point is recommended for the opportunity of seeing the best variety of birds. The road out to Cromane and back to Killorglin on the south side might be a good option in poor weather, as many birds can be seen from the car.

The harbour is best visited in winter as there is little bird interest at other times.

BIRDS

In winter, the bay attracts large numbers of Brent Geese and Wigeon. Both species favour the Inch area near the mouth of the estuary. A walk along the sand dunes at Inch Point is likely to produce a variety of wildfowl and waders, including a few Pintail. The sandy beach on the other side of the point often has a few Sanderlings, while Common Scoter and the occasional Long-tailed Duck can be seen on the sea. Great Northern Divers are regular offshore and in the deeper channels within the harbour.

BIRDS THROUGH THE SEASONS

ALL YEAR: Mallard, Oystercatcher, Ringed Plover and Peregrine.
SPRING: Lingering winter visitors.
SUMMER: A few terns use the harbour. The first Brent Geese and Wigeon arrive in late August.

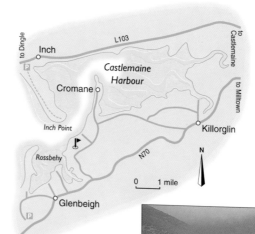

AUTUMN: As for winter.
WINTER: Great Northern Diver, light-bellied Brent Goose, Mallard, Wigeon, Teal, Shoveler, Pintail, Goldeneye, Scaup, Long-tailed Duck, Common Scoter, Red-breasted Merganser, Ringed Plover, Golden Plover, Lapwing, Dunlin, Sanderling, Bar-tailed Godwit, Redshank and a few Greenshank.

ACCESS: To reach Rossbehy, head south from Killorglin and take the right turn past the Towers Hotel signed to Rossbehy Strand. The estuary can be viewed from the car park here.

The road to Cromane and back to Killorglin runs alongside the estuary. From Glenbeigh, drive towards Killorglin on the N70 and turn left to Dooks Golf Links approximately half a mile from Glenbeigh just past the River Caragh. Follow this road, which eventually forks for Cromane Farm. Views of the estuary can be had from here and by carrying on to Killorglin.

Castlemaine Harbour.

To reach Inch Point, take the R561 from Castlemaine to Dingle. Park just beyond Inch at Inch Strand and walk to the point, by far the best site for a variety of birds.

DISABLED ACCESS: The sites on the south side between Glenbeigh and Killorglin provide the best opportunities for viewing from a vehicle. Otherwise, access is limited.

OTHER ATTRACTIONS

TO THE south of Dingle Bay lies the scenically spectacular Ring of Kerry. Mountains, rivers and bogs dominate the landscape. The Killarney National Park lies to the south-east.

TRALEE BAY is close to Castlemaine Harbour but, being substantially smaller, is more easily covered. Like most estuaries, it is best visited two or three hours before high tide during autumn and winter.

BIRDS
Similar species occur as at Castlemaine during winter, while during autumn there is often a variety of passage waders that have included a number of American vagrants in the past. One of the best sites for waders is at Blennerville. The rubbish dump in the village is worth a look in winter for Glaucous, Iceland and Ring-billed Gull.

Bar-tailed Godwit, Black-tailed Godwit, Grey Plover and Curlew. Arrival of winter wildfowl.
WINTER: Red-throated and Great Northern Diver, Whooper Swan, light-bellied Brent Goose, Wigeon, Teal, Shoveler, Goldeneye, Scaup, Common Scoter, Red-

windmill. Park here and scan the estuary. To view the outer estuary, travel back across the bridge, taking the first left turn to the end of the disused canal. The waterways and inlets on the Tralee side of the bridge should also be explored.

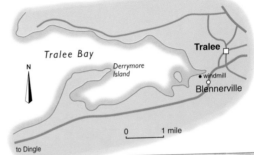

Tralee Bay.

BIRDS THROUGH THE SEASONS
ALL YEAR: Mute Swan, Mallard, Oystercatcher and Peregrine.
SPRING: A few waders. Lingering winter visitors.
SUMMER: *See* All year.
AUTUMN: Dunlin, Curlew Sandpiper, Little Stint, Ruff, Spotted Redshank, Red-shank, Lapwing, Curlew,

breasted Merganser, Ringed Plover, Golden Plover, Lapwing, Dunlin, Sander-ling, Bar-tailed Godwit, Greenshank, Redshank, Spotted Redshank, Glaucous Gull, Iceland Gull and Ring-billed Gull.

ACCESS: From the town of Tralee, take the R559 west. The road crosses the river at Blennerville by a large

DISABLED ACCESS: Viewing from a wheelchair is possible from Blennerville.

OTHER ATTRACTIONS

THERE IS a small tourist complex at Blennerville, also home to Ireland's only commercially run working windmill, located on the estuary shore.

RAHASANE TURLOUGH, to the east of Galway, is a wintering site for wildfowl. Turloughs are shallow limestone depressions that flood after autumn and winter rains. In recent years, steps have been taken to drain the lake, and the water-levels are now not as high as they once were. There is little bird interest during summer.

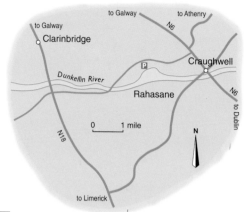

🦆 BIRDS

Wildfowl commute between here and sites in the Galway area. When there is human disturbance there may therefore be few birds, but when there is plenty of water wildfowl numbers can be high, with a few thousand Wigeon, often a small flock of Greenland White-fronted Geese, and both Bewick's and Whooper Swans. In autumn, the occasional rare wader may be spotted.

Bewick's Swans grace the turlough in winter.

Waders may be seen during winter, with large numbers of Golden Plover and Lapwing. Often, in spring, a few Icelandic Black-tailed Godwits stop off on their journey north.

🌸 OTHER ANIMALS AND FLOWERS

You are likely to notice large black and green lumps of moss; these are characteristic species of turloughs in Ireland. The Blackthorn in the hedgerows around the turlough support a colony of the Brown Hairstreak butterfly, a rarity in Ireland.

BIRDS THROUGH THE SEASONS

ALL YEAR: Grey Heron, Mallard, Kingfisher and Reed Bunting.
SPRING: Black-tailed Godwit and Whimbrel on passage.
SUMMER: *See* All year.
AUTUMN: Dunlin, Ruff, Black-tailed Godwit, Curlew and arrival of winter visitors. There is the chance of a rare wader.
WINTER: Whooper Swan, Bewick's Swan, Greenland White-fronted Goose, Teal, Shoveler, Wigeon, Pintail, Pochard, Tufted Duck, Golden Plover, Lapwing, Dunlin, Black-tailed Godwit and Redshank.

▶ ACCESS: If travelling from Galway to Limerick, turn left in Kilcogan towards Craughwell. Follow this road for 3 miles until you see the turlough on your right. There is a ruin and church past the phone box; turn down the lane opposite. Park at the end and view the area.

♿ DISABLED ACCESS: None.

OTHER ATTRACTIONS

A FEW miles to the west is the Burren, a spectacular limestone pavement with a rich flora.

The limestone pavements of the Burren are one of Ireland's natural wonders.

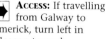

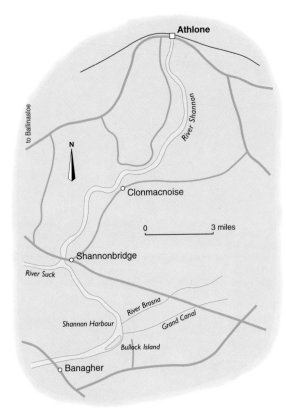

AUTUMN: Winter visitors arrive.

WINTER: Whooper Swan, Bewick's Swan, Greenland White-fronted Goose, Wigeon, Teal, Golden Plover, Lapwing, Redshank, Curlew, Snipe and Black-tailed Godwit.

Access: Between the bridges of Athlone and Shannonbridge, there are a number of access points. A good map will show you those places where roads run close to the river and the various access points used by fishermen. A good view of some of the meadows can be gained from Clonmacnoise.

Disabled access: Possible where roads run close to the river.

OTHER ATTRACTIONS

THE SHANNON is best explored by hiring a cruiser. The monastic ruins at Clonmacnoise are most impressive.

Corncrake.

THIS VAST area encompasses many unimproved low-lying meadows, inhabited by Corncrakes in summer. These meadows flood in winter, attracting thousands of wildfowl and waders.

Access is difficult in winter because of flooding, but in summer one of the best ways of exploring the area is to walk along the banks of the river or hire a boat for a few days.

BIRDS
In winter, Greenland White-fronted Geese and Bewick's and Whooper Swans use the fields. Most numerous are flocks of Wigeon and large numbers of Golden Plover and Lap-wing. During summer, apart from the Corncrakes that are almost impossible to see but easily heard, there are nesting Curlew, Redshank and Lapwing nesting.

For Corncrakes, the best time is from late May to early July, but generally the winter period provides the best bird-watching.

BIRDS THROUGH THE SEASONS
ALL YEAR: Little Grebe, Grey Heron, Mute Swan, Moorhen, Mallard, Curlew, Redshank, Lapwing, Snipe, Kingfisher and Reed Bunting.

SPRING: Lingering winter birds.

SUMMER: Corncrake.

CLARE

Cliffs of Moher

Close to the Burren are these 650-foot cliffs, home to a variety of nesting seabirds including over 1000 pairs of Puffins that nest on Goat Island. Chough, Rock Dove, Peregrine, Raven and Twite all breed. The visitor centre is off the R478. The nearby Burren has an outstanding flora.

Loop Head and Bridges of Ross

The area around the head regularly attracts rarities in autumn. However, the headland is best known as an excellent sea-watching site in westerly or north-westerly gales. For sea-watching, the Bridges of Ross are best; Sabine's Gulls, Grey Phalaropes and Leach's Storm-petrels are regular. Loop Head is reached off the R487 from Kilkee. The Bridges of Ross are on the north side of the head, about 2 miles before the lighthouse.

CORK

Cork Harbour

The harbour is best in winter when thousands of waders and wildfowl are present. Due to its large size, there are many access points.

Dursey Island

Dursey, off the tip of the Beara Peninsula, has become well known for turning up some impressive European and American vagrants, including Ovenbird and Great Snipe. The island is reached by cable car.

Mizen Head

This bleak promontory west of Cape Clear is a superb sea-watching site in autumn, and is always worth checking for migrants. A number of rarities have been recorded.

DONEGAL

Donegal Bay

The bay is excellent for divers, wildfowl and gulls. All three species of British diver winter. Long-tailed Ducks are annual in varying numbers. Red-breasted Merganser, Eider and large numbers of Common Scoter occur along the south side. The Scoter flocks should be checked thoroughly for both Velvet and Surf Scoters. The harbour at Killybegs, to the west of Donegal, regularly attracts both Glaucous and Iceland Gull.

Lough Swilly

This long lough, just west of Londonderry, attracts divers, wildfowl and waders in winter. Slavonian Grebes are regular off Inch Island, along with both Great Northern and Red-throated Divers. Corncrake breed near Inch, and Quail have been heard in recent summers.

Malin Head

Malin Head, directly north of Londonderry, is a superb sea-watching site in north-west winds. Sabine's Gull, Grey Phalarope, Leach's Storm-petrel, skuas and shearwaters are regular in autumn. In October, the head is a good site from which to watch arriving Barnacle Geese and Whooper Swans.

GALWAY

Galway Bay and Harbour

The bay supports a range of wildfowl and waders, especially in winter. In the harbour there are sometimes small flocks of Little Gull and often Iceland and Glaucous Gull. In the last few years the occasional Ross's Gull has been seen. Nimmo's Pier in Galway City provides a good viewpoint for searching for gulls.

Lough Corrib

Large numbers of wildfowl winter. A variety of breeding species includes gulls and wildfowl, notably a small population of Common Scoter. The lough

Grey Phalaropes are regularly recorded off west coast headlands in autumn.

is huge and has a number of access points easily reached from roads north of Galway City.

KERRY

Brandon Point

A good sea-watching point in north-westerly gales. Great and Sooty Shearwater, skuas, Sabine's Gull and Grey Phalaropes are all possible. Brandon Point lies west of Tralee Bay.

Skelligs

Great Skellig, measuring 119 acres, and Little Skellig, measuring 17 acres are important seabird colonies with particularly large numbers of Gannets. Boats depart from Valentia during the summer.

LOUTH

Clogher Head

Clogher Head, to the north of Drogheda, is a good sea-watching site. A variety of migrants occur in both spring and autumn. The harbour has both Glaucous and Iceland Gulls in winter, and Mediterranean Gulls are regular on the beach to the north of the head.

Dundalk Bay

The bay is a winter site with a variety of wildfowl, but is most important for the large numbers of waders it supports. The South Marsh west of Dundalk holds wintering Twite, while wader watching is particularly good from Ballymascanian, north of Dundalk, and at Annagassan on the south side of the bay.

MAYO

The Mullet

This remote, windswept promontory west of Sligo has a year-round attraction. In summer, waders such as Red-necked Phalarope nest at Annagh, while a few Corncrakes still survive. During autumn, rarities are likely, and there is good sea-watching. Winter visitors include Whooper Swans and Greenland White-fronted Geese.

NORTHERN IRELAND

Castlecaldwell Forest
RSPB Reserve

This RSPB reserve on Lower Lough Erne was once the centre of Ireland's breeding population of Common Scoter, but now just a few individuals summer. A few species of wildfowl and wader breed. Crossbill and Siskin inhabit the forest, and in winter there are Wigeon, Goldeneye and Whooper Swan. The reserve is 4 miles east of Belleek, and is reached off the A47.

Copeland Island Bird Observatory

Reached by boat from Donaghadee, permission to visit John's Island (one of three in the Copeland group and home to the observatory) is required from the Bookings Secretary, Neville McKee, 67 Temple Rise, Templepatrick, Antrim BT39 0AG. Tel: 01849 433068. The island is important for breeding colonies of Manx Shearwater. Migrants occur in spring and autumn. The island recorded Britain's first and only Fox Sparrow in 1961 and Britain's first Scarlet Tanager, as well as attracting much attention in 1994 when a White's Thrush was observed.

Green Island & Greencastle Point
RSPB Reserve

Green Island and Greencastle Point, a promontory in Carlingford Lough, are nesting sites for Common, Sandwich and Arctic Terns. Cranfield Point to the south-east has breeding Black Guillemots. Brent Goose, Scaup, Long-tailed Duck and a few grebes and divers are present on the lough in winter. The site is 5 miles south-west of Kilkeel.

Portmore Lough
RSPB Reserve

THIS LOUGH lies close to Lough Neagh and is a recent acquisition of the RSPB. The reserve on the western side of Portmore Lough covers grazing marsh

and reed beds. Since management work started, the value of the site has increased dramatically.

Waders and wildfowl are returning to breed. Marsh Harriers occasionally linger, and during winter a herd of Icelandic Whooper Swans uses the meadows.

Visiting is by appointment only. Contact the warden, Eddie Franklin, Tel: 01846 652406.

Ramore Head

This headland at Portrush is an excellent sea-watching site during north-westerly winds in autumn. A variety of skuas and shearwaters may be expected, and it is particularly good for Leach's Storm-petrel. Sabine's Gull is recorded annually.

WATERFORD

Dungarvan Harbour

Dungarvan Harbour, west of Waterford, shares many similar species with Tramore (see below). View it from the old swimming baths in the town.

Tramore and Brownstown Head

Tramore Bay and Backstrand is a winter site, especially good for waders and light-bellied Brent Geese. The town dump attracts large numbers of

gulls, including Iceland and Glaucous Gull. Near by, Brownstown Head can produce migrants in autumn and is a good sea-watching site. Tramore lies south of Waterford.

WEXFORD

Carnsore Point

Close to Lady's Island Lake. The point often has a few migrants in spring and autumn, and is well placed for observing seabirds moving from the Irish Sea and Atlantic. Pomarine Skuas pass in May.

Hook Head

Hook Head lies south-east of Waterford, and is good for spring and autumn migrants and as a sea-watching site. In May, Pomarine Skuas pass, while sea-watching in autumn is best in south-westerly winds when a variety of skuas, shearwaters and gulls are possible.

WICKLOW

Kilcoole

This area of marsh and low-lying pasture south of Dublin and close to Greystones attracts geese and swans, as well as a variety of wildfowl and waders in winter. Little Terns breed on the beach.

GLOSSARY

Auk – Family of seabirds that include Puffin, Guillemot and Razorbill.

Carr – Usually willow or alder woodland growing in water.

Crepuscular – Most active at dawn or dusk.

Diurnal – Active during the day, as opposed to nocturnal.

Drift migrant – A migrant that loses its course by being drifted by winds or inclement weather.

Fall – A mass arrival of birds, normally passerines, that are grounded due to adverse weather.

Feral – A species formally captive but living in a wild state.

Fleet – An inlet or creek by the coast.

Hirundine – Collective term for House and Sand Martins, and Swallows.

Inter-tidal mudflats – An expanse of mud regularly covered and exposed by the tide.

Internationally important numbers – Constitutes 1 per cent or more of the world population at one particular location.

Nationally important numbers – A term used to measure the importance of a specific site for birds. One per cent of the entire British population at a particular site constitutes a nationally important population. Most commonly used for wildfowl and waders.

NNR – Abbreviation for National Nature Reserve.

Passage migrant – A migrant passing through an area where it does not remain to breed or winter.

Passerine – A perching bird.

Phylloscopus warbler – Generic name for leaf warblers that include Willow Warbler, Chiffchaff and Wood Warbler.

Raptor – A bird of prey.

RSPB – Abbreviation for Royal Society for the Protection of Birds.

Saltmarsh – Inter-tidal mudflats colonised by salt-loving plants.

Sawbill – A family of fish-eating ducks that have a serrated edge to their bills. Family includes Red-breasted Merganser, Goosander and Smew.

Seaduck – Ducks that are commonly found on the sea in winter and include scoters, Red-breasted Merganser, Long-tailed Duck, Eider and Scaup.

Scrape – A shallow excavation designed to attract wildfowl and waders.

Vagrant – A rare visitor not native to the country in which it has strayed.

FURTHER READING

IDENTIFICATION GUIDES

Alstrom, P, *et al.* (1991) *A Field Guide to the Rare Birds of Britain and Europe.* Harper Collins.

Hayman, P (1979) *Birdwatcher's Pocket Guide.* Mitchell Beazley.

Heinzel, H, *et al.* (1995) *The Birds of Britain and Europe with North Africa and the Middle East.* Harper Collins.

Jonsson, L (1992) *Birds of Europe with North Africa and the Middle East.* Helm.

MISCELLANEOUS

Elphick, J, *et al.* (1995) *Atlas of Bird Migration.* Harper Collins.

Gibbons, D, *et al.* (1993) *The New Atlas of Breeding Birds in Britain and Ireland 1988-91.* Poyser.

Pemberton, J (ed.), *Birdwatcher's Yearbook and Diary.* Annual; packed with information.

MAGAZINES

Bird Watching, EMAP. Available monthly from newsagents.

Birding World. Available monthly on subscription from: Stonerunner, Coast Road, Cley-next-the-Sea, Holt, Norfolk NR25 7RZ.

Birds, magazine of the RSPB sent free to members quarterly.

Birdwatch, Solo Publishing Ltd. Available monthly from newsagents.

British Birds. Available monthly on subscription from: Fountains, Park Lane, Blunham, Bedford MK44 3NJ.

USEFUL ADDRESSES

The Royal Society for the Protection of Birds, The Lodge, Sandy, Bedfordshire SG19 2DL. Tel: 01767 680551

British Trust for Ornithology, National Centre for Ornithology, The Nunnery, Thetford, Norfolk IP24 2PU. Tel: 01842 750050

Wildfowl and Wetlands Trust, Slimbridge, Gloucester GL2 7BT. Tel: 01453 890333

Young Ornithologist's Club, (Junior section of the RSPB) same address as for RSPB.

BIRDWATCHER'S CODE OF CONDUCT

As OUR hobby grows, so the pressures on particular habitats and sites increase. We have a responsibility to conduct ourselves in a manner that brings no harm to the birds we watch. The following points comprise a recognised code of conduct to which we should all adhere.

1. The birds' welfare must come first, whatever your interest.

2. Damage to habitats must be avoided by our activities.

3. Disturbance of birds, especially nesting ones, should be kept to a minimum. Flushing from the nest may cause desertion or predation.

4. The discovery of a rare breeding bird should be reported to the RSPB if protection is required. Otherwise, it is best to keep the record secret. Disturbance at or near the nest of a species listed on the First Schedule of the Wildlife and Countryside Act 1981 is a criminal offence.

5. Rare migrants or vagrants must not be harassed. If on private land, seek the permission of the owners before releasing news of a rarity. If this is not forthcoming try contacting someone more experienced to negotiate and organise the arrival of birdwatchers to view the bird. Many small reserves have benefited financially from hosting a rarity by charging a viewing fee. Viewing, however restrictive, can usually be arranged at sensitive sites to the benefit of everybody concerned.

6. The Bird Protection Laws embodied in the Wildlife and Countryside Act must be upheld and abided by us all.

7. Respect the rights of landowners. If you are leading a group, give advance notice of an impending visit to a reserve. Obey permit schemes in operation on some reserves.

8. Have due consideration for other bird-watchers. Respect the rights of other users in the countryside. Abide by the Country Code.

9. Keep records. Much of our knowledge is due to the meticulous record-keeping of our predecessors. Send your records to the county recorder.

10. When abroad, behave as you would here. Well-behaved bird-watchers can be important ambassadors for bird protection.

SITE INDEX

SPECIES INDEX

The page numbers in **bold** denote sites especially good for watching particular species. References in *italic* are for photographs.